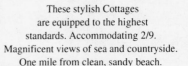

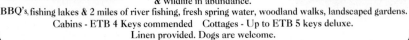

ST. MARGARET'S HOLIDAY PARK

Tel: (01726) 74283 Fax (01726) 71680

Family owned and run holiday park, set in six acres of beautiful parkland and offering good quality accommodation of varying sizes, from detached bungalows sleeping up to eight persons to self contained chalets nestling amongst the trees and sleeping from two to five people. Two of the bungalows are suitable for disabled persons. All property is well equipped including colour TV and microwave ovens. Launderette and pay phone on park. St. Austell golf course is 400 yards away and the Polgooth shops and inn are conveniently near. Well controlled pets allowed. Special rates early/late season or for two persons. Open March to December. Terms and colour brochure from: Mrs M. King, St. Margaret's Holiday Park, Polgooth, St. Austell, Cornwall PL26 7AX.

CHARACTER COTTAGES AND PINE LODGES

Fringe of Lake District, National Park. 3 lodges peacefully situated in our grounds in picturesque hamlet. Views over farmland to Caldbeck Fells, 30 minutes Lake Ullswater, Keswick or Gretna Green.

* 3 cottages, 1 heavily beamed with wood burning stove
* 1/2/3 Bedrooms (sleep 2/7)
* Shower/bath, second WC in 3-bedroom properties
* Heaters in all properties
* Colour TVs
* Microwaves
* Laundry
* Open all year, Winter Breaks
* Warm for your arrival
* Excellent quality throughout
* Direct dial telephones
* ♛♛♛♛ / ♛♛♛♛♛ up to Highly Commended

Featured in Good Holiday Cottage Guide. Terms £140-£440. For details and brochure:
Mrs Ivinson (SCF), Green View, Welton, Near Dalston, Carlisle CA5 7ES
Telephone: 016974 76230 Fax: 016974 76523

LAKELAND LEISURE PARK

call now for a free colour brochure
Open 24 hours - 7 days a week
01539 58556
or see your local travel agent

GATEWAY TO THE LAKE DISTRICT

* On the Furness & Cartmel Peninsula (Holiday Destinations Winner 1994)
* Luxury Holiday Homes for 2 - 8 people
* Heated Indoor & Outdoor Swimming Pools
* Bowling, Putting, Tennis, & Horseriding on Park
* Bradley Bear Kids Club and Teen Club
* Restaurants - Bars - Takeaway Food
* Live Family Evening Entertainment
* Touring and Tenting Pitches Available

★ A BRITISH HOLIDAYS PARK

WINDERMERE
10 minutes' walk from lake or village. Open all year. 10 fully equipped spacious apartments sleep 2-6. Pool, colour TV, central heating. Terms £105-£380.

COMMENDED

For brochure contact resident owners:
Bruce and Marsha Dodsworth,
Birthwaite Edge, Birthwaite Road,
Windermere LA23 1BS
Telephone: 015394 42861
*See self catering section –
Windermere, Cumbria*

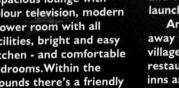

Patterdale Hall Estate

GLENRIDDING · PENRITH · CUMBRIA · CA11 0PJ
Telephone & Fax: Glenridding (017684) 82308 (24 hours)

In a magnificent mountain setting at the southern end of Ullswater, Patterdale Hall Estate is ideally situated for holidays and outdoor activities. Its spacious wooded grounds reach from the shores of the lake to the lower slopes of the Helvellyn range. The 300 acres contains a working hill farm, own private section of foreshore and 100 acres of private woodland and gardens. Sailing, fishing, canoeing, windsurfing and steamer trips on Ullswater, and the Estate makes an ideal base for touring the whole of the Lake District.

There are 16 self-catering units in various parts of the Estate.

Three	Two	Six	Two	Three

Apartments	Cottages	Cedar Chalets	Pine Lodges	Dairy & Bothies

Terms are from £112 to £381 per week including central heating and one tank of hot water per day. Other electricity metered. Linen hire available. Children welcome. Pets by arrangement in some accommodation. Colour TV in all units. Launderette on site.

**"Short Breaks"
available.
Telephone for
detailed brochure.**

For the widest choice of cottages in Devon ...

... and the best value you'll find anywhere

Contact us now for a free copy of our guide to the 500 best value cottages around Devon's unspoilt National Trust Coast. Spring and Autumn breaks in delightful Exmoor farm cottages from only £65 to luxury beachside homes with swimming pools at over £650 p.w. in Summer. All are regularly inspected and guaranteed to offer first class value.

Free leisure guide and £75 worth of discount shopping vouchers with every booking. Cottages for sale details and free hotel accommodation also available.

North Devon Holiday Homes

19 Cross Street, Barnstaple, EX31 1BD
Tel: (01271) 76322 (24 hrs)

A warm family .... *is here for you!*

Ever had too much to do?
... You will at

WELCOME FAMILY!

- ☺ Stylish **DOLPHIN CLUB** & Entertainment Centre
- ☺ Super Indoor Heated **NEPTUNE TROPICANA** Water Leisure Complex – four Feature-packed Pools, Solarium, Sauna, spectator viewing.
- ☺ **CRUISERS** adult Cocktail bar
- ☺ Children's **JOLLY ROGER** Club with Disco, Cinema & large Games arcade
- ☺ Short, level walk to safe sandy beach
- ☺ Great *Value - for - money* prices

- ☺ **FREE** Electricity, Linen, Colour TV
- ☺ Welcome T.V. – great films, local attractions, and more
- ☺ 2 Shops   ☺ Cafe
- ☺ 2 Takeaways
- ☺ Crazy Golf
- ☺ Adventure Playground
- ☺ Laundrette
- ☺ Hire Service with computer games
- ☺ Pets *Welcome* (at small charge)
- ☺ Choose from economy 4-berth to luxury 8-berth caravans.

One of the finest choices for your holiday in South Devon, *Welcome Family* offers all the facilities and atmosphere of a large holiday centre, but with the friendly, personal service of a small park. Situated in a very picturesque part of South Devon, only a short level walk to the famous safe sandy dunes and wildlife areas. Only 15 minutes from the M5, a half hour drive from a host of attractions, including Dartmoor, Torbay or Exeter.

WELCOME FAMILY HOLIDAY PARK
DAWLISH WARREN
SOUTH DEVON   EX7 0PH

RESERVATIONS   01626 862070
DIAL a BROCHURE 01626 888323

We look forward to making
YOU feel Welcome!

DARTMOOR NATIONAL PARK
Delightful accommodation in beautiful surroundings for two to eight persons

English Tourist Board
APPROVED

Accommodation comprises an 18th century granite barn converted into two fully self-contained apartments and a detached summer chalet in the grounds of Poltimore Country Hotel and providing direct access to the Moor. Also, close by, a superb detached bungalow surrounded by open moor and farmland with outstanding views.

The Old Barn: Each apartment has one double and one twin-bedded room, charming beamed sitting room with dining area, kitchenette and bathroom. Fully equipped and furnished to a high standard.

The Chalet: One twin-bedded room, sitting/dining room, kitchenette and shower room with WC. Fully equipped and furnished for two.

Detached Bungalow: One double and two twin bedrooms (one ensuite) enjoying open views from every room. Fully equipped and furnished to a high standard for eight. Large gardens with private swimming pool.

Open all year. Close to local shops and pubs, and providing a good base for touring, walking, fishing, golf. Meals can be taken in the hotel (subject to capacity). Children and dogs welcome.

Please write or telephone for full details.
Mr Wilkens, Poltimore, South Zeal, Okehampton, Devon EX20 2PD
Telephone: Okehampton (01837) 840209

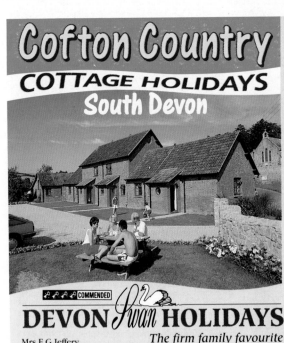

Cofton Country
COTTAGE HOLIDAYS
South Devon

COMMENDED

DEVON *Swan* HOLIDAYS

The firm family favourite

Mrs F G Jeffery,
Devon Swan Holidays, Starcross, Nr. Dawlish, South Devon EX6 8RP.

100 year old farm buildings, tastefully converted into self-contained cottages for 4–6 people. Overlooked by ancient Cofton Church and the woodlands behind, each cottage is fitted-out to a very high standard with colour co-ordinated funishings and with equipment of the latest design. Open all year.

- *Colour TV and Video plus TV point for your own portable.*
- *Kitchens inc. electric oven & hob, microwave, dishwasher etc.*
- *Full central heating and electricity – FREE.*
- *Use of all Park amenities during season.*

FOR 1996 Woodside Cottages, on the edge of Eastdon Woods overlooking the Exe Estuary and Dawlish Warren, will be available.

01626 890111

HEMSFORD
'A Country Holiday for All Ages'

Hemsford is ideally situated in the heart of South Devon, with Torbay, Dartmoor and the excellent beaches of the South Hams only a short drive away. Our 16 comfortable and well appointed cottages (one suitable for disabled guests) accommodate 2-10 people. All have night store heating and are available throughout the year. Own riding stables, heated indoor pool, sauna, solarium, games room, licensed bar, two all-weather tennis courts, 9-hole approach golf and children's play area. **Terms £95 to £875 per week.** Full colour brochure on request. Regret no pets.

**Hemsford Country Holidays, Hemsford, Littlehempston, Totnes, Devon TQ9 6NE
Telephone: 01803 762637**

Superb self catering accommodation in idyllic surroundings. Sea, river and hill view locations each with its own special charm.

PHONE: 01271 850611
for colour brochure

Short breaks available
Best Leisure, North Hill, Shirwell, Barnstaple, DEVON EX31 4LG
COMMENDED/HIGHLY COMMENDED

COTTAGES IN DEVON, CORNWALL & THE COTSWOLDS

RELAX IN PEACE
AND TRANQUILLITY

An Oasis of Tranquillity

ΨΨΨΨ Highly Commended

Nestling at the head of a valley, with magnificent views across Exmoor, yet only ten minutes from the beach. Watermill and stone barns in 8 acres of gardens and woodland, converted into 10 high quality cottages. Heated indoor swimming pool, sauna and fitness room.

Four posters, dishwashers, microwaves, central heating, wood stoves, home made meals, shop, laundry, children's playground, bed linen and maid service inclusive. Open March to November. Prices from £180 to £840 per week. Short Break holidays available off peak.

Wheel Farm Country Cottages,
Berrydown 12, Combe Martin, Devon EX34 0NT.
Telephone: 01271-882100

Torcross Apartment Hotel
At the water's edge on Slapton Sands overlooking the blue waters of Start Bay

Family self-catering in our Luxury Apartment Hotel. Ground floor Beachside apartments for two and really spacious Family Apartments. Superb sea views. Family owned and supervised ensuring a high standard of cleanliness. Village Inn and Waterside Family Restaurant with an extensive Menu including fresh local fish and a "Sunday Carvery". "Take-away" service available to the Apartments. Light entertainment some evenings. Baby listening. Games Room. Launderette/drying/ironing room. Central heating. Car Park. Colour brochure with pleasure.

**Torcross Apartment Hotel, (ref. SCH), Torcross, near Kingsbridge, South Devon
Telephone: (01548) 580206**

MANOR FARM HOLIDAY CENTRE
CHARMOUTH, BRIDPORT, DORSET

Situated in rural valley of outstanding natural beauty, Manor Farm has all the requisite amenities for an exciting yet carefree holiday. Shop, launderette, licensed bar with family room, swimming pool and children's pool, play area. Ten minutes' level walk to beach, safe for bathing and famous for its fossils. Golf, riding, tennis, fishing and boating all nearby. Accommodation in 3 bedroomed bungalow, 2 and 3 bedroomed houses, and luxury caravans. All units sleep 4/6, and are equipped with colour TV; parking.

**SAE to Mr. R. E. Loosmore
or Telephone 01297-560226**

KENT / SUSSEX
The area specialists

Converted granaries, oasts, barns and cosy cottages. All sizes, all prices from £75 to £650 per week. Year round availability. Flexilets from one week/one year. Friendly personal service. Free brochure on request.

FREEDOM HOLIDAY HOMES, Weaversden Cottage, Frittenden, Kent TN17 2EP
Telephone: 01580 852251; Fax: 01580 852455

FAIRHAVEN HOLIDAY COTTAGES

**Derby House, 123 Watling Street, Gillingham, Kent ME7 2YY
Phone & Fax (01634) 570157 (24 hours)**

Offering an extensive selection of personally inspected holiday homes, all shapes and sizes, situated in a variety of attractive locations . . . coast, countryside and town.

COTTAGES IN THE SOUTH OF ENGLAND & WALES

HOLIDAY IN OUR ENGLISH COUNTRY GARDEN

2 ACRES IN RURAL NORFOLK WITH RIVER NEARBY.

10 select and spacious family-run bungalows and lovely country farmhouse. Peacefully set in 2 acres of delightful gardens with Games room. Heated pool. Children's play area. Fishing, Boating, Riding and Golf nearby. Only 50 yards from River Staithe with access to Broads and well situated for touring. Car essential.

HEDERA HOUSE & Plantation Bungalows

For full details & colour brochure contact:
S.C.F.H. Delf, Thurne Cottage, The Staithe, Thurne, Norfolk NR29 3BU. Tel. (01692) 670242 or (01493) 844568.

NORFOLK

APPIN HOLIDAY HOMES
IN A NATURE LOVERS' PARADISE

CHALETS   COTTAGES   CARAVANS

Holiday Homes in a magical setting.
Ten chalet-bungalows, three traditional cottages, eight modern caravans.
All fully serviced and equipped. Sleep 2-6.

Between Oban and Fort William	Excellent Touring Centre	STB 🌸🌸🌸🌸 Commended

IDEAL FOR FAMILIES . . . ALSO HONEYMOONS!
DISCOUNT FOR COUPLES

FREE FISHING (salt and freshwater). Boating, sailing and great hill walks. Pony trekking and Licensed Inn nearby. Lots to do and see.

PLAY AREA   RECREATION ROOM   LAUNDERETTE   BABY SITTING
COLOUR TV, SOME WITH VIDEO AND MICROWAVE OVEN

Special Spring, Autumn and Winter Terms.
Please send SAE for colour brochure giving dates required.
OPEN ALL YEAR
Price guide . . . £135-£345 per unit weekly

**FHG
DIPLOMA
WINNER**

**Mr and Mrs C. Weir
Appin Holiday Homes
Appin, Argyll PA38 4BQ
Tel: 01631 730287**

ESTD
1964

ARDCHONNEL FARMS

Lochaweside, By Dalmally, Argyll PA33 1BW

Tel: 01866 844242   Fax 01866 844227

Enjoy fishing, hill walking, bird watching, boating, touring, golf or just relaxing in Ardchonnel Cottage, a spacious 4-bedroomed, very well equipped single storey house with 2 bathrooms sleeping up to 8 people, peacefully situated in its large garden halfway down the east side of Loch Awe. Centrally heated and double glazed throughout ensuring our visitors comfort whatever the time of year or weather! Cot and high chair available. One dog welcome. Contact **Mrs J. Mackay** who will be delighted to send further details.

EASDALE – Isle of Seil   HARBOUR COTTAGE

Modernised quarrier's cottage in the village of Easdale on the edge of the sea. It has a patio and private garden area. There are magnificent views from the kitchen and patio to the Islands of the Inner Hebrides. The Cottage was used in the film *Ring of Bright Water* and the TV series *Para Handy Tales*. There are two bedrooms (one with double bed, one with three single beds), a lounge (colour TV), dining room, bathroom

(bath/shower) and toilet; cooking by electricity; night storage heaters and two open fires. There is a steep boxed staircase which may cause problems for elderly visitors and small children. Rates are from £155 to £260 per week. Available all year. For details please write to:

Hank and Maureen Clare, Harbour Crafts, EASDALE,
by Oban PA34 4RQ or telephone
01852 300424 (01/04-31/10) or 0191 4880346 (01/11-31/03)

BRALECKAN HOUSE, INVERARAY, ARGYLL

👑👑👑👑 Commended

Built in mid 19th century, comprises three houses, carefully restored to provide a high standard of comfort. All electric, cots, high chairs, colour TVs and payphone. Large parking area. Peacefully situated on hill farm in an area rich in archaeology, natural history and famous gardens and with many sporting activities besides.

SAE, please, or telephone for details:
Mr & Mrs D. Crawford,
Brenchoille Farm, Inveraray, Argyll PA32 8XN   Telephone: Furnace (01499) 500662

A view from the castle

A selection of charming self-catering properties, each unique in its history and character, and enhanced by the natural beauty of Loch Crinan. All have been attractively modernised and furnished, with care taken in the retention of many traditional and historically interesting features. The properties offer varying accommodation for between two to five persons in comfort. Home cooked meals are available on the premises and eating out is no problem with many good restaurants nearby. Salmon fishing, hill walking, sandy beaches and bicycle hire available in the area. SAE requested: Write to –

Susan Malcolm, Duntrune Castle, Kilmartin, ARGYLL
Tel: 0154 6510283   👑👑👑👑 Highly Commended

ESCAPE TO ANOTHER WORLD

TO TIMBER BUNGALOWS on COLOGIN FARM

THREE MILES SOUTH OF OBAN

Yet set in a peaceful quiet glen amongst the hills in wild and open countryside. You can have a real country holiday away from it all in one of our Bungalows.

TWO OF OUR BUNGALOWS IN THE HILLS

Come and see why people come back here year after year. Here you'll find complete freedom – you can do something different every day, or nothing, just as you fancy. Use a dinghy (and fishing rods if you want them) on our trout loch in the hills. Go for a ride on a bike. Join in the singing on ceilidh night (Scottish entertainment with compere, singer, accordionist, fiddler, Highland dancer and bagpipes). The old farm and surrounding countryside have a lot of wildlife, from herons and hares to roe deer and foxes, and there are ducks, hens, guinea fowl, guinea pigs, a donkey, rabbits and a market garden on the old farm itself. You can play table tennis or pool in the games room. Within two or three miles there are excellent facilities for golf, diving, fishing, swimming, sauna, tennis, bowls, pony trekking, squash, sailing and walking. We serve outstanding home-made bar meals all day in our own country pub/restaurant and have a great reputation for good service and good value with our customers. There are also many other well recommended hotels and restaurants in the area where you will enjoy dining out. Our site is ideal for children, and pets are very welcome too and don't cost any extra either.

THE OLD BYRE ON COLOGIN FARM WHICH IS NOW A COUNTRY PUB/RESTAURANT

OPEN ALL YEAR ROUND

 and

Scottish Tourist Board COMMENDED Facilities

Scottish Tourist Board COMMENDED Facilities

Rates vary from £125 in winter to £340 in July and August per bungalow per week.

Every bungalow is centrally heated, double glazed and fully insulated. Each has an electric radiant fire as well as the panel heaters, an electric cooker (with oven and grill) and fridge. Livingrooms, bath and shower rooms, double/twin bedrooms and kitchens are all fully equipped. Shop and launderette on site, babysitting available. Bed linen, most of the electricity and colour TV are included in the rentals. No charge is made for cots, high chairs, or pets. Colour brochure from:

Henry and Val Woodman, Cologin Chalets, Lerags, by Oban, Argyll PA34 4SE
Telephone: Oban 01631 564501 any time. Fax: Oban 01631 566925.

Mackinnon Hathway, 'Seawinds', Church Road, Kyle of Lochalsh IV40 8DD
Tel: (01599) 534567 Fax: (01599) 534864

Peace and tranquillity by Scottish lochs. We offer a large range of high class holiday homes accommodating from four to twelve people, all fully furnished with colour TV and washing machines. Situated in ideal positions for touring Wester Ross and Isle of Skye. Pursuits include fishing, golf, pony trekking, sailing, hill walking or simply watching otters play, all available close by. Properties available from April to October. Varied prices. Please write for brochure to the above address.

· MYDROILYN ·

Stone farm buildings, recently converted into 4 cottages, providing modern standard of comfort in traditional setting. Sleep 2/3 (terms £90-£180) or 4/8 (terms £145-£300). Gas, electricity, linen included. All have shower room; fully equipped kitchen; colour TV; shared laundry room; facilities for children. Secluded rural area, abundant with wildlife and flowers; 5 miles from sandy beaches, picturesque harbours of Cardigan Bay, National Trust coastal paths; breathtaking mountain scenery; birdwatching, fishing, pony trekking, steam railway nearby.

WTB and AA Approved.   Open Easter to October.
Gil & Mike Kearney, Blaenllanarth Holiday Cottages, Mydroilyn, Lampeter, Dyfed SA48 7RJ. Telephone: Lampeter (01570) 470374.

LLANGURIG SCHOOL HOUSE
Llangurig, Llanidloes, Powys

A self contained centrally heated schoolhouse in a peaceful mid-Wales village, sleeping 6 plus a baby's cot. Colour TV. Enjoy excellent walking and superb scenery (the habitat of the rare red kite), visiting Aberystwyth and the Vale of Rheidol Steam Railway and going pony trekking or fishing. There is a well equipped leisure centre at Rhayader, some 8 miles to the south.

WTB Grade 3. Price includes all electricity and central heating. Pets welcome. Apply:
Gwen Edwards, Powys County Council, Powys County Hall, Llandrindod Wells, Powys LD1 5LG. Telephone: 01597 826055; Fax: 01597 826250.

Our World by the Sea

FOR INEXPENSIVE QUALITY

FEATURED BY B.B.C — **BEACH MODERN LUXURY HOLIDAY HOME** *or approved caravan*
Your own beach moments from your door. Top Grade 5 award. In an area of outstanding natural beauty, quiet secluded cove with sub-tropical plants confirming Gulf Stream mild climate, safe bathing, water sports, sea and river fishing. P.O. & shop. Ramble along the flat coastal strip. Nearby restaurants, Bar Snacks, Take Aways, golf, pony trekking, three modern leisure centres, nature trails. Tour beautiful Snowdonia and the famous Llŷn peninsula and beaches. Every comfort. 4-6 berth B type 2 bedrooms: 4-8 berth A type 2 bedrooms limited to 6: 6-10 berth A type 3 bedrooms limited to 8. Lounge, Kitchen/dinette. Bedrooms: 1st. one double; 2nd. Some have a single with a drop down bed, or 2 singles to make a double; 3rd, two Singles, some make a double. Request on phone and on white booking form. On some a double bed settee makes up in the lounge/dinette. Blankets & pillows provided. Bring linen & towels or own duvet? Bathroom, shower, wash basin, toilet. Well heated, remote control Colour T.V. Fridge/freezer. Large Cooker. Electric Blanket, Kettle & hoover. Featured by the BBC, Wales Tourist Board & British Holiday Home Parks. Families return to us year after year, with the new Dual expressway making the journey so easy. Superior Holiday Homes with heated Bedroom. £2 nightly. Come & view anytime, or video available. Try a £12 Minibreak Special.

	MARCH				APRIL				MAY				JUNE				JULY				AUGUST				SEPTEMBER				OCTOBER		
Date	4-6 berth	4-8 berth	6-10 berth	Date	4-6 berth	4-8 berth	6-10 berth	Date	4-6 berth	4-8 berth	6-10 berth	Date	4-6 berth	4-8 berth	6-10 berth	Date	4-6 berth	4-8 berth	6-10 berth	Date	4-6 berth	4-8 berth	6-10 berth	Date	4-6 berth	4-8 berth	6-10 berth	Date	4-6 berth	4-8 berth	6-10 berth
16	£35	£38	£40	6BH	£55	£79	£85	4BH	£49	£59	£65	1	£69	£89	£99	6	£109	£139	£149	3	£159	£199	£219	7	£69	£85	£89	5	£35	£45	£47
23	£37	£39	£42	13	£39	£49	£55	11	£49	£55	£59	8	£79	£95	£105	13	£125	£149	£159	10	£159	£199	£219	14	£59	£69	£75	12	£35	£45	£47
30GF	£45	£59	£65	20	£37	£47	£49	18	£55	£69	£75	15	£85	£105	£109	20	£159	£189	£209	17	£159	£199	£219	21	£49	£59	£63	19	£45	£65	£69
				27	£45	£55	£59	25BH	£99	£135	£159	22	£95	£115	£119	27	£159	£199	£219	24BH	£129	£169	£179	28	£39	£49	£53	26	£45	£65	£69
												29	£105	£125	£129									31	£79	£99	£109				

12 foot wide super luxury holiday homes, 20% more spacious. Add £35 to the above prices. Deposit £33p.w., & insurance £1 nightly. Sea View £2 nightly. Twin bedded room £2 nightly. Microwave £1 nightly. Superior Holiday Homes, with heated bedroom £2 nightly, latest model, recent model, up market model, double glazed model, central heating to 65°, special position, upgraded etc. £5 nightly each. Request quotation. Over 6 persons £4 per night each. (Dogs £2 nightly.) Prices in grid are standard models. Weekend, Midweek or Week Breaks Phone 01 286 660 400.

ANY 4 DAYS
BEACH MODERN LUXURY HOLIDAY HOME *any 3 nights*

	MARCH				APRIL				MAY				JUNE		
	4-6 berth	4-8 berth	6-10 berth	Date	4-6 berth	4-8 berth	6-10 berth	Date	4-6 berth	4-8 berth	6-10 berth	Date	4-6 berth	4-8 berth	6-10 berth
16	£21	£24	£27	6BH	£39	£55	£59	4BH	£29	£39	£43	1	£39	£49	£59
23	£24	£26	£29	13	£27	£29	£35	11	£29	£35	£39	8	£55	£69	£75
30GF	£27	£36	£39	20	£27	£29	£35	18	£35	£45	£49	15	£55	£69	£75
				27	£28	£35	£37	25BH	£59	£79	£95	22	£57	£75	£85
												29	£59	£79	£89

	JULY				AUGUST				SEPTEMBER				OCTOBER		
Date	4-6 berth	4-8 berth	6-10 berth	Date	4-6 berth	4-8 berth	6-10 berth	Date	4-6 berth	4-8 berth	6-10 berth	Date	4-6 berth	4-8 berth	6-10 berth
6	£65	£85	£89	3	£89	£125	£139	7	£45	£55	£59	5	£23	£35	£37
13	£69	£89	£99	10	£89	£125	£139	14	£39	£43	£45	12	£23	£29	£35
20	£79	£99	£129	17	£89	£115	£139	21	£29	£39	£43	19	£29	£49	£55
27	£89	£125	£150	24BH	£89	£99	£129	28	£25	£37	£39	26	£29	£49	£55
				31	£49	£69	£79								

Extra nights available. Fri., Sat., & Sun. add £3 p.n.
Instant Holidays Anytime
Should you be able to take a last minute break, please ring 01286 660400, and we will do our best to accommodate you - the same day if you wish.

Minibreak A few days, week-end or mid-week
4-6 Berth	£10 per night per Holiday Home, until weekly charge.	**B Type**
4-8 Berth	£12 per night per Holiday Home, until weekly charge.	**A2 Type**
6-10 Berth	£14 per night per Holiday Home, until weekly charge.	**A3 Type**
to 9th June, September & October. Fri., Sat., Sun., add £3 p.n.		

also Villa Chalet

Phone for Brochure

How to find us

Easter Week-end 3rd to 11th April

	4-6 Berth.	4-8 Berth.	6-10 Berth.
2 nights	£39	£75	£79
3 nights	£49	£79	£89
4 nights	£55	£85	£95

ALSO latest Model 12 foot wide super luxury holiday homes, 20% more spacious, 2 & 3 bedrooms. Villa Chalets, Bungalows + Executive Bungalows.

 also **for sale**

May Day Bank Holiday Week-end
	4-6Berth	4-8 Berth	6-10 Berth
2nd to 8th May			
Any 3 nights	£35	£49	£55

Whit Bank Holiday Week-end
	4-6Berth	4-8 Berth	6-10 Berth
23rd to 30th May			
Any 3 nights	£69	£105	£125

August Bank Holiday Week-end
	4-6Berth	4-8 Berth	6-10 Berth
22nd to 29th August			
Any 3 nights	£99	£129	£149

ALSO latest Model 12 foot wide super luxury holiday homes, 20% more spacious, 2 & 3 bedrooms. Villa Chalets &* Bungalows. Phone for details.

BEACH HOLIDAY, WEST POINT, THE BEACH, PONTLLYFNI, CAERNARFON, NORTH WALES, LL54 5ET

PERSONAL ATTENTION, BROCHURE
& RESERVATIONS — TEL. 01286 660400

Please mention FHG Self-Catering and Furnished Holidays when enquiring

Selected
Self Catering Holidays in Scotland 1996

from

THE ASSOCIATION OF SCOTLAND'S SELF CATERERS

Cleanliness, Comfort, Courtesy and Efficiency
Are Our Ideals

The Association of Scotland's Self Caterers is an organisation of owners of holiday properties from cottages and chalets to flats, lodges and castles, who must prove that they provide truly comfortable and pleasing accommodation before they are accepted for membership. Our Association works hand in glove with the Scottish Tourist Board to promote high standards in Self Catering.

Our Members are committed to making sure you enjoy your holiday.

Don't take pot luck! Look for the mark of Quality – ASSC.

The holiday properties on the following pages are a selection from the many hundreds available throughout Scotland.

Contact your choice of accommodation direct, save yourself agents' fees and be assured of an excellent holiday.

If you are an owner-operator and feel you can meet our high standards, why not contact our secretary for more details about ASSC?

Wilma Marshall, Secretary ASSC, Dalreoch, Dunning, Perth PH2 0QJ
Tel: 01764 684368. Fax: 01764 684633.

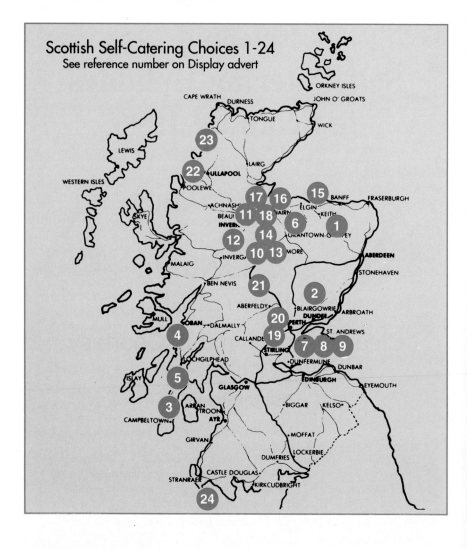

ABERDEENSHIRE

At the heart of the Scottish Highlands!

AVIEMORE
PINE BANK CHALETS
Dalfaber Road, Aviemore, Inverness-shire PH22 1PX

Cosy log cabins and quality chalets in lovely setting by Spey River and Cairngorm Mountains. Ideal touring base for exploring the best of the Scottish Highlands – Whisky Trail, Lochs and Castles. Activities include ski-ing, walking, cycling, watersports, bird-watching, fishing and golf. Close to all amenities including Steam Railway attraction. Country Inn and Leisure Pool nearby. Short Breaks available. Open all year. Pets welcome. Sky TV. Mountain Bikes.

A great value holiday! Brochure ...
Tel: 01479 810000;
Fax: 01479 811469.

EASTER DALZIEL FARM HOLIDAY COTTAGES
Dalcross, Inverness-shire IV1 2JL   Tel/Fax: 01667 462213
Up to 🏵️ 🏵️ 🏵️ 🏵️ Highly Commended

Relax in our stock/arable farm seven miles east of Inverness. Our three cosy traditional stonebuilt cottages are in a superb central location and make an excellent base from which to explore the Highlands. The area offers a wide range of activities to suit the sports minded, tourist or walker alike. The surrounding habitat provides a rich haven for wildlife. Look out for dolphins, roe deer and buzzards. Visit locally Cawdor Castle, Fort George, Culloden Battlefield and Loch Ness. Woodland and coastal walks. Fully equipped including linen and towels. Pets by arrangement. Cost – low season from £120, high season up to £350 per cottage per week. Recommended in the Good Holiday Cottage Guide. Long stays or short breaks – you are welcome all year. Brochure available on request.

South Loch Ness. 'Giusaichean', Ault-na-Goire, Errogie

Sleeps 4/6 plus cot. Secluded but not isolated. Giusaichean is a converted croft, three miles from the Falls of Foyers at Loch Ness, centally placed for touring the Highlands. Two double bedrooms upstairs, one with king-size bed, and double sofa bed in the study; also bathroom with bidet, shower and bath. Downstairs second WC and kitchen with electric hob and oven, microwave, washing machine, tumble dryer, dishwasher, fridge and freezer. Spacious lounge with wood-burning stove, colour TV and double-glazed 'cathedral' windows giving superb views. Oil central heating and electricity free. Payphone. Fenced garden, safe for pets and children. Open all year. Other self catering also in Loch Ness and Glen Affric area. **Brochure, contact Rosemary and Andy Holt, Wilderness Cottages, Island Cottage, Inverfarigaig, Inverness IV1 2XR. Tel/Fax: 01456 486631.**

Dell of Abernethy Cottages
Nethybridge, Inverness-shire PH25 3DL

Warm comfortable cottages, stonebuilt, of individual character, set in 2½ Acres of Lawn and Mature Woodland, and marked 'Dell Lodge' on maps. This area is a haven for walkers and naturalists, by Loch Garten of Speyside in the heart of the Abernethy Nature Reserve, part of the Ancient Caledonian Pine Forest famous for deer, red squirrels, capercaillie and other wildlife. 'Spey Valley' is also popular among hill-walkers, skiers and water-sports enthusiasts.

Further details are in the classified section under 'Inverness-shire'.

For colour brochure contact John F. Fleming
Tel: 01463 224358 or 01479 821643

LOGIERAIT PINE LODGES

by PITLOCHRY Perthshire PH9 0LH
Resident Proprietors: Mr and Mrs J. MacFarlane
Telephone & Fax: 01796 482253

So peaceful with wonderful views, these chalets are beautifully situated on the banks of the River Tay. Fitted out to the highest standard for self-catering comfort and open all year. Extremely warm with double glazing and electric heating. All have colour TV, refrigerators and full-size cookers, quality beds and fitted carpets. Bath and shower. Ideal centre for touring, golfing, bird-watching or just relaxing. Private fishing on River Tay, also coarse fishing free to residents. Shooting and stalking by arrangement. Colour brochure by return.

21

Aultbea, Ross-shire ... Oran Na Mara Holidays

Amidst beautiful Highland scenery, enjoy the peace of the crofting/fishing village of Aultbea, close by lovely Loch Maree, wild and magnificent Torridon, famous Gruinard Bay and the semi-tropical Inverewe Gardens. Two luxurious self-catering flats, each sleeping 2, fully equipped with separate entrances. Colour TV, bath, shower; all-electric with 50p meter; linen supplied. Ground-floor house, sleeping 8, all-electric with linen and central heating included. Shops, hotels nearby. Caravan also available.

To book, please contact
Mrs Lister, Oran Na Mara, Aultbea, Ross-shire IV22 2HU
Telephone: 01445 731394
Open all year. Pets and children welcome in house and caravan.

22

Baddidarroch Holiday Chalets

Superb redwood chalets in their own grounds overlooking Lochinver Bay with spectacular sea and mountain views. Comfortable and well-equipped with fully fitted kitchen, separate laundry room and electric heating. Each has two bedrooms, bath/shower room, colour TV and balcony. Ideal for walking, bird watching, fishing or just to enjoy the Highland life. Open all year. From £175 to £425 weekly. Short Breaks available. For colour brochure, please contact:

23

Mrs J.C. Macleod, 74 Baddidarroch, Lochinver IV27 4LP
Telephone: 01571 844457

HARBOUR ROW

Mull of Galloway, Wigtownshire

Row of five cottages and two houses completed in 1990 and designed to extend the village of Drummore. Patios at the rear benefit from the southerly exposure and open fires give evening relaxation. Only yards from sand and sea. Highest quality furnishings and equipment. Garden with children's playground. Open all year.
Colour brochure.
Prices £160-£395.

24

Contact Mrs Sally Colman, Harbour Row, Cailiness Road, Drummore, Stranraer DG9 9QY
Telephone 01776 840631.

SELF-CATERING HOLIDAYS IN BRITAIN 1996

Farms, Cottages, Houses, Chalets,
Flats and Caravans throughout Britain.

Includes Campus Holidays.

SELF-CATERING HOLIDAYS IN BRITAIN 1996

Farms, Cottages, Houses, Chalets, Flats and Caravans throughout Britain.

Includes Campus Holidays.

Other FHG Publications 1996

Recommended Short Break Holidays
Recommended Country Hotels of Britain
Recommended Wayside & Country Inns of Britain
Pets Welcome!
Bed and Breakfast in Britain
The Golf Guide: Where to Play/Where to Stay
Farm Holiday Guide England, Wales, Ireland & Channel Islands
Farm Holiday Guide Scotland
Britain's Best Holidays
Guide to Caravan and Camping Holidays
Bed and Breakfast Stops
Children Welcome! Family Holiday & Attractions Guide
Scottish Welcome

ISBN 1 85055 198 7 © FHG Publications Ltd. 1996
Cover picture: supplied by Still Moving Picture Co.
Design by Cyan Creative Consultants, Glasgow
(0141-638 4860)

Typeset by RD Composition Ltd., Glasgow.
Printed and bound by Benham's Ltd., Colchester.

Distribution – **Book Trade**: WLM, Downing Road, West Meadows Industrial Estate, Derby DE21 6HA.
(Tel: 01332 343332. Fax: 01332 340464).
News Trade: United Magazine Distribution Ltd, 16-28 Tabernacle Street, London EC2A 4BN.
(Tel: 0171-638 4666. Fax: 0171-638 4665).

Published by FHG Publications Ltd.,
Abbey Mill Business Centre, Seedhill, Paisley PA1 1TJ (Tel: 0141-887 0428. Fax: 0141-889 7204).

FHG

CONTENTS

GREAT BRITAIN
COUNTIES & REGIONS

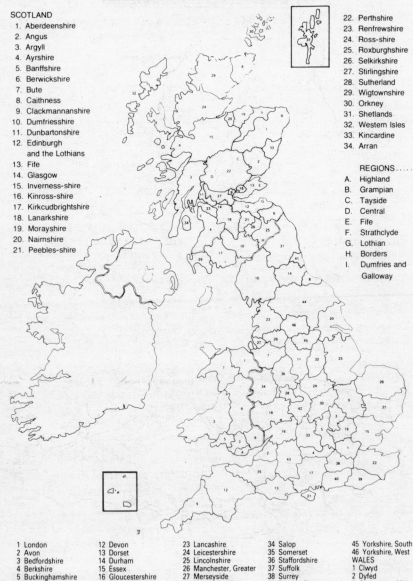

SCOTLAND
1. Aberdeenshire
2. Angus
3. Argyll
4. Ayrshire
5. Banffshire
6. Berwickshire
7. Bute
8. Caithness
9. Clackmannanshire
10. Dumfriesshire
11. Dunbartonshire
12. Edinburgh
   and the Lothians
13. Fife
14. Glasgow
15. Inverness-shire
16. Kinross-shire
17. Kirkcudbrightshire
18. Lanarkshire
19. Morayshire
20. Nairnshire
21. Peebles-shire

22. Perthshire
23. Renfrewshire
24. Ross-shire
25. Roxburghshire
26. Selkirkshire
27. Stirlingshire
28. Sutherland
29. Wigtownshire
30. Orkney
31. Shetlands
32. Western Isles
33. Kincardine
34. Arran

REGIONS.....
A. Highland
B. Grampian
C. Tayside
D. Central
E. Fife
F. Strathclyde
G. Lothian
H. Borders
I. Dumfries and
   Galloway

1 London
2 Avon
3 Bedfordshire
4 Berkshire
5 Buckinghamshire
6 Cambridgeshire
7 Cheshire
8 Cleveland
9 Cornwall
10 Cumbria
11 Derbyshire

12 Devon
13 Dorset
14 Durham
15 Essex
16 Gloucestershire
17 Hampshire
18 Hereford & Worcester
19 Hertfordshire
20 Humberside
21 Isle of Wight
22 Kent

23 Lancashire
24 Leicestershire
25 Lincolnshire
26 Manchester, Greater
27 Merseyside
28 Midlands, West
29 Norfolk
30 Northamptonshire
31 Northumberland
32 Nottinghamshire
33 Oxfordshire

34 Salop
35 Somerset
36 Staffordshire
37 Suffolk
38 Surrey
39 Sussex, East
40 Sussex, West
41 Tyne & Wear
42 Warwickshire
43 Wiltshire
44 Yorkshire, North

45 Yorkshire, South
46 Yorkshire, West
WALES
1 Clwyd
2 Dyfed
3 Glamorgan, Mid
4 Glamorgan, South
5 Glamorgan, West
6 Gwent
7 Gwynedd
8 Powys

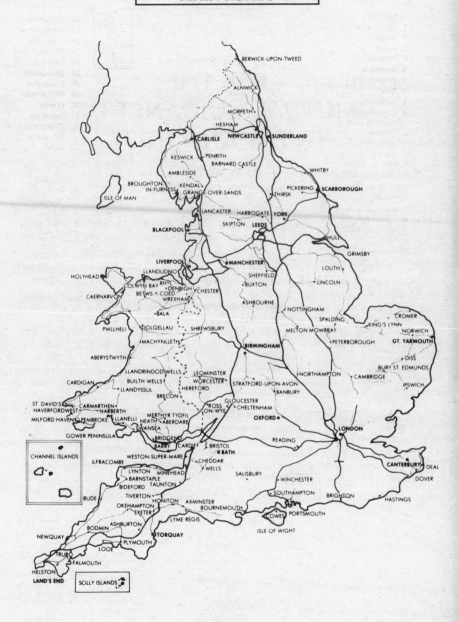

BOOKING

FOR THE
MUTUAL GUIDANCE OF
GUEST AND HOST

Every year literally thousands of holidays, short-breaks and overnight stops are arranged through our guides, the vast majority without any problems at all. In a handful of cases, however, difficulties do arise about bookings, which often could have been prevented from the outset.

It is important to remember that when accommodation has been booked, both parties — guests and hosts — have entered into a form of contract. We hope that the following points will provide helpful guidance.

GUESTS: When enquiring about accommodation, be as precise as possible. Give exact dates, numbers in your party and the ages of any children. State the number and type of rooms wanted and also what catering you require — bed and breakfast, full board, etc. Make sure that the position about evening meals is clear — and about pets, reductions for children or any other special points.

Read our reviews carefully to ensure that the proprietors you are going to contact can supply what you want. Ask for a letter confirming all arrangements, if possible.

If you have to cancel, do so as soon as possible. Proprietors do have the right to retain deposits and under certain circumstances to charge for cancelled holidays if adequate notice is not given and they cannot re-let the accommodation.

HOSTS: Give details about your facilities and about any special conditions. Explain your deposit system clearly and arrangements for cancellations, charges, etc, and whether or not your terms include VAT.

If for any reason you are unable to fulfill an agreed booking without adequate notice, you may be under an obligation to arrange alternative suitable accommodation or to make some form of compensation.

While every effort is made to ensure accuracy, we regret that FHG Publications cannot accept responsibility for errors, omissions or misrepresentation in our entries or any consequences thereof. Prices in particular should be checked because we go to press early. We will follow up complaints but cannot act as arbiters or agents for either party.

FHG

FOREWORD

SELF-CATERING HOLIDAYS IN BRITAIN 1996

Self-catering holidays in Britain are benefiting from the general growth of visitor attractions, outdoor and indoor leisure opportunities, resort facilities and improved choice and quality for 'eating out'. Free from hotel routines and set meal-times, there is usually plenty to see and do when it suits you. Activities for adults, diversions for children, fun for families when and where you please. Our Readers' Offer Vouchers are hopefully an appetiser for what is becoming a rich menu of holiday entertainment across the country.

For 1996 we have another wide selection of all kinds of holiday properties throughout Britain to help you to enjoy all the advantages of self-catering. When you use the Direct Booking contacts in *SELF-CATERING HOLIDAYS IN BRITAIN*, you benefit from the economy and flexibility this allows. By booking Direct you can make big savings on your holiday costs. You can also discuss a range of possible dates and other personal requirements with your prospective host without completing forms and ticking boxes and coping with an often anonymous central reservation service.

When you are making your enquiries and bookings, you should bear the following points in mind.

ENQUIRIES AND BOOKINGS. Give full details of dates (with an alternative), numbers and any special requirements. Ask about any points in the holiday description which are not clear and make sure that prices and conditions are clearly explained. You should receive confirmation in writing and a receipt for any deposit or advance payment. If you book your holiday well in advance, especially self-catering, confirm your arrival details nearer the time. Some proprietors, especially for self-catering, request full payment in advance but a reasonable deposit is more normal.

CANCELLATIONS. A holiday booking is a form of contract with obligations on both sides. If you have to cancel, give as much notice as possible. The longer the notice the better the chance that your host can replace your booking and therefore refund any payments. If the proprietor cancels in such a way that causes serious inconvenience, he may have obligations to you which have not been properly honoured. Take advice if necessary from such organisations as the Citizen's Advice Bureau, Consumer's Association, Trading Standards Office, Local Tourist Office, etc., or your own solicitor.

COMPLAINTS. It's best if any problems can be sorted out at the start of your holiday. If the problem is not solved, you can contact the organisations mentioned above. You can also write to us. We will follow up the complaint with the advertiser – but we cannot act as intermediaries or accept responsibility for holiday arrangements.

FHG Publications Ltd. do not inspect accommodation and an entry in our guides does not imply a recommendation. However our advertisers have signed their agreement to work for the holidaymaker's best interests and as their customer, you have the right to expect appropriate attention and service.

HOLIDAY INSURANCE. It is possible to insure against holiday cancellation. Brokers and insurance companies can advise you about this.

THE FHG DIPLOMA. Every year we award a small number of Diplomas to holiday proprietors who have been specially recommended to us by readers. The names of our 1995 Diploma winners are listed in this book and we will be happy to receive your recommendations for 1996.

Please mention *SELF-CATERING & FURNISHED HOLIDAYS* when you are making enquiries or bookings and don't forget to use our Readers' Offer Voucher/Coupons if you're near any of the attractions which are kindly participating.

Peter Clark
Publishing Director

SELF-CATERING HOLIDAYS IN BRITAIN 1996

READERS OFFER VOUCHERS

On the following pages you will find vouchers which offer free and/or reduced rate entry to a selection of Visitor Attractions.
Readers should simply cut out the coupons and present them if they are visiting any of the attractions concerned.
Please let us know if you have any difficulty.

READERS' OFFER 1996 VALID during 1996

Sacrewell Farm and Country Centre

Thornaugh, Peterborough, Cambridgeshire PE8 6HJ Tel: (01780) 782222

One **FREE** admission with each paid entry of similar age group (adult/child)

NOT TO BE USED IN CONJUNCTION WITH ANY OTHER OFFER

 READERS' OFFER 1996 VALID during 1996

RAILWAY AGE

Vernon Way, Crewe, Cheshire CW1 2DB Telephone: 01270 212130

£1 off adult or child admission; **£2** off family ticket.

NOT TO BE USED IN CONJUNCTION WITH ANY OTHER OFFER

 READERS' OFFER 1996 VALID 10/4 to 30/9 1996 (not Bank Holidays)

CORNISH SEAL SANCTUARY

Gweek, Near Helston, Cornwall TR12 6UG Tel: 01326 221361

One FREE child (4-14 incl.) when accompanied by two full-paying adults

NOT TO BE USED IN CONJUNCTION WITH ANY OTHER OFFER

 READERS' OFFER 1996 VALID during 1996

DAIRYLAND FARM WORLD

Summercourt, Near Newquay, Cornwall TR8 5AA Tel: 01872 510246

One child **FREE** when accompanied by adult paying full admission price

NOT TO BE USED IN CONJUNCTION WITH ANY OTHER OFFER

 READERS' OFFER 1996 VALID during 1996

COARSE FISHING AT CROSSFIELD

Crossfield, Staffield, Kirkoswald, Cumbria CA10 1EU Tel: 01768 898711

ADMIT two children for the price of one; three adults for the price of two

NOT TO BE USED IN CONJUNCTION WITH ANY OTHER OFFER

The fascinating story of farming and country life with working watermill, gardens, collections of bygones, farm and nature trails. Excellent for young children. Campers and Caravanners welcome.

DIRECTIONS: off A47, 8 miles west of Peterborough.

OPEN: daily all year.

FHG PUBLICATIONS, ABBEY MILL BUSINESS CENTRE, PAISLEY PA1 1TJ

Railway Museum and operating centre

DIRECTIONS: adjacent to Safeway supermarket in town centre; follow brown-and-white tourist signs.

OPEN: daily 10am to 4pm (21st February to 21st December 1996).

FHG PUBLICATIONS, ABBEY MILL BUSINESS CENTRE, PAISLEY PA1 1TJ

Europe's leading marine animal rescue centre, dedicated to the rescue and release of pups found around the coastline; also home to a colony of adult seals and sealions.

DIRECTIONS: from Helston follow A3083, past RNAS Culdrose turn left at roundabout and follow tourist signs to Gweek (approx. 5 miles).

OPEN: daily (except Christmas Day) from 9am.

FHG PUBLICATIONS, ABBEY MILL BUSINESS CENTRE, PAISLEY PA1 1TJ

Britain's premier farm attraction - milking parlour, Heritage Centre, Farmpark and playground. Daily events include bottle feeding, "Pat-a-Pet" and rally karts.

DIRECTIONS: 4 miles from Newquay on the A3058 Newquay to St Austell road.

OPEN: from early April to end October 10.30am to 5pm. Also open from early December to Christmas Eve 12-5pm daily.

FHG PUBLICATIONS, ABBEY MILL BUSINESS CENTRE, PAISLEY PA1 1TJ

Relax, escape and enjoy a great day out - Carp, Rudd, Tench, Bream, Crucians, Ide, Roach and (for fly) Rainbow and Brown Trout

DIRECTIONS: from Kirkoswald follow signs for Staffield, turn right (signposted Dale/Blunderfield); Crossfield is 200m up narrow road via cattle grid.

OPEN: April to November open daily; November to April weekends only

FHG PUBLICATIONS, ABBEY MILL BUSINESS CENTRE, PAISLEY PA1 1TJ

FHG

READERS' OFFER 1996

VALID during 1996

THE CUMBERLAND TOY AND MODEL MUSEUM

Banks Court, Market Place, Cockermouth, Cumbria CA13 9NG Tel: 01900 827606

One person **FREE** per full paying adult

NOT TO BE USED IN CONJUNCTION WITH ANY OTHER OFFER

FHG

READERS' OFFER 1996

VALID April to September 1996

Lowther Leisure and Wildlife Park

Hackthorpe, Penrith, Cumbria CA10 2HG   Tel: 01931 712523

£2 off standard admission price (per person) up to maximum of 5 persons

NOT TO BE USED IN CONJUNCTION WITH ANY OTHER OFFER

FHG

READERS' OFFER 1996

VALID to end October 1996

HEIGHTS OF ABRAHAM

Matlock Bath, Derbyshire DE4 3PD Telephone: 01629 582365

FREE child entry with one full paying adult

NOT TO BE USED IN CONJUNCTION WITH ANY OTHER OFFER

READERS' OFFER 1996

VALID during 1996

National Tramway Museum

Crich, Matlock, Derbyshire DE4 5DP Telephone: 01773 852565

Admit one child **FREE** with full paying adult (not valid for Santa Specials)

NOT TO BE USED IN CONJUNCTION WITH ANY OTHER OFFER

READERS' OFFER 1996

VALID Easter to October 1996

TOTNES MOTOR MUSEUM

Steamer Quay, Totnes, Devon TQ9 5AL Telephone: 01803 862777

One child **FREE** when accompanied by full-paying adult

NOT TO BE USED IN CONJUNCTION WITH ANY OTHER OFFER

100 years of mainly British toys including working tinplate Hornby trains, Scalextric cars, Lego etc. Free quiz.

DIRECTIONS: just off the market place in Cockermouth

OPEN: daily 10am to 5pm from 1st February to 30th November

FHG PUBLICATIONS, ABBEY MILL BUSINESS CENTRE, PAISLEY PA1 1TJ

Attractions, rides, adventure play areas, circus and wildlife - all set in undulating parkland amidst beautiful scenery - make Lowther the Lake District's premier all-day attraction.

DIRECTIONS: travelling North leave M6 at J39, follow brown signs; travelling South leave at J40, follow brown signs. A6 Shap Road, 6 miles south Penrith.

OPEN: March/April to September 10am to 5/6pm.

FHG PUBLICATIONS, ABBEY MILL BUSINESS CENTRE, PAISLEY PA1 1TJ

Cable car return journey plus two famous show caverns. Tree Top Visitor Centre with restaurant, coffee and gift shops; nature trails and children's play areas.

DIRECTIONS: signposted from all nearby major trunk roads.On A6 at Matlock Bath.

OPEN: daily Easter to end October 10am to 5pm (later in High Season).

FHG PUBLICATIONS, ABBEY MILL BUSINESS CENTRE, PAISLEY PA1 1TJ

Outdoor action with indoor attractions! Unlimited vintage tram rides through period street to open countryside, plus video theatre, exhibition hall, cafe, picnic areas, shops.

DIRECTIONS: 15 miles north of Derby, 6 miles from Matlock, 8 miles from Junction 28 M1

OPEN: April to October 10am to 5.30pm daily (6.30pm weekends and Bank Holidays); March and November Sundays only

FHG PUBLICATIONS, ABBEY MILL BUSINESS CENTRE, PAISLEY PA1 1TJ

Vintage, sports and racing cars, motorbikes, bicycles; 1920s picnic, 1930s garage; video showing old racing film. Something for everyone!

DIRECTIONS: Totnes town centre. Follow brown tourist signs.

OPEN: Easter to October 10am to 5.30pm

FHG PUBLICATIONS, ABBEY MILL BUSINESS CENTRE, PAISLEY PA1 1TJ

43

READERS' OFFER 1996

VALID during 1996

THE BIG SHEEP

Bideford, Devon EX39 5AP   Telephone: 01237 472366

Admit one **FREE** with each paid admission

NOT TO BE USED IN CONJUNCTION WITH ANY OTHER OFFER

READERS' OFFER 1996

VALID Easter to end Oct. 1996

Dorset Heavy Horse Centre

Edmondsham, Verwood, Dorset BH21 5RJ Telephone: 01202 824040

Admit one adult **FREE** when accompanied by one full-paying adult

NOT TO BE USED IN CONJUNCTION WITH ANY OTHER OFFER

READERS' OFFER 1996

VALID April to October 1996

Killhope Lead Mining Centre

Cowshill, Upper Weardale, Co. Durham DL13 1AR Tel: 01388 537505

Admit one child **FREE** with full-paying adult

NOT TO BE USED IN CONJUNCTION WITH ANY OTHER OFFER

READERS' OFFER 1996

VALID during 1996

Cotswold Farm Park

Guiting Power, Near Stow-on-the-Wold, Gloucestershire GL54 5UG Tel: 01451 850307

Admit one child **FREE** with an adult paying full entrance fee

NOT TO BE USED IN CONJUNCTION WITH ANY OTHER OFFER

READERS' OFFER 1996

VALID during 1996

NATIONAL WATERWAYS MUSEUM

Llanthony Warehouse, Gloucester Docks, Gloucester GL1 2EH Tel: 01452 318054

20% off all tickets (Single, Family or Shopper).

NOT TO BE USED IN CONJUNCTION WITH ANY OTHER OFFER

"England for Excellence" award-winning rural attraction combining traditional rural crafts with hilarious novelties such as sheep racing and duck trialling.

DIRECTIONS: on A39 North Devon link road, 2 miles west of Bideford Bridge

OPEN: daily all year, 10am to 6pm

FHG PUBLICATIONS, ABBEY MILL BUSINESS CENTRE, PAISLEY PA1 1TJ

Heavy horse and pony centre, also Icelandic riding stables. Cafe, gift shop. Facilities for disabled visitors.

DIRECTIONS: signposted from the centre of Verwood, which is on the B3081

OPEN: Easter to end October 10am to 5pm

FHG PUBLICATIONS, ABBEY MILL BUSINESS CENTRE, PAISLEY PA1 1TJ

Britain's best preserved lead mining site - and a great day out for all the family, with lots to see and do

DIRECTIONS: alongside A689, midway between Stanhope and Alston in the heart of the North Pennines.

OPEN: April 1st to October 31st 10.30am to 5pm daily

FHG PUBLICATIONS, ABBEY MILL BUSINESS CENTRE, PAISLEY PA1 1TJ

The home of rare breeds conservation, with over 50 breeding flocks and herds of rare farm animals. Adventure playground, pets' corners, picnic area, farm nature trail.

DIRECTIONS: M5 Junction 9, off B4077 Stow-on-the-Wold road. 5 miles from Bourton-on-the-Water.

OPEN: daily 10.30am to 5pm April to September (to 6pm Sundays, Bank Holidays and daily in July and August).

FHG PUBLICATIONS, ABBEY MILL BUSINESS CENTRE, PAISLEY PA1 1TJ

The history of 200 years of inland waterways by means of interactive exhibits, working engines, and two quaysides of floating exhibits. Special school summer holiday activities.

DIRECTIONS: Junction 11 or 12 off M5 - follow brown signs for Historic Docks. Railway and bus station 10 minute walk.

OPEN: Summer 10am to 6pm; Winter 10am to 5pm. Closed Christmas Day.

FHG PUBLICATIONS, ABBEY MILL BUSINESS CENTRE, PAISLEY PA1 1TJ

The No.1 Zoological Park in the South, dedicated to breeding endangered species.
1000 animals in 100 acres of parkland - ideal for all ages.

DIRECTIONS: 6 miles south-east of Winchester, clearly signposted from M3 and M27.

OPEN: daily from 10am (closed Christmas Day).

FHG PUBLICATIONS, ABBEY MILL BUSINESS CENTRE, PAISLEY PA1 1TJ

One of the UK's largest collections of rare farm animals, plus deer, llamas, miniature
horses, waterfowl and poultry in 30 beautiful coastal acres.

DIRECTIONS: on main south coast road A3055 between Ventnor and Niton.

OPEN: Easter to end October open daily 10am to 5.30pm;
Winter open weekends only 10am to 4pm

FHG PUBLICATIONS, ABBEY MILL BUSINESS CENTRE, PAISLEY PA1 1TJ

Award-winning science and industry museum. Fascinating colliery tours and
"hands-on" displays including a robot, holograms, tornado and virtual reality.

DIRECTIONS: 10 minutes from Junction 22 M1 and Junction 13 M42/A42.
Well signposted along the A50.

OPEN: April to Oct.10am to 6pm; Nov. to March 10am to 5pm. Closed 25/26 Dec.

FHG PUBLICATIONS, ABBEY MILL BUSINESS CENTRE, PAISLEY PA1 1TJ

Lions, snow leopards, chimpanzees, penguins, reptiles, aquarium and lots more,
set amidst landscaped gardens.

DIRECTIONS: on the coast 16 miles north of Liverpool; follow the brown tourist signs.

OPEN: daily except Christmas Day. Summer 10am to 6pm; Winter 10am to 4pm.

FHG PUBLICATIONS, ABBEY MILL BUSINESS CENTRE, PAISLEY PA1 1TJ

Beautiful walled garden with nearly 900 types of herbs, woodland walk, nursery, shop.
Guide dogs only.

DIRECTIONS: 6 miles north of Hexham, next to Chesters Roman Fort.

OPEN: daily March to October/November.

FHG PUBLICATIONS, ABBEY MILL BUSINESS CENTRE, PAISLEY PA1 1TJ

47

A modern working farm with over 3000 animals including ducklings, deer, bees, rheas, piglets, snails, lambs (all year). New pet centre.

DIRECTIONS: off the A614 at Farnsfield, 12 miles north of Nottingham. From M1 Junction 27 follow "Robin Hood" signs for 10 miles.

OPEN: daily all year round.

FHG PUBLICATIONS, ABBEY MILL BUSINESS CENTRE, PAISLEY PA1 1TJ

Traditional cider made on the premises (Oct/Nov) on sale all year- sample before you buy. Shop with pottery and gifts; garden section; museum of farm tools, wagons and photos.

DIRECTIONS: approx. 2 miles from Ilminster off A303, 3 miles from Cricket St Thomas.

OPEN: all year except Sunday afternoons.

FHG PUBLICATIONS, ABBEY MILL BUSINESS CENTRE, PAISLEY PA1 1TJ

---

* Britain's most spectacular caves * Traditional paper-making * Fairground Memories *
* Penny Arcade * Magical Mirror Maze *

DIRECTIONS: from M5 Junction 22 follow brown-and-white signs via A38 and A371. Wookey Hole is just 2 miles from Wells.

OPEN: Summer 9.30am to 5.30pm; Winter 10.30am to 4.30pm. Closed 17-25 December.

FHG PUBLICATIONS, ABBEY MILL BUSINESS CENTRE, PAISLEY PA1 1TJ

See woodland with new eyes at this family-run working wood; fascinating and fun for all the family. Trails, adventure playground, exhibition, picnic areas, BBQs for hire, teas.

DIRECTIONS: on main A272 in Hadlow Down village, 5 miles north-east of Uckfield.

OPEN: daily all year.

FHG PUBLICATIONS, ABBEY MILL BUSINESS CENTRE, PAISLEY PA1 1TJ

World of Natural History including World of Dinosaurs and Fossil Museum.

DIRECTIONS: signposted "Garden Paradise" off A26 and A259

OPEN: all year, except Christmas Day and Boxing Day.

FHG PUBLICATIONS, ABBEY MILL BUSINESS CENTRE, PAISLEY PA1 1TJ

49

Europe's only indoor theme park with rollercoaster, McDonald's Party Express, live entertainment, and lots more - a great day IN.

DIRECTIONS: A1(M), south of Newcastle-upon-Tyne

OPEN: daily all year round.

FHG PUBLICATIONS, ABBEY MILL BUSINESS CENTRE, PAISLEY PA1 1TJ

Working narrow gauge steam railway, railway museum and over 70 replica brasses to rub.

DIRECTIONS: on the A447 six miles north of Hinckley.

OPEN: second Saturday each month

FHG PUBLICATIONS, ABBEY MILL BUSINESS CENTRE, PAISLEY PA1 1TJ

England's largest craft village, cafe, butcher's and farm shops, antiques centre (no charge). Rare breeds farm, pets' corner, nature trail, guinea pig village, falconry displays.

DIRECTIONS: 3 miles north of Warwick, 5 miles south of Knowle, just off Junction 15 of M40 via A46/A4177

OPEN: daily 10am to 5.30pm

FHG PUBLICATIONS, ABBEY MILL BUSINESS CENTRE, PAISLEY PA1 1TJ

A unique museum transporting you back in time to wartime Britain

DIRECTIONS: at junction of A64 York to Scarborough road and A169 Malton to Pickering road.

OPEN: February 14th to December 23rd 9am to 5pm (last admission 4pm). Allow at least 3 hours for a visit.

FHG PUBLICATIONS, ABBEY MILL BUSINESS CENTRE, PAISLEY PA1 1TJ

Three-dimensional animated feline characters with entertaining scripts in a woodland themed environment. Video theatre, coffee house and gift shop. Disabled access.

DIRECTIONS: on the A657 out of Shipley (250 yards)

OPEN: daily except Christmas Day 10am to 5.30pm (last admission 4.45pm)

FHG PUBLICATIONS, ABBEY MILL BUSINESS CENTRE, PAISLEY PA1 1TJ

READERS' OFFER 1996   VALID during 1996

STORYBOOK GLEN

Maryculter, Aberdeen, Aberdeenshire AB1 OAT   Telephone: (01224) 732941

10% Discount on all entry fees on production of voucher.

NOT TO BE USED IN CONJUNCTION WITH ANY OTHER OFFER

READERS' OFFER 1996   VALID April to October 1996

SCOTTISH MARITIME MUSEUM

Harbourside, Irvine, Ayrshire KA12 8QE Telephone: (01294) 278283

One adult FREE with each paid adult entry

NOT TO BE USED IN CONJUNCTION WITH ANY OTHER OFFER

READERS' OFFER 1996   VALID during 1996

MYRETON MOTOR MUSEUM

Aberlady, East Lothian EH32 0PZ Telephone: 01875 870288

One child **FREE** with each paying adult

NOT TO BE USED IN CONJUNCTION WITH ANY OTHER OFFER

READERS' OFFER 1996   VALID April 1996 to April 1997

EDINBURGH CRYSTAL VISITOR CENTRE

Eastfield, Penicuik, Midlothian EH26 8HB Telephone: 01968 675128

OFFER: Two for the price of one (higher ticket price applies).

NOT TO BE USED IN CONJUNCTION WITH ANY OTHER OFFER

READERS' OFFER 1996   VALID during 1996

HIGHLAND FOLK MUSEUM

Duke Street, Kingussie, Inverness-shire PH21 1JG Tel: 01540 661307

One **FREE** child with accompanying adult paying full admission price

NOT TO BE USED IN CONJUNCTION WITH ANY OTHER OFFER

28 acre landscaped park with over 100 life-sized models of nursery rhymes.

DIRECTIONS: 5 miles west of Aberdeen on the B9077

OPEN: 1st March to 31st October: daily 10am to 6pm.
1st November to end February: Saturday and Sunday only 11am to 4pm

FHG PUBLICATIONS, ABBEY MILL BUSINESS CENTRE, PAISLEY PA1 1TJ

Historic vessels open to the public including a "puffer" and a steam yacht; "There Is A Cow In My Cabin" exhibition, plus world's oldest clipper "Carrick" under restoration.

DIRECTIONS: follow signs to Irvine and then signposts for harbourside.

OPEN: 1st April to 31st October - 10am to 5pm

FHG PUBLICATIONS, ABBEY MILL BUSINESS CENTRE, PAISLEY PA1 1TJ

Motor cars from 1896, motorcycles from 1902, commercial vehicles from 1919, cycles from 1880, British WWII military vehicles, ephemera, period advertising etc.

DIRECTIONS: off the A198 near Aberlady.

OPEN: daily October to Easter 10am to 5pm; Easter to October 10am to 6pm.
Closed Christmas Day and New Year's Day.

FHG PUBLICATIONS, ABBEY MILL BUSINESS CENTRE, PAISLEY PA1 1TJ

Visitor Centre with Exhibition Room, factory tours, Crystal Shop, gift shop, coffee shop. Facilities for disabled visitors.

DIRECTIONS: 10 miles south of Edinburgh on the A701 Peebles road; signposted a few miles from the city centre.

OPEN: Visitor Centre open daily; Factory Tours weekdays all year, plus weekends April to October.

FHG PUBLICATIONS, ABBEY MILL BUSINESS CENTRE, PAISLEY PA1 1TJ

One of the oldest open air museums in Britain! A treasure trove of Highland life and culture. Live events June to September.

DIRECTIONS: Easily reached via the A9, 68 miles north of Perth and 42 miles south of Inverness.

OPEN: Easter to October: open daily. November to March: open weekdays.
Closed Christmas and New Year.

FHG PUBLICATIONS, ABBEY MILL BUSINESS CENTRE, PAISLEY PA1 1TJ

READERS' OFFER 1996

VALID during 1996

CREETOWN GEM ROCK MUSEUM

Chain Road, Creetown, Near Newton Stewart, Kirkcudbrightshire DG8 7HJ
Telephone: 01671 820357

20% off admission prices

NOT TO BE USED IN CONJUNCTION WITH ANY OTHER OFFER

READERS' OFFER 1996

VALID during 1996

NEW LANARK VISITOR CENTRE

New Lanark Mills, Lanark, Lanarkshire ML11 9DB Tel: (01555) 661345

One child **FREE** with each full paying adult

NOT TO BE USED IN CONJUNCTION WITH ANY OTHER OFFER

READERS' OFFER 1996

VALID April to October 1996

MUSEUM OF LEAD MINING

Wanlockhead, By Biggar, Lanarkshire ML12 6UT Telephone: (01659) 74387

One child **FREE** with each paying adult

NOT TO BE USED IN CONJUNCTION WITH ANY OTHER OFFER

READERS' OFFER 1996

VALID May to September 1996

DARNAWAY FARM VISITOR CENTRE

Brodie, Forres, Morayshire Telephone: (01309) 641469

A **FREE** pot of tea if full admission has been paid

NOT TO BE USED IN CONJUNCTION WITH ANY OTHER OFFER

READERS' OFFER 1996

VALID 1st March to 30th September 1996

FINLAYSTONE

Langbank, Renfrewshire PA14 6TG Telephone: 01475 540505

One adult admitted **FREE** with each paying adult

NOT TO BE USED IN CONJUNCTION WITH ANY OTHER OFFER

STB award-winning museum designed to stimulate interest and wonder in the fascinating subjects of gems, crystals and mineralogy. Exciting audio-visual display.

DIRECTIONS: 7 miles from Newton Stewart, 11 miles from Gatehouse of Fleet; just off A75 Carlisle to Stranraer road.

OPEN: Open daily Easter to 23rd December; January and February weekends only.

FHG PUBLICATIONS, ABBEY MILL BUSINESS CENTRE, PAISLEY PA1 1TJ

200-year old conservation village with award-winning Visitor Centre, set in beautiful countryside

DIRECTIONS: one mile south of Lanark; well signposted from all major routes.

OPEN: daily all year round 11am to 5pm

FHG PUBLICATIONS, ABBEY MILL BUSINESS CENTRE, PAISLEY PA1 1TJ

Museum and Visitor Centre with tearoom and gift shop. Guided tours of real lead mine and period cottages. New for 1996: Lead Miners' Library.

DIRECTIONS: signposted off A76 at Mennock and off M74 at Abington.

OPEN: 11am to 4.30pm daily 1st April to 31st October. November to March by appointment.

FHG PUBLICATIONS, ABBEY MILL BUSINESS CENTRE, PAISLEY PA1 1TJ

A family day out. Exhibitions of vintage tractors and machinery, lots of animals and poultry. Extensive woodland walks, play area and coffee shop.

DIRECTIONS: signposted on the A96 three miles west of Forres.

OPEN: daily 1st May to mid-September 10am to 5pm.

FHG PUBLICATIONS, ABBEY MILL BUSINESS CENTRE, PAISLEY PA1 1TJ

---

100 acres of beautiful woodlands, 10 acres of renowned gardens, Visitor Centre and shop, Clan MacMillan Centre, tearoom.

DIRECTIONS: west of Glasgow, on the A8 10 minutes from Glasgow Airport.

OPEN: daily 10am to 5pm. Tearoom open daily 11am to 5pm April to September.

FHG PUBLICATIONS, ABBEY MILL BUSINESS CENTRE, PAISLEY PA1 1TJ

READERS' OFFER 1996   VALID until 30th September 1996

LLANGOLLEN RAILWAY

The Station, Abbey Road, Llangollen, Clwyd LL20 8SN Tel: (01978) 860979

One child **FREE** with each full fare-paying adult

NOT TO BE USED IN CONJUNCTION WITH ANY OTHER OFFER

READERS' OFFER 1996   VALID during 1996

Big Pit Mining Museum

Blaenafon, Gwent NP4 9XP Telephone: (01495) 790311

Admit one child **FREE** per voucher with two full-paying adults.
(not to be used with family ticket).

NOT TO BE USED IN CONJUNCTION WITH ANY OTHER OFFER

READERS' OFFER 1996   VALID March to October 1996

PILI PALAS - BUTTERFLY PALACE

Menai Bridge, Isle of Anglesey, Gwynedd LL59 5RP Tel: 01248 712474

One child **FREE** with each adult paying full entry price

NOT TO BE USED IN CONJUNCTION WITH ANY OTHER OFFER

READERS' OFFER 1996   VALID during 1996

Llanberis Lake Railway

Llanberis, Gwynedd LL55 4TY Telephone: 01286 870549

One child travels **FREE** with two full fare-paying adults

NOT TO BE USED IN CONJUNCTION WITH ANY OTHER OFFER

READERS' OFFER 1996   VALID during 1996

CENTRE FOR ALTERNATIVE TECHNOLOGY

Machynlleth, Powys SY20 9AZ Telephone: 01654 702400

One child **FREE** when accompanied by paying adult (one per party only)

NOT TO BE USED IN CONJUNCTION WITH ANY OTHER OFFER

Preserved railway with steam and diesel engines, diesel multiple units and coaching stock; cafes and shops.

DIRECTIONS: A539 on left past river bridge in Llangollen; A5 turn right at traffic lights and left across river bridge - station is immediately on left.

OPEN: 10am to 6pm

FHG PUBLICATIONS, ABBEY MILL BUSINESS CENTRE, PAISLEY PA1 1TJ

Underground tours of original colliery workings by experienced miners. On the surface: exhibitions, forge, stables, craft shop and licensed cafeteria.

DIRECTIONS: M4 Junction 6, then A4042/3 to Pontypool and Blaenafon. From M50, A449 to Raglan, then A40 to Abergavenny and A4246 to Blaenafon.

OPEN: daily March to November. Phone for Winter opening times. Last admission 3.30pm

FHG PUBLICATIONS, ABBEY MILL BUSINESS CENTRE, PAISLEY PA1 1TJ

Visit Wales' top Butterfly House, with Bird House, Snake House, Ant Avenue, Creepy Crawly Cavern, shop, cafe, adventure playground, picnic area, nature trail etc.

DIRECTIONS: follow brown-and-white signs when crossing to Anglesey; one-and-a-half miles from the Bridge.

OPEN: March to end October 10am to 5pm daily; November/December 11am to 3pm.

FHG PUBLICATIONS, ABBEY MILL BUSINESS CENTRE, PAISLEY PA1 1TJ

A 40-minute ride on a quaint historic steam train along the shore of Llyn Padarn. Spectacular views of the mountains of Snowdonia.

DIRECTIONS: just off the A4086 Caernarfon to Capel Curig road. Follow the "Padarn Country Park" signs.

OPEN: most days March to October. Free timetable available from Railway.

FHG PUBLICATIONS, ABBEY MILL BUSINESS CENTRE, PAISLEY PA1 1TJ

Europe's leading Eco-Centre. Water-powered cliff railway, interactive renewable energy displays, beautiful organic gardens, animals; vegetarian restaurant.

DIRECTIONS: two-and-a-half miles north of Machynlleth on the A487 towards Dolgellau.

OPEN: From Easter to October inclusive: open daily 10am to 5pm; times may vary in Winter.

FHG PUBLICATIONS, ABBEY MILL BUSINESS CENTRE, PAISLEY PA1 1TJ

ENGLAND

LONDON

LONDON. Clarendon House, Ealing, London W5 5RJ. ♀♀ to ♀♀♀♀ *COMMENDED.* An elegant

Victorian town-house providing a choice of three apartments. Located in a fashionable residential area just half a mile from South Ealing Station (Piccadilly Line). Easy access to both Heathrow and Central London (20 minutes away), making the apartments ideal for holidays or business. The house has a secluded garden for alfresco meals or relaxation. Excellent shops, restaurants, theatres and places of interest are all at hand. Each apartment sleeps TWO, but this can be extended. All bed linen and towels are provided, and the rental is fully inclusive of heat and power. A detailed brochure is available on request. Rentals from £225 to £285. Brochure, all correspondance to: **Mr and Mrs C.A. Pedley, 21E Harewood Close, Bexhill-on-Sea, East Sussex TN39 3LX or Tel/Fax: 01424 212954 (24 hours answerphone).**

AVON

BATH near. Myrtle Cottage, Goose Green, Near Bristol. ♟♟♟♟ *HIGHLY COMMENDED.* **Sleeps 6 plus infant.**

250 year old country cottage overlooks meadows, situated in pleasant rural area midway between Bristol and Bath. Ideal centre for visiting the Cotswolds, Slimbridge, Longleat, Weston-super-Mare, Cheddar and Wells. Bath with its Georgian architecture and Roman remains is only 15 minutes' drive, as is Bristol, with Brunel's Suspension Bridge and S.S. Great Britain. Leisure centre nearby for swimming, badminton and squash. Modernised and equipped to a high standard. Sleeps six in one double bedroom, two twin-bedded rooms. Fully fitted kitchen/diner with automatic washing machine/dryer, dishwasher, freezer, microwave, etc. Lounge with inglenook fireplace, colour TV and telephone. Bathroom. Garden. Garage. Night storage heating inclusive. Linen an optional extra. Children welcome, but sorry, no pets. Terms from £195 to £315 per week. Open all year. Brochure from **Mrs S. Thompson, Myrtle House, Goose Green, Syston Hill, Warmley, Near Bristol BS15 5LU (0117 956 4961).**

BATH. Mrs P. Harward, Tyning House, Freshford, Bath BA3 6DR (01225 723288). ♟♟♟♟ *COMMENDED.* **Sleep 4/6.**

Large Victorian house and coachhouse with four comfortable and spacious apartments, self-contained units each sleeping four to six persons (one ground floor) set in seven acres of organically-run gardens and grounds. Rare breed and domestic animals to enjoy, large garden to relax in, hard tennis court, games room, seasonal produce for sale. Very pretty stone village, serviced by train and bus, six miles from Bath; extremely beautiful countryside, classified as an Area of Outstanding Natural Beauty. Lovely walks, canal rides, nice pubs, great variety of places to visit including Stonehenge, Salisbury, Longleat, Wells, Bristol, the Cotswolds, Weston super Mare, etc. Brochure available.

CORNWALL

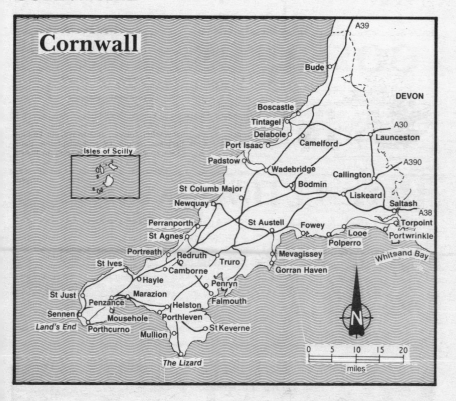

BODMIN. Tom Chadwick, Skisdon, St. Kew, Bodmin PL30 3HB (01208 841372). Charming flats in lovely old country manor house, Grade II Listed. Spacious gardens, lawns, streams and woodlands in peaceful valley only four miles from spectacular North Coast. Outstanding local coastline and countryside; many unspoiled stretches are National Trust owned. Bathing, surfing, sailing, sailboarding, golf, hill walking, fishing, pony trekking, cycleways, tennis, squash and modern sports centre all within easy reach — Camel Estuary, Polzeath, Daymer, Rock, Port Isaac and Bodmin Moor. Spacious self contained flats sleep from one to seven (for larger parties interior doors can be opened). Fully equipped kitchen, colour TVs, night storage heaters, communal laundry facilities. Popular village pub serving excellent food only 200 yards away, shops one mile, market town (Wadebridge) five miles. Prices from £110 to £330. Brochure available on request.

BODMIN (Liskeard). Janet and Malcolm Barker, Rivermead, Twowatersfoot, Liskeard PL14 6HT (01208 821464). Nestling in the beautiful Glynn Valley, midway Liskeard and Bodmin, off A38, amidst 30 acres of meadows and watermeadows. Ideally situated within reach of both North and South coasts and moors. Our two-bedroomed flats in the old stone barns sleep up to four. The old farm cottage sleeps six in three bedrooms with wood-burner in the lounge and electric blankets on all beds. Trout and salmon fishing available on our own single bank stretch of River Fowey at only £20 per week, limited to our guests. Well behaved pets welcome at no extra charge. Short Breaks October to mid-December and February to May excluding Bank Holidays.

A recently modernised old Cornish cottage with exposed beams situated in the centre of a delightful village which has shops and a pub just around the corner. Within easy reach of many beautiful walks, sandy beaches and places of interest including Tintagel (land of King Arthur), Port Isaac (an historic village), horse riding (three miles), boating (nine miles), surfing (seven miles), golf course (2 miles). The cottage is open March to October and has two double bedrooms, bathroom/toilet, sitting room, kitchen/diner with electric cooker, refrigerator, washing machine etc. A colour TV is also provided and, along with bed linen and power, included in the rental. Children welcome. Sorry, no pets. Parking space alongside cottage. Rates from £180 per week. SAE please for details.

Mrs J. C. Davey, "Churchtown", Fore Street, St. Teath, Bodmin PL30 3JA. Telephone: (01208) 850080

Churchtown

BOSCASTLE. Mrs Cheryl Nicholls, Trerosewill Farm, Paradise, Boscastle PL35 0DL (Tel & Fax: 01840 250545). ♀♀♀♀♀ *COMMENDED.* **Sleeps 2/10.** Self catering bungalow set in grounds of working dairy farm, overlooking picturesque fishing village. Situated in the heart of the Heritage Coast, close to the South-West Way. Panoramic sea and rural views. Bungalow is comfortable and equipped to high standard. Centrally heated. Linen and electricity all inclusive. Large gardens with children's play area. Badger watching available. Golfing breaks organised with concessionary rates on five local courses. On arrival we can supply a welcome pack and fresh eggs and milk from farm. Evening Meal is available at farmhouse. Regret no pets or smokers. Prices from £25 per person per week.

BOSCASTLE. Gull Cottage, Penally Terrace, Boscastle. Sleeps 5. In a sunny position, on coastal footpath immediately overlooking the tiny ancient harbour, a National Trust beauty spot, the cottage is peacefully situated and removed from through traffic. Splendid cliff walks and walks into the Valency Valley immediately from the cottage. Also many sandy beaches and lovely coves within easy reach. Cottage sleeps five people comfortably in four bedrooms — one double and three single. Separate diningroom and sittingroom; bathroom with shaver point, two toilets. TV, night storage heater. Roomy kitchen has cooker, fridge, waterheater, etc. Electric fires. Coin meter. Ample blankets provided, but guests must bring own linen. Regret, no pets or children under five years. Private covered parking. Small terraced garden. Milkman calls. Village shops five minutes' walk. Open all year. Terms approximately £100 to £365 weekly. Short Breaks available. SAE, please, for details from

Mrs Jewkes, 5 Headon Gardens, Countess Wear, Exeter, Devon EX2 6LE (01392 55191).

See also Colour Display Advertisement BOSCASTLE near. **David and Karen Claugh, Courtyard Farm Cottages, Lesnewth, Near Boscastle (01840 261256; Fax: 01840 261794).** A warm welcome awaits you at a group of delightful 17th century traditional stone cottages, converted original Corn Mill and buildings. Overlooking the Valencey Valley; some have sea views. The cottages are furnished and equipped to very high standards. Table tennis and snooker available. Beaches within easy reach. Children welcome. Dogs by arrangement. Terms from £105 to £595. Short breaks available. Colour brochure sent on request.

See also Colour Display Advertisement BUDE. **Houndapitt Farm Cottages, Sandymouth, Bude EX23 9HW (01288 355455).** Beautifully designed cottages, with magnificent views of bay and countryside, situated three-quarters of a mile from the beach. They accommodate two/nine persons in comfort. Amenities include launderette, games room etc, membership of Leisure Club with indoor heated pool. Farm activities include clay pigeon shoot, pony rides and daily feeding of lambs and small animals. Sorry no pets. Contact resident owners **Mr and Mrs A. Heard.**

LOWER KITLEIGH COTTAGE
Week St. Mary, Near Bude, Cornwall
Sleeps 7 plus cot

Pretty listed farmhouse in unspoilt country near magnificent coast. Newly renovated with all conveniences, yet retaining its charm, it stands in a peaceful grassy garden with picnic table and own parking. The sittingroom has period furniture, inglenook fireplace, free logs and colour TV. The fully equipped kitchen has fridge/freezer, double sink, electric cooker and new washer/tumble dryer. Three bedrooms with panoramic views, cot, duvets. Well-controlled dogs allowed. Riding nearby, golf, safe beaches, surfing, Cornish Moors, markets, cliff walks. All electricity inclusive, and central heating ensures a cosy stay throughout the year. Prices from £150 to £325 weekly.

Mr and Mrs T. Bruce-Dick, 114 Albert Street, London NW1 7NE   Tel: 0171-485 8976

CADGWITH COVE. **Mrs Andrea Betty, High Massetts, Cadgwith Cove, Helston TR12 7LA (01326 290571). Sleeps 2.** Fully equipped self-contained flat ideal for couples and only 200 yards from the sea. Situated in the picturesque village of Cadgwith on The Lizard Peninsula, the flat is attached to a large family residence, set in its own attractive grounds overlooking the sea. The flat comprises sleeping and living accommodation for two people with modern kitchen/dining facilities and separate shower room and toilet. Cadgwith is an unspoilt village and the cove offers safe bathing, fishing, skin diving and boating. A pub and small restaurant provide a good choice of food. Shopping and garage facilities within half a mile. Superb cliff walks along coastal paths. Golf and riding available locally. Please phone for further details.

CAMBORNE. **Wheelwrights Cottage, Carnhell Green, Camborne. Sleeps 4 adults; 1 child, plus cot.** This recently converted cottage in centre of village with Post Office/Stores and pub, is two-and-a-half miles inland from St. Ives Bay. On the ground floor there is a large lounge with multi-fuel stove and colour TV, a spacious kitchen/diner with automatic washing machine, and a cloakroom with washbasin and WC. Upstairs there is a double-bedded room, a twin-bedded room and a single-bedded room. A cot can be provided, on request. Duvets and covers are provided but not sheets and towels. There is a garage and parking for two cars, and a patio area. Electricity is deducted from the security deposit. We regret pets are not allowed. Terms from £135 to £320. Please apply to **Mr and Mrs G.N.F. Broughton, Orchard House, Wall, Gwinear, Hayle TR27 5HA (01736 850201; Fax: 01736 850046).**

COVERACK. Mill House Flat, Coverack. Sleeps 5. The self-contained first floor flat is centrally situated

close to the beach, shops and cafe. The accommodation comprises lounge/diner, comfortably furnished including colour TV, doors opening onto balcony with steps; three bedrooms (one with twin beds and sea view, one with bunk beds, one with single bed); all have washbasin, wardrobe and dressing table; cot available. Kitchen equipped with electric cooker, fridge and washing machine; bathroom has heated towel rail and razor point. Private parking for two cars. Electricity by coin meter. Dogs by arrangement with owner. From £125 weekly. All enquiries and further details from **Mrs C.H. Bishop, 2 Mill Lane, Smeeton Westerby, Leicester LE8 0QL (0116 2792180).**

COVERACK. Harbour Cottage, Coverack. Sleeps 6. Cosy 18th century cottage in the beautiful village of

Coverack. A most comfortable little cottage with three bedrooms, all with washbasins; small bathroom, separate toilet. Washing machine, TV and telephone. For the past 23 years guests have returned year after year. Fishing, safe bathing and wonderful walks all nearby, 10 minutes from market town of Helston. For further details contact **Mrs E. Parr, Beach House, Coverack TR12 6TE (01326 280621).**

CRACKINGTON HAVEN (North Cornwall Coast). Crackington Haven Holiday Cottages. ♀♀♀/

♀♀♀♀ APPROVED & COMMENDED. **Properties sleep 4/6.** Superior cottages situated in cliff-top hamlet with spectacular views surrounded by National Trust land. Accommodation for four/five/six, sleeping only two per bedroom. One room has four-poster and early pegged roof; all very well equipped and furnished; fine timber ceilings, some dating back to Tudor period. Livingrooms have attractive stone fireplaces, colour TV. Background central heating available; also laundry facilities and linen hire. Each cottage has its own private garden and ample parking space. Sandy beach within walking distance; splendid cliff walks. Excellent choice of home-cooked take-away meals available. SAE **Mrs P. Preller, Broomhill, Rosecare, St. Gennys, Bude EX23 0BE (01840 230310).**

CUSGARNE. Joyce Clench, Saffron Meadow, Cusgarne, Truro TR4 8RW (01872 863171). Sleeps 2 or 2 plus child. The Studio sited within the grounds of Saffron Meadow is a cosy single storey detached dwelling with own enclosed garden and safe parking. Secluded and surrounded by wooded pastureland. Well appointed main bedroom with vanity unit. Small child's bedroom. Fully tiled shower, WC and LB suite. Well equipped kitchen/diner, compact TV room. Hot water galore and gas inclusive. Metered heaters, blanket, toaster, fridge etc, plus use of washing machine. Post shop, Inn a short walk. Central to Truro, Falmouth, Perranporth with beaches and golf courses. Rates from £100 to £250.

FALMOUTH. Mrs J. Matthews, Boskensoe Farm Holiday Bungalows, Mawnan Smith, Falmouth

TR11 5JP (01326 250257). Sleep 6/8. Bungalows overlook farm on edge of village. Three bedrooms. Colour TV. Electric cooker, fridge/freezer, washing machine and microwave. Fitted with storage heaters and electric fires. Spacious gardens and ample parking for cars and boats. Situated in the picturesque village of Mawnan Smith, Falmouth five miles, one and a half miles from lovely Helford River famous for beautiful coastal walks, gardens and scenery. Several quiet safe beaches for bathing. Also excellent sailing and fishing facilities. Terms from £130 to £375. Apply for brochure.

FALMOUTH. Mrs J.B. Jewell, Pennance Mill Farm, Maenporth, Falmouth TR11 5HJ (01326 312616/317431). √ √ √ Four Cedarwood chalets furnished to a high standard. Also 50 spaces for caravans and tents. Situated on a dairy farm with a milking parlour viewing gallery. Maenporth beach half a mile, Falmouth two miles; golf nearby. Children and pets welcome. Shower facilities and shop on site. Open March to December. Chalets from £110 to £270 per week; Camping £6.60 per night. SAE, please, for colour brochure.

FALMOUTH. Nantrissack, Constantine, Falmouth. Sleeps 8. NANTRISSACK is an impressive farmhouse standing in a delightful garden. It is ideally situated for touring this lovely southern coast of Cornwall. Being two miles from Gweek — the little creek of the Helford River — it is also ideal for visiting Falmouth and the Lizard Peninsula. The farm and small woodland with a freshwater stream is available for those who wish to walk. The furnishings are nice, and beds are new divans. Bathroom; hot and cold water in all bedrooms. Partial central heating. New 30ft sun lounge. Colour TV. Fully equipped with all linen except towels. Kiddies welcome, also well-behaved dog. Premises thoroughly cleaned and checked by owners between each let. Sea about four and a half miles. Illustrated brochure available. SAE please. Terms from £180 to £400 including VAT per week. **Mr T.P. Tremayne, "The Home", Penjerrick, Falmouth TR11 5EE (01326 250427 and 250143).**

FLUSHING. Quayside Cottage, Flushing, Near Falmouth. This comfortable, furnished cottage, sleeping up to six in three bedrooms, is situated on beautiful Falmouth Harbour. The village pubs, restaurants and shops are all close by, as is the ferry to Falmouth. The sandy beach is about 10 minutes' walk. Colour TV, cooker and microwave, bath with shower, separate utility room. Night storage heaters, double glazing and high insulation for holidays at any time of the year. Views across the harbour. Children and pets welcome. Terms from £100 to £335 per week; electricity by slot meter. Full details available from **Mr A. Bromley, 22 Gravel Lane, Ringwood, Hampshire BH24 1LN (01425 476660).**

Key to Tourist Board Ratings

The Crown Scheme
(England, Scotland & Wales)

Covering hotels, motels, private hotels, guesthouses, inns, bed & breakfast, farmhouses. Every Crown classified place to stay is inspected annually. *The classification:* Listed then 1-5 Crown indicates the range of facilities and services. Higher quality standards are indicated by the terms APPROVED, COMMENDED, HIGHLY COMMENDED and DELUXE.

The Key Scheme
(also operates in Scotland using a Crown symbol)

Covering self-catering in cottages, bungalows, flats, houseboats, houses, chalets, etc. Every Key classified holiday home is inspected annually. *The classification:* 1-5 Key indicates the range of facilities and equipment. Higher quality standards are indicated by the terms APPROVED, COMMENDED, HIGHLY COMMENDED and DELUXE.

The Q Scheme
(England, Scotland & Wales)

Covering holiday, caravan, chalet and camping parks. Every Q rated park is inspected annually for its quality standards. The more √ in the Q – up to 5 – the higher the standard of what is provided.

HAYLE. Honeysuckle Cottage, 14 Chenhalls Close, St. Erth, Hayle. Sleeps 4 adults; 2 children. St.

Erth is an attractive village with granite church, hospitable pub and Post Office/stores. The cottage is in a small terrace of four on a quiet rural development and is within easy reach of St. Ives, Penzance and Helston, and many safe sandy beaches close by. The cottage is very warm with night storage heaters and has three bedrooms (one double, one twin and one with bunk beds); bathroom with bath, toilet, washbasin and electric shower; large lounge with open fire and colour TV; kitchen/diner with electric cooker, automatic washing machine and fridge/freezer; downstairs toilet. Duvets and covers provided, but not sheets, pillowcases or towels. Car essential, garage. Regret no animals. Electricity included. Terms from £145 to £340. Apply: **Mr and Mrs G.N.F. Broughton, Orchard House, Wall, Gwinear, Hayle TR27 5HA (01736 850201; Fax: 01736 850046).**

HAYLE TOWANS. Sleeps 8/9. Detached four bedroomed Bungalow with sea views across St. Ives Bay. Beach 100 yards, three miles of soft golden sand, backed by rolling sand dunes. Ideal for children and for two families wishing to holiday together. Located in an area of Cornwall noted for its scenery and attractions. Local supermarket, or Hayle town shops five minutes by car. Accommodation comprises kitchen, lounge/dining room with colour TV, four bedrooms sleeping eight. Folding bed and cot available. Bathroom with shower, plus additional toilet. Fenced garden. Metered electricity. Off road parking for two/three cars. Weekly terms £100 to £285. **Mrs Langford, 1 Fleetway, Thorpe, Surrey TW20 8UA (01932 560503).**

HAYLE. Count House Farm Cottage, Wheal Alfred, Hayle. Sleeps 2 adults; 2 children. This cottage,

adjoining farmhouse set in 35 acres, is completely self-contained. Situated two miles inland from Hayle beach it is within easy reach of most of the popular resorts and numerous good sandy beaches. Accommodation for two adults and two children with one big bedroom containing a double bed and a pair of bunk beds. A single bed can also be put in here and a cot, if required. Sheets/duvet covers are provided but other linen and towels are not. Lounge with colour TV and storage heater. A large kitchen with fridge, electric cooker and spin dryer, etc. Electricity included. Downstairs bathroom with bath/shower, WC and washbasin. Regret, no pets. Terms from £105 to £215. **Mr and Mrs G.N.F. Broughton, Orchard House, Wall, Gwinear, Hayle TR27 5HA (01736 850201; Fax; 01736 850046).**

HELSTON. Fuchsia Cottage, Tregarne, Manaccan, Helston. Sleeps 6. Secluded, spacious country

bungalow (owners' home) in large mature garden, one mile from quiet fishing cove of Porthallow. The well carpeted, fully equipped accommodation includes three double bedrooms, two with double beds, one with bunks/twin beds, all with Continental quilts; large dining/kitchen with electric cooker, twin-tub washing machine, fridge/freezer, electric water heater and toaster. Large lounge, inglenook with stone fireplace, TV, radio. Cot available on request. Electricity by meter. Car essential. Access is down a private lane. Ample car parking. Lovely area for walking, touring, boating, fishing, coastal path. Shop, pub, beach one mile. Ideal for a peaceful holiday. Great for children. Pets by arrangement. Available April to October. Special rates for Senior Citizens, except during June, July and August. Telephone for further details after 4pm. **Mrs P.M. Jones, Avisford, Chase Road, Brocton, Stafford ST17 0TL (01785 662470).**

See also Colour Display Advertisement **HELSTON. Anne Viccars, Flushing Cottage, Flushing Cove, Gillan, Manaccan, Helston TR12 6HQ (Tel & Fax: 01326 231244). Sleep 2/9.** Sample the peace and privacy of Creekside cottages, set around a private beach in the mouth of the Helford River. The area is renowned for its beautiful walks, wonderful sailing, interesting birds, rare plants and superb fishing. We offer a variety of cottages to sleep from two to nine in great comfort. All cottages are well equipped to a very high standard and are set in mature gardens, sloping down to the creek with its secluded sand and shingle beach. Plenty of parking. Linen, high chairs and cots available for hire. Sorry, no pets.

HELSTON. Wheal Sara/Wheal James, Lanjowan, St. Johns. Two newly built apartments with full gas central heating, double glazing, off road parking space and close to town centre. Wheal Sara is on the ground floor, sleeps three and has large lounge/diner with electric fire and colour TV; small fitted kitchen with electric cooker, fridge and washing machine; one double-bedded room, one single bedroom, and bathroom with bath, toilet, washbasin and electric shower. Wheal James is on the first floor and sleeps four persons. There is a very large lounge/diner with colour TV and electric fire; one twin-bedded room, one double-bedded room; fitted kitchen with electric cooker, fridge and washing machine, and large bathroom with bath, toilet, washbasin and electric shower. Duvets/covers provided. Visitors asked to bring bottom sheets and towels. Gas and electricity included in the rental. A cot can be provided if required. Regret animals not allowed. Terms from £120 to £275. Please apply to **Mr and Mrs G.N.F. Broughton, Orchard House, Wall, Gwinear, Hayle TR27 5HA (01736 850201; Fax: 01736 850046).**

See also Colour Display Advertisement **HELSTON. Mr and Mrs H. Donald, "Halwyn", Manaccan, Helston TR12 6ER (01326 280359 or 565694). Properties sleep 2/12.** Situated in an area of outstanding natural beauty, "Halwyn" is an ancient Cornish farmstead with the original old farmhouse and former farm buildings converted to a choice of holiday homes for two to 12. There are two acres of delightful gardens including an indoor heated swimming pool with sauna and solarium, small lake with boat, badminton court, children's play area and a putting green. A perfect away-from-it-all holiday retreat, ideal for relaxing and forgetting the pressures of everyday life. Open all year with special low rates, log fires and storage heaters out of season. Stamp for colour brochure.

HELSTON. Mrs A.G. Farquhar, Porthpradnack, Mullion, Helston TR12 7EX (01326 240226). At Mullion Cove on the Lizard Peninsula is Porthpradnack, a well built house with two flats, each accommodation four/six persons. A 10 minute walk from house to Mullion Cove and three other beaches. Both flats have fully equipped kitchens with all modern facilities. Colour TV. Each flat has separate front door. Pets permitted by arrangement. Car essential, large car park. Panoramic rural views from all rooms. One acre gardens at tenants' disposal. Weekly terms from £100 to £265. Other holiday accommodation also available, please enquire.

HELSTON. Ruthdower Cottage, Godolphin Cross, Helston. A most unusual and attractive cottage in peaceful sheltered position, 200 yards from the centre of the village, three miles from the beach at Praa Sands on the south coast. Cottage has full central heating from an open multi-fuel stove in the lounge plus storage heaters. Tastefully furnished, mainly in stripped pine. Downstairs fitted kitchen/diner with electric cooker, dishwasher and microwave; utility room with fridge/freezer, automatic washing machine and tumble dryer; large diningroom; lounge with colour TV, video and doors leading to patio area and a cloakroom with toilet and washbasin. Upstairs there is a double-bedded room and two twin-bedded rooms; bathroom with bath, toilet, washbasins and electric shower. Garage and parking for two cars. Large safe garden. All linen provided. Meters read before and after your holiday and the electricity used is deducted from security deposit. Sorry no pets. Terms £215 to £395. **Mr and Mrs G.N.F. Broughton, Orchard House, Wall, Gwinear, Hayle TR27 5HA (01736 850201; Fax: 01736 850046).**

HELSTON near. The Oaks, 9 Forth Vean, Godolphin Cross, Helston. Sleeps 4 adults; 2 children.

This luxury bungalow is situated 100 yards from the centre of the village with fine open views of surrounding countryside. There are two twin-bedded and one double bedrooms; bathroom with electric shower; separate WC; large kitchen/diner with fridge/freezer, electric cooker and automatic washing machine, and lounge with open fire and colour TV. Full oil-fired central heating and double glazing. Ideal for early/late holidays. Car essential, garage. Duvets/covers provided, but not sheets, pillowcases and towels. All electricity included. The village is two and a half miles from south coast. Good local walking. Regret no animals. Terms from £170 to £365. AA Listed. SAE to **Mr and Mrs G.N.F. Broughton, Orchard House, Gwinear, Hayle TR27 5HA (01736 850201; Fax: 01736 850046).**

HELSTON near. Troon Cottage, Breage, Near Helston. Sleeps 2/5. Take an early or late break in this

charming old cottage, attractively furnished to a high standard and situated in a quiet country lane near the sea. Modern kitchen, microwave, tumble dryer, colour TV, oil-fired central heating, beds made up ready. Secluded garden, patio, garage. Children welcome, cot provided. Breage is an ideal centre for exploring the numerous beaches and National Trust coastal walks in the area and within easy motoring distance of Land's End, The Lizard, Helford, Falmouth, Penzance, St. Ives and many other well known beauty spots. Sorry, no pets. Telephone or write to **Mrs A.M. Graham, Long View, Maple Avenue, Bexhill-on-Sea, East Sussex TN39 4ST (01424 843182).**

LISKEARD. Mrs L.F. Arthur, Rosecraddoc Lodge, Liskeard PL14 5BU (Tel & Fax: 01579 346768).

Up to ♀♀♀♀ *COMMENDED.* Enjoy a peaceful holiday in beautiful South East Cornwall in one of our modern but traditionally built two/three bedroom bungalows. They are set in lawned gardens and woodland, in countryside at the foot of Bodmin Moor yet only 10 miles from the coasts and 20 miles from Plymouth. Each bungalow is furnished and equipped to a high standard including bathroom with bath and shower. Night storage heating. Many have microwave ovens and videos. Ideally situated for fishing, golf, walking, beaches, touring Cornwall and Devon. Suitable for disabled visitors, two bungalows specially adapted for wheelchair users. Terms from £120 to £340 per week. Please write, telephone or fax for brochure.

LOOE. Mrs Chapman, Trenant Park Cottages, Trenant Lodge, Sandplace, Looe PL13 1PH (01503

263639/262241). Exclusive cottages set in tranquil grounds of historic estate with abundant wildlife. Linen, dishwasher, washing machine, microwave, video, etc. Traditional and antique furnishings. Private garden and country walks accessible. Heating and log fires. Open all year, plus Short Breaks from 1st November till Easter. Dogs welcome. Looe one and a half miles. Near Coastal Path walks. Brochure available.

LOOE. Flat 10, Nailzee Point, Looe. Sleeps 2. Situated in this charming Cornish fishing town central for touring Cornwall and Devon. Entrance by exterior stairs to first floor flat. One double bedroom, sleeps two, occasionally three. Fully furnished and equipped including colour TV, electric cooking facilities and microwave. Bath and shower. Large balcony. This attractive flat overlooks sea and coastline. Dog welcome at £10 per week. Easy parking facilities. Terms from £140 to £180 per week. Contact **Mrs Miller 01752 661915.**

MARAZION near. Mrs D. Hutchinson, "An Gwythow", Perranuthnoe, Penzance TR20 9NB (01736 711523). Sleeps 4. Accommodation in spacious, modern, self-contained apartment with central heating, situated in beautiful, quiet, unspoilt village of Perranuthnoe, 250 yards from sandy beach. Central for St. Ives, Marazion, Falmouth, Land's End, etc. Perran Sands faces due south and is sheltered by low cliffs, has rocky pools, sandy beaches and superb cliff walks. Accommodation comprises lounge with beautiful view and breakfast bar through to modern kitchen with microwave. One double bedroom, one twin bedroom (cot available). Bathroom. Local farm providing eggs, vegetables and cream. Weekly terms from £80.

MARAZION near. Mrs W. Boase, Trebarvah Farm, Trebarvah Lane, Perranuthnoe, Penzance TR20 9NG (01736 710361). Sleeps up to 4.  "Tue Brook" is a detached bungalow with magnificent views across Mount's Bay and St. Michael's Mount. It overlooks the village of Perranuthnoe (two and a half miles east of Marazion) in this beautiful holiday area with Penzance the local centre. Perranuthnoe beach is both sandy and sheltered and easily accessible on foot and by car. Accommodation comprises one double and one twin-bedded room, both with pillows and blankets; please supply own linen; kitchen/diner, bathroom and sitting room leading to a large conservatory overlooking the sea; front and rear gardens; well behaved dogs welcome; fully equipped electrically with £1 prepayment meter. Colour TV. Terms from £140 to £270 per week. Available April to October.

MEVAGISSEY. Mr and Mrs T. Dudley, Polhaun Holiday Apartments, Polkirt, Mevagissey PL26 6UU (01726 843222). Apartments are situated high on the hill with patios overlooking the quaint little fishing harbour and bay. Each apartment is completely self-contained with its own car park. Sleeps two to four with bed linen and hot water supplied free. Modern kitchen with electric cooker, fridge, etc. Bathroom with shower and WC. Electric heating and TV. Sorry no pets. There are plenty of safe beaches nearby. Beautiful coastal walks, restaurants and shops, etc within five minutes' walk. Open all year. Brochure on request.

`See also Colour Display Advertisement` **MEVAGISSEY. Mr and Mrs F. Seamark, Treloen Holiday Apartments, Polkirt Hill, Mevagissey PL26 6UX (Tel & Fax: 01726 842406). ♟♟♟ up to** *HIGHLY COMMENDED.* **Sleep 2/6.** Offering unrivalled sea views, all apartments are modern, self-contained with private patios/balconies and fully equipped to a high standard including colour TV, to accommodate two to six people. Situated on the cliff tops in a quiet and secluded position within a few minutes' walk of sandy beach, shops and picturesque harbour. Central heating, pleasant gardens, sun patios and balconies, private car park, launderette and barbecue facilities; games room, children's play area, babysitting. Part week bookings in low season. Ideally located for exploring Cornwall. Weekly terms per apartment from £99 to £389 including VAT (17.5%). **Open all year.** Personally run and maintained to a high standard by resident proprietors. Colour brochure from **Mrs F. Seamark.**

CORNWALL — FROM COAST TO COAST
Stretching for some 300 miles, Cornwall's north and south coastlines are equally spectacular in different ways. The North is a paradise for those who enjoy watersports, with the Atlantic Ocean crashing onto long stretches of beautiful beach, while the more sheltered South Coast, with its picturesque fishing villages and sheltered coves, is ideal for a break at any time of year. Stretch your legs along the South West Coast Path and see for yourself!

MEVAGISSEY. Mr A.H. Robins, Invermore, School Hill, Mevagissey PL26 6TQ (01726 843352).
Four traditional self contained flats to let in the centre of Mevagissey, a quaint old Cornish fishing village. Each flat will sleep up to six people and all are fully equipped. Two double bedrooms and cot, bathroom, toilet, lounge with bed settee, dining room, kitchen. Everything provided except linen. Close to shops and just two minutes from the harbour. Free parking available. Pets permitted. Open all year and personally supervised by Cornish owners. Cornish Tourist Board registered. Weekly terms from £110 to £220 VAT exempt. SAE please.

MOUSEHOLE. Wharfside Cottage, Mousehole. Charming well furnished two-bedroomed harbourside cottage sleeping four persons, 20 yards from small sandy beach.

From the side entrance, there is a quarry tiled lobby leading to downstairs cloakroom; open plan kitchen/diner with electric oven/grill, ceramic hob, fridge/freezer and dishwasher; tastefully furnished lounge with colour TV, granite fireplace with multifuel stove and superb views to St. Michael's Mount. Upstairs there are two double-bedded rooms; dressing room, and bathroom with bath/shower over, toilet and washbasin. There are night storage heaters in the property. All linen is provided. Electricity is charged for on the meter reading at the end of the holiday. Regret pets not allowed. A cot can be provided on request. A parking ticket is provided for visitors. Terms from £145 to £340. Please apply to **Mr and Mrs G.N.F. Broughton, Orchard House, Wall, Gwinear, Hayle TR27 5HA (01736 850201; Fax: 01736 850046).**

MOUSEHOLE. Sleeps 4/5 or 2. Traditional Fisherman's two bedroomed cottage and cosy character ground floor flat. Both close to harbour and all amenities.

Regret no pets. Clean, comfortable and well equipped. Parking. Colour TV; washing machine, microwave. Convenient for beaches/touring. Central heating (seasonal). Cottage from £95 to £350 per week. Studio flat from £50 to £190 per week. Contact: **Mr A.G. Wright, 100 Wensley Road, Woodthorpe, Nottingham NG5 4JU (0115 9639279).**

MULLION. Mr T.R. Leach, "Venton Arriance", Trewoon Road, Mullion TR12 7DT (01326 240514).

Sleep 4. Three self contained holiday homes in a converted 17th century farmhouse, stable and barn, each sleeping four comfortably. Quiet country position, yet just 10 minutes' walk up the lane to Mullion village which has all the essentials including a launderette. Mullion Cove, sandy beaches, cliff walks, riding and golf all within a couple of miles; Helston, famous for its Floral Dance in May, seven miles, Falmouth and Penzance half an hour's drive. All units are carpeted and have good sized open plan kitchen/living rooms with electric cooker, fridge, colour TV, electric fire. One double bedroom and one twin bedroom in each, heating if required. Bathrooms have bath, washbasin, toilet, wall heater. Bed linen and towels not supplied. Short breaks of three or more days October to June. Weekly terms from £80 to £220.

MULLION COVE (Lizard Peninsula). Mullion Cove Bungalows, Mullion. Bungalows sleep 2/4.

Situated in secluded gardens overlooking Mullion Cove, close to sandy and surfing beaches. Picturesque harbour and magnificent scenic walks, mainly over National Trust land. Just 100 yards from Cornish Coastal Footpath. Riding, golf, fishing and sailing all close by. The bungalow accommodation comprises: lounge with colour TV, all-electric kitchenette, bathroom, toilet, and two bedrooms to sleep up to four persons. Terms £99 to £285 weekly. For further details and colour brochure write or phone **Mrs V. Law, 1 The Alders, Cheltenham, Gloucestershire GL53 0PX (01242 574068).**

NEWQUAY. Mr I. Davison, "Oyster Sands", 38 Henver Road, Newquay TR7 3BN (01637 850630).

Sleep 2/8. The flats/flatlets are situated amongst residential property on the quieter side of Newquay and enjoy an ideal position for beaches, shops, pubs and buses. All are well furnished, equipped, maintained and supervised with the security of a night warden. Resident owner who greets all guests, invites you in and, later on, explains the facilities and shows you around. Facilities: linen and towels supplied, eight channel colour TV (four Satellite), free car transport to and from stations, laundry with automatic washer/dryer, wet suits, surf and body boards, instant showers, microwaves and barbecues, video, central heating, easy private parking. Terms: from £7 per person per night; High Season Saturday/Saturday bookings only.

NEWQUAY. Mr Alexander, Rettorick Mill, St Mawgan, Newquay TR8 4BH (01637 860460). Cottage ♀♀♀ *APPROVED,* **Bungalows ♀♀** *APPROVED.* Stone built single storey cottage — formerly the old mill — and six two-bedroomed holiday bungalows sleeping up to five. Set in nine acres in secluded wooded valley, one mile from the large sandy beach at Mawgan Porth, six miles from Newquay and nine miles from the old fishing port of Padstow. Children's play area and woodland nature walk. Riding and golf both within a couple of miles. Attractive coastal walks in National Trust land at nearby Bedruthan Steps. Most pets welcome. From £80 to £290 weekly.

NORTH CORNWALL. North Cornwall "Holidays", 101 Coventry Road, Coleshill, Warwick B46 3EK. A small, friendly agency offering quality self catering

accommodation in Padstow, Polzeath, Port Isaac and other lovely locations in beautiful North Cornwall. Properties include a Victorian farmhouse, modern townhouses, apartments overlooking the sea, estuary or harbour, converted barns and olde worlde cottages. Country, town or coastal situations to suit couples, families and larger groups. All personally inspected by agency proprietor. Pets and children welcome at most properties. Prices from £75 to £700. Out of season mini breaks available Please telephone **"Holidays" 01675 463588** for a copy of our illustrated brochure.

PENRYN. Mrs B. Newing, Glengarth, Burnthouse, St. Gluvias, Penryn TR10 9AS (01872 863209). Ideally situated for touring Cornwall and furnished to a high standard, a centrally heated first-floor flat in a delightful detached Cornish house, the owner living on the ground floor. Accommodation comprises two double bedrooms and one room with two full-size bunk beds. All rooms have washbasins and all beds have duvets. Electric fire and colour TV in the comfortable lounge. The kitchen/diner is fully equipped with crockery, cutlery, electric cooker, fridge/freezer, microwave oven and spin dryer plus iron and ironing board. Bathroom with toilet plus shower room with toilet, bidet and shaver point. Hot water, electricity, bed linen and towels included in tariff. Cot and high chair available. Garden and ample parking. Pets welcome. Write for brochure.

PENZANCE. Mrs Catherine Wall, Trenow, Relubbus Lane, St. Hilary, Penzance TR20 9EA (01736

762308). Property sleeps 2. Wing of old Cornish House standing in an acre of ground with picturesque large garden — wide views of surrounding rural district and away beyond. Mini bungalow available for holiday letting. Comfortably furnished. Linen not provided. Accommodation for two people in one double bedroom; sitting/diningroom with colour TV; shower, toilet; kitchen with electric cooker, fridge, etc. Sporting activities and beaches within easy reach. Great area for birdwatching. No pets. Parking. Terms from £70 weekly. Open from March to October and Christmas. Send for details.

PENZANCE. Penwith Cottages, Chyandour Office, Penzance TR18 3LW (01736 741112). ♀♀♀/ ♀♀♀♀ *COMMENDED/HIGHLY COMMENDED.* **Sleep 3/8.**

Carefully selected, high quality holiday cottages and farmhouses all registered with English Tourist Board. Set in beautiful Cornish countryside within easy reach of sea and with freedom to walk your dogs in surrounding fields and woods. Sleeping three to eight people and very well equipped. Children and pets welcome. Most properties have lawned gardens. Send SAE for brochure to above address, or telephone for friendly help and advice to choose your perfect holiday.

PENZANCE. The Engine House, Plain-an-Gwarry. This Cornish Engine House was built in the late 19th century and has recently been converted into an unusual and attractive holiday property. It is situated near the village of Goldsithney, one and a half miles from Marazion and St. Michael's Mount and four miles from Penzance. It has an attractive lounge with colour TV; one double-bedded room; one bunk bedded room and shower room with shower, washbasin and toilet. A spiral staircase leads down from the lounge to the well-fitted kitchen/diner with electric hob, microwave oven, fridge/freezer and automatic washing machine. There are night storage heaters in the property. The house is not suitable for toddlers or elderly people in view of the staircase. Linen is not provided. There is plenty of parking space and a small dog is allowed, but please speak to us first. Electricity is charged on meter reading at the end of the holiday. Terms from £110 to £240. Please apply to **Mr and Mrs G.N.F. Broughton, Orchard House, Wall, Gwinear, Hayle TR27 5HA (01736 850201; Fax: 01736 850046).**

FOR THE MUTUAL GUIDANCE OF GUEST AND HOST

Every year literally thousands of holidays, short-breaks and overnight stops are arranged through our guides, the vast majority without any problems at all. In a handful of cases, however, difficulties do arise about bookings, which often could have been prevented from the outset.

It is important to remember that when accommodation has been booked, both parties — guests and hosts — have entered into a form of contract. We hope that the following points will provide helpful guidance.

GUESTS: When enquiring about accommodation, be as precise as possible. Give exact dates, numbers in your party and the ages of any children. State the number and type of rooms wanted and also what catering you require — bed and breakfast, full board, etc. Make sure that the position about evening meals is clear — and about pets, reductions for children or any other special points.

Read our reviews carefully to ensure that the proprietors you are going to contact can supply what you want. Ask for a letter confirming all arrangements, if possible.

If you have to cancel, do so as soon as possible. Proprietors do have the right to retain deposits and under certain circumstances to charge for cancelled holidays if adequate notice is not given and they cannot re-let the accommodation.

HOSTS: Give details about your facilities and about any special conditions. Explain your deposit system clearly and arrangements for cancellations, charges, etc, and whether or not your terms include VAT.

If for any reason you are unable to fulfil an agreed booking without adequate notice, you may be under an obligation to arrange alternative suitable accommodation or to make some form of compensation.

While every effort is made to ensure accuracy, we regret that FHG Publications cannot accept responsibility for errors, omissions or misrepresentation in our entries or any consequences thereof. Prices in particular should be checked because we go to press early. We will follow up complaints but cannot act as arbiters or agents for either party.

ONE MINUTE STROLL TO THE BEACH!

MARINE COURT
SELF CATERING FAMILY LEISURE FLATS

Situated in the centre of Perranporth. Level and adjacent to the shops and three-mile sandy beach, with private car park. The flats accommodate 2-6 persons and are supervised by the owners living close by. We welcome your enquiry and will be delighted to send our Brochure.
Please state property required.

Terms: From £90 per week (including VAT) according to season. Reductions small parties. Includes colour television.

R. T. & S. RILSTONE, MARINE COURT,
8 Pentreve, Wheal Leisure, Perranporth, Cornwall TR6 0EY
or Telephone 01872 572157

Extensive holiday home in the centre of Perranporth and only 50 yards from the sandy surfing beach. This spacious family flat has all the facilities for 2-8 persons to have a seaside holiday in comfort. 4 bedrooms (H&C), 2 bathrooms and separate shower room, large dining room, modern fully fitted kitchen with split level cooker, fridge etc. Large lounge. All rooms (including bedrooms) with TV sockets. Cots available. Completely self contained and boasting full central heating in every room. Supervised by owner living close by. Colour television. Secluded bungalow, centrally heated, with gardens plus garage and parking. Sleeps 2-6. From £90 (VAT inclusive). Brochure with pleasure.
Please state property required.

Mrs S. Rilstone, Seathrift Seaside Flat, 8 Pentreve, Wheal Leisure Road, Perranporth TR6 0EY.

Sea Thrift

Opposite the beach. Sleeps 2/8.

PERRANPORTH. Four lovely one and two bedroomed character apartments — Poldark, Grenville, Godolphin and Trelawney — accommodate from two to six persons. All well equipped, decorated and furnished to a high standard, including colour TV and always beautifully clean. Garage, cots and high chairs, linen (for duvets) are all available. We also welcome pets. Gull Rock is less than two minutes' walk from the beach, village and cliffs with three apartments enjoying superb sea views and views over the village and boating lake. Terms from £88 to £330 per week (VAT exempt). Personally supervised by resident proprietors **Richard and Ann Snow, Gull Rock Holiday Apartments, Tywarnhayle Road, Perranporth TR6 0DX (01872 573289).**

PERRANPORTH. Cornish coast between Newquay and St. Ives. Two adjacent semi-detached houses at PERRANPORTH; one with six bedrooms sleeping eight to 12, the other with four bedrooms sleeping six to 10; lounges with colour TV; bathrooms with bath and shower. Walled gardens; garages and parking. Only quarter of a mile from magnificent sandy beach. From £150 per week per house. Also to let a small wooden chalet at PORTHTOWAN sleeping four to six and only two minutes from a sandy beach. From £60 per week. Apply **Dorothy Gill-Carey, 3 Penwinnick Road, St. Agnes TR5 0PA (01872 552262).**

PERRANPORTH. Sand Bay Holiday Flats, St Pirans Road, Perranporth TR6 0BH (01872 572081). ♀♀ *APPROVED.* **Sleep from 4 to 10.** A select and recent development of fully equipped high class flats and villas adjacent to Perranporth's lovely beach. First class accommodation is offered for groups of between 4 and 10 persons. Colour TV; full electric cooker and fridge are standard equipment. Located on the edge of the beach, the town centre is within a couple of minutes' easy walking distance. Private car parking included. We can also offer launderette facilities within the complex. Prices range from £115 to £450 weekly. For full information and tariff, please contact the resident proprietor JON MANSFIELD. SAE would be appreciated.

PLEASE ENCLOSE A STAMPED ADDRESSED ENVELOPE WITH ENQUIRIES

PORT ISAAC. Mrs Taylor, Sea Vista, Lundy Road, Port Isaac PL29 3RR (01208 880283). Delightful approved self catering Bungalows accommodating two to four; House for five to seven; two newly built Bungalows for two to five persons. Modern amenities, colour TV, own parking. Amidst glorious beaches, lovely scenery and fishing harbour. Port Isaac, unspoilt and picturesque, lies between Bude and Newquay. This coast has the finest beaches. Lovely walks, Floral Dance weekly by local band through village. Shops, pubs, cafes all handy. Terms from £65 to £295 weekly. £95 to £125 weekly early and late season.

PORT ISAAC. Mr and Mrs H. Symons, Trevathan Farm, St. Endellion, Port Isaac PL29 3TT (01208 880248). ♛♛♛♛/♛♛♛♛♛ **up to** *HIGHLY COMMEN-DED.* Open all year. Winter Breaks available. A warm welcome awaits you on our working family farm. Our cottages have panoramic views of the countryside and are furnished to a high standard having microwaves, washer/dryers, central heating, double glazing, etc. There are glorious walks on the farm and very friendly animals which you may enjoy helping to feed. We have games and fitness rooms, also hard tennis court and volleyball court on the farm. Golf and moors two miles, sea five miles; sailing, surfing, fishing are all available in the area, also excellent pubs. Near Camelford we have a large period house sleeping 12 plus cots, containing five double bedrooms; two bathrooms and shower room. There are 60 acres of land on which you may wander or perhaps enjoy a picnic by the river. Open all year. For details please telephone or send SAE.

PORT ISAAC. Mrs M.E. Warne, Tresungers Farm, Port Isaac PL29 3SY (01208 880307). Working farm. Sleeps 6. Ideal spot for anyone desiring quiet holiday, this farmhouse on 160 acres of mixed farmland offers furnished self-contained wing for self catering holidays from March to November. Approximately 400 yards from B3314 coast road, just over two miles from sea at Port Isaac. Accommodation for five/six people in two double bedrooms, one with extra single bed; also cot available; bathroom, toilet; sitting/dining room; well equipped kitchen with electric cooker, fridge, etc. Terms include bed linen. Shops just over two miles. Car essential, parking. Electricity on meter. Golf, bathing and surfing within easy reach. St. Endellion Church about one and a half miles away. Terms on receipt of SAE, please.

CORNWALL – SOMETHING FOR EVERYONE!

Sea, sand, cliffs and quite often the sun, but that's not all you will find in this interesting county. Cornwall has many fascinating places to visit, such as the Charlestown Shipwreck Centre, the Tropical Bird Gardens at Padstow, Cornwall Aeronautical Park near Helston, Botallack Tin Mine, The Cornish Seal Sanctuary, Perranporth and of course, St. Michael's Mount.

PORT ISAAC. Mrs Christine Everett, "Halcyon Flats", 7 The Terrace, Port Isaac PL29 3SG (01208 880378). Flats sleep 6. Port Isaac nestles in a coastal valley, unspoilt and little affected by its 600 years' history. Narrow alleys and streets lead down to the harbour where you can watch the local catch being landed and buy fresh crab, lobster and mackerel. Port Isaac and neighbouring Port Gaverne offer safe bathing and both are a short walk from the flats, as are a number of pubs and eating places. Halcyon Flats stand high on the cliff top and all lounges enjoy magnificent views of sea and surrounding coast. Each flat has its own front door and key and is equipped to a high standard with full-sized electric cooker, fridge, colour TV; parking. Children and pets welcome. Linen supplied. CTB and ETB registered. Brochure available. Weekly terms from £100 to £400; out of season reductions for couples.

Port Isaac Bay, North Cornwall.

PORT ISAAC. Carn Awn, Port Gaverne, Port Isaac. Sleeps 6. Carn Awn stands on its own in the hamlet of Port Gaverne and overlooks the harbour and sea. Fishing, swimming, boating and delightful rock pools for the children. Magnificent coastline where you can walk for miles along coastal paths. Many beaches within reach. Plenty of shopping facilities. Car essential, parking. Accommodation for six people in three double bedrooms; bathroom, separate toilet; sitting/diningroom; kitchen. Cot available. Linen may be hired. All electric, coal fire. Well behaved dogs welcome. Open all year. For terms contact **Mrs S.A. May, Orcades House, Port Gaverne, Port Isaac PL29 3SQ (01208 880716).**

PORT ISAAC. Salters and Penny Cottages, Port Gaverne, Port Isaac. Sleep 4/6. On National Trust Land, Port Gaverne is a hamlet adjoining Port Isaac on an inlet in the magnificent rugged north coast, and its shingle beach is one of the safest bathing beaches in Cornwall. Salters and Penny Cottages are about 100 yards from the sea, made from the old fishermen's netting lofts and fish cellars, dating from the days when Port Gaverne had a flourishing herring and pilchard trade. The cottages are fully equipped and most comfortably furnished and Penny, being all on the ground floor, is most suitable for the elderly or disabled. Salters Cottage has a piano which is tuned each Spring. I will be most happy to send you full details of rents and all vacant dates on receipt of SAE. **Mrs M.M. Cook, The Beach House, Port Gaverne, Port Isaac PL29 3SQ (01208 880296).**

PORT ISAAC. The Lodge, Treharrock, Port Isaac. Sleeps 6. Pleasant south facing and convenient bungalow, set in its own small natural garden and surrounded by fields and woodland with streams. About two miles inland from Port Isaac, a sheltered, secluded spot at the end of driveway to Treharrock Manor. Rugged North Cornish cliffs with National Trust footpaths and lovely sandy coves in the vicinity. Excellent sandy beach at Polzeath (five miles), also pony trekking, golf, etc in the area. South facing sun room leads to terrace; TV. Accommodation for six plus baby in three double bedrooms with washbasins; cot. Linen extra. Sorry, no pets. Car essential — parking. Terms from £150 to £300 per week (heating included). SAE to **Mrs E.A. Hambly, Home Farm House, Little Gaddesden, Berkhamsted, Hertfordshire HP4 1PN (0144-284 3412).**

CORNWALL – FUN FOR ALL THE FAMILY

Colliford Lake Park, Bolventor, Bodmin; Flambards Triple Theme Park, near Helston; Goonhilly Satellite Earth Station, near Helston; Lappa Valley Railway and Leisure Park, Newquay; Merlin's Magic Land, Lelant, St. Ives; Paradise Park, Hayle; Poldark Mine, Helston; St. Michael's Mount, Marazion; Tamar Otter Park, near Launceston; Tunnels Through Time, Newquay; Tropical Bird Gardens, Padstow; World of Model Railways, Mevagissey.

CORNISH COAST

Welcome to the Green Door

This well-known ETB ♥♥♥♥ Commended Cornish Coastal Inn offers six comfortably renovated beamed character cottages, sleeping 4/6 persons, each with central heating throughout; spacious lounge with log burner, completely equipped fitted kitchen with gas hob and electric oven, colour TV, telephone, free parking; enclosed sheltered garden. One large flat to sleep eight. Elevated position on cliff, overlooking the Cove. Central heating/Washing machine/Tumble dryer/Dishwasher/Colour TV/Direct-dial telephone. No meters, everything included in price. Convenient to the fully licensed, internationally recognised Port Gaverne Hotel. Port Isaac half-a-mile; beach 50 yards. Golf, fishing, sailing, riding nearby. Cornish Coastal Path passes the door. OPEN ALL YEAR.

For Brochure Freephone 0500 657867

or write to Midge Ross, Port Gaverne Hotel,
Near Port Isaac PL29 3SQ. Tel: 01208 880244 Fax: 01208 880151

COMMENDED

PORT QUIN. 1 The Fishcellars, Port Quin, Near Port Isaac. Sleeps 6. Luxury Fisherman's Cottage situated at the top of the slipway in Port Quin, an old fishing and mining hamlet between Port Isaac and Polzeath. Although off the beaten track all amenities are in the vicinity. Swimming, diving, fishing at Port Quin and sailing, water ski-ing, surfing, golfing and pony trekking nearby. Ideal for walkers as the property is on North Cornwall Coastal Footpath, peacefully surrounded by National Trust cliffs and farmland. The cottage, which affords beautiful sea views, is tastefully furnished. Two bedrooms (sleep up to six; duvets on all beds). Fully equipped kitchen — automatic washing machine, microwave oven, etc. Large lounge/diner with open fire, colour TV. Bathroom and shower. Night storage heaters. Car essential, parking. From £165 to £300 per week. For brochure contact **Mrs P.E. Yelland, Dunveth Cottage, St. Breock, Wadebridge PL27 7JR (Tel & Fax: 01208 814550).**

PORTSCATHO. Trewince Manor, Portscatho, South Cornwall. Peter and Liz Heywood invite you to take your self-catering or touring holiday at their Georgian Manor House estate in this undiscovered and peaceful corner of Cornwall. Luxury lodges, cedarwood chalets, cottage and small touring site available. Spectacular sea views, our own quay and moorings. Relaxing lounge bar and restaurant, shop, launderette, games rooms. Superb walking and sailing; abundance of wildlife. Dogs welcome. Please write or telephone for further information **Freephone 0500 657861.**

FREE and REDUCED RATE Holiday Visits! See our Reader's Offer Vouchers for details!

PRAA SANDS. Rustic Cottage, Praa Sands. Sleeps 4/9. Relax and recharge in a cottage to fall in love

with. RUSTIC COTTAGE is a charming, open beamed farmhouse set in four acres of peaceful Cornish countryside. A short distance by car driving through pretty country lanes takes you to the sandy beach and sea at Praa Sands. Penzance, Helston and the ever-popular St. Ives are roughly equidistant. Ideal for walking, touring or just lounging and lazing enjoying clean air, magnificent views and very comfy accommodation. Booking from Saturday to Saturday. From £200 to £225 weekly. Please telephone **0181-661 7865** preferably after 9pm or Sundays.

PRAA SANDS. Mrs June Markham, Broom Farm, Packet Lane, Rosudgeon, Penzance TR20 9QD (01736 763738). Sleeps 2/4. Broom Farm Cottage, a

comfortable detached cottage converted from a granite barn and set on three-acre smallholding. Well furnished, sleeps two/four, children welcome. There is a full size cooker, fridge, colour TV. Covered car space leading to patio overlooking field. Shop, post office, village pub, fish and chip shop and bus stop at end of the lane. Perfect for summer holidays or an out-of-season break. Award-winning goats' cheese made in the farmhouse. Two miles Praa or Perran Sands, one mile Prussia Cove, Penzance six miles. Weekly terms from £90 to £220. SAE for illustrated brochure, stating holiday period preferred.

RUTHERNBRIDGE, Near Bodmin. Ruthern Valley Holidays, Ruthernbridge, Bodmin PL30 5LU (01208 831395; Freephone 0500 151610). Only eight

modern timber lodges, four cedarwood bungalows and six holiday caravans set in seven and a half acres of beautiful, spacious lawns, shrubs, colour and woodlands. An abundance of bird and wild life — feed the squirrels direct from your window. **The Perfect Family Retreat,** holding a 1994 AA Excellence Award for Attractive Environment, yet centrally based for beaches on both north and south coasts. Cycling, fishing, riding and excellent walking all within two miles including Saints Way and the Camel Trail — once described by Betjeman as "the best journey in England". All units have two bedrooms, colour TV, well equipped kitchen, bathroom with shower and mains facilities. Lodges also have verandahs and picnic tables for eating "al fresco". From £110 weekly. Resident proprietors **Brian and Christine Smith.**

See also Colour Display Advertisement ST. AUSTELL. Mrs J. King, St. Margaret's Holiday Park, Polgooth, St. Austell PL26 7AX (01726 74283; Fax: 01726 71680). √ √ √ √ √ BHP Approved. Family owned and run Holiday Park set in six acres of beautiful parkland and offering good quality accommodation of varying sizes, from detached bungalows (sleep up to eight) to self-contained chalets (sleep two to six). Two bungalows suitable for disabled visitors. All the properties are well equipped with the usual facilities. Colour TV and fitted carpets. Launderette and pay phone on site. Golf course is 400 yards away and the Polgooth shops and inn are conveniently near. Well controlled pets allowed. Special rates available. Open March to December. Terms from £85 to £415. Colour brochure available.

ST. AUSTELL BAY. Mrs A. Buckingham, 16 Haddon Way, Carlyon Bay, St Austell PL25 3QG

(01726 815566). ♀ ♀ ♀ ♀ *COMMENDED.* **Sleep 1/5.** Two charming 18th century cottages, one harbourside only yards from the sea and one in delightful countryside setting, both superb locations in the unspoilt, unchanged, coastal village of Charlestown. Sleep 1-4. Two detached seaside bungalows, one at Carlyon Bay with its award winning blue flag beach, coastal walks and clifftop golf course and the other only five minutes' walk from Par Sands and the wildlife pond. Pets welcome by arrangement. All at good coastal locations with parking; all personally supervised. From £100 to £350.

See also Colour Display Advertisement **ST. AUSTELL BAY. Mr and Mrs F.H.G. Milln, Bosinver Farm, St. Austell PL26 7DT (01726 72128). ♀ ♀ / ♀ ♀ ♀ ♀ up to** *COMMENDED.* **Properties sleep 2/3/4/5/6/11.** Bosinver is a small farm and holiday centre one mile from St. Austell (on main BR line) with cinemas, recreation centre, and within easy reach of several beaches. The 16th century thatched farmhouse has six bedrooms and there are three modernised cottages sleeping four/five and 14 bungalows sleeping two, three, four or five people. Another bungalow sleeping up to six has a second bathroom and is designed to take wheelchairs. All are superbly equipped and have electric cooking/heating with bath/shower and colour TV. Cots can be hired and dogs are permitted. Attractions within Cornwall are displayed with many suggestions of what to do. Many people prefer to relax amid the garden surroundings, walk by the lake or watch the fan-tailed pigeons in flight. County Council and English Tourist Board Approved. Please write or telephone **Mr and Mrs Milln.**

ST. COLUMB MAJOR, Near Newquay. Mrs E.J. Ford, Glenfield, 1 Trekenning Road, St. Columb

TR9 6RR (01637 880619). Sleeps 2/6 plus cot. Glenfield is a high standard detached modern bungalow in St. Columb Major village, seven miles from the beaches at Newquay; beaches at Watergate Bay and Mawgan Porth are five miles. Accommodation comprises one double bedroom with en suite shower, washbasin, WC; one double bedroom and a twin-bedded room; bathroom; lounge/diner with colour TV; kitchen with breakfast bar, gas cooker, microwave, fridge and washing machine. Linen inclusive (quilts). Central heating. £1 electric slot meter and £1 gas meter. Sorry, no pets. Baby-sitting by arrangement. Open all year. Prices from £160 to £439 depending on week. £50 deposit on booking.

ST. ISSEY. Cannalidgey Villa Cottages, St. Issey, Wadebridge. ♀ ♀ ♀ *APPROVED/COMMENDED.* **Sleep 4 adults, 2 children.** Modernised farm cottages, situated in a quiet agricultural area, but not isolated. Ideal centre for touring, walking, cycling on scenic Camel Trail, also coastal walks. Six miles Padstow, sandy beaches, boat trips, swimming, golf; local shops, post office, pub with restaurant and parish church one and a half miles. Each cottage has a large walled garden, ideal for children. Modern electric kitchen with all necessary equipment. Well furnished diner and lounge. Night storage heater, electric heaters, open fire, colour TV. Bathroom with toilet. Each cottage has family room with double and single beds and twin bedded room. All rooms are carpeted except kitchen. Cot available. Open all year round. No pets. Terms from £95 to £300 No VAT. Brochures available from **Mrs E.D. Old, Rosmere, Little Petherick, Wadebridge PL27 7RX (01841 540212).**

ST. IVES. Mrs E.J. Jefferies, "Chy-an-Veor", Hellesveor, St. Ives TR26 3AD (01736 795372). Country cottage situated one mile from St. Ives on the Land's End coast road. Three bedrooms: two double rooms and one room fitted with adult-sized bunk beds. Fully equipped kitchen including microwave, fridge, cooker, etc. Lounge with colour television. Victorian bathroom, open beams, slate floor. Large garden and garage. Horse riding, golf, walking, beaches, fishing are all within easy reach. Available June to September.

ST. IVES. Messrs J. Husband and Sons, Consols Farm, St. Ives TR26 2HN (01736 796151). Properties sleep 4/6/8. A selection of four properties is available. Large cottage set in garden in quiet surroundings, sleeps eight people, sittingroom with TV; fully fitted kitchen (fridge, electric cooker, etc); bathroom; five bedrooms: from £120 per week. Also annexe flat in garden grounds; one double bed, one set bunk beds in family room; kitchen; lounge; bathroom, toilet, etc; small garden and patio: £70 per week. Ample parking. Situated one mile from St. Ives: Cottage flat sleeping four at end of farmhouse, on working farm. Sittingroom with TV; two bedrooms; kitchen; bathroom, toilet, etc: from £120 per week. Flat in town of St. Ives sleeps five. One large attic room with panoramic view, one small double room, one single bedroom; kitchen, lounge; bathroom and toilet. From £120 per week. Parking in town car park. Full details on request.

ST. MAWGAN. Mrs J.A. Wake N.D.D., Polgreen Farm, St. Mawgan, Near Newquay TR8 4AG (01637 860700). Sleeps maximum 5 plus cot. Tradi-

tional Cornish farmhouse set in rural valley designated of Great Landscape Value within walking distance of beach/ cliffs and conservation village of St. Mawgan. The adjoining cottage offers, upstairs: one double, two single/double bedrooms, bathroom/WC (bath with shower, heated towel rail); downstairs: sunny sittingroom (coal-effect electric fire, colour TV), all-electric kitchen/diningroom (fully automatic washer dryer), second WC with basin. Fitted carpets. Duvets/ central heating when required. Private parking, lawn, cottage garden with culinary herbs, patio. Additional accommodation in farmhouse. Badminton lawn. Opportunities for drawing/painting, natural history studies/birdwatching, visits to National Trust properties, galleries, gardens etc, plus golf, walking, riding, fishing. From £80 (Short Breaks) to £290 (four persons high season).

ST. TUDY. Chapel Cottages, St. Tudy. Four listed cottages situated at St. Tudy near remarkable coastal

CHAPEL
COTTAGES

scenery, good beaches and beautiful Bodmin Moor. Carefully modernised whilst retaining their character and charm. Sleeping up to five, each cottage is tasteful, warm and comfortable. Garden and private parking. Rental from £90 to £295 per week. Also two smaller cottages at Blisland, suitable for couples, converted from a 17th century barn. These are situated in a peaceful farming hamlet along a private lane, well away from traffic. Rental from £90 to £220 per week. Linen, colour TV, cots and high chairs are included with all cottages. Regretfully no pets. Brochure available from **Mr and Mrs C.W. Pestell, "Hockadays", Tregenna, Near Blisland PL30 4QJ (01208 850146).**

TINTAGEL. Kate and Peter West, Chilcotts, Bossiney, Tintagel PL34 0AY (Tel & Fax: 01840 770324). Without stepping onto a road, slip through the

side gate of your 16th century listed cottage into a landscape owned by the National Trust and designated as an area of outstanding natural beauty. Closest cottages to nearby Bossiney beach for rockpools, surfing, safe swimming and caves to explore. Walk the cliffpath north to famous Rocky Valley or onwards to the picturesque Boscastle Harbour. Southwards takes you to the ruins of King Arthur's Castle and onwards to Trebarwith Strand. Notice you have not stepped onto a road yet? Group of three friendly old country cottages, largest ideal for six. Low beamed ceilings and exposed stonework. Double and family bedrooms, all linen supplied. Comfortable lounges, colour TVs. Fully equipped kitchens, night storage heating throughout. Terms £100 to £300. Short winter breaks or Bed and Breakfast (from £14) also available. Directions: Bossiney adjoins Tintagel on B3253 (coast road). "Chilcotts" adjoins large layby with old red phonebox.

WIDEMOUTH BAY/BUDE. Mrs J.C. Marks, Widemouth Bay, Bude EX23 0DG (01288 361210).

♀ ♀ ♀ ♀ COMMENDED. **Working farm.** Panoramic sea and country views from all windows of Penhalt Farmhouse. Sleeps up to nine in comfortable and well equipped accommodation with open fire. There is one downstairs bedroom, sitting room with TV and video, and a shower room. Upper floor has three bedrooms, large lounge/dining room with TV, separate toilet and bathroom and fully fitted kitchen. The upper floor alone is ideal for smaller parties at a reduced rate. Outside games room, children's play area and telephone. Pets welcome. We are a working farm and visitors are welcome to look around. The beach is within walking distance along the coastal path. Terms from £95 per week.

CORNWALL

There's much more to Cornwall than just sand and sea. Take time to explore the traces of the past at Chysauster Ancient Village, near Penzance, a collection of huge stone houses dating from prehistoric times, and Pendennis Castle, Falmouth, built by Henry VIII to guard against invasion. The legend of King Arthur lives on at Tintagel Castle and at Dozmary Pool, Bodmin Moor, reputed to be where he threw back the sword, Excalibur.

CUMBRIA — including "The Lakes"

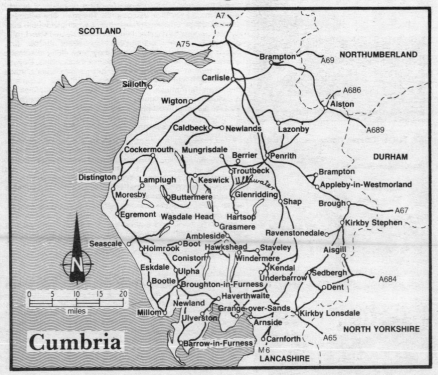

Cumbria

AMBLESIDE. **Peter and Anne Hart, Bracken Fell, Outgate, Ambleside LA22 0NH (015394 36289).** **Sleeps 2/4.** Bracken Fell Cottage is situated in beautiful open countryside between Ambleside and Hawkshead in the picturesque hamlet of Outgate. The two bedroomed accommodation has central heating, is immaculately furnished and has a fully equipped kitchen. Linen and electricity included. Patio area. Ideally positioned for exploring the Lake District. All major outdoor activities catered for nearby. Ample parking and two acres of gardens. Open all year. Terms from £140 per week. Sorry, no pets or children under eight years. Bed and Breakfast accommodation also available. Two Crowns Commended. Non smoking. Write or phone for brochure and tariff (015394 36289).

Bracken Fell

AMBLESIDE. **Mr Evans, Ramsteads Coppice, Outgate, Ambleside LA22 0NH (015394 36583).** Six timber lodges of varied size and design set in 15 acres of mixed woodland with wild flowers, birds and native wild animals. There are also 11 acres of rough hill pasture. Three miles south west of Ambleside, it is an ideal centre for walkers, naturalists and country lovers. No pets. Children welcome. Open March to November.

AMBLESIDE. **2 Lowfield, Old Lake Road, Ambleside. Sleeps 4/5.** Ground floor garden flat situated half a mile from town centre. The accommodation comprises lounge/dining room, kitchen, bathroom/WC, two bedrooms with twin beds. Linen supplied. Children and pets welcome. Ample private parking. Bookings run from Saturday to Saturday. Terms from £80 to £155 per week. Contact: **Mr P.F. Quarmby, 3 Lowfield, Old Lake Road, Ambleside LA22 0DH (015394 32326).**

Terms quoted in this publication may be subject to increase if rises in costs necessitate

AMBLESIDE. "The Eyrie", Lake Road, Ambleside. Sleeps 6. A really delightful, characterful flat

nestling under the eaves of a converted school with lovely views of the fells, high above the village. Large airy living/dining room with colour TV. Comfortably furnished as the owners' second home. Well equipped kitchen with spacious airing cupboard; three bedrooms sleeping six; attractive bathroom (bath/WC/shower) and lots of space for boots and walking gear. Colour TV, fitted carpets, gas central heating, use of separate laundry room. Terrace garden with fine views. Sorry, but no pets. Weekly rates or short breaks. Many recommendations. Brochure available. Telephone **Mrs Clarke 01844 212293.**

APPLEBY near. "The Yews", Long Marton, Appleby. Sleeps 3 adults; 2 children. This is a

comfortable old cottage, fully modernised, well furnished with fitted carpets throughout. Situated in a small village three miles from Appleby where swimming, golf and riding are available. Ideal for walkers with Fells nearby, also within easy reach of lakes and Dales. Accommodation comprises double bed, twin beds and single bed in three bedrooms. Cot also available. Well equipped kitchen; cooker, fridge and spindryer. Sittingroom, diningroom, coal or electric fire, colour TV. Linen provided. Attractive garden. Children especially welcome. One dog only. Available all year. Terms from £120 to £185 weekly. Weekend/Short Breaks available. Contact **Mrs B.M. Sowerby, Hawthorn Cottage, Long Marton, Appleby CA16 6BT (017683 61392).**

**APPLEBY-IN-WESTMORLAND. Mrs M.J. Burke, Milburn Grange, Knock, Appleby-in-Westmorland

CA16 6DR (Tel & Fax: 017683 61867; Vodaphone 0836 547130).** ♀♀♀/♀♀♀♀ *COMMENDED.* **Properties sleep 2/7.** Milburn Grange is a tiny hamlet nestling at the foot of the Pennines enjoying extensive views over Lakeland Hills and Pennines. Six quality cottages (three beamed) equipped to highest standards set within two acres. All cottages have either their own washing machine or use of utility room with washing machine, dryer and ironing facilities. Linen included free of charge; cots and high chairs; babysitting available. Children's safe play area, picnic tables, guests' garden and barbecue. Shop/PO/garage close by, selection of public houses in area. Well behaved pets welcome at £10 per week per pet. Two other cottages available in nearby idyllic villages. Nearest Lake 11 miles (Ullswater), also Children's Fun Park. Appleby five miles (castle, swimming, golf, tennis, fishing). Open all year. OFF SEASON BARGAIN BREAKS and LOW LOW WEEKLY RATES FROM NOVEMBER TO MARCH excluding Christmas and New Year. Terms from £80 to £350. SAE please for brochure.

APPLEBY-IN-WESTMORLAND near. "Jubilee Cottage". Sleeps 5/6. 18th century cottage, fully equipped, except linen. Two bedrooms (sleep five plus small child). Bathroom, lounge with colour TV and kitchen/diner with electric cooker, automatic washer, fridge, iron, etc. Economy 7 storage heater. Carpeted throughout. Situated between North Lakes and the Pennines. Car essential, off road parking for two cars in front of the cottage. Open March to November. Well behaved pets welcome. Terms £125 to £160. Price includes all electricity. **Miss L.I. Basten, Daymer Cottage, Lee, Near Ilfracombe, Devon (01271 863769).**

BOWNESS-ON-WINDERMERE. 43A Quarry Rigg, Bowness-on-Windermere. Sleeps 4. Ideally situated in the centre of the village close to the Lake and all amenities, the flat is in a new development, fully self-contained, and furnished and equipped to a high standard for owner's own comfort and use. Lake views, ideal relaxation and touring centre. Accommodation is for two/four people. Bedroom with twin beds, lounge with TV and video; convertible settee; separate kitchen with electric cooker, microwave and fridge; bathroom with bath/shower and WC. Electric heating. Parking for residents. Sorry, no pets. Terms from £125 to £195. Weekends and Short Breaks also available. SAE, please, for details to **E. Jones, 45 West Oakhill Park, Liverpool, Merseyside L13 4BN (0151-228 5799).**

BOWNESS-ON-WINDERMERE. Mrs P.M. Fanstone, Deloraine, (Dept. F), Helm Road, Bowness-on-Windermere LA23 2HS (015394 45557). ♀♀♀/ ♀♀♀♀ *COMMENDED.* Disabled Scheme Category 2 (first in Cumbria). Deloraine spells seclusion, space, convenience and comfort for all seasons, while exploring Lakeland heritage. Parties of two/six have choice of five apartments within an Edwardian mansion, and a detached cottage with four-poster bed. Set in one and a half acres of private gardens, yet only a few minutes' walk from Bowness centre and water sports. Each unit has distinctive qualities and character. Two command dramatic views of the Langdale Pikes and Lake at 300 foot elevation. Ground floor flat and cottage include disabled facilities. All properties have free parking, private entrances, full equipment, colour TV, electric heaters and central heating. Double glazing. Fire Prevention systems. Payphone. Washing machine. Barbecue. Sun room. Cot hire.

Linen included. Free swim tickets. No pets. Resident owners. Brochure on request. Terms from £95 to £340 per week. Winter Breaks available. Inspected by Lakeland Self-Caterers' Association.

BOWNESS-ON-WINDERMERE. Fernville, 6 Queens Drive, Bowness-on-Windermere. Sleeps 5 adults; 1 child. Fernville is in the centre of a terrace built in Lakeland stone and in a quiet residential road off the main Windermere-Bowness bus route. Two minutes away a delightful path leads to the lake in about 20 minutes' walk. There is a hall, living and dining rooms, with sliding doors between; kitchen; one double and two single bedrooms; attic bedroom with twin beds; cot also available. Comfortably furnished, electric heating, TV, modern kitchen with fridge, dishwasher and electric cooker. Fully equipped except linen. Well behaved pets allowed. Shops half a mile. Small paved garden at front. Parking at rear. Swimming, golf, fishing, water ski-ing, riding, etc. available nearby. Bowness is a very pleasant resort on Lake Windermere. Terms approximately £200 per week according to season etc. SAE, please, or phone. **Mrs Christine Walmsley, Godferhead, Loweswater, Cockermouth CA13 0RT (01900 85013).**

BOWNESS-ON-WINDERMERE. 45 Quarry Rigg, Lake Road, Bowness-on-Windermere. Sleeps 4. This flat is in a new development with lake views. Ideally placed in the centre of the village for shops, restaurants, etc. Parking for tenants. Within easy reach of tennis, boating, fishing, golf. Ideal for touring and walking. Modern self contained second floor flat comprising lounge/diner with kitchenette; two bedrooms (one twin, one double); bathroom. Furnished and equipped to a high standard for owner's personal use including colour TV, fridge, cooker, etc. Continental quilts. Electric heating including storage heaters. Metered electricity. No pets or children under 10 years. SAE for further details. **Mrs J. Kay, 11 Sommerville Close, The Belfry, High Legh, Near Knutsford, Cheshire WA16 6TR (01925 755612).**

BRAMPTON. Mrs Annabel Forster, High Nook Farm, Low Row, Brampton CA8 2LU (016977 46273). Sleeps 2/4. Small wooden chalet situated in beautiful Irthing Valley near Hadrian's Wall, convenient for touring Lakes, Northumbria and Scottish Borders. One double bedroom; lounge/kitchen with full electric cooker, fridge, water heater; fire, black and white TV; toilet. Fully equipped except linen. Nicely furnished, clean and comfortable. Open May to October. Terms from £70 per week plus electricity. Also Bed and Breakfast available in the farmhouse.

BUTTERMERE. Mr A. Beard, Wilkinsyke Farm, Buttermere, Near Cockermouth CA13 9XA (017687 70237/70232). Working farm. Sleeps 5. Wilkinsyke Farm Cottage is a comfortable 18th century cottage attached to a working fell farm, situated in Buttermere village — and only a short walking distance from Buttermere Lake itself. Ideally situated for walking, fishing and touring. The accommodation comprises: Ground Floor — bathroom, kitchen and livingroom; First Floor — two bedrooms sleeping a maximum of five people. Sorry, no dogs or children under five years of age. Terms from £100 to £200 per week.

WHEN MAKING ENQUIRIES PLEASE MENTION
FARM HOLIDAY GUIDES

CARLISLE. Mrs J.T. James, Midtodhills Farm, Roadhead, Carlisle CA6 6PF (Tel & Fax: 016977 48213). Up to ♛♛♛♛♛ *HIGHLY COMMENDED.* **Working farm.** Situated overlooking the beautiful Lyne Valley on the Cumbria/Scottish border. On a traditional 320 acre working farm guests are welcome to join in and learn about life on a farm. Ideally situated for touring Hadrian's Wall, Kielder, Carlisle, Gretna Green and Lakes. Good fishing and walking area. **Arch View** sleeps eight in five bedrooms, new sandstone barn conversion, kitchen/diner, shower room, lounge, twin bedroom. First floor two double rooms with vanity units, two single bedrooms and bathroom. **Riggfoot** sleeps four/five, detached cottage, open plan kitchen/lounge, log fire, one double (four-poster bed), one twin bedroom, cot and high chair; bathroom. Properties have dishwasher, microwave, fridge, cooker, washer/dryer, colour TV, video, radio. Storage heaters. Garden with barbecue and furniture. Prices from £120. £415 for eight people/five bedrooms. Linen included. Use of swimming pool May to September.

`See also Colour Display Advertisement`

CARLISLE. Mrs Ivinson (FHG), Green View, Welton, Near Dalston, Carlisle CA5 7ES (016974 76230; Fax: 016974 76523). ♛♛♛♛ & ♛♛♛♛♛ up to *HIGHLY COMMENDED.* **Properties sleep 2/7.** Three superb Scandinavian pine lodges, surprisingly spacious, two 17th century oak beamed cottages, one with wood burning stove, also delightful pine panelled converted chapel for two. Tiny picturesque rural hamlet, unspoilt open views to Caldbeck Fells three miles away. Every home comfort provided for a relaxing country holiday in peaceful surroundings. Own gardens. All properties have shower/bath, colour TV, microwave, telephone, laundry, central heating, linen and towels. Second WC in three bedroomed properties. Within half an hour's drive of Keswick, Lake Ullswater or Gretna Green. Golf five miles. Dogs permitted. Open all year. Ideal for an off season break, warm for your arrival. Resident owners. Weekly terms from £135 to £440. Car essential. Accommodation is suitable for accompanied disabled visitors.

CARLISLE. Mrs D. Carruthers, University of Northumbria, Old Brewery Residencies, Bridge Lane, Caldewgate, Carlisle CA2 5SW (01228 597352). The University of Northumbria's self-catering holiday flats are set in the attractive surroundings of the restored Theakston's Old Brewery on the banks of the River Caldew and adjacent to Carlisle Castle. The recently built self-contained flats are ideal for holiday accommodation with a choice of four, five or six bedrooms and comprise shower room, bathroom with WC, separate WC, a well fitted kitchen/dining room with microwave, electric cooker and fridge/freezer. Bed linen and tea towels are provided but not personal towels. Disabled visitors accommodated. Children welcome but sorry, no pets. The pedestrianised city centre is only a few minutes' walk away and features high quality shopping centres and a Victorian covered market. Weekly terms from £196 to £284.

CONISTON. Thurston House, Coniston. ♛♛♛ *APPROVED.* **Flats sleep 2/5.** Self-contained flats designed to help you have a relaxing holiday, including one ground floor flat suitable for disabled visitors. Full fire precautions. The flats are comfortable, clean and well proportioned. Background heating early and late season. Carefully maintained by the owners. Open all year. Children welcome, cot provided. Pets by prior arrangement. Parking. Shopping close by. From most flats there are scenic views. Quiet situation. Special low season rates (from £70 weekly). Spring Short Breaks available. Enquiries to **Smith, Woodhow, Staveley-in-Cartmel, Near Ulverston LA12 8NH (015395 31223).**

OUT AND ABOUT IN CUMBRIA

Take a trip back in time on a narrow-gauge railway: The Lakeside and Haverthwaite runs through the beautiful Leven Valley, Ravenglass and Eskdale travels 7 miles from the coast up into the fells, and the South Tynedale Railway offers a journey through a beautiful North Pennine Valley.

The perfect way to appreciate the magnificent Lakeland scenery is on a leisurely Lake cruiser — Ullswater, Coniston, Derwentwater all have scheduled services daily in season.

CONISTON near. Mrs J. Halton, "Brookfield", Torver, Near Coniston LA21 8AY (015394 41328).

♀ ♀ APPROVED/COMMENDED. **Sleeps 2/4.** "Brookfield" is a large attractive modern bungalow property in a rural setting with lovely outlook and extensive views of the Coniston mountains. The bungalow stands in its own half acre of level garden and grounds. The inside is made into two completely separate self-contained units (semi-detached). The holiday bungalow accommodation consists of large sitting/dining room, kitchen, utility room, two good bedrooms (one twin and one double), bathroom. Good parking. Well equipped except for linen. Lovely walking terrain. Two village inns with restaurant facilities approximately 300 yards. One small dog by arrangement only. Terms from £125 to £215. Special rates for two persons. Further details on request with SAE please.

CONISTON. Low Arnside Cottage, Coniston. Working farm. Sleeps 6. Low Arnside Cottage is a 16th

century farm cottage comprising three bedrooms — two double (one with cot) and one twin-bedded. Bathroom. Sittingroom with coal fire. Kitchen. Bring your own linen. Parking is available for two cars. The cottage is situated in a good area for walking; three miles from Coniston and five miles from Ambleside. Good views of Coniston and Langdale Fells. Coniston is famous for its Lake, where Donald Campbell set his water speed records, and for its mountain, the 2635 ft Coniston Old Man. Further details and terms contact: **Mrs T. Holliday, High Arnside, Coniston LA21 8DW (015394 32261).**

DERWENTWATER. Derwent House and Brandelhowe, Portinscale, Keswick. ♀♀♀ *COMMENDED.*

Sleeps up to 6. In the picturesque village of Portinscale, Keswick, Derwent House with Brandelhowe is a traditional stone Lakeland building renovated and converted to four self-contained comfortable well appointed holiday suites, each with parking. BRANDELHOWE COTTAGE SUITE on ground floor has two double bedrooms both with en suite shower/WC. SHIRE, HUNTER AND COB SUITES have views south over Derwentwater. Central heating included. Colour TV. All bed linen provided. Children and pets welcome. Open all year. Prices from £90 to £290 per week. Some reductions for two people. Short breaks available. SAE for brochure to **Mary and Oliver Bull, Stone Heath, Hilderstone, Staffordshire ST15 8SH (01889 505678; Fax: 01889 505679).**

ELTERWATER. Lane Ends Cottages, Elterwater. ♀♀♀ *COMMENDED.* Three cottages are situated next to "Fellside" on the edge of Elterwater Common. Two cottages accommodate a maximum of six persons: double bedroom, twin bedded room; large lounge with studio couch, open fire, electric fire, colour TV; fully equipped kitchen/diningroom; bathroom. Third cottage sleeps five: as above plus single bedroom and separate diningroom. Electricity by meters. The cottages provide an ideal base for walking/touring holidays with Ambleside, Grasmere, Hawkshead and Coniston within a few miles. Parking for one car per cottage, additional parking opposite. Open all year, out of season long weekends available. Rates from £150 per week. Brochure on request (SAE please). **Mrs M.E. Rice, "Fellside", Elterwater, Ambleside LA22 9HN (015394 37678).**

ENGLISH LAKES & EDEN VALLEY. Selection of fully furnished apartments, cottages and houses situated in the Lake District and in the popular Eden Valley Villages, all within easy access of the M6 motorway. Pets by arrangement. For brochure and further details contact **Lowther Scott-Harden, 4 St Andrew's Churchyard, Penrith, Cumbria CA11 7YE (01768 864541 24 hours).**

ENNERDALE. Mrs E.J. Vickers, Mireside Farm, Ennerdale, Cleator CA23 3AU (01946 861276). ♀♀♀ *APPROVED.* **Sleeps 6.** Comfortable country cottage near beautiful Ennerdale Lake (one field away) surrounded by mountains with spectacular views and many interesting walks. The cottage adjoins the farmhouse at Mireside Farm and is completely self contained. Open all year. Car essential. Parking. Accommodation for six in three double bedrooms. Children welcome and cot available. Sitting/diningroom, bathroom/toilet, kitchen with electric cooker. Linen is supplied. All kitchen equipment provided, fridge etc. Central heating throughout. Electric fire, colour TV. Weekly rates from £120 (low season) to £220 (high season). SAE for brochure please.

CUMBRIA – THE GREAT OUTDOORS

Lakes, rivers, mountains and moors (and a mild climate) make Cumbria a paradise for the outdoor enthusiast — with something to suit every age group and every level of ability. Practically every kind of watersport can be enjoyed — if you haven't tried water ski-ing, canoeing, windsurfing or yachting, then now's your chance! Climbing, abseiling, walking, cycling, mountain biking, pony trekking, fishing, orienteering . . . the list is endless!

TEL. MRS J. HALL (019467) 23319

SELF-CATERING IN STYLE

Three Pine Lodges & two stone cottages share an acre of orchard on this Lakeland farm. Each is very well equipped, with three bedrooms, bathroom, lounge with colour TV and fully fitted kitchen area with electric hob, microwave combination oven & dishwasher. The barn has been converted to provide a **Sports Hall** with Badminton, Short Tennis, etc.; a **Games Room** with Table Tennis, Pool, Snooker, Darts; and a **Laundry** and **telephone.** There is an **Adventure Playground** with zip-wire, assault course, and two **ponds with rafts.**

And we have our own station on the **Ravenglass & Eskdale miniature railway!**

Ideal for couples wanting peace and tranquillity, for families with energetic kids, and for dog-lovers – pets are very welcome.

Brochure on request. ETB ↑↑↑↑ Commended.

FISHERGROUND FARM ESKDALE CUMBRIA CA19 ITF

GLENRIDDING. Roma Rigg, Glenridding, Penrith. ↑↑ *COMMENDED.* **Sleeps 6/8.** Slate/stone bungalow in large private garden, with views of mountains on all sides and Lake Ullswater in front. Fishing, boating (including Lake steamer), ski-ing, fell walking, pony trekking and sailing nearby. Good bar meals, hotels and shops within 500 yards. Well-furnished accommodation sleeping eight (six on ground floor and additional two in Loft Studio); cot and high chair available. Facilities for disabled. Central heating and open fire. Everything provided except linen. Pets allowed. Terms from £180 to £395 per week, inclusive of central heating and hot water. Other electricity is by coin-slot meter. SAE, please, to **Mrs M.J. Matthews, Thornthwaite Vicarage, Braithwaite, Keswick CA12 5RY (017687 78243).**

HAWESWATER. Goosemire Cottages. Lovely Lakeland self catering cottages for two to eight people. Furnished and equipped to a high standard, set in one of Lake District's loveliest corners, the tranquil Lowther Valley lies between Haweswater and Ullswater. An ideal base for walking, fishing, bird watching, visiting historical sites or just relaxing in a beautiful and peaceful setting. Local pubs and post office/shop nearby. Log fires and central heating. Heating, electricity, bed linen included in the tariff. Open all year. Short Breaks available. Details and brochure from **Anne Frith, "Goosemire", The Mews, Bampton, Penrith CA10 2RE (01931 713245).**

HAWKSHEAD. Peter and Anne Hart, Bracken Fell, Outgate, Ambleside LA22 0NH (015394 36289). Sleeps 2/4. Bracken Fell Cottage is situated in beautiful open countryside between Ambleside and Hawkshead in the picturesque hamlet of Outgate. The two bedroomed accommodation has central heating and is immaculately furnished. Fully equipped kitchen. Linen and electricity included. Patio area. Ideally positioned for exploring the Lake District. All major outdoor activities catered for nearby. Ample parking and two acres of gardens. Open all year. From £140 per week. Sorry, no pets or children under eight years. Bed and Breakfast accommodation also available. Two Crowns Commended. Non smoking. Write or phone for brochure and tariff (015394 36289).

Bracken Fell

HIGH WRAY. J.R. Benson, Tock How Farm, High Wray, Ambleside LA22 0JF (015394 36481). HOLE

HOUSE, High Wray, is a charming detached 17th century Lakeland cottage set in idyllic surroundings overlooking Blelham Tarn with magnificent panoramic views of the Langdale Pikes, Coniston Old Man, the Troutbeck Fells and Lake Windermere. High Wray is a quiet unspoilt hamlet set between Ambleside and Hawkshead making this an ideal base for walking or touring. This charming cottage which once belonged to Beatrix Potter has the original oak beams and feature stone staircase. It has recently been restored to provide very comfortable accommodation without losing its olde worlde charm. Accommodation consists of one double and two twin bedrooms; bathroom with shower; large spacious lounge with Sky TV and video; fitted kitchen with microwave oven, fridge freezer, tumble dryer, automatic washing machine and electric cooker. Storage heating included in the cost. Play area. Ample parking. Please write, or phone, for further details.

HIGH WRAY. Chestnuts and Beeches, High Wray, Ambleside. Sleep 6. Two charming cottages

converted from a former coach house set in idyllic surroundings overlooking Lake Windermere with magnificent panoramic views of Langdale Pikes, Coniston Old Man and the Troutbeck Fells. High Wray is a quiet unspoilt hamlet set between Ambleside and Hawkshead making this an ideal base for walking and touring. Both cottages have large lounges with dining area, electric fire, colour TV and double glazed French doors to balcony overlooking the Lake. Fully fitted kitchens have electric cookers, microwaves and fridges. Chestnuts has one double and two twin bedrooms, Beeches has one double, one twin and one full size bunk bedded room. All bedrooms have fitted wardrobes and dressing tables. Fully tiled bathrooms with three piece bathroom suite and electric shower. Night store heaters. Ample parking. Contact: **J.R. Benson, Tock How Farm, High Wray, Ambleside LA22 0JF (015394 36481).**

Key to
Tourist Board Ratings

The Crown Scheme
(England, Scotland & Wales)

Covering hotels, motels, private hotels, guesthouses, inns, bed & breakfast, farmhouses. Every Crown classified place to stay is inspected annually. *The classification:* Listed then 1-5 Crown indicates the range of facilities and services. Higher quality standards are indicated by the terms APPROVED, COMMENDED, HIGHLY COMMENDED and DELUXE.

The Key Scheme
(also operates in Scotland using a Crown symbol)

Covering self-catering in cottages, bungalows, flats, houseboats, houses, chalets, etc. Every Key classified holiday home is inspected annually. *The classification:* 1-5 Key indicates the range of facilities and equipment. Higher quality standards are indicated by the terms APPROVED, COMMENDED, HIGHLY COMMENDED and DELUXE.

The Q Scheme
(England, Scotland & Wales)

Covering holiday, caravan, chalet and camping parks. Every Q rated park is inspected annually for its quality standards. The more √ in the Q – up to 5 – the higher the standard of what is provided.

HOLMROOK. G. and H.W. Cook, Hall Flatt, Santon, Holmrook CA19 1UU (019467 26270). Working farm. Sleeps 7. This comfortably furnished house is set in own grounds with beautiful views. The approach road is a short but good lane off Gosforth/Santon Bridge road. Ideal centre for climbers and walkers. Within easy reach of Muncaster Castle and Narrow Gauge Railway from Ravenglass to Eskdale, about three miles from the sea and Wastwater. Accommodation comprises two double bedrooms, two single and child's bed; cot; bathroom, two toilets; sittingroom, dining room; all electric kitchen with cooker, fridge, kettle, immersion heater, stainless steel sink unit. Fully equipped except for linen. Open Easter to Christmas. Pets by arrangement. Shopping about two miles and car essential. Electricity by 50p meter. SAE, please, for weekly terms.

KENDAL. The Barns, Field End, Patton, Kendal. ♀♀♀♀ *COMMENDED.* **Properties sleep 6/8.** Two

detached barns converted into five spacious architect-designed houses. The Barns are situated on 200 acres of farm, four miles north of Kendal in a quiet country area with River Mint passing through farmland, and lovely views of Cumbrian Hills. Many interesting local walks, with the Dales Way passing close by; central to Lakes and Yorkshire Dales, National Parks. Fishing is available on the river. The Barns consists of four houses each with four double bedrooms, and one house with three double bedrooms. Each house has full central heating for early/late holidays, lounge with open fire, diningroom; kitchen with cooker, microwave, fridge and washer; bathroom, downstairs shower room and toilet. Many interesting features include oak beams, pine floors and patio doors. Electricity at cost. Pets and children welcome. Terms from £120 to £290. For brochure apply to **Mr and Mrs E.D. Robinson, 1 Field End, Patton, Kendal LA8 9DU (01539 824220 or 0378 596863).**

KENDAL. Mrs H.E. Gardner, Barn House, Natland Mill Beck Lane, Kendal LA9 7LQ (01539 729333).

Stable Cottage is a recently restored stone-faced farm cottage which has been modernised to create a very comfortable holiday home, whilst still retaining the charm and character of the original cottage. Ideally situated in the south side of Kendal only one and a half miles from the centre of the town, with easy access to local shops and amenities. An ideal base for walking and touring in the Lake District and Yorkshire Dales. Nicely furnished throughout with central heating; one double and one twin-bedded room, cot available; bathroom with bath or electric shower, WC and wash-basin; livingroom with colour TV; modern fully fitted kitchen. Bed linen provided. Terms from £170 to £250 per week. Please write or telephone for further details.

KENDAL. Dora's Cottage, Natland, Kendal. ♀♀♀*COMMENDED.* **Sleeps 2/4.** Adjoining farmhouse in a

peaceful village south of Kendal, this delightful cottage overlooks the garden amid the Lakeland Fells. Ground floor bedrooms, TV, fridge, ironing facilities, electric cooker, central heating and linen provided to help make the most of a country holiday with the hills and Dales nearby. Golf, riding, inns, restaurants, leisure centre, historic visits within easy distance. Pets and children welcome. Car parking. Terms from £180 to £275 per week. Short Breaks can be arranged. Farmhouse Bed and Breakfast also available. For further details apply to **Mrs Val Sunter, Higher House Farm, Oxenholme Lane, Natland, Kendal LA9 7QH (Tel & Fax: 015395 61177).**

KENDAL near. "Jasmin Cottage", Church View, Natland, Near Kendal. Sleeps 6. Comfortable cottage, accommodating six people, available from January to December. Lovely views overlooking the village green, church and Lakeland Fells. Kendal two miles; Arnside, Grange, Kirkby Lonsdale and Windermere eight miles. Riding centre one mile. Leisure centre and Asda only a short distance away. Two double bedrooms, bathroom and toilet. Sittingroom, fully equipped kitchen with dining area, sun lounge. Fitted carpets. Bed settee. Colour TV, gas central heating, extra if required. Bed linen supplied and beds made up. Parking space. Village shop and post office. 50p meter for electricity. Garden and lawn. Weekly terms from £130 to £190. SAE for details to **Mrs M.E. Moorhouse, High House, Helm Lane, Natland, Near Kendal LA9 7QW (015395 60564).**

FUN FOR ALL THE FAMILY IN CUMBRIA

Muncaster Mill, near Ravenglass; World of Beatrix Potter, Bowness-on-Windermere; Carlisle Castle; Wordsworth Museum, Dove Cottage, Grasmere; Appleby Castle Conservation Centre; Cumberland Toy and Model Museum, Cockermouth; Wildlife Oasis, near Milnthorpe; Brockhole National Park Centre, near Windermere; Cumberland Pencil Museum, Keswick; Windermere Steamboat Museum.

KESWICK. Mrs B. Brownrigg, "Spoutclose Cottage", Millbeck, Keswick CA12 4PS (017687 73697). Cottages sleep 5/8. These attractive oak-beamed Lakeland cottages are situated on the slopes of Skiddaw with good views of the Derwent Valley. Accommodation is for five/eight persons in three double bedrooms; one cot is also available. There is a bathroom, toilet; sittingroom, diningroom, and an all-electric fully equipped kitchen. No linen is supplied. Pets are allowed. Car is not essential but there is parking space. Shops are two miles away. The village community is very friendly and this is a good centre for fell-walking while being within easy reach of town facilities. Open Easter to November. Terms from £120 to £140 per week, plus electricity.

◦ KESWICK ◦

'AYSGARTH', CROSTHWAITE ROAD, KESWICK

Aysgarth is a lovely secluded semi-detached house on the outskirts of Keswick – the jewel of the Lake District. Furnished to a high standard, Aysgarth features a 27' long sitting room with colour TV, kitchen, bathroom and 3 bedrooms sleeping up to 6. There is a lovely garden, and ample private parking. The centre of the town with its shops and attractions is a 10 minute walk through the park, and Lake Derwentwater, with all sorts of boating, just 15 minutes' walk. Pets and children welcome and well catered for.

Apply to: Mrs J. Hall, Fisherground Farm, Eskdale CA19 1TF. Tel: 019467 23319

KESWICK. 1 Church Row, Threlkeld, Keswick. Sleeps 5. The cottage, in the centre of the village of Threlkeld (four miles east of Keswick), is an ideal base for touring the Lake District. Village amenities and services are all within easy walking distance. Golf, fishing, tennis, pony trekking available within a short distance. For hill climbers the cottage is situated on the lower slopes of Blencathra. Fully equipped to accommodate five people in one double, one family bedrooms; bathroom, toilet; diningroom. Colour TV. Fitted kitchen with electric cooker, fridge/freezer, electric kettle, automatic washing machine, etc. Linen is supplied. Children welcome. Garage available if required. Parking provided; garden to rear of cottage. Weekly rates £125 to £240. Enquiries to **Mrs G.I. Stevens, Chapel House, Threlkeld, Keswick CA12 4TY (017687 79391).**

KESWICK. Mrs M. Beaty, Birkrigg Farm, Newlands, Keswick CA12 5TS (017687 78278). Sleeps 4. ♀♀♀ COMMENDED. The cottage at our dairy and sheep farm, adjoining the farm guest house, is extremely nice with an excellent outlook. Situated very pleasantly and peacefully amongst beautiful mountain scenery in the lovely Newlands Valley in the heart of Cumbria. Five miles from Keswick, between Braithwaite and Buttermere. Perfect base for hill walking, central for touring the Lake District. Clean and comfortable, comprising lounge, TV, kitchen, fridge freezer, cooker, one double and one twin room, shower/toilet. Linen and towels provided. Oil central heating, electric stove-type fire. Available all year. Ample parking. No dogs. Short breaks out of season. £160 — £230 weekly.

KESWICK. 3 Catherine Cottages, Keswick. ♀♀ **Sleeps 5.** Pleasant holiday cottage situated in the beautiful Lake District. Modern conveniences include colour television and refrigerator, and the town centre is just five minutes away. Children welcome, but sorry, no pets. Space for car parking. Open all year. Owner maintained. Terms from £100 — £190 (all inclusive). SAE for details to **Mrs D. Allison, 2 Raven Lane, Applethwaite, Keswick CA12 4PW (017687 74153).**

CUMBRIA – LAKELAND SPLENDOUR!

The Lake District has for long been a popular tourist destination; however, the Fells and Pennine areas are also worth exploring. The many attractions of Cumbria include the Ennerdale Forest, St. Bees Head, Langdale Pikes, Bowness-on-Solway, the market town of Alston, Lanercost Priory, Scafell Pike – England's highest mountain – and the Wordsworth country around Ambleside, Grasmere and Cockermouth.

KIRKBY LONSDALE (Whittington). Church Cottage, Whittington, Kirkby Lonsdale, Via Carnforth. Sleeps 4 adults; 2 children. Church Cottage is situated in the quiet village of Whittington, two miles from Kirkby Lonsdale. It makes an ideal base for touring the Lake District, Yorkshire Dales, Ingleton and Morecambe. Accommodation for six persons in two double bedrooms and one room with two single beds; cot available. Bathroom, toilet; sittingroom with colour TV; diningroom. Both public rooms have coal fires (fuel extra), plus storage heater. Kitchen equipped with electric cooker, fridge, iron, kettle etc. No linen supplied. Children welcome. Pets allowed. Car essential, parking. Terms on request. Cottages sleeping two/eight people also available. **Mrs M. Dixon, Harrison Farm, Whittington, Kirkby Lonsdale, Via Carnforth LA6 2NX (015242 71415).**

KIRKOSWALD. Elaine and Colin Eade, Howscales, Kirkoswald, Penrith CA10 1JG (01768 898666;

Fax: 01768 898710). ♀♀♀ & ♀♀♀♀ *HIGHLY COMMENDED.* **Sleep 2/4.** Four cottages for non-smokers. Howscales is a non-working farmstead built in local red sandstone, and the cottages are grouped around a pretty courtyard. Located in a rural setting, one and a half miles from Kirkoswald. Three cottages are two storey, with the lounge, dining area and kitchen on the first floor, and the bedrooms and bathroom on the ground floor. One is single storey, suitable for accompanied disabled guests, with accommodation in two en suite double bedrooms. All cottages are furnished and equipped to a high standard. Bed linen, all towels and tablecloths are included in the tariff. No pets. Children 12 years and over welcome. All cottages are notably warm and well insulated — making them a good choice for a holiday at any time of the year. Colour brochure available. Terms from £140 to £400 weekly.

KIRKOSWALD. Crossfield Cottages and Leisure Fishery. Accessible secluded tranquil cottages overlooking small trout lake, amid Lakeland's beautiful Eden Valley countryside. Only 30 minutes' drive equidistant from Ullswater, North Pennines, Hadrian's Wall and Scotland's Borderlands. You will find beds freshly made up for your arrival, tranquillity and freedom in your surroundings, and good coarse and game fishing at hand. Accommodation is guaranteed clean, well equipped and maintained. Centrally located, good fishing and walking. Relax and escape to "YOUR" home in the country, why settle for less! Pets welcome. No silly rules. **Telephone 01768 896275, Fax available 24 hours; brochure line 01768 898711 (manned most Saturdays), or SAE Crossfield Cottage, Kirkoswald CA10 1EU for details.**

LAMPLUGH. Nos 1 and 2 Hodyoad Cottages, Lamplugh. Cottages sleep 5. Hodyoad stands in its own

private grounds, with extensive views of the surrounding fells in peaceful rural countryside. Mid-way between the beautiful Lakes of Loweswater and Ennerdale, six miles from Cockermouth and 17 from Keswick. Fell walking, boating, pony trekking and trout fishing can all be enjoyed within a three and a half mile radius. Each cottage is fully centrally heated and has two bedrooms to sleep five plus cot. All linen provided. Lounge with colour TV. Kitchen with fitted units, cooker and fridge. Bathroom with shower, washbasin, toilet, shaver point. Laundry room with washing machine and tumble dryer. Car essential, ample parking. Sea eight miles. Open all year. For further details please contact: **Mrs J.A. Cook, Hodyoad House, Lamplugh, Workington CA14 4TT (01946 861338).**

LITTLE LANGDALE. Highfold Cottage, 3 Greenbank Terrace, Little Langdale. ♀♀♀ *COMMENDED.*

Sleeps 5 plus cot. Comfortable, well equipped three bed-roomed Lakeland terrace cottage in magnificent mountain scenery. Excellent walking area, central for touring. Central heating, open fire, fitted carpets throughout. All beds have duvets and will be made up for your arrival. Children and pets welcome. There is a lockable outside shed for bikes, etc., and parking available a few yards from cottage. Rates from £175 to £295 weekly. Winter Breaks available from November to March (minimum three nights). For further information or bookings please contact: **Mrs C. Blair, 8 The Glebe, Chapel Stile, Ambleside LA22 9JT (015394 37686).**

LOWESWATER. Nether Close, Loweswater, Cockermouth. ♀♀♀ **Sleeps 6 plus cot.** Country cottage with large garden, located in picturesque countryside between Loweswater Lake and Crummock Water, within easy reach of Buttermere and other lakes and comfortable walking distance of local inn which serves bar meals. Fur-

nished to a comfortable standard with three bedrooms (one double and four single beds). Two reception rooms with storage heaters, one open fire (fuel supplied) and an electric fire. Metered electricity, colour TV, electric cooker, fridge, tumble dryer and coin box telephone. No pets. Terms from £100 to £230 per week. For further details contact: **Mrs E. Vickers, Howside, Ennerdale, Cleator CA23 3AU (01946 861334).**

LOWESWATER. Jenkinson Place Cottage, Loweswater. Sleeps 4/6. Jenkinson Place is a 17th century Lakeland farmstead, but no longer a working farm. The holiday cottage has been carefully and tastefully constructed from a former stable building to provide a maximum of six guests plus infant with comfortable, modernised accommodation while retaining those traditional period features. The proprietors resident in the farmhouse are able to give guests personal help and attention if or when required. Linen not supplied. Sorry, no pets. Ideal location for a quiet, relaxing holiday away from the crowds yet within easy reach of Crummock Water, Ennerdale, Buttermere, the old market town of Cockermouth, Keswick and the lovely West Cumbrian coast. Available April to October. Weekly terms from £100. Further details on request from **Mrs E.K. Bond, Jenkinson Place, Loweswater, Cockermouth CA13 0SU (01946 861748).**

MELMERBY. Mrs J. Gettins, Melmerby Caravan Park, Melmerby, Penrith CA10 1HE (01768 881311). Sleeps 2/4 plus cot. A newly renovated sandstone cottage in the fellside village of Melmerby. Furnished to a high standard with central heating, modern fitted kitchen, colour TV, radio cassette and bathroom with over bath shower. Parking and garden area. Ideal base for walking and touring in the North Pennines, Eden Valley, Lake District and Hadrian's Wall. Two minutes' walk to shop, pub and bakery/restaur-ant. Heating and electricity included. Open all year. Short Breaks available. Write or telephone for brochure.

MORESBY. Swallows Return and Owls Retreat, Moresby. ♀♀♀♀ *HIGHLY COMMENDED.* Sorry no

smokers, no pets. Maintained with loving care by the owners who live within two minutes' walking distance, recently converted 19th century farm buildings tastefully furnished to a high standard in a courtyard setting within a rural hamlet. Two miles from Georgian Whitehaven with its antiquarian bookshop, half a mile from Rosehill Theatre and Restaurant. Easily reached: Ennerdale, Wastwater, Loweswater, Crummock and Buttermere, St. Bees with its red sandstone cliffs, Ravenglass and miniature railway, Muncaster Castle and Owl Centre. Full gas central heating, living flame gas fires, double glazing. Open all year. Each property sleeps four, cot available. Ample parking. Brochure available on request from **James and Joyce Moore, Moresby Hall Cottage, Moresby, Whitehaven CA28 6PJ (01946 64078).**

MUNGRISDALE. Copy Hill, Mungrisdale, Penrith. An 18th century farm cottage, recently renovated to a

high standard featuring oak beams and open fireplace. Situ-ated in the quiet and unspoilt village of Mungrisdale over-looking the fells, eight miles from Keswick and 10 miles from Penrith. An ideal base for touring the Lakes or walking in the hills. Comprises comfortable lounge/dining room, fully equipped kitchen, cloakroom with shower, three bedrooms (one family/double, one double and one twin), bathroom. Price from £175 to £300 per week including electricity, central heating, colour TV and bed linen. Ample parking. Sorry, no pets. Available all year. SAE or telephone for details **Mrs Wilson, High Beckside, Mungrisdale, Penrith CA11 0XR (017687 79636).**

NEAR SAWREY. Delightful accommodation in Beatrix Potter's Lakeland village. Accommodation

for two and four people, equipped to high standard. High Fieldside comprises kitchen/diner; payphone; sittingroom; two bedrooms (double, twin); bathroom including shower. Low Fieldside has livingroom; kitchen; double bedroom; bathroom. Two small lawned gardens, car parking. Water heating and cooking by electricity, storage heaters included in the rental of £140 to £260 per week. Excellent food at nearby village pub owned by National Trust. Regret no pets. Year round letting. Personally supervised by the owner: **Mrs Margaret Hall, Castle Cottage, Near Sawrey, Ambleside LA22 0LF (015394 36216).**

NEWBIGGIN (near Stainton). Sycamore Cottage, Newbiggin, Stainton. Penrith — Gateway to the Lakes. Three bedroomed detached limestone cottage, newly converted to highest standard and fully equipped. Central heating with open fire. Lounge through to conservatory with patio door leading to lawned garden. Main bedrooms leading onto balcony with breathtaking views over Cumbria Fells. Garage. Within easy reach of Keswick; Lake Ullswater four miles; golf facilities, driving range, open and indoor swimming pools, pony trekking, extensive walks, historic castles, sailing/boating, fell climbing, etc all available nearby. Wide range of interesting restaurants and local inns. Market town with individual type shops, Lowther Park five miles. Separate dog accommodation included. From £350 weekly. Bed linen, etc fully inclusive. Telephone **Miss R. Harrop 017684 83998 or 0860 711411.**

PENRITH. Town End Farm Cottage, Little Salkeld, Penrith. ♀♀♀♀ COMMENDED. Charming red

sandstone country cottage with garden and views across the countryside. Situated on working farm in Eden Valley village, seven miles from M6 and Penrith. The cottage, with oak beams, sleeps six in three bedrooms (one double, one twin and one adult bunks). Bathroom with four piece bathroom suite, plus shower. Bed linen provided and cot and high chair. Kitchen/diningroom with electric cooker, fridge, dishwasher, kettle, etc. Comfortable lounge with open fire, colour TV and video. Utility room with washer/dryer. Full central heating. Electricity by meter reading. Sorry, no pets. Ample parking. Open all year. Terms from £200 to £320 per week. For further details and brochure please write or telephone **Mrs J. Hebson, Town End Farm, Little Salkeld, Penrith CA10 1NN (01768 881336).**

TROUTBECK (Windermere). Mrs M. Tyson, Troutbeck Park, Troutbeck, Windermere LA23 1PS (015394 33398). Working farm, join in. Troutbeck Park Holiday Cottage adjoins the farmhouse on this 2,574-acre hill farm, one mile off the main road. Situated at the head of Troutbeck Valley, it was once owned by Beatrix Potter, who left it to the National Trust. A beautiful place with an abundance of wildlife, from flowers and plants to a large selection of animals. Peaceful and relaxing, yet handy for shopping areas. One family bedroom (one double and one single beds); cot on request. Flush toilet; shower and washbasin; sittingroom with double bed; kitchen-diningroom with electric cooker, fridge etc. No linen supplied. Shops one and a half miles. No pets. Car essential — parking. Open all year. Terms on request.

See also Colour Display Advertisement **ULLSWATER. The Estate Office, Patterdale Hall Estate, Glenridding, Penrith CA11 0PJ (Tel & Fax: 017684 82308 24 hours). Apartments** ♀♀♀♀ COMMENDED; **Cottages** ♀♀♀ APPROVED; **Pine Lodges** ♀♀♀ COMMENDED; **Cedar Chalets** ♀ COMMENDED; **The Dairy and Bothies** ♀ COMMENDED. Our range includes three very comfortable large apartments, two stone built cottages with open fires, two three-bedroomed pine lodges, six two-bedroomed cedar chalets, a unique, detached converted dairy and two converted gardeners' bothies which make ideal, low cost accommodation for two people. All set in a private 300 acre Estate between Lake Ullswater and Helvellyn and containing a working hill farm, a Victorian Waterfall Wood, private lake foreshore for guests to use for boating and fishing and 100 acres of designated ancient woodland for you to explore. Children welcome. Dogs by appointment in some of the accommodation. Colour TV, central heating, launderette; daytime electricity metered. Linen hire available. Weekly prices from £112 to £381. Please phone for full brochure.

WASTWATER LAKE. Mrs J. Burnett, Greendale, Wasdale CA20 1EU (019467 26243). ♀♀♀

COMMENDED. **Sleep 4/5.** Lakeland Cottage style apartments to sleep four/five people, half a mile from Wastwater Lake. All apartments have one double and one twin bedded room, and some have a third bedroom with a small single bed. Bathroom with shower. Colour TV. Electric heating and hot water. Linen supplied. Electricity included in the weekly price, £180 to £275. Fell walkers and mountaineers alike will be attracted to the impressive peaks within easy reach, Great Gable, Scafell etc. Other places of interest include Ravenglass Miniature Railway and Muncaster Castle. Golf, fishing, pony trekking may be enjoyed in the area. Sandy beaches eight miles away. Full details on request.

WHICHAM VALLEY. Jim and Susan Capstick, Whicham Hall Farm, Silecroft, Millom LA18 5LT (01229 772637). Sleeps 7/8 plus baby. Working farm, join in. Nestling on the side of Bootle Fell with magnificent views over surrounding mountains and farmland. This charming farmhouse is on a working beef and sheep farm of 850 acres — visitors are welcome to watch or take part in various farm activities. Fellside has its own private road leading to courtyard. The house is excellently equipped and centrally heated by Rayburn cooker and open fires for winter visitors. TV, fridge/freezer, electric cooker, washing machine. Play safe garden. Linen not supplied. There is also a playroom with full size table tennis. Cot and high chair available. Pets welcome by arrangement. The property is throughly cleaned after each let by owner. From £100 to £250 weekly. Also available are a six-berth mobile home and Bed and Breakfast accommodation on the main farm.

FELLSIDE FARM

FHG DIPLOMA WINNERS 1995

Each year we award a small number of diplomas to holiday proprietors whose services have been specially commended by our readers and the following advertisers were our FHG Diploma winners for 1995.

ENGLAND

Mrs Cheryl Nicholls, Trerosewill Farm, Paradise, Boscastle, Cornwall

Mr & Mrs Atkinson, Bank Head Farm, Underbarrow Road, Kendal, Cumbria

Mr & Mrs Cox, the Beaumont Hotel, Holly Road, Windermere, Cumbria

Jill Shears, Glen Cottage, Rock Road, Chudleigh, Devon

Rosie & Dick Pell, Verulam House, 181 Wilton Road, Shirley, Southampton, Hampshire

Mrs Turton, Wychwood, 7 Bearley Road, Martock, Somerset

Philip and Janet Maricic, Rose Farm, Mill Street, Middleton, Saxmundham, Suffolk

Mr & Mrs J. Searancke, Chequers Hotel, Church Place, Pulborough, West Sussex

Paul and Caroline Hooks, Copperwood Guest House, Massetts Road, Horley, Surrey

Mrs E. Payne, North Pasture Farm, Brimham Rocks, Summerbridge, Harrogate, N. Yorks

SCOTLAND

Moira Bartrop, Tigh-na-Cloich Hotel, Larchwood Road, Pitlochry, Perthshire

WINDERMERE. Birthwaite Edge Apartments, Windermere.

♀♀♀ *COMMENDED*. Situated in extensive grounds in one of the most exclusive areas of Windermere, 10 minutes from village and Lake, this is the perfect all year round holiday base. 10 self catering apartments for two to six people. Resident proprietors personally ensure the highest standards of cleanliness and comfort. Swimming pool open May to September. Colour TV. Well equipped kitchens. Hot water included. Coin metered electricity for lighting, cooking and electric fires. Background central heating during winter. Duvets and linen provided. High chairs and cots extra. Ample car parking. Regret, no pets. Terms from £105 to £380. Brochure from **Bruce and Marsha Dodsworth, Birthwaite Edge, Birthwaite Road, Windermere LA23 1BS (015394 42861).**

WINDERMERE. Mr Ray Hood, Spinnery Cottage, Fairfield Country House Hotel, Brantfell Road, Bowness-on-Windermere LA23 3AE (015394 44884; Fax: 015394 46565). Up to ♀♀♀ *HIGHLY COMMENDED*.

Sleep 2 to 4. These apartments are part of the attractive Fairfield Hotel which is one of Lakeland's original country house hotels. The Spinnery Cottage is over 200 years old and was originally the stables. In the last century it was in full production with full-time weavers operating eight looms. Now it contains four self catering apartments, all tastefully decorated and furnished. All bed linen and towels, etc are provided. Weekend and short breaks can be arranged. Local leisure club facilities are available. There is a private car park. Children and pets welcome. Weekly terms from £165 to £285.

WINDERMERE. Mr and Mrs J.N. Pickup, The Heaning, Heaning Lane, Windermere LA23 1JW (015394 43453). ♀♀♀/♀♀♀♀ **up to** *COMMENDED*. **Flats sleep 4.** This accommodation is in a Victorian mansion in seven acres of own grounds with panoramic views of the fells. Converted into six self-contained apartments, each comfortably furnished. Colour TV. Open all year. Short stays at reduced rates out of season. Croquet lawn. Children over five years welcome. Pets accepted by arrangement. Each flat accommodates four comfortably. Attractive weekly terms, from £120; linen hire on request. Short Breaks possible November to March. Available all year with electric heating (extra). Also four one-bedroom cottages from 17th century barn conversion.

WINDERMERE. Mr and Mrs F. Legge, Pinethwaite, Lickbarrow Road, Windermere LA23 2NQ (Tel & Fax: 015394 44558). ♀♀♀ **&** ♀♀♀♀ *COMMENDED*.

Properties sleep 2/7. Pinethwaite offers more than just somewhere to stay for your Lake District holiday. Our unique Cottages and Apartments nestle in the heart of our private woodland, the haunt of roe deer, red squirrels and extensive bird life. A tranquil location, yet only one mile from Windermere and Bowness villages. Superb viewpoints close by. Lovely walks in our grounds and local footpaths (Cumbrian Way) through surrounding farmland and fell. Well equipped accommodation (colour TVs, microwaves, electric heating, log fires). Central washing machine/dryer. Private parking. Children welcome, but not pets. Open all year. Short Breaks available in the Low Season. Tariffs from £140 to £400 per week. Full details in our brochure, sent on request.

DERBYSHIRE

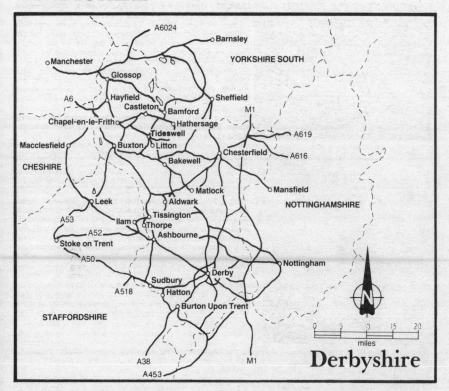

Derbyshire

ALKMONTON. Mr and Mrs A. Harris, Dairy House Farm, Alkmonton, Longford DE6 3DG (01335 330359). ♀♀♀♀ *HIGHLY COMMENDED.* Two cottages, formerly Victorian Pigsty (sleeps four plus baby), and Looseboxes (sleeps two plus baby), dating back to 1878. Both properties have been tastefully converted, finished and furnished to a very high standard, retaining beams and other original features. Situated on 81 acre working farm in the tranquil countryside of South Derbyshire yet not far from Ashbourne, eight miles; Derby nine miles; Alton Towers eight miles. Close to the Peak District. Facilities for both cottages — night storage heaters, metered electricity, linen and towels provided, colour TV, microwave, fridge freezer, autowasher, shaver point, cot and high chair. Outside there is a patio with garden furniture. Ample parking for two cars next to each property. No smokers. No pets. Weekly terms: The Pigsty £160 to £250; Looseboxes £120 to £200.

ASHBOURNE. Mrs Linda Adams, Park View Farm, Weston Underwood, Ashbourne DE6 4PA (01335 360352). Sleeps 6. HONEYSUCKLE COTTAGE is a truly delightful country cottage set in its own secluded garden with wonderful views over the Derbyshire countryside. Full of character and charm, furnished to a very high standard, with beamed sitting room, antique furnishings and pretty four-poster bed. Three bedrooms. Linen provided. Colour TV, microwave, automatic washing machine and tumble dryer. Terms from £90 to £350 per week. Smaller village cottage also available.

ASHBOURNE. Dove Cottage, Church Lane, Mayfield, Ashbourne. ♀♀♀ *APPROVED.* **Sleeps 8.**

Modernised 200-year-old cottage in Mayfield Village. Children welcome, pets by arrangement. Gas central heating. Garage and parking. Fenced garden overlooks farmland. Comfortably furnished, well equipped; TV, fridge, automatic washing machine. Convenient for shops, pubs, busy market towns, sporting facilities, lovely Dove Valley, Alton Towers, Peaks and Staffordshire Moorlands and many other places of interest. Available long and short lets, also mid-week bookings. Terms and brochure on request from **Arthur Tatlow, Ashview, Ashfield Farm, Calwich, Ashbourne DE6 2EB (01335 324443 or 324279).**

ASHBOURNE. Clifton Edge, Clifton, Ashbourne. Sleeps 4/5. Groom's cottage of individual character, carefully and tastefully converted to provide a comfortable well-equipped base for a relaxing holiday. Idyllic setting overlooking the beautiful grounds of a quiet country house in the Valley of the Dove, close to Dovedale on the edge of the Peak District National Park and well placed for exploring the Derbyshire Dales. Peaceful village just one and a half miles from Ashbourne. Chatsworth and Haddon Hall within easy reach. Alton Towers just 10 minutes away. Shop and good village pub 200 yards. Twin bedroom with adjacent bathroom; double bedroom with shower room en suite. Linen provided. Colour TV, dishwasher, woodburner, gas central heating. Garden furniture, barbecue. BARGAIN BREAKS out of season. Details from **Mr and Mrs B. Davison, Clifton Cottage, Clifton, Ashbourne DE6 2GL (01335 343915).**

ASHBOURNE. Nos. 2 & 3 Trinity View, Clifton. ♀♀♀ *COMMENDED.* **Sleeping 4 to 8.** These charming 300 year old cottages, recently refurbished to the highest standards, provide every modern comfort whilst retaining their original old world cosiness and character. They are both fully equipped with lounge/diner, separate kitchen, bathroom and two bedrooms each (a double and a twin bedded). They have large secure rear gardens and no parking problems. The tranquil and charming village of Clifton is on the southern edge of the Peak District and is convenient for Alton Towers, Carsington Water, Chatsworth, Kedleston, etc. The cottages are situated opposite the church, overlooking the golf course to the rear, with the village pub, which serves meals, and local shop nearby. Terms from £100 to £250 weekly. Leaflets available. Contact: **Mrs M.J. Davies, Clifton Hall, Clifton, Ashbourne DE6 2GL (01335 342265).**

ASHBOURNE. Mrs E.J. Harrison, Little Park Farm, Mappleton, Ashbourne DE6 2BR (01335 350341). ♀♀♀ *APPROVED.* **Working farm.** Merryfields farmhouse is situated half a mile from the village of Kniveton overlooking the beautiful Derbyshire hills. Easy access to Carsington Waters, cycle hire, Alton Towers Theme Park and the Derbyshire Dales. Downstairs: lounge with electric or open fire (coal provided); dining kitchen with cooker, microwave and fridge. Upstairs are two double bedrooms, one twin bedroom and bathroom with washbasin, toilet and bath/shower. Overall heating is provided by storage heaters. There is ample car parking and a large lawned garden. Electricity and bed linen are also included in the rental price of from £110 to £270 weekly.

DERBYSHIRE – PEAK DISTRICT AND DALES!

The undulating dales set against the gritstone edges of the Pennine moors give Derbyshire its scenic wealth. In the tourists' itinerary should be the prehistoric monument at Arbor Low, the canal port of Shardlow, the country parks at Elvaston and Shipley, the limestone caves at Creswell Crags and Castleton and the market towns of Ashbourne and Bakewell. For walkers this area provides many excellent opportunities.

ASHBOURNE near. Tony and Linda Stoddart, Cornpark Cottage, Swinscoe, Near Ashbourne DE6 2HR (01335 345041). Adjacent to our old farmhouse, overlooking the hills of Dovedale and with views over three counties, this exciting barn conversion, set beside a pond, affords privacy with easy access to all of the Derbyshire/Staffordshire attractions. Dovedale and Alton Towers 15 minutes. Converted to use all of the ground floor and part of the first floor, the barn sleeps four/five. All necessary modern conveniences provided in a beamed setting. Large gardens, tennis court, barbecue all surrounded by open countryside. Well behaved pets welcome. Linen provided, electricity is metered. Car essential. Open March to November, Saturday to Saturday bookings. Terms from £85 to £190. Also available, static van (on mains services) ideal for two people. Also Bed and Breakfast from £15. Phone or write for brochures.

ASHBOURNE near. Yeldersley Hall, Ashbourne. ♀♀♀♀ *COMMENDED* to ♀♀♀♀♀ *DE LUXE.* We have two delightful flats (each to sleep two) in the stable block and a fabulous apartment (to sleep four) in the East Wing of our historic Georgian house two miles from Ashbourne. This is an operational country house with horses in the stables and 12 acres of gardens and grounds to explore. Each flat is furnished and equipped to a very high standard with full heating, colour TV, microwave, payphone, etc. Use of washing machine and dryer. All linen and electricity included. Cot available. Regret no pets or children under 12 years except baby in cot. Terms from £140 per week. Further details and brochure from **Ms J. Bailey, Yeldersley Hall, Ashbourne DE6 1LS (01335 343432).**

ASHBOURNE near. Mrs Sylvia Foster, Shirley Hall Farm, Shirley, Ashbourne DE6 3AS (01335 360346). Up to ♀♀♀ *COMMENDED.* Three lovely properties in the Derbyshire Dales. Bungalow on the edge of peaceful Shirley village overlooking farmland comprises three double bedrooms, bathroom, large lounge/dining room, kitchen with washing machine, fridge, cooker, microwave. Colour TV. Night storage heaters. First floor barn conversion comprises family bedroom, bathroom, living-room with kitchen, electric cooker, fridge, microwave. Colour TV. Night store heaters. In nearby hamlet of Mercaston secluded farmhouse in gentle rolling countryside sleeping up to eight in four bedrooms. Modern kitchen with washing machine, cooker, fridge, microwave. Colour TV in beamed sitting room, log burner. Night store heaters. All properties have free coarse fishing. From £150 to £350 per week.

ASHBOURNE near. Mrs A.M. Hollingsworth, Mount Pleasant Farm Cottage, Mount Pleasant Farm, Snelston, Near Ashbourne DE6 2QJ (01335 342330). Sleeps 6. Modern self catering farm cottage at Snelston (off the A515 Sudbury to Ashbourne road), in beautiful setting ideal for walking and touring in the Peak District. Market town of Ashbourne two miles; Alton Towers eight miles; golf course half a mile. Available all year, the cottage is fully equipped to accommodate six holidaymakers and linen is supplied. Three double bedrooms plus cot; bathroom, toilet. Large lounge with colour TV; dining room/kitchen includes refrigerator, electric cooker. Electric heating. Pets welcome. Large garden for the children, also babysitting provided if required. Car essential, parking. Please write or telephone for further details and terms (including fuel).

ASHBOURNE/DOVEDALE. Very picturesque stone holiday cottage with superb views in delightful setting by river and close to Dovedale. Ideally situated for quiet, peaceful holidays walking/touring in the Peak District with stately homes, cycling, trekking, fishing and Alton Towers close for those who seek a more active holiday. This property has been sympathetically modernised to a high standard, retaining its old beams and character. It sleeps up to six and has fitted carpets, electric cooking/heating and all modern conveniences, cots, Satellite TV, etc. Available for weekly periods at prices between £100 and £280 per week. Leaflet giving full detailed information from **Mrs Y. Bailey, 4 Woodland Close, Thorpe, Ashbourne DE6 2AP (01335 350447).**

FREE and REDUCED RATE Holiday Visits! See our Reader's Offer Vouchers for details!

BAKEWELL. Jan and Tony Staley, Bolehill Farm, Monyash Road, Bakewell DE45 1QW (Tel & Fax: 01629 812359). ♀♀♀♀ *COMMENDED.* **Sleep 2/8 adults plus 2 children.** AWARD WINNING COTTAGES. Charming collection of eight stone cottages grouped around an attractive courtyard and incorporating high quality furnishings and equipment. Situated in 20 acres of open fields and woodland with magnificent views over Lathkill Dale (Bakewell two miles). Leisure facilities include sauna, solarium, table tennis, pool table, children's play area and barbecue. From £175 to £460 weekly. Winner of East Midlands Tourist Board Self-Catering Holiday of the Year Award.

BAKEWELL (Peak District). Mrs E. Hague, Dale End Farm, Gratton, Youlgreave, Bakewell DE45 1LN (01629 650453). ♀♀♀ **&** ♀♀♀♀ *COMMENDED.* Charming period cottage (sleeps two/four) and delightful bungalow (sleeps two/seven) located in peaceful, picturesque, rural surroundings of Gratton Dale. Ideal for walking, local well dressings and crafts; Chatsworth, Haddon Hall, Arbor Low and the beautiful Derbyshire Dales within easy distance. Both properties spacious, fully carpeted, centrally heated. All amenities, washing machine, fridge, colour TV. One and three bedroom accommodation with washbasins and bathrooms. Properties renovated, comfortable and maintained to a high standard. Cots provided. Tennis, garden, patio, ample parking. Bed linen/towel hire. Shops two miles. Telephone nearby. Weekend Breaks. Open all year. Low Season rates per week: Cottage from £125, Bungalow from £155; High Season rates per week: Cottage from £155, Bungalow from £235.

BUXTON near. Mrs Lawrenson, Grove House, Elkstone, Longnor, Buxton SK17 0LU (01298 84223 or 01538 300487). ♀♀♀ *COMMENDED.* Stable Cottage is a delightful fully equipped oak beamed cottage situated in a small, quiet village near Manifold Valley and Dovedale. Patio garden, parking space. Ideal for a couple plus put-u-up for third person; cot available. Good walking and cycling area and convenient for National Trust properties in Derbyshire and Staffordshire. The perfect location for the true country lover. Sorry, no pets. Weekly terms from £125 to £195.

CUTTHORPE. Birley Grange Farm, Cutthorpe. Three cottages and converted barn, tastefully converted and retaining original beams and stone wherever possible. Bramble Cottage has twin bedded room; Acorn Cottage has double bedded room; Haywain Cottage has double bedded room and room with bunk beds; the Barn has family room and twin-bedded room. All the dwellings are comfortably furnished and carpeted and are completely self contained, with refrigerator, cooker and TV. Heating and cooking by 50p meter. Well behaved pets welcome. Ample parking space. Situated at the edge of the Peak National Park, eight miles from Bakewell. Many interesting places to visit — Chatsworth House, Matlock, Buxton and Chesterfield. Terms from £70 to £175. Further details from **Mrs M. Ward, Birley Grange Farm, Cutthorpe, Near Chesterfield S42 7AY (01246 583292).**

Birley Grange Cottages

PUBLISHER'S NOTE

While every effort is made to ensure accuracy, we regret that FHG Publications cannot accept responsibility for errors, omissions or misrepresentation in our entries or any consequences thereof. Prices in particular should be checked because we go to press early. We will follow up complaints but cannot act as arbiters or agents for either party.

DERBY. Mrs E.M. Foster, Burley Meadows Farm, Duffield, Derby DE6 4FQ (01332 840125).

Cottage sleeps 4. A working mixed farm (arable, dairy, beef cattle and "pick your own" soft fruit), set in the beautiful Derwent Valley. Situated on the A6 Derby to Matlock road approximately 15 miles from Chatsworth and Haddon Hall and three miles from Kedleston Hall. Three local golf courses and fishing; local shops. Self catering flat with one bedroom sleeping four. Fully equipped with linen, etc; gas cooker and fire, fridge, colour TV. Bathroom with toilet, washbasin and shower. Own entrance and key. From £80 to £120 per week. Bed and Breakfast accommodation also available from £13.50 per person.

DERBY. Bank Cottage, 3 The Hollow, Mickleover, Derby. ♀♀♀ *HIGHLY COMMENDED.* **Sleeps 4 plus**

cot. Bank Cottage is a delightful 18th century oak-beamed cottage in a quiet Conservation Area of Derby. Many places of interest are easily reached by car including the Peak District and Derbyshire Dales. The cottage is centrally heated and is clean and comfortable, being personally maintained to a high standard by the owner. It has good quality furnishings and accommodation comprises a well-equipped kitchen, bow-windowed sittingroom, bathroom and two pretty bedrooms (one double, one twin). The cottage is inspected annually by the English Tourist Board. Open all year. No pets. Cot available. Weekly terms from £170 including bed linen, gas and electricity; colour TV. **Mrs P.K. Pym, 2 The Hollow, Mickleover, Derby DE3 5DG (01332 515607).**

DOVEDALE/ASHBOURNE. Alstonefield Holiday Homes, Post Office House, Alstonefield, Ash-

bourne DE6 2FX (01335 310201). ♀♀♀/♀♀♀♀ A choice of five properties sleeping two/six people, all situated in the quiet picturesque limestone village of Alstonefield, five times winner of the Best Kept Village Award. Complete with a 13th century church, an old coaching inn and village shop. An ideal base to explore the Peak National Park situated between Dovedale and Manifold Valleys, also near the attractions of Alton Towers, Chatsworth House, etc. All accommodation recently modernised and tastefully furnished in country style to a high standard. Ideal for those Winter Breaks. Children and pets welcome. Terms from £95 to £150 low season, £150 to £375 high season, per week. Three nights midweek from £50.

EDALE. ♀♀♀ *COMMENDED.* **Cottages sleep 2/4.** Edale, in the heart of the Derbyshire Peak District,

well-known as the start of the Pennine Way, is renowned for its beautiful scenery, and is a paradise for walking, climbing and touring. Two cottages on working hill farm sleep two/four, plus cot. Bathroom, one bedroom with double bed and bunk beds, kitchen/lounge. Well equipped, with central heating, double glazing, colour TV, immersion heater. Bed linen and towels provided. Electricity by coin meter. Children welcome. Terms from £130 to £185 per week. Weekend and short breaks out of season. Details from **Mrs S. Gee, Cotefield Farm, Edale, Near Sheffield S30 2ZG (01433 670273).**

WHEN MAKING ENQUIRIES PLEASE MENTION
FARM HOLIDAY GUIDES

HOPE. Crabtree Cottages, Crabtree Meadow, Aston Lane, Hope, Via Sheffield. ♀♀♀♀ *HIGHLY*

COMMENDED. **Four cottages sleep 2/6.** Four beautifully converted well-equipped cottages in the grounds of a country house in Peak District National Park, sleeping two to six persons. Beautifully fitted kitchens with microwave ovens. Colour TV's. Laundry. Payphone. Central heating, fuel and linen included in rental. Ample off road parking but car not essential. Superb walking country and facilities in area for golf, tennis, climbing, gliding, fishing, pony trekking and caving. Convenient for shops and pubs, visiting historic houses. Weekly all year £140 to £330. Short breaks in winter from £55. **Mrs P.M. Mason, Crabtree Meadow, Hope, Via Sheffield S30 2RA (Tel & Fax: 01433 620291).**

MATLOCK. Darwin Forest Country Park, Two Dales, Matlock DE4 5LN (01629 732428).

√ √ √ √ √ Situated in the heart of the Peak District, Darwin Forest is set in 44 acres of magnificent woodland. It is the ideal place to spend a family holiday. As well as the beautiful countryside, the area boasts many attractions including Alton Towers, Heights of Abraham and Chatsworth House. Our luxury "Pinelodge" self catering holiday lodges vary in size to accommodate up to eight adults. Equipped with a superb bar and meals facility, laundry, shop, children's playground and games room, the park has recently been complemented by a luxurious indoor heated swimming pool. Please apply for colour brochure and terms.

MILLDALE. Old Millers Cottage, Milldale, Near Ashbourne. ♀♀♀ *COMMENDED.* **Sleeps 4.** Situated in the beautiful hamlet of Milldale, beside the River Dove, with its famous Packhorse Bridge, the cottage is an ideal starting point for exploring the 'Peak National Park'. This cosy 18th century Miller's Cottage (sleeping four) has been beautifully renovated to a very high standard, to retain all its charm and character, with exposed beams and featured limestone walls. Accommodation fully furnished and equipped except for linen. Children and pets welcome. Colour TV, electricity for storage heating and cooking included in the rental of £135 to £175 per week. Open all year. Details on request from: **Mrs P.M. Hewitt, 45 Portway Drive, Tutbury, Burton-on-Trent, Staffordshire DE13 9HU (01283 815895).**

THORPE. Hawthorn Studio, Thorpe, Ashbourne. Sleeps 2. A compact stone built holiday home in the heart of Thorpe, a pretty village near Dovedale in the Peak District Park, offers romantic and beautifully appointed accommodation with superb views. There are fine walks from the door, cycling on the Tissington Trail with the market town of Ashbourne and the National Trust village of Ilam all a few minutes away. Alton Towers, Chatsworth House, Carsington Water all within easy reach. Electric storage heaters and shower, colour TV, bed linen and towels provided. Weekly and short break rates £50 to £200, electricity included. Details **Suzanne Walton, Hawthorn Cottage, Church Lane, Thorpe, Ashbourne DE6 2AW (01335 350494).**

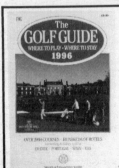

DEVON

Devon

APPLEDORE. Sea Birds Cottage, Appledore. Sea edge, pretty Georgian cottage facing directly out to the open sea, Sea Birds is a spacious cottage with large lounge, colour TV; dining room with french windows onto garden; modern fitted kitchen with washing machine; three double bedrooms; bathroom, second WC downstairs. Lawned garden at back overlooking the sea with garden furniture. Sea views from most rooms and the garden is magnificent: views of the open sea, boats entering the estuary, sunset, sea birds. Appledore is still a fishing village — fishing trips from the quay, restaurants by the water. Area has good cliff and coastal walks, stately homes, riding, swimming, golf, surfing, excellent beaches. Off peak heating. From £95. Other cottages available. **Ring 01237 473801** for prices and vacancies or SAE to **F.S. Barnes, Boat Hyde, Northam, Bideford EX39 1NX.**

The view from Mariners' Cottage Garden

APPLEDORE. Mariner's Cottage, Irsha Street, Appledore. Sleeps 6. Elizabethan fisherman's cottage right at the sea edge — the high tide laps against the garden wall. Extensive open sea and estuary view of ships, lighthouses, fishing and sailing boats. The quayside, beach, shops, restaurants and fishing trips are all close by. Riding, sailing, tennis, golf, sandy beaches, historic houses and beautiful coastal walks, and the Country Park, are all near. Mariner's Cottage (an historic Listed building), sleeps six, plus baby, in three bedrooms, and has a modern bathroom, fitted kitchen, washing machine; diningroom and large lounge with colour TV. Children's play house. Gas central heating makes Mariner's good for winter holidays from £95 per week. Pet welcome. Picture shows view from garden. SAE, please, for brochure of this and other cottages to **Mrs S.A. Barnes, Boat Hyde, Northam, Bideford** or phone **(Bideford [01237] 473801) for prices and vacancies.**

ASHBURTON. Mrs Angela Bell, Wooder Manor, Widecombe-in-the-Moor, Near Ashburton TQ13 7TR (01364 621391). ♀♀♀♀ *COMMENDED.*

Modernised granite cottages and converted coach house, on 108-acre working family farm nestled in the picturesque valley of Widecombe, surrounded by unspoilt woodland, moors and granite tors. Half a mile from village with post office, general stores, inn with dining room, church and National Trust Information Centre. Excellent centre for touring Devon with a variety of places to visit and exploring Dartmoor by foot or on horseback. Accommodation is clean and well equipped with colour TV, central heating, laundry room. Children welcome. Large gardens and courtyard for easy parking. Open all year, so take advantage of off-season reduced rates. Weekend lets also available. One property suitable for disabled visitors. Brochure available.

ASHWATER. Anne and George Ridge, Braddon Cottages, Ashwater, Beaworthy EX21 5EP (Tel & Fax: 01409 211350). ♀♀♀♀ *COMMENDED.* **Sleep 6 to 12.** Six English country cottages in quiet countryside of meadow and woodland on 500 acre site. Four barn conver-

B RADDON

ASHWATER   BEAWORTHY

DEVON   EX21 5EP UK

Tel/Fax 01409 211350

George & Anne Ridge

sions and two purpose built houses; all of highly original character surrounded by gardens, featuring lawns facing south with views over lake to Dartmoor. All weather tennis court (with basketball). Well equipped games field and games room. Very comfortable, gas central heating, wood fires, dishwashers, washing machines, clothes dryers, microwaves, payphones. Bed linen and towels supplied. Pleasant walks around lake and woodland; large summer house with barbecue, benches, picnic table, free fishing and firewood. Resident owners. Colour brochure. Open 12 months of the year. Midweek/Weekend/Short Breaks available. Prices from £40 winter to £500 at peak holiday periods. Credit cards accepted.

AXMINSTER. Cider Room Cottage, Hasland Farm, Membury, Axminster. Sleeps 4. This delightfully

converted thatched cider barn, with exposed beams, adjoins main farmhouse and overlooks the outstanding beauty of the orchards, pools and pastureland, and is ideally situated for touring Devon, Dorset and Somerset. Bathing, golf and tennis at Lyme Regis and many places of interest locally, including Wildlife Park, donkey sanctuary and Forde Abbey. Membury Village, with its post office and stores, trout farm, church and swimming pool is one mile away. The accommodation is of the highest standard with the emphasis on comfort. Two double rooms, cot if required; shower room and toilet; sitting/diningroom with colour TV; kitchen with electric cooker, microwave, fridge, kettle and iron. Linen supplied if required. Pets by arrangement. Car essential. Open all year. Terms from £115. SAE, please, to **Mrs Pat Steele, Hasland Farm, Membury, Axminster EX13 7JF (01404 881558).**

See also Colour Display Advertisement **BARNSTAPLE. Best Leisure, North Hill, Shirwell, Barnstaple EX31 4LG (01271 850611; Fax: 01271 850693).** ♀♀♀♀ *COMMENDED* and *HIGHLY COMMENDED.* Superb self-catering accommodation in idyllic surroundings. Sea, river and hill view locations each with its own special charm. Children welcome. Pets by arrangement. Short breaks available. Terms from £201 to £659 per week including power and linen. Colour brochure on request.

See also Colour Display Advertisement **BARNSTAPLE. North Devon Holiday Homes, 13 Cross Street, Barnstaple EX31 1BD (01271 76322 24-hour brochure service).** With our Free Colour Guide and unbiased recommendation and booking service, we can spoil you for choice in the wide sandy beaches and coves of Devon's National Trust Coast. Choose from over 500 selected properties, including thatched cottages, working farms, beachside bungalows with swimming pools, luxury manor houses, etc. From only £60 per week in Spring and Autumn. First class value assured. Contact above.

BARNSTAPLE (Exmoor). Hillcroft, Natsley Farm, Brayford, Barnstaple. This bungalow is an ideal holiday centre, being near the moors and within easy reach of the coasts. Hillcroft is situated beside a quiet country road in the Exmoor National Park. Lovely walks, touring, pony trekking available locally or just relax and enjoy the glorious views. Lawn at front and back of bungalow. Three double bedrooms and cot available. Children and pets welcome. Sittingroom, dining room; bathroom, toilet; kitchen with electric cooker. Available all year round. Electric heating metered. Everything supplied except linen. Terms from £75 to £200 weekly. Please apply to **Mrs M.E. Williams, Natsley Farm, Brayford, Barnstaple EX32 7QR (01598 710358).**

Terms quoted in this publication may be subject to increase if rises in costs necessitate

BERRYNARBOR. Mr and Mrs T. Massey, Wheel Farm Country Cottages, Berrydown 2, Near Combe Martin EX34 0NT (01271 882100). ♀♀♀♀ *HIGHLY COMMENDED.* **Properties sleep 2/6.** Nestling at the head of a valley, with magnificent views across Exmoor, yet only five minutes from the beach. Watermill and traditional stone barns in eight acres of gardens and woodland, converted into 10 high quality cottages. Indoor heated swimming pool and sauna. Four-poster beds, dishwashers, microwaves, central heating, woodburning stoves, home made meals service, shop, laundry, children's playground. Bed linen and maid service inclusive. Open March to November. Prices from £180 to £840 per week. Short Break holidays available off peak.

Enjoy the
FREEDOM
of a self catering or farmhouse holiday

Farm & Cottage HOLIDAYS

D iscover the delights of self catering and farmhouse holidays in Cornwall, Devon and Somerset. Many are farm based and offer fun for the children and space and freedom for you.

Or consider a half board holiday where English breakfast and a three course evening meal is provided each day.

Whatever your preference Farm and Cottage Holidays offers a large selection of properties to choose from. Please call us (24 hrs a day) for a free colour brochure on:

(01237) 479698

or write to

Dept FHG, 12 Fore Street, Northam, Bideford, Devon EX39 1AW

BIDEFORD. Webbery Cottages, Webbery, Alverdiscott, Bideford. Once the home farm and stables of the old Manor of Webbery, our architect-designed conversions of farm buildings offer a high degree of modern comfort and luxury. Set in a peaceful walled garden at centre of private five-acre grounds with views extending to Exmoor, Bideford Bay and Lundy Isle. Two all-electric two-bedroomed cottages. One centrally heated three-bedroom cottage. All tastefully furnished. Colour TV. Fitted carpets. Fridge, toaster, coffee maker, etc. Separate laundry room. Ample parking. Quietly situated between market towns of Bideford and Barnstaple. Beaches, bird watching, fishing, golf, riding, sailing, surfing and walks nearby. Brochure with pleasure. **Mrs B.M. Wilson, Webbery Garden Cottage, Webbery, Alverdiscott, Bideford EX39 4PU (01271 858430).**

BIDEFORD near. West Titchberry Farm Cottage, Hartland, Near Bideford. Sleeps 5 adults, 1 child.

♀♀♀ *COMMENDED.* Situated on the coast near Hartland Point (follow signs to Hartland Point Lighthouse), this recently renovated farm cottage comprises (upstairs) double and family rooms (plus cot); bathroom, toilet. Downstairs is a fully fitted kitchen with dining area. Electricity for the cooker, fridge/freezer, microwave oven and washing machine is on a 50p meter. In the lounge the settee converts into a double bed; colour TV, video, wood burning stove (logs provided free), central heating downstairs (no charge), portable heaters upstairs. The lounge door opens onto a small enclosed garden. The cottage is carpeted throughout and well appointed. Open all year. Guests have freedom of this 150 acre mixed farm. A nearby cliff path leads to the National Trust beauty spot of Shipland Bay, a sandy cove at low tide. Clovelly six miles; Hartland three miles. Sorry, no pets. Terms approximately £80 to £290 weekly according to season. SAE please **Mrs Yvonne Heard, West Titchberry Farm, Hartland, Near Bideford EX39 6AU (01237 441287).**

BIDEFORD. The Pines at Eastleigh, Near Bideford EX39 4PA (01271 860561). Set in the grounds of a

small country house hotel; seven acres of gardens, orchard and fields with glorious views to the sea at Hartland Point and Lundy Island. Vine Cottage: sleeps four plus cot in two bedrooms, bathroom, shower room, lounge/kitchen/diner with patio doors to garden. Terms £150 to £350 per week. Treetops: sleeps two plus cot. Bedroom, shower room, lounge/kitchen/diner with super views. Patio, raised garden. Terms £110 to £250. Cooker, microwave, fridge, colour TV, direct dial telephones (baby listening to hotel). Bed linen, towels, electricity included. Freezer and laundry room. Central heating.

BIGBURY BAY. "Waves Edge", Challaborough. Sleeps 8. "Waves Edge" is a detached four-bedroom bungalow in a magnificent position overlooking the sea. It is situated in a large lawned garden leading on to a low cliff with direct access to the sandy beach. First class furnishings and equipment include a modern kitchen complete with automatic washing machine and tumble dryer, also a large lounge with picture windows. Fully centrally heated. Ample parking. No pets. Challaborough is part of a beautiful coastline including superb sandy beaches such as Bigbury, Bantham and Thurlestone. Walkers can explore for miles along scenic cliffs or surf, sail, swim and fish to their heart's content. SAE **Mrs C. Cooper, The Oaks, Woolston, Loddiswell, Kingsbridge, Devon TQ7 4DU (01548 550511 or 01548 810704).**

BUCK'S MILLS. No.5 Forest Gardens, Buck's Mills, Near Bideford. ♀ ♀ ♀ *APPROVED.* **Sleeps 4 + cot.**

Cosy, traditional, comfortable, well equipped Devon cottage, three minutes' walk from the beach, in the quiet conservation village of Buck's Mills. Two bedrooms, bathroom, livingroom with old but very efficient coal burning range, plus storage heaters. Kitchen with electric cooker, fridge, toaster etc. Buck's Mills beach has sand, pebbles and rocks with lovely rock pools — catch your own prawn cocktail! — safe swimming. Coastal Path leaves the village in both directions: Peppercombe one way, Clovelly the other. Small village shop which also serves excellent snacks; larger shop and Post Office, half a mile. Terms from £70 to £325. 10% discount for previous visitors. Details: **Mrs J. Stevens, Court Barn Cottage, West Bradley, Near Glastonbury, Somerset BA6 8LR (01458 850349).**

HELP IMPROVE BRITISH TOURIST STANDARDS

You are choosing holiday accommodation from our very popular FHG Publications. Whether it be a hotel, guest house, farmhouse or self-catering accommodation, we think you will find it hospitable, comfortable and clean, and your host and hostess friendly and helpful. Why not write and tell us about it?

As a recognition of the generally well-run and excellent holiday accommodation reviewed in our publications, we at FHG Publications Ltd. present a diploma to proprietors who receive the highest recommendation from their guests who are also readers of our Guides. If you care to write to us praising the holiday you have booked through FHG Publications Ltd. – whether this be board, self-catering accommodation, a sporting or a caravan holiday, what you say will be evaluated and the proprietors who reach our final list will be contacted.

The winning proprietor will receive an attractive framed diploma to display on his premises as recognition of a high standard of comfort, amenity and hospitality. FHG Publications Ltd. offer this diploma as a contribution towards the improvement of standards in tourist accommodation in Britain. Help your excellent host or hostess to win it!

FHG DIPLOMA

We nominate ....

....

Because

Name ....

Address ....

.... Telephone No. ....

Devoncourt is a development of 24 self-contained flats, occupying one of the finest positions in Torbay, with unsurpassed views. At night the lights of Torbay are like a fairyland to be enjoyed from your very own balcony.

EACH FLAT HAS:

Marina views	Heating	Sea views over Torbay
Private balcony	Own front door	Separate bathroom and toilet
Separate bedroom	Bed-settee in lounge	Lounge sea views over Marina
Kitchenette – all electric	Private car park	Opposite beach
Colour television	Overlooks lifeboat	Short walk to town centre
	Open all year	Mini-Breaks October to April

DEVONCOURT HOLIDAY FLATS
BERRYHEAD ROAD, BRIXHAM TQ5 9AB
01803 853748 (24 hours)

COMBE MARTIN/BERRYNARBOR. Mrs E.D. Allen, "Bali-Hai", Sterridge Valley, Berrynarbor, Near Ilfracombe EX34 9TB (01271 882491). Sleeps 5 plus cot. This fully self-contained holiday flat is built on the back of the family bungalow which stands in one and a half acres of landscaped garden, situated in the beautiful Sterridge Valley. The flat has its own entrance leading to the first floor which has a lounge/diningroom with TV and electric fire. There are two double bedrooms, both with double beds, washbasins and shaver points. A single bed is also available in one room. Bedlinen is provided. The kitchen has an electric cooker, fridge and stainless steel sink unit. High chair and cot on request. Sorry, no pets. Ample parking — car is desirable, although village with Post Office stores, pub and restaurant half a mile away. Coast two miles, Combe Martin three and Ilfracombe four, with golf course, fishing and boating. Ideal centre for walking and exploring Exmoor National Park. Terms on request with SAE, please.

CROYDE BAY. "Sandyholme". Sleeps 6. Chalet bungalow, comfortably furnished and carpeted.

Lounge/diner, colour TV, good selection of books, maps and games. Bathroom with separate shower. Well equipped all electric kitchen including microwave, fridge, cooker, spin dryer. Situated on quiet private road, safe for children with enclosed garden, ample parking. Just five minutes through sand dunes leads to the superb sheltered bay with golden sands and rock pools. The old world village with quaint cottages, pubs and restaurants just five minutes' amble away. Set amidst National Trust protected countryside offering wonderful walks. Excellent base for touring beautiful North Devon. Sorry, no pets. Brochure on request from **Mrs J. Pearce, 59 Avonmead, Greenmeadow, Swindon, Wiltshire SN2 3NY (01793 723521).**

FREE and REDUCED RATE Holiday Visits!
See our Reader's Offer Vouchers for details!

DARTMOOR NATIONAL PARK. Dartmoor Country Holidays, Magpie Leisure Park, Bedford Bridge, Horrabridge, Yelverton PL20 7RY (01822 852651). Pine

lodges sleeping two to seven, available all year round, in peaceful woodland setting next to the River Walkham. The Lodges have been purpose-built and blend tastefully into the surroundings. The interior specification and furnishings are to a very high standard and include a fully fitted kitchen with oven, hob, microwave, dishwasher, etc. Small and uncrowded, the Park is one of those hard-to-find places where you can relax and switch-off, idle by the river bank or take pleasant strolls among seasonal flowers and trees. The village and shops are a short walk away and there are two golf courses within easy reach by car. Fishing is available in the River Walkham and horse riding can be enjoyed nearby. Dogs are permitted in all accommodation. In all, ideal holidays for golfers, walkers and lovers of unspoilt countryside. **Telephone for free brochure: 01822 852651.**

DARTSIDE Holidays

Waterside self-catering accommodation in Dartmouth, Devon and St. Ives, Cornwall.

TEL: (01803) 832093
FAX: (01803) 835135

The Dartmouth area is ideal for holidays throughout the year. The narrow streets, long flights of steps, over-hanging medieval houses, old quays, and breathtaking views delight the visitor. **Dartside Holidays** offer you high quality self-catering apartments in five prime locations in this area. An ideal holiday guaranteed for everyone with plenty to see and do. *Brochure and tariff on request. Open all year.*
RIVERSIDE COURT, SOUTH EMBANKMENT, SOUTH DEVON TQ6 9BH

WEST COUNTRY TOURIST BOARD MEMBER

DARTMOUTH. Allan and Marcia Green, Gara Mill, Slapton, Kingsbridge TQ7 2RE (01803 770295). Properties sleep 1/7. We offer eight comfortable cedar

lodges in this idyllic setting on a sunny slope above the River Gara. There are also two cosy self-contained flats within the 16th century mill building. The mill and lodges are set in four acres along a quiet lane, sheltered and peaceful yet convenient for Dartmouth and Kingsbridge. Colour TVs, children's play area, outdoor badminton court, games room, launderette. Cots available. Dogs welcome. Woodland walks on your doorstep. Two miles to beaches and spectacular coastline. Daily rates for short breaks out of season. From £130 to £275 per week. Free brochure on request.

PUBLISHER'S NOTE

While every effort is made to ensure accuracy, we regret that FHG Publications cannot accept responsibility for errors, omissions or misrepresentation in our entries or any consequences thereof. Prices in particular should be checked because we go to press early. We will follow up complaints but cannot act as arbiters or agents for either party.

DARTMOUTH. Mr Ryan, Park West Holiday Bungalows, Stoke Fleming, Dartmouth TQ6 0RZ

(01548 580072). A small attractive site of 11 purpose built chalet/bungalows surrounded by lawns in an old walled garden. Situated only one mile from lovely Blackpool Sands and two miles from Dartmouth. On the edge of the village, a quiet site with private car park. Children welcome. Sorry, no pets. Terms from £85 to £249 per week. No VAT to pay.

DARTMOUTH. Mrs S.R. Ridalls, The Old Bakehouse, 4 Broadstone, Dartmouth TQ6 9NR (01803 832109). ♀♀♀ **up to** COMMENDED. Three cottages with exposed beams and stone fireplaces, one cottage with four-poster bed, tucked away in a residential side street but only two minutes' walk from the river front, Royal Avenue Gardens and Coronation Park, restaurants and shops. Staying in this historic town gives you opportunities for boating, fishing, sailing and swimming. There are River Cruises, ferry boats to small coves for bathing, coastal and inland walks in National Trust countryside. Dartmouth and the surrounding villages have many restaurants and old inns. The properties are fully equipped to meet English Tourist Board recommendations. Cot, high chair and babysitting available. Dogs welcome. Terms from £100 to £340 per week.

See also Colour Display Advertisement

DAWLISH near. Mrs F.G. Jeffery, Cofton Country Cottage Holidays, Starcross, Near Dawlish EX6 8RP (01626 890111). ♀♀♀♀ COMMENDED. Old farm buildings, dating back over 100 years, tastefully converted into delightful self-contained cottages for parties of four/six people. Overlooked by ancient Cofton Church and the woodlands behind, each cottage is fitted out to a very high standard with colour co-ordinated furnishings and with equipment of the latest design. Colour TV and video plus TV point for your own portable. Kitchen includes electric oven and hob, microwave, dishwasher, etc. Full central heating and electricity FREE. Use of Cofton Country Holiday Park amenities in season. Open all year. Weekly from £150. **For 1996 Woodside Cottages, overlooking the Exe Estuary and Dawlish Warren, will be available.**

A warm family WELCOME is here for you!

* ★ Stylish **DOLPHIN CLUB** & Entertainment Centre
* ★ Super Indoor Heated **NEPTUNE TROPICANA** Water Leisure Complex – four Feature-packed Pools, Solarium, Sauna, spectator viewing.
* ★ **CRUISERS** adult Cocktail bar
* ★ Children's **JOLLY ROGER** Club with Disco, Cinema & large Games arcade
* ★ Short, level walk to safe sandy beach
* ★ Great *Value - for - money* prices

* ★ **FREE** Electricity, Linen, Colour TV
* ★ Welcome T.V. – great films, local attractions, and more
* ★ 2 Shops ● Cafe
* ★ 2 Takeaways
* ★ Crazy Golf
* ★ Adventure Playground
* ★ Laundrette
* ★ Hire Service with computer games
* ★ Pets *Welcome* (at small charge)
* ★ Choose from economy 4-berth to luxury 8-berth caravans.

See our MAIN AD in the colour section!

WELCOME FAMILY HOLIDAY PARK DAWLISH WARREN SOUTH DEVON EX7 0PH

DEVON & CORNWALL. Sweetcombe Cottage Holidays. For some years Sweetcombe Cottage Holidays have carefully selected holiday homes in Devon and Cornwall for their brochure and are able to offer a wide range of coastal and country cottages, farmhouses and flats, all beautifully presented and well equipped ready for your carefree holiday visit. Many visitors return year after year because of the high standards and personal attention which is given to everyone. Cottages and apartments accommodate from two to 10 people and most have cot, washing machine, freezer, microwave and colour TV. Terms start from £115 per week and off season short breaks can be arranged. Please contact **Tracy Jones** who will be delighted to send the illustrated brochure or answer any queries you may have. Colour video available on request. **Sweetcombe Cottage Holidays, "Rosemary Cottage", Weston, Near Sidmouth EX10 0PH (01395 512130; Fax 01395 515680).**

DREWSTEIGNTON. Mrs A. Bowden, Bowbeer Farm, Drewsteignton, Exeter EX6 6PD (01647 281239). Working farm, join in. Sleeps 4 plus cot. Wing of old Devon farmhouse, full of character and charm. Spacious accommodation consists of one double and one twin room, bathroom, lounge, kitchen/diner. Central heating. Garden with swing, slide and trampoline. Linen and towels provided. Colour TV, microwave, fridge, electric cooker, washing machine. Evening meals provided on request. Situated one mile from picturesque village of Drewsteignton. Fishing available on nearby farm, and guests are welcome to join in the activities on the working and pony farm. Children welcome, cot available. Sorry, no pets. Terms from £80 to £200. Further details available on request.

EXETER near. Mrs R.F. Horsman, Oxen Park Farm, Lower Ashton, Exeter EX6 7QW (01647 252461). Sleeps 2. Ground floor flat in modern farmhouse with wheelchair access. 50 acre working farm with suckler cows and sheep in scenic Teign Valley. Sunny conservatory, bedsitting room, kitchen, bathroom with bath and separate shower. Central heating, electric cooker, fridge, colour TV. Linen supplied. Shared garden, ample parking. Sorry, no pets or smokers. Eight miles west of Exeter; easy reach coast and Dartmoor; good local wildlife and walks; golf course one mile; quarter of a mile to thatched village with post office/shop and excellent pub meals. Terms from £140; full weeks preferred but need not be Saturdays.

PLEASE ENCLOSE A STAMPED ADDRESSED ENVELOPE WITH ENQUIRIES

EXMOUTH. Mrs Christine Duncan, 24 Raleigh Road, Exmouth EX8 2SB (01395 266967). Properties sleep 4/10. Small selection of self catering houses and flats in residential roads near sea and shops. Available July, August and September only. Examples: Flat for five in September from £200 per week; House for 10, washbasins all five bedrooms; huge lounge; excellent car parking, etc. — August £460 per week. Linen can be hired. Exmouth has two miles of sandy beach and safe bathing, the town is unspoilt, the Exe estuary full of interest and there is a wide range of water sports and other activities, including new sports centre and swimming pools. There are children's play parks, some evening entertainment and many places of interest and beauty to visit.

See also Colour Display Advertisement

HOLSWORTHY. Glebe House Luxury Cottages, Bridgerule, Holsworthy EX22 7EW (01288 381272). ♛♛♛♛ *HIGHLY COMMENDED.* Beautiful Georgian, tranquil five acre estate on the Devon/Cornwall border, 10 minutes' drive spectacular coast, sandy beaches. Seven cottages of historic interest with exposed beams, sleeping two to 10, meticulously maintained and equipped. Open all year. Full central heating. Some cottages with four-posters and double size whirlpool baths with power showers. Variety of amenities including residents' Olde Worlde Cellar Bar. Ideal for families or couples wishing to relax in comfort and explore coast, moors and quaint fishing villages. Three golf courses within 10 minutes' drive.

HOPE COVE. Craigwell Cottage, Hope Cove, Near Salcombe. Craigwell Cottage is situated in picturesque fishing village of Hope Cove, a few minutes' walk from two delightful beaches and with lovely country views overlooking National Trust land. The accommodation, which sleeps six, consists of three bedrooms, two twin-bedded and one with bunk beds, all with fitted carpets; bathroom with toilet; large lounge/dining room with colour TV and radio; kitchen with pine units, electric cooker, fridge/freezer, microwave, dishwasher, washing machine; walk-in pantry. Outside toilet. Plenty of parking space. The cottage is ideal for your Summer holiday, but also cosy for that welcome winter break, as there is an oil-fired Rayburn and radiators in all rooms. Sorry no pets. Terms from £150 to £395. **Mrs Pedrick, Barton Cottage, Hope Cove, Near Kingsbridge TQ7 3HT (01548 561296).**

ILFRACOMBE. Mrs Valerie Watts, Chartwood Holiday Flats, Torrs Park, Ilfracombe EX34 8AZ (01271 864590). Sleeps 2/6. Chartwood Flats are all completely self contained with separate entrances from the gardens which surround this south-facing property with panoramic views across Ilfracombe to the sea. Backing onto National Trust lands and cliff top walks yet within walking distance of the town, beaches and harbour. Fully equipped one, two or three bedroomed flats are available with colour TV, games room and laundry room. Car parking. Children welcome, pets by arrangement. Special offers for two persons plus short breaks with prices from £45 to £250 per week.

ILFRACOMBE. Mr J.W.M. Kempson, Post House Holiday Flats, Portland Street Post Office, Ilfracombe EX34 9NN (01271 862204). Flats sleep 4. Situated in a terrace overlooking the town of Ilfracombe and its picturesque harbour, the properties enjoy breathtaking panoramic views of the Bristol Channel and Ilfracombe Harbour. They are decorated in tasteful modern style with modern furnishings. Cleanliness guaranteed by resident proprietors. Choice of two flats each offering accommodation for up to four persons. Both have kitchen/diner with electric cooker, hot and cold water, fridge. Lounge with settee, colour TV, portable radio etc. Children welcome; cot, high chair. No pets. Town's High Street only five minutes away, as are harbour area and Esplanade. Weekly terms from £60 to £180. Details on application.

ILFRACOMBE near. Mrs M. Cowell, Lower Campscott Farm, Lee, Near Ilfracombe EX34 8LS (01271 863479). Four excellent holiday cottages on a 90 acre dairy farm with a delightful one mile walk down to the beach at Lee Bay. The cottages have been converted from the original farm buildings and are equipped to a high standard. Two of the cottages will accommodate four people, one will accommodate up to six people and the large one will take eight/10 people. Laundry room; linen included in the price. We also have a large self-contained six-berth caravan to let with Bed and Breakfast in the farmhouse. Children welcome but regret no pets. Terms from £129 weekly. Spring Mini Breaks (three nights) from £70.

IVYBRIDGE. Strashleigh Annexe, Ivybridge. ♀♀♀ *APPROVED.* **Sleeps 2 adults plus cot.** Peacefully set with views of Dartmoor, Strashleigh Annexe is a one level self-contained wing of the farmhouse. Strashleigh is a working farm set between Dartmoor and Bigbury Bay; being easily accessible it's a perfect base for touring, city entertainment, horse riding, golf and many other attractions. One double room with en-suite bathroom, newly fitted kitchen with dishwasher, washing machine and a cosy open plan living area with a beautiful granite mullion window. In the winter you can treat yourself to a cosy evening by the log burning stove. Small private garden and garage available. Linen inclusive. 50p meter, logs sold by the bag. Cot available. Terms from £160 to £240 per week. Bed and Breakfast also available. Brochure on request. FHB Member. **Mrs Paula Salter, Strashleigh Farm, Ivybridge PL21 9JP (01752 892226).**

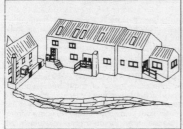

KING'S NYMPTON. Mrs Martin, Venn Farm Cottages. ♀♀♀♀ COMMENDED. **Sleep 6 plus cot.** Delightful holiday cottages converted from old stone barn on small working farm set in beautiful Devon countryside. The children will love to feed the lambs and goat kids. Nearly 50 acres of rolling fields to wander over with views to Exmoor and Dartmoor. The cottages are furnished and equipped to a high standard, have patios with picnic table and barbecue and have two or three bedrooms sleeping up to six plus cot. One cottage is suitable for disabled visitors. Bed linen provided. Laundry room and adventure playground. Pets welcome. Prices from £110 to £390. For brochure apply to: **Mrs I. Martin, Venn Farm, King's Nympton, Umberleigh, Devon EX37 9TR (01769 572448).**

KINGSBRIDGE. Anne Rossiter, Burton Farm Cottages, Burton Farm, Galmpton, Kingsbridge TQ7 3EY (01548 561210). ♀♀♀♀ *APPROVED.* **Sleep 4/5/6.** Cob and slate cottages situated in pretty hamlet, three miles Salcombe. Two/three bedrooms, bathroom. Many original features have been retained such as open fireplace. Garden. Takeaway meals. Guests welcome to enjoy farm activities. Children and pets welcome. Open all year. Terms from £100 to £400 per week.

KINGSBRIDGE. Mr and Mrs H.D. Ide, Fairfield, Wallingford Road, Kingsbridge TQ7 1NF (01548 852441). Sleeps 2/5. "Garden Flat" situated in a quiet position within easy walking distance of the town centre. Direct access to secluded well fenced garden, ideal for children and/or dogs. A garden seat, table and deck chairs are ready for outdoor meals. Colour TV. Bed linen provided. No charge for heating, all other electricity metered. Parking space. The Coastal Path, National Trust land and the Ramblers' Association all help to make a walking holiday easy and pleasurable. Open all year. A friendly welcome and cream tea await you. From £140 to £180 per week.

KINGSBRIDGE. Mr and Mrs M.B. Turner, Cross Farm, East Allington, Near Kingsbridge TQ9 7RW (01548 521327). Working farm, join in. Sleeps 11 plus 2 cots.

Get away from the hustle and bustle of everyday life and enjoy the peace and tranquillity of Cross Farm, surrounded by South Hams countryside of outstanding natural beauty. Children love to help feed the animals while you take a leisurely farm walk or relax in the garden. Lovely 17th century part farmhouse and delightful coverted barn, both sleep 11 in four bedrooms; equipped to very high standard including colour TV, dishwasher, microwave, washing machine, dryer, fridge freezer, showers, duvets and linen. Cleanliness guaranteed. Play area and recreation barn. Heating included for early/late holidays. Only four miles to Kingsbridge (one mile to village pub!) and close to many lovely coves and beaches. Central for Dartmoor, Salcombe, Darmouth, Torbay; riding, fishing, golf, etc. Ideal touring area. Rough shooting on farm in season. Brochure available.

KINGSBRIDGE. Vine Cottage, Towns Lane, Loddiswell, Kingsbridge. Sleeps 6, plus cot. Self catering cottage with garden in lovely South Hams area, four miles from Bantham. Ideal beach for small children, several other sandy and shingle beaches in area. Within easy reach of Dartmoor and the surrounding countryside for pleasant walks and picnics. Children welcome. Dog allowed if well-trained. Cottage sleeps six, cot also available. Two bedrooms, bathroom and toilet, lounge, kitchen/diningroom, TV. Bring own linen. All electric. Car space. Shops and post office close by. Terms from £90. Please send SAE for reply. **Mrs N.R. Baker, Vine House, Towns Lane, Loddiswell, Kingsbridge TQ7 4QY (01548 550224).**

KINGSBRIDGE. Mr and Mrs F.C. Wright, Lower Norton Barn, East Allington, Near Totnes TQ9 7RL (01548 521361).

Situated in a peaceful valley adjoining farmland in the centre of the magnificent South Hams. The barn is completely surrounded by lush rolling countryside, and close by is a stretch of coastline between Dartmouth and Plymouth, boasting unspoilt beaches, sandy coves and cliff walks. Approximately four miles away is the market town of Kingsbridge and estuary stretching to Salcombe with its quaint streets and harbour. The Nature Reserve at Slapton is some four miles away whilst the sophistication of Torbay is close at hand. The beautiful moors of Dartmoor are within easy reach. Locally there are facilities for excellent sea and fresh water fishing, sailing, horse riding and there are 18 hole golf links at Thurlestone and Bigbury. The accommodation comprises self contained apartments each with its own private entrance/patio. Mainly two bedroomed, lounge with TV, well equipped kitchen, bathroom/toilet. All electric. Pets allowed out of main season. Open all year. Special terms off season.

See also Colour Display Advertisement **KINGSBRIDGE near. TORCROSS APARTMENT HOTEL.** ♀♀♀ *APPROVED.* At the water's edge on Slapton Sands overlooking the blue waters of Start Bay. Family self catering in our Luxury Apartment Hotel ranging from our ground floor Beachside apartments for two to our really spacious family apartments. Superb sea views. Family owned and supervised ensuring a high standard of cleanliness. Village Inn and Waterside Family Restaurant with an extensive menu including fresh local fish and a Sunday Carvery. Light entertainment some evenings. Children and pets welcome. Baby listening. Games room. Launderette/drying/ironing room. Bargain Breaks. Central heating. Car park. West Country Tourist Board Member. Colour brochure with pleasure. Terms on request. **Mrs F.J. Signora, REF SC, Torcross Apartment Hotel, Torcross, Near Kingsbridge TQ7 2TQ (01548 580206).**

KINGSBRIDGE. 1 New Buildings, South Milton, Kingsbridge. Sleeps 4. This is a modernised end terraced cottage overlooking the little village of South Milton. The property faces south with garden running down the hill towards an attractive 13th century church. The cottage dates from about 1830 and has a winding staircase. Lounge has large open Devon fireplace. Salcombe is four miles away for sailing and fishing. Dartmoor is 15 miles away; excellent game fishing. Nearest rivers Avon and Dart. Kingsbridge is an excellent shopping centre and many villages have delightful eating out places. Thurlestone (one mile) offers magnificent golf course and tennis facilities. Nearest beach, Thurlestone Sands, one mile, now a Premier Seaside Award area, is ideal for children, very safe, clean bathing, large stretches of rock pools. Let from Easter to end September. Terms from £100 to £220. Free car parking at Beach Cottage. **Mrs J.M. Turner, Beach Cottage, South Milton, Kingsbridge TQ7 3JR (01548 560354).**

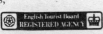

See also Colour Display Advertisement **KINGSBRIDGE. Mrs M. Cuming, "Ocean View", c/o Atlantic Lodge, Hope Cove, Kingsbridge TQ7 3HH (01548 561873).** ♕♕♕♕ *HIGHLY COMMENDED.* This is a new luxury bungalow situated in the small fishing village of Hope Cove. Four double bedrooms plus cloakroom, two bathrooms, superb kitchen with electric cooker, hob, fan extractor, fridge, freezer, automatic washing machine; spacious lounge. Economy 7 heating for off season guests. Parking. Open all year. Brochure available. Special rates for early/late holidays.

KINGSBRIDGE near. Knap Mill, Loddiswell, Near Kingsbridge. Self contained apartment in country house, comprising one bedroom with double bed and a second bedroom with double bed and bunk beds, cot available; bathroom and toilet; lounge/diningroom with TV; kitchen with electric cooker, fridge, kettle, washing machine/dryer, etc. Fully equipped, except linen. Own transport is essential, parking space available. Sorry, no pets. This accommodation is situated in the Avon Valley, between Loddiswell and Aveton Gifford. The beaches are within easy reach, also various coastal walks. We are three miles from the main shopping centre of Kingsbridge. SAE, please, for terms to **Mrs L.M. Elliot, Knap Mill, Loddiswell, Near Kingsbridge TQ7 4AQ (01548 550313).**

LYNTON/LYNMOUTH. Mr H.D. King-Fretts, West Lyn Farm, Barbrook, Lynton EX35 6LD (01598 753618). Farmhouse sleeping eight/nine and one cottage sleeping four on a traditional 134 acre working sheep farm, with Shire horses, ponies, vintage machinery, goats and poultry. Adjoining coastal footpath and National Trust woodland with breathtaking views across the Bristol Channel. Farmhouse has four bedrooms, one double, one family, one twin, one bunks. Two bathrooms. Cottage has one double and one twin bedrooms, colour TV and all amenities. Ample gardens and parking. Shop/launderette within walking distance. Long SAE for brochure and tariff for friendly farm holidays.

PLEASE SEND A STAMPED ADDRESSED ENVELOPE WITH ENQUIRIES

HOLIDAY FLATS

* Comfortably furnished – sleep up to 6 * Ample parking in own car park
* All modern amenities, TV, constant hot water, garden, panoramic sea
views * Beaches and National Trust walks – 2 minutes * Regret no dogs

Brochure from: **C. Arnold**
Crows Nest, Mortehoe,
Devon EX34 7EA
Tel. Woolacombe (01271) 870230

CROWS NEST
Mortehoe

MORTEHOE. Hillcrest, Chapel Hill, Mortehoe. Three self-contained flats fully equipped to sleep four to six persons. Children and dogs welcome; no single groups. Central heating, fully carpeted. Parking. Colour TV, refrigerator, microwave. No meters. Surrounded by National Trust grounds with many coastal walks. Facing south, overlooking beaches and Woolacombe Bay. Reduced terms for early and late holidays. Weekly rates from £150 to £425 (no extras). SAE please to **Mrs D. Vause, Woodend, Highcotts Lane, West Clandon, Surrey GU4 7XA** or telephone **(01483 222644).**

NEWTON ABBOT. Mrs Angela Dallyn, Bulleigh Park Farm, Ipplepen, Newton Abbot TQ12 5UA (01803 872254). Sleeps 2/4. A two bedroom self-contained ground floor apartment. Situated on a small family farm in a delightful rural setting with panoramic views of the Devon countryside. Offering peace and quiet, but centrally located for Torbay, Totnes (10 minutes), Dartmoor and the sea; also sporting facilities — golf (one and a half miles), tennis and local shop. The accommodation is tastefully newly decorated and furnished, with double glazing; superb kitchen with electric cooker, hob, extractor fan, fridge, automatic washing machine and microwave. Spacious shower room with power shower; lounge/diner with colour TV. Cot and high chair available. Secure and secluded garden. Parking. Electricity by meter reading. Linen provided. Price from £125.

NEWTON ABBOT. Mrs E.V. Whale, Roselands, Totnes Road, Ipplepen, Newton Abbot TQ12 5TD (01803 812701). The three Roselands self catering detached chalets are set in a peaceful private garden within easy reach of all South Devon beaches and attractions and the beauty of Dartmoor. The chalets are completely self contained and offer accommodation for two to four adults or two adults and two/three children. We love dogs and they are made most welcome at Roselands with the freedom of the garden to play in if they are friendly and sociable. Roselands is ideal for those seeking a peaceful restful holiday with their young children and/or pets. We are within easy walking distance of churches, shops, local hostelries (offering good pub meals) and a pay and play golf course. Safe parking.

FREE and REDUCED RATE Holiday Visits!
See our Reader's Offer Vouchers for details!

NEWTON ABBOT near. Mrs Y. Tully, Dunscombe Farm, Chudleigh, Near Newton Abbot TQ13 0BS

(01626 853149). Working farm. A 150 acre mixed farm situated in a valley just under Haldon Moor, midway between Exeter and Newton Abbot. Chudleigh one and three-quarter miles away; main road A380. Ideal position for touring moors and also within easy reach of the sea, riding, climbing and golf. The accommodation comprises kitchen, large living/dining room which has a bed settee, bathroom with wash-basin, bedroom (large) with double and bunk beds. Separate toilet. TV in livingroom. Calor gas cooking. Electricity metered. Linen available by arrangement. Children and pets welcome. Prices from £120 weekly. SAE, or telephone, for further details.

NEWTON ABBOT. Mrs M.R. Chitty, Bittons, Ipplepen, Newton Abbot TQ12 5TW (01803 812489). Sleeps 4. Year round self-catering accommodation in an attractive modern chalet, delightfully situated in the grounds of a private guest house. Fully furnished and equipped for four people. Ideal touring centre within easy reach of sea, moorland and many sporting activities including several golf courses (nearest one mile), tennis, pony trekking and riding. One double bedroom, one room with bunk beds; cot and high chair available, if required. Bathroom, toilet. Sittingroom. Kitchen facilities include gas cooker, double burner, plus oven. Everything supplied including linen. Electric/Calor gas heating. Sorry, no pets. Car essential — parking. Shopping half a mile. Weekly terms from £130 to £150 (including gas). Please write or telephone for further details.

See also Colour Display Advertisement **OKEHAMPTON. Mr P. Wilkens, Poltimore, South Zeal, Okehampton EX20 2PD (01837 840209).** ♀♀♀ *APPROVED.*

Situated in the Dartmoor National Park, the comfortable and attractive accommodation is set in beautiful and tranquil surroundings and sleeps from two to eight persons. Children and dogs are welcome and a cot is available. One luxury bungalow (sleeps eight in one double and two twin rooms), barn apartments (sleep four in one double and one twin room) and a summer chalet (sleeps two) situated on Ramsley Common. There is ample car parking. All accommodation is fully equipped and furnished to a high standard. Village shops are within walking distance. Terms according to season and accommodation. Write or telephone for brochure and tariff.

OKEHAMPTON. East Hook Cottages, Okehampton. Cottages sleep 2/6. In the heart of Devon, on the fringe of Dartmoor, with woodland surroundings, two comfortably furnished holiday cottages. One mile north of the A30 at Okehampton, quiet and peaceful, 50 yards from a country road. Ample car parking space. The accommodation comprises a pleasant sittingroom with a television set; kitchen with electric cooker and refrigerator; modern bathroom with shaver point; three bedrooms. Visitors are requested to supply their own bed linen. Electricity by 50p meter. Children and pets welcome. Terms from £90 to £150 per week. Open all year. Midweek/weekend breaks possible. **Mrs M.E. Stevens, West Hook Farm, Okehampton EX20 1RL (01837 52305).**

PUTSBOROUGH/WOOLACOMBE. Mrs S.J. Cook, Pickwell Barton Holiday Cottages, Georgeham, Braunton EX33 1LA (01271 890987/890994). Do you like to be on holiday by the sea, away from the crowds? If so we live in the ideal spot. Pickwell Barton and Sunnyside are two spacious well equipped farm cottages (three bedrooms) close to Putsborough and Woolacombe's golden sandy beaches. Gorgeous walks across our fields for breathtaking views. Reductions early and late season. Why not spend a long weekend with cosy coal fires in the autumn and winter? Ideal for surfing and golf at nearby Saunton Championship Golf Course. Open all year. Terms on request.

SALCOMBE. Mrs Molly Lonsdale, Fern Lodge, Hope Cove, Kingsbridge TQ7 3HF (01548 561326).

Sleeps 4. Fern Lodge, a modern first floor flat, comprises a through lounge with magnificent views over the Cove and Bolt Tail. One double bedroom, second bedroom with adult bunk beds; both have colour TV and own keys; kitchen; bathroom. Linen is supplied at no extra cost. Cleanliness assured. The flat is situated in an unspoilt area of the South Hams, set in a picturesque fishing village. Three minutes' stroll to the sea and sandy beaches. The village has a post office, shop and two inns and is surrounded by miles of National Trust land providing superb coastal and country walks. Terms from £250. Write or telephone for full details.

See also Colour Display Advertisement **SALCOMBE near. Rock House Marine Hotel Apartments, Thurlestone Sands, Near Salcombe TQ7 3JY (01548 561285).** ♀♀♀/♀♀♀♀ up to *COMMENDED.* A touch of luxury on the waterside in a beautiful secluded bay. Holiday apartments and cottages. Amenities include heated pool, games room, fully licensed bar and restaurant. Pets welcome by arrangement. Write or telephone for brochure.

SEATON. Mrs Elsie Pady, Higher Cownhayne Farm, Cownhayne Lane, Colyton, Near Seaton EX13 6HD (01297 552267). Working farm. Properties sleep 4/8. Higher Cownhayne is a family working farm. Accommodation consists of three self catering farmhouse holiday apartments which are open all year round. Each apartment has all modern conveniences with its own dining room, kitchen, bathroom and WC (no linen is provided). Caravan site on farm with four-berth caravan, fully equipped. Farm produce is available including milk from a brucellosis-free herd, eggs, etc. Babysitting can be provided by arrangement. Trout/fly fishing on farm. Leisure facilities available to visitors include badminton, squash, gymnasium, sauna, solarium, swimming pool; licensed restaurant. Air strip on farm for small plane enthusiasts. No pets. Terms on application, at a price families can afford to pay.

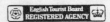

See also Colour Display Advertisement **SEATON. Mrs E.P. Fox, "West Ridge", Harepath Hill, Seaton EX12 2TA (Tel & Fax: 01297 22398). ♀♀♀ *COMMENDED*. Sleeps 5.** "West Ridge" bungalow stands on elevated ground above the small coastal town of Seaton. It has one and a half acres of lawns and gardens and enjoys wide panoramic views of the beautiful Axe Estuary and the sea. Close by are Axmouth, Beer and Branscombe. The Lyme Bay area is an excellent centre for touring, walking, sailing, fishing, golf, etc. This comfortably furnished accommodation is ideally suited for three to five people. Cot can be provided. Available March to October, £125 to £315 weekly (fuel charges included). Full gas central heating. Colour TV. SAE for brochure.

DEVON – ENDLESS CHOICES!

People never tire of visiting Devon. There's so much to do, like visiting Alscott Farm Museum, Berry Head Country Park, Bickleigh Mill Farm, Farway Countryside Park, Haytor Granite Railway, Kent's Cavern, Dartmoor National Park, Exmoor National Park and of course Plymouth and its Hoe.

SIDMOUTH. Mrs J.M. Jackson, Hawkerland Valley Cottages, Stoneyford Cottage, Stoneyford, Colaton Raleigh, Sidmouth EX10 0HY (01395 568843 Fax: 01395 567085). Sleeps 5 plus cot. STUDIO COTTAGE. An old Devon Barn tastefully converted and set amidst beautiful countryside with Budleigh Salterton and Sidmouth five miles and the Cathedral City of Exeter 10 miles away. The cottage is furnished, decorated and equipped to a high standard including a microwave, spin dryer and colour TV. The woodburner and night storage heater in the sitting-room make it cosy for all the year round holidays. Sleeps five in double, twin and single-bedded rooms. TV, electricity and wood for the fire included in the rental. From £135 per week. Special rates for two people. Parking for two cars, garden and patio. Cot and high chair available on request. SAE for details please.

SIDMOUTH. John and Lucille Baxter, Lower Knapp Farm, Sidbury, Sidmouth EX10 0QN (01404 871438). ♀ ♀ ♀ Properties sleep 2/9. Luxury self catering cottages, set in 16 acres of accessible East Devon. Sidmouth five miles, Seaton, Lyme Regis and Exmouth 30 minutes. Children and pets welcome. Delightful walking country, the farm being on the East Devon Way. Indoor heated swimming pool, sauna, solarium, children's play area. All cottages have fully fitted kitchens, microwaves; some have dishwashers. Colour TV, central heating. Cots, high chairs, video players available. Some four-poster beds. Linen supplied, laundry room. Fishing, golf, riding available locally. Open all year. Prices from £159 to £924 per week. Please telephone for free colour brochure.

SOUTH MOLTON. Mrs Ruth Ley, Drewstone Farm, South Molton EX36 3EF (01769 572337). ♀ ♀ ♀ ♀ COMMENDED. Escape to farm tranquillity in the foothills of Exmoor. The farmhouse is perched like an eagle's nest looking out over a wooded valley two miles from the village of North Molton. Red deer, foxes, badgers and a variety of birds can be seen at crack of dawn. The breathtaking view extends to Dartmoor 40 miles away. The accommodation consists of four bedrooms, one en suite; fitted kitchen with autowasher, dryer, deep freeze, fridge, electric cooker, microwave and dishwasher. Dining room; lounge; bath/shower room; three toilets. Furnished and equipped to the highest standards, carpeted and heated throughout, the house has double glazing, colour TV, phone and log fire. Patio doors lead on to lawn. Guests may wander among the farm animals, enjoy country walks, games room, clay shooting, trout fishing. Terms from £130.

SOUTH MOLTON near. Court Green, Bishop's Nympton, Near South Molton. Sleeps 5. A most attractive well equipped, south-facing cottage with large garden, on edge of the village of Bishop's Nympton, three miles from South Molton. Ideal holiday centre, easy reach of Exmoor, the coast, sporting activities and places of interest. Three bedrooms — one double, one twin-bedded, one single with washbasins. Two bathrooms with toilets and shower. Sitting and dining rooms, large kitchen. Central heating, wood-burning stove, TV. One mile sea trout/trout fishing on River Mole. Well behaved pets welcome. Terms April to October £100 to £200. **Mrs J.D. Greenwell, Tregeiriog, Near Llangollen, Clwyd LL20 7HU (01691 600672).**

Terms quoted in this publication may be subject to increase if rises in costs necessitate

TAVISTOCK. Mrs Rose Bacon, April Cottage, Mount Tavy Road, Tavistock PL19 9JB (01822 613280). Sleeps 6/8. Character Victorian cottage on the

western edge of Dartmoor built 1857 and beautifully restored. In a unique setting on the banks of the River Tavy only two minutes' level walk from town. Flower gardens/patios overlook river. Extensive range of local facilities, ideal centre for touring moors and coast. Extremely comfortable accommodation with quality furnishings. All three bedrooms (two double, one twin) are en suite with colour TVs, etc. Central heating. Double glazing. Fully equipped kitchen. Electricity included. Ample parking. Maid service if required. Linen supplied. Small pet by arrangement. Children welcome. Special rates for out of season breaks. Bed and Breakfast also available from £15 (✿ ✿ *HIGHLY COMMENDED*). Self-catering property from £180 weekly. Telephone for brochure.

THURLESTONE SANDS. Seamark Holiday Apartments, Thurlestone Sands, Kingsbridge TQ7 3JY (01548 561300). We are situated on the Coastal Path and

have five well equipped apartments — four with two bedrooms, one with three bedrooms — all with outstanding sea views. There are spacious lawns with a children's play area, a 56ft games room with table tennis, snooker and darts; a laundry room; payphone. Ample parking. Linen available. Safe beaches, windsurfing, golf course all nearby. Well-behaved dogs are welcome. Terms range from £120 to £410. Please phone and ask for our colour brochure.

FOR THE MUTUAL GUIDANCE
OF GUEST AND HOST

Every year literally thousands of holidays, short-breaks and overnight stops are arranged through our guides, the vast majority without any problems at all. In a handful of cases, however, difficulties do arise about bookings, which often could have been prevented from the outset.

It is important to remember that when accommodation has been booked, both parties — guests and hosts — have entered into a form of contract. We hope that the following points will provide helpful guidance.

GUESTS: When enquiring about accommodation, be as precise as possible. Give exact dates, numbers in your party and the ages of any children. State the number and type of rooms wanted and also what catering you require — bed and breakfast, full board, etc. Make sure that the position about evening meals is clear — and about pets, reductions for children or any other special points.

Read our reviews carefully to ensure that the proprietors you are going to contact can supply what you want. Ask for a letter confirming all arrangements, if possible.

If you have to cancel, do so as soon as possible. Proprietors do have the right to retain deposits and under certain circumstances to charge for cancelled holidays if adequate notice is not given and they cannot re-let the accommodation.

HOSTS: Give details about your facilities and about any special conditions. Explain your deposit system clearly and arrangements for cancellations, charges, etc, and whether or not your terms include VAT.

If for any reason you are unable to fulfil an agreed booking without adequate notice, you may be under an obligation to arrange alternative suitable accommodation or to make some form of compensation.

While every effort is made to ensure accuracy, we regret that FHG Publications cannot accept responsibility for errors, omissions or misrepresentation in our entries or any consequences thereof. Prices in particular should be checked because we go to press early. We will follow up complaints but cannot act as arbiters or agents for either party.

TORRINGTON. Mrs R.M. Wood, Lake Farm, Langtree, Torrington EX38 8NX (01805 601320). Lake

Farm is a working farm with calves, cows, sheep, ducks, etc. It is within easy reach of Westward Ho!, Clovelly, RHS Rosemoor Gardens and the Moors, one and a half miles from holiday route. Near the Tarka Trail and fishing is available on the farm. Indoor heated swimming pool at Torrington. Here at Lake Farm a stream runs through the yard, and there is a large flower garden and lawn. Accommodation for six in two double bedrooms and one twin-bedded room; sitting/dining room with colour TV; bathroom/toilet; fully fitted electrically equipped kitchen. Children are welcome and there is a cot and a high chair. Pets by arrangement. Available all year with electric heating; fully equipped except linen. Own transport essential, ample parking. Shops one and a quarter miles. Electricity by meter. Weekly terms from £95 to £135 per week.

TOTNES. Hemsford Country Holidays, Hemsford, Littlehempston, Totnes TQ9 6NE (01803

762637). "Hemsford — A Country Holiday for All Ages". Ideally situated in the heart of South Devon, with Torbay, Dartmoor and the excellent beaches of the South Hams only a short drive away. Our 16 comfortable and well appointed cottages (one suitable for disabled guests) accommodate two to 10 people. All have night store heating and are available throughout the year. Facilities include our own riding stables, heated indoor pool, sauna, solarium, games room, licensed bar, two all-weather tennis courts, 9 hole approach golf and children's play area. Terms from £95 to £875 per week. Full colour brochure on request. Regret no pets.

TOTNES. Mr and Mrs D. Christie-Mutch, Lower Well, Broadhempston, Totnes TQ9 6BD (01803 813417). Charming, comfortable, well-equipped self-contained one and two bedroomed cottages, formerly part of Georgian farm (not working farm). Colour TV; laundry facilities; cot and high chair available. Orchard garden. Linen is not provided. Well behaved dogs accepted. Lovely unspoiled Devon village with two pubs, church and shop, situated between Dartmoor and the Torbay coast with easy access to the beautiful South Hams, historic Totnes, Dartington and Exeter etc. Telephone or write for details.

TOTNES near. Mrs B. Anning, Lower Blakemore Farm, Higher Plymouth Road, Totnes TQ9 6DN

(01803 863718). ♛ ♛ ♛ ♛ *HIGHLY COMMENDED.* **Sleeps 6/7 plus cot.** Tastefully converted Cider House on working farm two miles from Totnes. Central for exploring South Devon. Accommodation: Ground floor — one twin room, one double/family room with washbasin; bathroom with bath, toilet and basin; separate shower room; utility area with washer/dryer. First floor — twin room, separate toilet and basin; light and airy open plan living room with sofas and armchairs, colour TV; kitchen/diner is fully fitted with gas cooker, microwave and fridge/freezer. Lovely views from upstairs. Gas central heating. Linen provided. Gas and electricity metered. Large garden. Undercover and ample outside parking. Sorry no dogs in house. £155 to £380 per week. Brochure available.

DEVON – FROM COAST TO COAST

Dramatic cliffs, hidden coves, rolling surf and traditional family holiday resorts are some of the attractions which make holidaymakers return year after year to the unspoiled coastline of North Devon. There are unparalleled opportunities for watersports of all kinds, and, for the less energetic, picturesque fishing villages to explore and hidden coves for sunbathing.

The sheltered South Coast has been dubbed the "English Riviera", with an exceptionally mild climate and lively resorts offering amenities and attractions for all the family.

DORSET

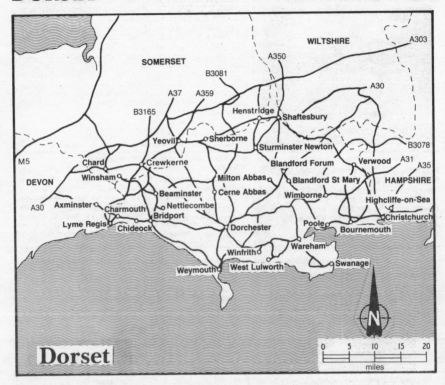

Dorset

BEAMINSTER. 33A St. Mary Well Street, Beaminster. Sleeps 5. Lovely two bedroomed bungalow in heart of "Hardy's Wessex". Peaceful position yet only 200 metres from market square with shops, restaurants, pubs, etc. Each bedroom has washbasin; one contains a double bed and the other two singles; Z-bed and cot available. Separate WC and bathroom. Colour TV in lounge. Gas cooker, microwave, fridge/freezer in well furbished kitchen/diningroom. Utility room has WC, shower and automatic washing machine. Patio garden and large car park. Hardy's Cottage, Parnham House, Forde Abbey, Cricket St. Thomas and many other places of interest nearby. The beautiful unspoilt coast is eight miles away. Terms from £90 to £240. For brochure, SAE to **Mrs L. Watts, 53 Hogshill Street, Beaminster DT8 3AG (01308 863088).**

BEAMINSTER. "Orchard End", Hooke, Beaminster. ♀♀♀♀ Sleeps 6. Hooke is a quiet village nine

miles from the coast. Good walking country and near Hooke Working Woodland with lovely woodland walks. Trout fishing nearby. Bungalow is stone built with electric central heating and double glazing. It is on a working dairy farm and is clean and comfortable. Three bedrooms, all beds with duvets. Cot available. Large lounge/diningroom with colour TV. Well equipped kitchen with electric cooker, microwave, fridge freezer and automatic washing machine. Bathroom and separate toilet. Carpeted. Payphone. Large garden, garage. Terms £160 to £280 per week inclusive of electricity, bed linen and VAT. ETB registered. Contact **Mrs P.M. Wallbridge, Bridge Farm, Hooke, Beaminster DT8 3PD (01308 862619).**

BEXINGTON. Mrs Josephine Pearse, Tamarisk Farm, West Bexington, Dorchester DT2 9DF (01308 897784). ♀♀/♀♀♀ On Chesil Beach between Abbotsbury and Burton Bradstock. Farm slopes down to sea. One large and two smaller bungalows and two chalets. Sleep four to eight. Terms from £105 to £410. Each one stands in own garden. Glorious views along West Dorset and Devon Coasts. Lovely walks by sea and inland. Mixed organic farm with arable, sheep, cattle, horses and market garden — vegetables and herbs available. Sea fishing, riding in Abbotsbury, lots of tourist attractions and good markets in Bridport (six miles), Dorchester, Weymouth and Portland (all 13 miles). Good centre for touring Thomas Hardy's Wessex. Safe for children and pets can be quite free.

BLOXWORTH. Bloxworth Holiday Cottages. Large Georgian farmhouse and thatched cottages sleeping five/12 respectively. Bloxworth is a quiet village on the edge of Wareham Forest, close to the Isle of Purbeck beauty spots and numerous beaches along the Dorset coast. Beautiful Poole Harbour 10 miles. Pleasant walks nearby. Good country pubs in the area. Well furnished and equipped except for linen and towels. Electricity by coin meter. Dogs welcome. Open all year round. Ideal for winter weekends. SAE, please, **Mr and Mrs P.G. MacDonald-Smith, Bloxworth Estate, Near Wareham BH20 7EF (Tel & Fax: 01929 459442).**

BOURNEMOUTH. Bournemouth Holiday Bureau, Henbury View, Dullar Lane, Sturminster Marshall BH21 4AD (01258 858580). For more than a quarter of a century, Bournemouth's oldest self catering holiday accommodation agency has been providing a letting service for scores of privately owned houses, cottages, bungalows, flats, caravans and chalets in Bournemouth, Poole, Ringwood, Christchurch and about 20 miles around. All inspected before acceptance and accurately described. Prices to suit every pocket. Most properties welcome children and many accept pets. Colour brochure on request.

BOURNEMOUTH HOLIDAY BUREAU

BOURNEMOUTH. Mr and Mrs A.E. Pascoe, Seaway Holiday Flats, 41 Grand Avenue, Southbourne, Bournemouth BH6 3SY (01202 300351). Self contained holiday flats with exercise area in garden. Situated in a most popular family position just three minutes' level walk between shops and cliffs, with lift to fine sandy beach. Clean, well fitted. Colour TV. Car park. Most reasonable terms early and late season.

BOURNEMOUTH. Mr and Mrs D. Rapson, Sark Lodge Holiday Flatlets, 3 Herbert Road, Alum Chine, Bournemouth BH4 8HD (01202 763827). Properties sleep 2. Sark Lodge is a quiet building which specialises in accommodation for couples. Each flatlet has its own modern en-suite facilities of shower, toilet and hand-basin, kitchenette, refrigerator and colour television. We supply bed linen and parking is available. Free hot water is provided as is central heating when appropriate. Sark Lodge is within walking distance of the beach (through Alum Chine), shops and buses. Terms from £48 to £76 per person per week May to October according to season. Easter Break and May Day Break £38 per person. Special low rates in May/June. Resident Proprietors. Stamp please, for brochure, or telephone.

FUN FOR ALL THE FAMILY IN DORSET
Brewers Quay, Weymouth; Deep Sea Adventure, Weymouth; Dinosaur Museum, Dorchester; Dinosaurland, Lyme Regis; Maiden Castle, Dorchester; Natural World, Poole Aquarium; Sea Life Centre, Weymouth; Upton Country Park, Poole; Waterfront Museum, Poole.

BOURNEMOUTH. Questors and St. George's Holiday Flats. Both establishments are very well equipped, decorated and clean, have spacious private parking, laundry, television, payphones. Bed linen, cots and highchairs available; dogs and children welcome. Questors is beautifully located on the Bournemouth Upper Gardens in Surrey Road. Westbourne shops are ten minutes' walk away, municipal golf course nearby. Walk through the gardens past tennis courts to Bournemouth centre, about a mile. Bus stop outside. St. George's, Cecil Road, is 100 yards from Boscombe's pedestrianised shopping and new mall. 400 yards to fine sandy beach. Frequent buses to Bournemouth centre. Terms from £75 to £384 per week. **Sandra and Barry Glenard, 45 Branksome Wood Road, Bournemouth BH4 9JT (01202 763262).**

BOURNEMOUTH. Mr and Mrs T. Lambert, Lyttelton Lodge, 16 Florence Road, Bournemouth BH5 1HF (01202 304925 or 01425 474007). Apartments sleep 1/10. The accommodation has recently been extensively altered and refurbished to make all units self-contained with new kitchens and bathrooms. Ideally situated only a short walk from beach and shops. The apartments sleep one to 10 persons. They are all furnished and equipped to a high standard. Constant free hot water and central heating for the winter. Colour TV included. Car parking space for each apartment and lock-up garages also available. Visitors' telephone. Discounts for bookings of two weeks or over. Children and pets welcome. Write or telephone for brochure and terms from Proprietors (please state numbers in party and dates required).

BRIDPORT. ♀♀♀ COMMENDED. Bungalow: modern, spacious and fully equipped to a high standard. Available all year. Situated between Bridport, West Bay Harbour, Chesil Beach and The Dorset Coastal Path. Lounge/diningroom featuring picture window with south-westerly aspect. Two double/twin bedrooms with en-suite toilet/washbasins. Bathroom. Large kitchen. Utility room. Garden. Own parking. Ideal base for walking holidays or enjoying/visiting the many places/attractions with varying interests in the area. Swimming, Sea Fishing, Golf (preferential green fees), numerous Cliff and Inland walks, Fossil Hunting. Value for Money Terms inclusive of gas/electricity/linen/towels, even a starter pack of milk, etc. From £140 to £320 per week (discounts for longer holidays). For brochure/photograph/availablility telephone **Bridport (01308) 422941.**

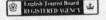
DORSET – OUTSTANDING NATURAL BEAUTY

Almost all the coastline and much of the inland county has been designated an Area of Outstanding Natural Beauty, with fine sandy beaches and sheltered coves backed by undulating chalkland and unspoiled moorland. The county retains many traces of its rich heritage e.g. Maiden Castle, the finest known example of an Iron Age hill fort, and Dorchester, rich in Roman remains. The region was immortalised by Thomas Hardy in his Wessex novels — follow the "Hardy Trail" to Bere Regis ("Kingsbere") and Bournemouth ("Sandbourne").

MANOR FARM HOLIDAY CENTRE
Charmouth, Bridport, Dorset

Situated in a rural valley, ten minutes' level walk from the beach.

1983 Built Luxury Two-Bedroomed Houses: *Sleep 4-6 *Lounge with colour T.V. *Fully fitted kitchen/diner *Fitted carpets *Double glazing *Central heating *Parking space.

Three-Bedroomed House and Bungalow: *Sleep 4/6 each *Lounge with colour T.V. *Central heating available *Parking within grounds *Enclosed garden.

Luxury six-berth Caravans: *One or two bedrooms *Toilet *Shower *Refrigerator *Full cooker *Television *Gas fire.

FULL CENTRE FACILITIES AVAILABLE INCLUDING SWIMMING POOL, SHOP, FISH AND CHIP TAKEAWAY, BAR, LAUNDERETTE, ETC.

Send SAE for colour brochure to **Mr R. E. Loosmore** *or Tel.* **01297 560226**
See also Colour Display Advertisement in this Guide.

Willowhayne Farm
LUXURY SELF-CATERING MEWS COTTAGES

CHIDEOCK, DORSET Tel: 01297 489042

This exclusive development of 6 Mews cottages opened in 1988, built in mellow stone to a modern design, represents the highest standards in accommodation, furnishing and equipment. The farm nestles quietly in a fold of Dorset's rolling hills only 15 minutes' walk across the fields from the beach at Seatown. The village of Chideock and its services lies half-a-mile away. The cottages, all facing south, have 2 bedrooms, luxury bathroom and a large, comfortable lounge/dining/room with french doors to your private patio and formal gardens. The oak kitchens are fully equipped including washing machine and tumble dryer. All heating, electricity and linen are provided free of charge. 𝄆𝄆𝄆𝄆 **Highly Commended**

DORCHESTER near. Pitt Cottage, Ringstead Bay, Near Dorchester. Sleeps 6. An attractive part-thatched stone-built cottage, surrounded by farmland and situated on the edge of a small wood about quarter of a mile from the sea, commanding outstanding views of Ringstead Bay on the Dorset Heritage Coast. The cottage has been renovated and is equipped to sleep six: three bedrooms (two beds in each), two bathrooms, sittingroom (with open fire); large kitchen/dining area. Cot/high chair; washing machine; TV; electric radiators in all rooms. Car essential. Available from £85 per week. For details, please send SAE with Ref. SCFH to: **Mrs S.H. Russell, 14 Brodrick Road, London SW17 7DZ or telephone 0181-672 2022.**

PITT COTTAGE

FERNDOWN. Lyndale, 11 Fernlea Avenue, Ferndown. Sleeps 4. The bungalow has a large, pleasant garden with garage and is situated just half a mile away from the village in a quiet residential area. Buses from Ferndown run to Bournemouth and surrounding areas. The New Forest is within easy reach for picnics and beautiful walks. The bungalow is centrally heated and well equipped throughout. Bed linen and towels excepted. Children are welcome. Cot available on request. Regrettably this property is not suitable for the disabled. Small pets are accepted by arrangement. Further details and terms from **Mrs S. MacKay (01768 865091) or Mrs Loader (01202 873895).**

FREE and REDUCED RATE Holiday Visits!
See our Reader's Offer Vouchers for details!

LYME REGIS. 1 Wellhayse, Marine Parade, Lyme Regis. Our chalet is in one of the finest settings in

Lyme Regis, yards from the beach and harbour overlooking the famous Cobb with panoramic views of the Golden Cap coastline and Portland Bill. Fossil hunting, golf, sailing, bowls and cliff walks are all close by. The newly refurbished holiday chalet has a lounge with balcony, small kitchen, double bedroom, shower room and bunk bedroom. Linen is provided, electricity by coin meter. Private parking is two minutes away. Wellhayse is reached by steps straight off Marine Parade and has its own terraced garden with barbecue. Small dogs are welcome. Terms from £70 to £350 per week. Please send for brochure from **Mrs Pamela Boyland, Barn Park Farm, Stockland Hill, Near Cotleigh, Honiton, Devon EX14 9JA (01404 861297).**

LYME REGIS. Mrs S.M. Denning, Higher Holcombe Farm, Uplyme, Lyme Regis DT7 3SN (01297 443223). Sleeps 6 plus cot. Completely separate part of the farmhouse on the working dairy farm, which was once a Roman Settlement. Surrounded by pleasant country walks; golf, fishing, horse riding and safe sandy beaches are all nearby. There are three bedrooms — one double and two twin; two bathrooms; lounge with inglenook fireplace, kitchen/dining room with electric cooker, microwave, fridge/freezer, dishwasher, etc; use of washing machine and tumble dryer. Electric heating by 50p slot meter. Plenty of parking. One mile from village shops and pub, two miles coast of Lyme Regis. Winter Breaks. Linen provided. One pet by arrangement.

LYME REGIS. Mrs M.J. Tedbury, Little Paddocks, Yawl Hill Lane, Lyme Regis DT7 3RW (01297 443085). Sleeps 3. A chalet situated in the garden of a smallholding which overlooks Lyme Bay and surrounding countryside for perfect peace and quiet. Two-and-a-half miles Lyme Regis, three-and-a-half miles Charmouth. Easy driving distance Seaton, Beer, Sidmouth. The chalet sleeps three but is ideal for two people liking plenty of room; it has a double bedroom and is fully equipped except linen. Mains water, hot and cold, flush toilet and shower, electric light, fridge, fire, TV. Fresh eggs. Parking space for cars. Pets welcome. Terms from £65. Also six berth caravan from £80. SAE, please.

LYTCHETT MINSTER. East Cottage, Organford Manor, Lytchett Minster, Near Poole. A three-

bedroomed, red brick cottage in the wooded grounds of a Manor house, with its own garden. Within easy reach of the Purbecks and the sea, and only 10 miles from the amenities and entertainment of Bournemouth. Four miles from Wareham and Hardy country, five miles from Poole with its harbour and sandy beaches. Two double bedrooms and third room with bunk beds and a single bed. Cot and high chair available. All-electric, by 50p meter, including automatic washing machine. No linen provided. Available April to October from £100 to £250 per week. Send SAE for further details. **Mrs M.E. Waterman, Organford Manor, Poole BH16 6ES (01202 622202).**

MARNHULL. Mrs K. Cook and Mrs J. Williams, Walton Elm House, Marnhull, Sturminster Newton

DT10 1QG (01258 820553). Situated in the heart of Thomas Hardy country, offering accommodation of one, two or three bedrooms each with colour TV, shower or bath and usual kitchen facilities. Surrounded by countryside of outstanding natural beauty yet within easy reach of Yeovil, Blandford and Shaftesbury with its famous Gold Hill, perfect for a relaxing holiday. Available at no extra cost is a solar heated swimming pool, tennis court, badminton room and table tennis whilst for a small charge adults can enjoy the full size snooker table. Offering a warm family welcome — we can provide cots, high chairs and babysitting service if required. Pets welcome by prior notice. Terms from £120 to £315 per week.

Pool Cottages

**WHEN MAKING ENQUIRIES PLEASE MENTION
THIS *FHG* PUBLICATION**

MILTON ABBAS. Mrs V.O. Davey, Little Hewish Farm, Milton Abbas, Blandford DT11 0LH (01258 880326). ♀♀♀ COMMENDED. Cottages sleep 4/5/6.

Little Hewish Farm offers accommodation in three modernised farm cottages. Situated in Hardy country, it is one mile from the unique village of Milton Abbas with its picturesque thatched cottages, lake and Abbey. One and a half miles from Milborne St. Andrew which is eight miles west of Blandford on A354. It is within easy driving distance of the coast with sandy beaches at Bournemouth, Studland, Swanage and Weymouth with many coastline walks between; farm walk also. Accommodation comprises sittingroom; dining/kitchen fully equipped including fridge and spin dryer; bathroom and separate toilet. Comfortably furnished and fully carpeted. Colour TV. £1 electric meter. Nightstore heaters. Linen extra. Cot and high chair available. Laundry room. Sorry, no pets. Car essential with ample parking. Available all year. Terms approximately £90 to £245 weekly. Please telephone or SAE for details.

MILTON ABBAS. Primrose Cottage, 29 Milton Abbas, Blandford Forum. ♀♀♀ HIGHLY COMMEN-

DED. Sleeps 6. Primrose Cottage is one of the semidetached cob and thatched houses that make up a unique village created around 1770 by Lord Milton and landscaped by Capability Brown. The model village itself is said by many to be one of the prettiest in England. Certainly each house has individual charm whilst the winding valley setting with its lake at the bottom is the ideal base for walking through the Dorset countryside. The cottage, which sleeps four to six, has everything you would expect from a Grade II Listed building. The beamed sitting room, of course, has an inglenook fireplace with wood stove. Low doors remind you of the building's age but the 20th century has taken over everywhere else, from modern kitchen and bathroom to the two bedrooms. Non-smoking accommodation available. Really it's a cottage in which romantics can relax. Weekly rates from £165 to £325. Contact: **Mr R.A. Garvey, 16 Mole Road, Hersham, Surrey KT12 4LU (01932 220395).**

POOLE. The Old Mill Holiday Flats, The Quay, and Cinnamon House Flats & Mews House. The Old

Mill Holiday Flats are situated on Poole's historic Quay, while Cinnamon House is in the old town 100 yards from the Quay. There is plenty to do and see, for all ages, within easy walking distance. The flats have been created with the holidaymaker in mind, with car parking for each flat on the premises. They are fully furnished with bathroom, kitchen, livingroom and bedroom(s) and sleep from two to eight. Terms from £105 to £360 per week. For details and brochures: **Anthony and Wendy Yeatman, Court House, Corfe Mullen, Wimborne BH21 3RH (01258 857328; Fax: 01258 858171).**

SHERBORNE. Mrs S.J. Wade, Popes House, Milborne Wick, Sherborne DT9 4PW (01963 250318).

Sleeps 8. Old farmhouse in idyllic position on edge of small hamlet. There are open fireplaces and inglenook, TV and dart board. High chair. Own entrance (own key); private lawn, swing seat and badminton equipment. Free range eggs, good shops one-and-a-half miles with no parking restrictions. Local fishing (trout and coarse), tennis courts, golf and riding. Top class local restaurants. Several interesting houses open to the public. Sherborne with Abbey, two castles and almshouses three miles; Worldwide Butterfly Farm. This is a small farm and can accommodate guests' own horses. Open all year. Accommodation for seven/eight in three double bedrooms, including attic; cot; bathroom, toilet; sittingroom, diningroom; well-equipped kitchen, electric cooker, fridge, auto kettle, etc. Linen for hire. Sea 27 miles. Pets allowed. Car essential, parking. Electricity by £1 meter. Weekly terms from £90, attic extra. Open for weekends. SAE, please.

SWANAGE. 3 Rocklands, Stafford Road, Swanage. Sleeps 6. Luxury first floor flat in an elevated position with superb sea views. Situated 200 yards from the town centre and 500 yards from a sandy beach. It is furnished to a high standard and consists of a hall/third single bedroom, large comfortable lounge, both overlooking the sea, two further spacious bedrooms, fitted kitchen/diner and bathroom/WC with shower, with wall-to-wall carpeting throughout. Facilities include TV, cot, heating, washing machine, telephone and refrigerator. Bed linen and towels are not supplied, but there is an ample supply of blankets and pillows. Reserved car parking. Electricity included in price. Local amenities include cliff-walking, sailing, patrolled beach, diving and wind surfing school, bird reserves on Poole Harbour and Corfe Castle. SAE to **Mr and Mrs D.F. Williams, Hartfield, 18 Down Lane, Bathampton, Bath, Avon BA2 6UE (Tel & Fax: 01225 466945).**

WAREHAM near. Mrs M.J.M. Constantinides, "Woodlands", Hyde, Near Wareham BH20 7NT (01929 471239). Secluded house, formerly Dower House of Hyde Estate, stands alone on a meadow of the River Piddle in four-and-a-half acres in the midst of "Hardy Country". The maisonette comprises: upstairs lounge with colour TV; one bedroom (two single beds); downstairs large kitchen-diner, small entrance hall, bathroom; electric cooker (in addition to Aga cooker), refrigerator. Independent side entrance. Extra bedroom (two single beds) on request at £22 per week. Visitors are welcome to use house grounds; children can fish or play in the boundary stream. Pleasant walks in woods and heath nearby. Golf course half-a-mile; pony trekking/riding nearby. All linen included, beds ready made and basic shopping arranged on arrival day. Aga will be lit and maintained on request. Ideal for a quiet holiday far from the madding crowd. Cot and high chair available and children welcome to bring their pets. SAE, please, for terms and further particulars.

WAREHAM near. "Dormer Cottage", Woodlands, Hyde, Near Wareham. Sleeps 5. This secluded cottage, cosy and modern, is a converted old barn of Woodlands House. Standing in its own grounds, it is fronted by a small wood with a walled paddock at the back. Pleasant walks in woods and forests nearby. In the midst of "Hardy Country" and ideal for a family holiday and for those who value seclusion. All linen included, beds ready made on guests' arrival and basic shopping arranged on request. Aga will be lit if required. Amusements at Bournemouth, Poole and Dorchester within easy reach. Five people and a baby can be accommodated in two double and one single bedrooms; cot and high chair available. Bathroom, two toilets; lounge and diningroom, colour TV. Kitchen with cooker, fridge; washing machine, small deep freeze etc. Pets welcome. Open all year. Golf course half-mile; pony trekking/riding nearby. SAE, please, for terms. **Mrs M.J.M. Constantinides, "Woodlands", Hyde, Near Wareham BH20 7NT (01929 471239).**

DURHAM

DARLINGTON. Mr R. Lauder, Newbus Grange Ltd., The Old Brickworks, Throstlenest Avenue, Darlington DL1 2BH (01325 466742). Situated close to the banks of the River Tees in a peaceful, rural location these eight immaculate properties were formerly the stabling and grooms' quarters of a large country house, and now form part of a small group of tasteful holiday homes. Attractively furnished and equipped to a very high standard. Overlooking open fields there are walks along the riverside. The small village of Hurworth with its elegant Georgian houses offers everyday shopping, restaurants and country inns. Golf and tennis available locally; games room is provided. Ideally placed for touring the Yorkshire Dales and North Pennines to the west and the North York Moors to the east — an excellent holiday location. Rates depending on season and property. Please write, or telephone, for further details.

Stables Bungalow,   (Sleeps 5/6)
Neasham, Nr Darlington

GLOUCESTERSHIRE

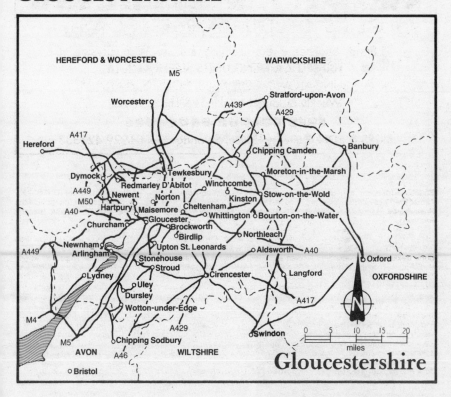

Gloucestershire

BADMINTON AREA (Gloucestershire/Avon). Delightful, small detached stone cottage, quiet surroundings. One double bedroom. All facilities, electricity, linen included. Convenient M4/M5, Bath, Bristol etc. £120 per week; £25 per day (minimum three days). Sorry no pets. **Mrs A. Elliott, Tally-Ho, Inglestone Common, Badminton GL9 1BX (01454 294385).**

CHELTENHAM. Mike and Janice Cotterill, Magnolia Cottage Apartment, Lansdowne, Bourton-on-the-Water, Cheltenham GL54 2AR (01451 821841). ♛♛♛♛ Quality first floor apartment. Fitted carpets throughout. Comfortably furnished, with colour TV and video and gas log-effect fire. Two bedrooms each with twin beds and washbasins. All linen and towels provided. Electric blankets if required. Fully fitted oak kitchen with microwave, electric oven and hob, fridge and dishwasher, full central heating all included. Bathroom fitted with electric shower. Lobby with washer/dryer. Pay phone. Small welcome pack on arrival. Sorry no pets. Parking in courtyard. Minutes' walk to local shops, inns, restaurants. Terms from £210 to £290 per week. Short Break terms on request. Will accept Access or Barclaycard. Sorry, not suitable for children under 10 years. Mike and Janice Cotterill look forward to your visit. SAE, please, for brochure.

CHELTENHAM. Mr and Mrs J. Close, Coxhorne Farm, London Road, Charlton Kings, Cheltenham GL52 6UY (01242 236599). ♛♛♛ COMMENDED. **Sleeps 3.** Eastern outskirts of Cheltenham. Self catering in a well equipped studio apartment of Annexe adjoining farmhouse on working dairy farm. Accommodation consists of large lounge with sleeping for three plus extra bed on request. Gas fire and full central heating. Comfortable chairs and colour TV. Large fully fitted kitchen and en suite bathroom. Steps from kitchen leading to garden and plenty of parking space. Sorry, no smoking or pets. Children welcome. Electricity and linen included in rental. Ideal location for touring and walking Cotswolds. The farm is situated half a mile off the Cotswold Way with lovely views. Terms from £120 to £160 per week.

CHIPPING CAMPDEN. Mrs D. Brook, Tod Cott, Noel Court, Calf Lane, Chipping Campden GL55

6BS (01386 841127). The most beautiful village in the country. Cotswold stone ground floor apartment in quiet mews. One minute from High Street for shops, inns and restaurants. Comfortably furnished with old world charm. Full central heating and carpets throughout. One bedroom with four-poster bed as seen on BBC Holiday Programme. Superb fully fitted kitchen, washer/dryer, microwave, fridge/freezer, electric oven and hob. Bathroom complete with shower; pleasant lounge, stone fireplace, gas fire, colour TV, sofa bed. Includes heating and linen. Parking and small garden. Convenient for touring Cotswolds and Shakespeare country. From £200 per week.

COLEFORD. "Greystones", Marsh Hill, Sling, Near Coleford. ♀♀♀ *COMMENDED.* **Sleeps 4/5.** Guaranteed immaculate two bedroom detached modern bungalow, sleeps four/five. Quiet position on outskirts of Forest of Dean village (Coleford two miles) standing in maintained lawned grounds with panoramic views. Garage and parking. Easy access Wye Valley, Wales, Cotswolds, Avon etc. Golf, riding, fishing, swimming, walks in area. Bungalow is excellently equipped, furnished and carpeted. Twin bedroom, double bedroom, kitchen/diner, bath/shower/WC, lounge with colour TV and Z-bed. Electric cooker, fridge, kettle, iron, vacuum, spin dryer etc. Five electric heaters, two storage heaters. No children under six. No pets. Terms £150 to £240 (four persons) per week. Electricity metered. Linen hire. Garage hire. SAE please to **Mrs P. Pendrey, Pen-y-Dale, Marsh Hill, Clements End Road, Sling, Near Coleford GL16 8JW (01594 834906).**

COTSWOLDS. Wainlodes Hill, Norton, Near Gloucester. Sleeps 4. Pretty holiday cottage, overlooking the River Severn. Furnished to high standard with inglenook fireplace. All electric, no meters, pine kitchen, pretty garden, colour TV, fully equipped except linen. Suitable for four persons. Excellent fishing, beautiful surroundings, good centre for touring the Cotswolds and Severn Valley and numerous other places of interest. Open all year. Prices on request. Enquiries to **Mrs Joan Mitchell, Wainlodes Hill, Norton, Near Gloucester (01452 730251).**

DURSLEY near. Gerald and Norma Kent, Hill House, Crawley Hill, Uley, Dursley GL11 5BH (01453

860267). Sleeps 2. The flat is a separate part of this Cotswold stone house which stands in four and a half acres and is situated on top of a hill with beautiful views of the surrounding countryside. The accommodation consists of double bedroom, kitchen with cooker, microwave, fridge, etc., lounge with TV and video, toilet and shower. Car port and garden area. We supply a comprehensive set of maps and tourist information as well as routes to the many places of interest in the area. Bed linen and towels not supplied. Electricity by meter. Open all year. Sorry, no pets. Please phone, or write, for a brochure.

GLOUCESTER near. Mrs J.P. Whitaker, Overtown Farmhouse, Cranham, Near Gloucester GL4 8HQ (01452 862573). "Shepherds Piece" is a twin unit mobile home with two double bedrooms. Lounge with colour TV; kitchen; bathroom and diningroom. Fitted carpets and double glazing. Parking and small garden. Necessary household requisites are supplied except linen and electricity which is metered. Situated adjoining the common and near the nature reserve common woods. There are attractive walks. Cranham is in a good position for touring the Cotswolds. Children and pets welcome. Terms £55 to £155.

STOW-ON-THE-WOLD. "Greystones" — Yew Tree Cottages. ♀♀♀♀ *HIGHLY COMMENDED.* **Sleeps**

4/5 plus cot. Charming 18th century traditional stone cottage, sympathetically refurbished to a very high standard, with beamed ceilings and a Cotswold fireplace. Luxuriously fitted and furnished. Well fitted bathroom and en suite shower room, plus ground floor cloakroom. Fully fitted kitchen, colour TV, video, hi-fi and payphone. Glorious views across the Evenlode valley from every window and all parts of the lovely, south-facing garden and large patio. Garden furniture and portable barbecue supplied. Available all year round. Full weeks from £290, short breaks from £180, inclusive of insurance, gas, electricity, linen and towels. Colour leaflet from **Liz and Ian James, 30a Albemarle Road, Beckenham, Kent BR3 2HJ (0181-658 8267).**

STOW-ON-THE-WOLD. Cottage in the Country, Forest Gate, Frog Lane, Milton-under-Wychwood, Oxon OX7 6JZ (01993 831495/831743; Fax: 01993 831095). A good selection of personally known holiday homes in Stow-on-the-Wold, Moreton-in-the-Marsh, Burford and many more Cotswold villages. Available all year, with many offering short winter breaks. Prices range from £150 to £750. Other similarly well appointed properties throughout central/middle England. TB Registered Agency. Free brochure available.

HAMPSHIRE

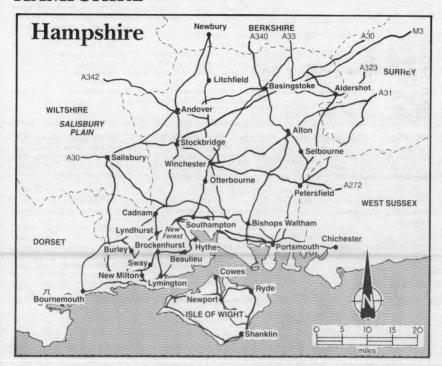

Hampshire

LOCKERLEY. No. 2 Thatched Cottage, Carter's Clay, Lockerley, Near Romsey. Sleeps 5. Delightful thatched self-catering cottage. Set in beautiful countryside, in rural hamlet four miles from Romsey. Ideally situated for exploring New Forest and within easy reach of many places of interest and tourist attractions. Cottage has modern conveniences — TV, fridge etc. - with linen provided. It is clean, homely and very comfortable with a large garden. A warm welcome awaits all visitors, including children and pets. Terms from £120 to £196 weekly. For further details SAE to: **Mrs R.J. Crane, 1 Thatched Cottage, Carter's Clay, Lockerley, Romsey SO51 0GN (01794 340460).**

LYMINGTON (New Forest). Greenacre, Woodenhouse Lane, Pilley Bailey, Lymington. Sleeps 6/7.

Delightful self catering thatched cottage about 150 years old, in peaceful village on lane leading down to shallow stream and open forest. Few miles from the sea and attractive harbour town. Ideal for walking, sailing, boat trips, pony riding, etc. Suits families, set in a garden, with living room and dining room with open fireplaces, breakfast room/kitchen downstairs; upstairs bathroom, three bedrooms (one room double and single beds and cot, one twin-bedded room, one room with bunk beds). Traditional furnishings. Duvets provided but no sheets or towels. Children and pets welcome. Weekly terms from £190 to £390. Details from **Mrs Alison Du Cane, Hanover Lodge, 14 Lansdowne Road, London W11 3LW (0171-727 5463; Fax: 0171-221 3936).**

LYMINGTON. 1 Hamilton Mews, Gosport Street, Lymington. ♀♀♀ *COMMENDED.* Spacious well equipped luxury Mews House, sleeping four comfortably. Pleasant situation, town centre — one minute quay, station, excellent shops, restaurants, pubs. Easy reach New Forest, Bournemouth. Lounge; dining area/kitchen; all electric, eye-level oven, hob, microwave, fridge/freezer, automatic washing machine. One double and one twin bedroom; bathroom; central heating, garaging. Colour TV. Terms inclusive of heating and electricity from £155 to £325 per week. Winter Breaks special rates. Unsuitable for pets. Enquiries: **Mrs S. Smith (01483 770444) or SAE Wey Lodge, 24 Potters Lane, Send, Woking, Surrey GU23 7AH.**

MILFORD-ON-SEA. Mrs Jean Halliday, Westover House, Westover Road, Milford-on-Sea, Lymington SO41 0PW (01590 642077). Sleeps 6. Westover House is a partly thatched period house 300 yards from the sea and half a mile from Milford's village green. Its East Wing, available for letting throughout the year, is self-contained and equipped for six, with modern services yet retaining an air of mature tranquillity reminiscent of a past age. There is a sheltered informal half-acre garden of unusual botanical interest, outstanding for its spring flowers. Milford is near the old-world market town of Lymington and the New Forest, yet is also convenient for Bournemouth and many popular holiday attractions of central Southern England. Terms from £105 per week, full tariff available on request.

WESTOVER HOUSE, MILFORD-ON-SEA

NEW FOREST. Twin Oaks, Redlynch, Salisbury. Sleeps 8/11. This completely modernised brick house is situated on rural Hampshire/Wiltshire border, only quarter of a mile from the New Forest. River Avon, fishing, golf, riding, etc nearby. Conveniently placed for visits to Beaulieu Motor Museum, Salisbury Cathedral, Wilton House, Old Sarum, Stonehenge, Broadlands House, Romsey Abbey, Breamore House, Downton, Mottisfont, Winchester, Marwell Zoo, Christchurch, Bournemouth and Weymouth. Many country walks and beautiful views. Accommodation: four bedrooms sleeping eight to 11 and cots. Large lounge, diningroom. Fully equipped kitchen, fitted carpets, bathroom, utility room, shower room, two WCs, conservatory. Washing machine, gas cooker, microwave, hot water, electric fires. Colour TV. Duvets with bed linen. Central heating extra. Payphone. Garage. Electricity by 50p meter. No pets. Available all year. Terms from £110 low season up to £450 maximum per week for eight in high season. Friday to Friday preferred. Winter Breaks from £100 for three nights. Write or phone for brochure to **Mr J. Leach, Newton, Whiteparish, Salisbury, Wiltshire SP5 2QQ (Tel & Fax: 01794 884428).**

SWAY, Lymington. Mrs H.J. Beale, Hackney Park, Mount Pleasant Lane, Sway, Lymington SO41 8LS (01590 682049). Two very comfortable and modern self-catering apartments and Coach House Cottage sleep two/six people (further bedrooms available). Colour TV. Bed linen and electricity included. Hackney Park is situated in a commanding and tranquil setting, two miles from Lymington and the village of Sway. It is a delightful residence standing in its own extensive grounds adjoining New Forest Heath with superb walks, rides and drives from the property. We have first class stables for those wishing to bring their own horse and there are excellent riding facilities within walking distance. There are many famous places of interest nearby; close to the Isle of Wight ferry and within six miles of sandy beaches. Pets by prior arrangement. Open all year.

HEREFORD & WORCESTER

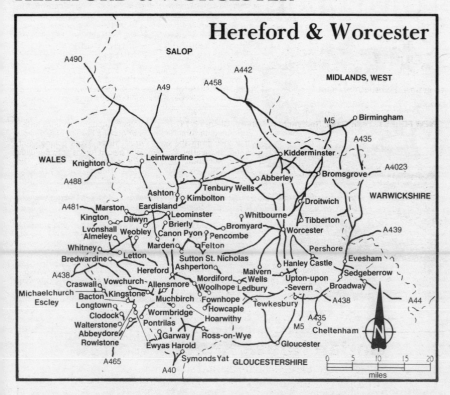

Hereford & Worcester

BROMYARD. **Mr and Mrs R.M. Bradbury, Cowarne Hall Cottages, Much Cowarne, Bromyard HR7 4JQ (01432 820317).** ♀♀♀♀ *COMMENDED.* A splendid, historic, Gothic hall with beams, open fireplaces, arched windows and doorways has been sensitively converted with support from the English Tourist Board to provide luxurious holiday cottage accommodation. Situated in the Malvern Hills area of Herefordshire 'twixt the hills and Wye Valley. In a quiet country lane location with hopfields, meadows, orchards and woods, yet within easy reach of the historic towns of Malvern, Bromyard, Hereford and Worcester. The cottages are centrally heated and have a patio, garden and parking. A box file provides details of the area's attractions including a working farm and Cider Mill. Free colour brochure. Terms from £90.

GREAT MALVERN. **Mr and Mrs D.G. Coates, Mill House, 16 Clarence Road, Great Malvern WR14 3EH (01684 562345). Sleeps 6/8.** Delightful Mill Cottage is situated at the foot of the beautiful Malvern Hills in the tranquil grounds of Mill House. A few minutes' walk from the town centre, hill walks, leisure pool and Great Malvern Station. Central heating, colour TV, microwave, dishwasher, etc., linen and towels provided. Two sitting rooms, one with patio window with superb view of hills; three bedrooms; two bathrooms, one en suite. Garden. Well behaved children and pets welcome. Parking within grounds of Mill House. Non-smokers preferred. Terms from £220 per week inclusive (no meters!). SAE please.

THE LODGE

The Lodge, being the former Verger's cottage, can be found in a tranquil setting just eight miles north of the historic cathedral town of Hereford. Peacefully located next to the Parish Church, guests can enjoy the pleasure of the gardens of Felton House, the stone built former Rectory, now a guest house. The Lodge has been completely renovated and restored to its Victorian character but with the convenience of central heating, a modern kitchen, two shower rooms, a dining room and a sitting room with TV. There are three bedrooms with accommodation for five people (one double room, one twin, one single), and in addition a cot is available. Linen may be hired. Children, and pets with responsible owners, are most welcome. Private parking, patio and garden. The Lodge is a cosy, restful cottage, spotlessly clean. Short Breaks catered for and weekly terms range from £125 to £225 per week, exclusive of electricity. Brochure available.

Marjorie and Brian Roby, Felton House, Felton HR1 3PH Tel: 01432 820366

HEREFORD near. Poolspringe Farm Cottages, Much Birch, Near Hereford. ♀♀♀♀ **Cottages sleep 2/7.** Five delightfully converted cottages on secluded 17th-century, 50-acre farm, amongst the orchards of South Hereford. Situated midway between Hereford and Ross-on-Wye, it is an ideal location for touring the Wye Valley, the Forest of Dean and mid-Wales. Visitors have the use of INDOOR HEATED SWIMMING POOL, sauna and solarium, and are invited to self pick fruit in season; large garden, games and coarse fishing available. Two to seven accommodated. All properties are fully equipped and furnished including colour TV; kitchens with fridges etc.; everything supplied for your holiday needs. Linen may be hired at extra charge. Children and pets welcome (walks for dogs). Ample parking. Terms £80 to £280 per week. Available all year. Please apply: **David and Val Beaumont, Poolspringe Farm, Much Birch, Hereford HR2 8JJ (Tel & Fax: 01981 540355).**

KINGTON. Ridge View Cottage, Bradnor Green, Kington. WTB 3 Dragons Award. Sleeps 5/7 plus cot. A detached 17th century stone cottage beautifully located on Bradnor Hill (National Trust), a mile above the border market town of Kington. Outstanding views to the Brecon Beacons, superb walks from the door (Offa's Dyke at top of garden) and a golf course within easy walking distance; 600 yards to pub/restaurant. Double and 2'6" twin bedrooms, with a single room at the bottom of the stairs leading to a double room; ground floor bath/shower room. All electric kitchen, sitting room with open fire and TV, lounge/diner in spacious extension. Washing machine, storage heaters, patio set. Not so suitable for infirm as quite steep access from parking (garage 200 yards if required). Pets welcome. Linen and solid fuel provided. Terms from £120 to £180 per week. Apply: **Mr K. Thomas, 228 Mary Vale Road, Bournville, Birmingham B30 1PJ (0121-628 0154).**

LEDBURY. Mrs Jane West, Church Farm, Coddington, Ledbury HR8 1JJ (01531 640271). ♀♀♀ **Sleeps 4.** Beautiful spacious cottage situated in quiet hamlet; Ledbury and Malvern Hills four and five miles respectively. Equidistant Hereford, Worcester, Ross-on-Wye and Gloucester. This former cider house, recently completely renovated to a very high standard, retains all the charm of exposed timberwork and beamed ceilings with views over the surrounding countryside. Fishing, swimming, riding, golfing nearby. Ample parking. Economy 7 central heating. Colour TV, radio, electric cooker, washing machine, dishwasher. Woodburner in lounge; downstairs cloakroom. French window onto patio. Open all year. £175 to £300 per week. Short Breaks out of season. Excellent Bed and Breakfast accommodation also available at farmhouse. Send SAE for full brochure.

DOCKLOW MANOR

HOLIDAY COTTAGES IN RURAL HEREFORDSHIRE FOR 2-6 PEOPLE

Quietly secluded in 10 acres of garden/woodland, the delightfully renovated stone cottages are grouped around an attractive stone-walled pond amidst shrubs, roses and honeysuckle. The cottages are homely, cosy and spotlessly clean. Fitted carpets, well equipped kitchens, colour TV, electric blankets. Laundry facilities. Bed linen is provided and beds are made up for your arrival. Wander round our rambling gardens and meet our friendly peacock, ducks, hens and goats. The more energetic can play croquet, lawn tennis, table tennis or take a dip in our **outdoor swimming pool**. Docklow is an ideal base for Ludlow, the Welsh border castles and market towns, Wye Valley, Brecon and Malvern hills. OPEN ALL YEAR INCLUDING CHRISTMAS & NEW YEAR. SHORT BREAKS LOW SEASON.

For Colour brochure and tourist map telephone 01568 760643.
Carol and Malcolm Ormerod, Docklow Manor, Leominster, Herefordshire.

LEINTWARDINE near. Mr and Mrs R.G. Cutler, Lower House, Adforton, Near Leintwardine, Shropshire SY7 0NF (01568 770223). ♀♀♀ Cottages sleep 4. "Oats" and "Barley" are two self-catering cottages tastefully converted from the 17th century oak-beamed former granary of Lower House. Both are fully equipped for four people. Linen, electricity and colour TV are provided. Dinner is available in the guesthouse diningroom which features exposed beams and a magnificent inglenook fireplace. Lower House is situated in peaceful and unspoilt countryside between Ludlow and the Welsh border and away from busy roads. The area is one of outstanding natural beauty and most suitable for walking, fishing, bird watching, etc. Ample parking. Terms from £95 to £210. Brochure available. Regret, no pets.

LUCTON. Mrs S.M. Sampson, Puddlecroft, Lucton HR6 9PH (01568 780537). ♀♀ COMMENDED. Our self-contained detached first floor "black and white" loft flat is ideally suited for two. It is in the grounds of the main house "Puddlecroft", and a private sitting out area complete with brick built barbecue is provided. Our own fields, where our free range chickens and sheep roam, provide lovely views from the flat and of course there is plenty of private parking. Puddlecroft is set in its own grounds on the edge of Lucton, a small peaceful hamlet which lies in North Herefordshire, close to borders of Wales and Shropshire. The area is ideally suited for walkers and as a central base for trips into Wales, Shropshire and Herefordshire. Terms from £80 to £160 per week. Available for weekly and weekend bookings throughout the year. Brochure available.

WHITEWELLS FARM COTTAGES

Seven award-winning cottages, including one for disabled, converted from an interesting old hop kiln and historic farm buildings set in nine acres of unspoilt Herefordshire countryside. Scrupulously clean. Full of charm and character with exposed beams, each cottage is fully furnished and equipped to the highest standards. Ideal base for touring Herefordshire, Worcestershire, Cotswolds, Welsh Mountains, Shakespeare country. Short breaks in low season. Dogs welcome. Prices include all linen, heating and lighting, colour TV, etc. Brochure and terms available on request.

David and Jane Berisford, Ridgway Cross, Near Malvern WR13 5JS Tel/Fax: (01886) 880607).

♀♀♀♀ **HIGHLY COMMENDED**

MALVERN. Greenbank Garden Flat, Malvern. ♀♀♀♀ *COMMENDED.* Greenbank Garden Flat is situated in the Malvern Hills overlooking Herefordshire. It is self contained and fully equipped with gas cooker, fridge, TV, immersion heater. Sleeping two/four, it has a double bed and studio couch which converts for two; cot and Z-bed are available by arrangement. The inclusive charge covers bedlinen for the double bed, towels and all fuel etc. Post office, supermarket and public house within five minutes' walk of Greenbank. Terms £95 — £150 weekly; shorter lets available. Guests have the use of our garden. An excellent base. Dogs welcome by arrangement, £10 charged per pet. Apply: **Mrs S.M. Matthews, Greenbank, 236 West Malvern Road, Malvern WR14 4BG (01684 567328).**

PEMBRIDGE. Rowena and Nurse's Cottages, East Street, Pembridge. ♀♀♀ *COMMENDED.* Two Black and White Cottages situated in Pembridge, which is noted for its ancient butter market and church with its detached belfry. One of Herefordshire's finest old black and white villages, Pembridge is situated on the River Arrow, midway between Leominster and Kington. It is an ideal touring centre for Border countryside. Riding, gliding and fishing are available nearby. Rowena Cottage sleeps four/six persons and Nurse's Cottage sleeps four/five persons. The properties are comfortably furnished and equipped with TV, fitted carpets, storage heaters and open fires. Each has a small garden. Weekly terms from £140 to £220. Short Breaks available. For further information please contact **Mrs D. Malone, The Cottage, Holme, Newark, Nottinghamshire NG23 7RZ (01636 72914).**

ROSS-ON-WYE. Mrs H. Smith, Old Kilns, Howle Hill, Ross-on-Wye HR9 5AP (01989 562051). ♀♀♀ *COMMENDED.* WTB 4 Dragons. Sleeps 10/12. 17th century character cottage perched high above the valley has superb views of the surrounding countryside. A short walk away is a magnificent view of Symonds Yat and the ruined 12th century red sandstone Goodrich Castle. Shop and pub half a mile. Central for Malverns, Cotswolds and Stratford. Furnished and equipped to high standard with central heating and open fires. One bedroom with king size bed and en suite shower and vanity unit, one double bedroom and one twin-bedded room. Two double bed settees in lounge; dining room; fully fitted kitchen with washing machine and fridge/freezer. Colour TV and radio. Garden furniture and barbecue. Cot, high chair, babysitting. Children and pets welcome. Fishing, riding, golf, canoeing, tennis, etc. Also smaller properties and smallholding with animals available.

PLEASE ENCLOSE A STAMPED ADDRESSED ENVELOPE WITH ENQUIRIES

ROSS-ON-WYE. Mrs J. Scudamore, Llangarron Court, Llangarron, Ross-on-Wye HR9 6NP (01989 770243).

♀♀♀ Surrounded by open farmland and glorious views, No.2 Potacre Cottage with its garden and lawn enjoys the best scenery in unspoilt Herefordshire. Ross-on-Wye is five miles away, the Cathedral at Hereford is 14 miles away and houses the "Mappa Mundi", while Symonds Yat is three miles away. The cottage is comfortably furnished and comprises sittingroom, kitchen/dining room, bathroom and loo downstairs, while upstairs there are three bedrooms sleeping five/six. Cot on request. Electricity by £1 coin meter; linen hire £3.50 per bed. Terms and brochure on request.

ROSS-ON-WYE. Mrs Pauline Amos, Oaklands, Llangarron, Ross-on-Wye HR9 6NZ (01989 770277).

♀♀♀ *APPROVED.* The cottage shown has a view of five counties, while the others are also situated in beautiful countryside; two are on a farm. Private enclosed gardens. They are all within three miles of Symonds Yat, six miles from Ross-on-Wye. Personally supervised. All have colour TV; central heating; cots, high chairs; upstairs and downstairs WCs, modern bathrooms; kitchens with many facilities including microwaves; sittingrooms; diningrooms; bedrooms sleeping two/seven people. Ample parking space. Two properties have a garage, two have large enclosed private lawns. Children and pets welcome. You are free to wander over our farm and sit by our beautiful lake, surrounded by trees and wild flowers. Lovely walks, horse riding, canoeing, fishing, golf, ballooning and many other facilities within the area. Terms from £95 per week. Telephone **Mrs Pauline Amos** for details.

ROSS-ON-WYE. Bill Mill Cottages, Bill Mill, Ross-on-Wye HR9 5TH (01432 840390; Fax: 01989 750760). ♀♀♀♀/♀♀♀♀♀ *COMMENDED/HIGHLY COMMENDED.* **Sleep up to 6.** Five very high standard

converted cottages around a 15th century Listed watermill. In the heart of the country, these lovely cottages are an ideal centre for the Wye Valley, Forest of Dean and Welsh Mountains. Each spacious cottage is furnished and equipped to the highest standard including full central heating, TV, video, open fires and excellent kitchens. There are very large natural grounds with stream and wild flower areas. Barbecue, badminton and croquet lawn. Full washing facilities and table tennis room adjacent. Linen, fuel, etc are available. Children and pets very welcome. For brochure and terms contact **Christine Jenkins.**

ROSS-ON-WYE near. Kiln House, Yatton, Near Ross-on-Wye. Sleeps 6. The Kiln House is a converted hop kiln, situated just off the A449 in the peace and quiet of lovely Herefordshire countryside. The historic towns of Ledbury and Ross-on-Wye are nearby, as well as the Wye Valley, Forest of Dean, Malvern Hills and many more places of interest. The accommodation sleeps six in three bedrooms — two with double beds and one with bunk beds. Cot and high chair available. Large lounge with woodburner and TV; well-equipped kitchen; downstairs toilet, bathroom and toilet upstairs. Airing cupboard with immersion heater. Garden and ample parking, car essential. Children welcome. Sorry, no pets. Available all year. SAE for terms and further details to: **Mrs P.A. Ruck, Lower House, Yatton, Near Ross-on-Wye HR9 7RB (01531 660280).**

ROSS-ON-WYE. Yew Tree Cottage, Symonds Yat West. Sleeps 4 adults; 2 children. 200 year old stone cottage situated in three-quarters of an acre orchard with elevated position overlooking River Wye. Modernised and refurbished to a high standard; all electric; fitted kitchen; night storage heaters; fitted carpets; bathroom (plus shower); three bedrooms (one double, one twin, one with bunk beds); magnificent views; open patio and conservatory. Ample parking. Charming riverside inns with good food nearby; Forest of Dean, delightful scenic walks, hiking/climbing, pony trekking, canoeing. Village shop 20 minutes walk. Monmouth four miles, Ross seven miles (both have swimming and tennis facilities). Children over five welcome. Sorry, no pets. Available all year. From £125 to £275 per week. **Mrs M.D. Ball, 126 Abbey Road, Westbury on Trym, Bristol BS9 3RB (0117 962 1494).**

SYMONDS YAT. Mrs J. Rudge, Hilltop, Llangrove, Near Ross-on-Wye (01600 890279). Sleeps 4. Chalet bungalow with magnificent views over surrounding countryside. One mile off A40 dual carriageway and within easy reach of Forest of Dean, Monmouth and Black Mountains. The chalet stands in the gardens of a seven-acre smallholding, enjoying peace and quiet, yet close to local shops, public houses and the local attractions. Livingroom with TV. Kitchen and bathroom with all amenities. Two bedrooms, one with two single beds and one with double bed. Patio, sun lounge, garden. Children welcome. No pets. Accommodation particularly suitable for the elderly. No linen supplied. 50p meter. Terms from £140 to £180. SAE, please.

SYMONDS YAT. Langstone Court Farm, Llangarron, Ross-on-Wye. Up to ♀♀♀♀ *COMMENDED.* Beautiful 14th century farmhouse home near Golden Valley, Hay-on-Wye, Black Mountains, Malverns, Wye Valley. Two night break for family celebrations — up to 24 people anytime except August, local caterers available. Beamed wings for two to 10 people. Ground floor twin room en suite for disabled guests. Central heating. Large flat garden, summer house, barbecue. Log fires. Payphone. Laundry, microwave, dishwasher, freezer. Mountain bike lock up after cycling in nearby Forest of Dean. Whole house only at Christmas and New Year but book early. FREE Christmas tree, logs, all fuel and hamper of home baking. Contact: **Doris Wilding, Linden House, Vowchurch Common HR2 0RL (01981 550360).**

WORCESTER. Worcester College of Higher Education, Worcester. Self catering flats on a quiet rural college campus two miles from Worcester's centre, within easy reach of Junction 7 of the M5. The fully equipped flats, comprising bath/shower/WC and lounge/kitchen area, sleep six people in separate rooms and are available from mid July to mid September. The location provides an excellent base for touring the Heart of England, being close to Stratford-upon-Avon, Warwick, Gloucester and the magnificent scenery of the Cotswolds and the Malvern Hills. Worcester city provides many interests, from the world famous porcelain factory to its splendid Cathedral on the banks of the River Severn. Older children welcome, (not suitable for infants/toddlers) but sorry, no pets. Terms £235 per week. Further details from **Colin Fry, Head of Residential Services, Worcester College of Higher Education, Henwick Grove, Worcester WR2 6AJ (01905 855000).** Please quote FHG.

HERTFORDSHIRE

SOUTH MIMMS. Mr W.A.J. Marsterson, The Black Swan, 62/64 Blanche Lane, South Mimms, Potters Bar EN6 3PD (01707 644180). Up to ♀♀♀

COMMENDED. **Sleep 2/6.** The Black Swan, a timber framed building dating from 1600, looks across the village green in South Mimms. Once a village inn, it is now our home. We have two flats and a cottage, convenient for M25 and A1(M), half an hour's drive, tube or train from central London. Near Junction 23 on M25. Follow signs to South Mimms village. Stay with us to see London and the South-East or use us as a staging post to or from the Channel Ports. We offer self-catering accommodation or overnight stay with Breakfast supplied. Self catering from £120 to £250 per week. Bed and Breakfast from £25. Children and pets welcome. Non-smoking accommodation available.

KENT

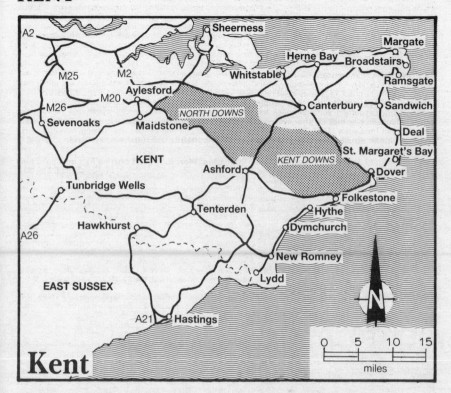

Kent

CANTERBURY. Woodcroft, Broad Oak, Canterbury. Sleeps up to 6. A cedarwood bungalow on the edge of the village. Three bedrooms; large lounge, bathroom/WC, kitchen. Gas central heating and cooking; woodstove (free wood). Big garden. Adjoining orchards and woodland. No pets, no smoking. Terms from £110 to £125 per week. Brochure available. **Mr and Mrs R. Jackson, Cedar Cottage, 50 Shalloak Road, Broad Oak, Canterbury CT2 0QE (01227 710284).**

GOUDHURST. Risebridge Farm Holiday Cottages, Goudhurst, Near Cranbrook. ♀♀♀♀ *COMMEN-*

DED. A group of 10 spacious, comfortable cottages, sleeping from two to eight, converted from an Oasthouse and traditional farm buildings on a 100 acre farm amidst beautiful countryside. Private facilities including indoor heated pool, sauna and jacuzzi, tennis, squash, badminton, gymnasium and horse riding. Children's play area and games room, farm shop and nature trail. Easy access to coast, London, historic castles and gardens. All cottages are fully equipped with pine furniture, colour TV, heating, carpeting and free linen. Weekly from April to end October (£200 to £720 per week), Short Breaks in winter (£125 to £265 three nights). Brochure from **Richard and Lindie Hillier, Risebridge Farm, Goudhurst, Cranbrook TN17 1HN (01580 211775; Fax: 01580 211984).**

HARRIETSHAM. St Christopher, Autumn and Dial Cottages, Harrietsham, Maidstone. ♀♀♀♀

HIGHLY COMMENDED. Three properties in village conservation area. Near local shops, pubs and transport (75 minutes to London, hourly trains). Excellent touring location for Kent and Sussex; Leeds Castle three miles. DIAL COTTAGE: cosy, ground floor flat with one bedroom. Mini garden. Central heating; £100 to £150. AUTUMN COTTAGE (1738): three bedrooms sleeping five, beams and inglenook fireplace. Lawned garden; £150 to £260. ST. CHRISTOPHER: very comfortable, spacious Victorian house, two bedrooms, sleeps five. Pretty, secluded garden; £150 to £260. All properties have central heating. Large car park. Washing machine, dryer and payphone on site. Bed linen inclusive, towel hire available. Open all year. Non-smokers preferred. **Mrs Margaret J. Bottle, Dial House, East Street, Harrietsham, Maidstone ME17 1HJ (01622 859622).**

HAWKHURST. Mrs L.C. Johnson, "Highwell", Heartenoak Road, Hawkhurst, Cranbrook TN18 5EU

(01580 752152). Sleeps 2. Enjoy a peaceful holiday in the spacious self contained annexe (own entrance) to our attractive Edwardian house. The accommodation is furnished and equipped to a very high standard and provides a large, comfortable sittingroom with delightful country views, kitchen with washing machine, microwave, etc, double bedroom, bathroom. Linen, TV, central heating, telephone. Set in an acre of secluded gardens down a country lane yet only half a mile from Hawkhurst village, "Highwell" offers an ideal base for touring Kent and East Sussex with a wealth of famous gardens, castles, coastline and picturesque scenery within easy reach. Terms from £90 to £185 weekly. Sorry no pets.

LYDD-ON-SEA. 98 Coast Drive, Lydd-on-Sea, Romney Marsh. Sleeps 5 adults, 2 children. Lydd-on-

Sea is a small hamlet on the south coast near New Romney/Dungeness. We offer a three bedroomed bungalow situated opposite the sea front with uninterrupted sea views from the sun lounge/diner. There is an inner lounge; colour TV is provided. A separate bathroom and toilet. Lawns to front and rear plus expanse of natural garden. Small patio to rear with garden furniture. Easy access to Dover and Folkestone for cross-Channel trips. The ancient towns of Rye and Hastings are a short distance away. Good sea fishing off Dungeness Point. Romney, Hythe and Plymouth small gauge railway passes rear of the house and buses stop a few yards away. Children welcome. Weekly terms from £95 to £200. Contact: **Mrs Frances I. Smith, Holts Farm House, Coopers Lane, Fordcombe, Near Tunbridge Wells TN3 0RN (01892 740338).**

KENT – THE GARDEN OF ENGLAND!

The pleasant landscape of Kent, including The North Downs and The Weald, is the host of many engaging places to visit. These include Chiddingstone – the half-timbered village, the sophisticated spa town of Tunbridge Wells and Swanton Mill. There are also day trips to the continent and for railway enthusiasts, The Sittingbourne & Kensley Light Railway, The Kent & East-Sussex Railway and the 'World's Smallest Public Railway' from Hythe to Dungeness.

MAIDSTONE near. Mr & Mrs J. Barker, Gore Court, Church Road, Otham, Maidstone ME15 8RF

(01622 863029). Private recently refurbished apartment in Listed Tudor Hall House — setting for many films including "Kind Hearts and Coronets" and Disney's "Bejewelled". Heavily beamed open plan lounge/dining/kitchen (10 × 6m). Separate utility room. Fully equipped — oven, hob, dishwasher, washing machine, tumble dryer, etc. Covered terrace for "al fresco" meals. Fine oak staircase leading to two "French style" bedrooms with vaulted 18th century plastered ceilings (each 5 × 5m). One double with en suite bathroom (bath/shower, WC and washbasin), one twin adjoining. Good sofa bed in lounge. Cot. Set in 13 hectares of private grounds; sheep pastures, woodland walk, extensive lawns. Very peaceful with open views. Quality furnishings throughout. Near Leeds Castle, South coast, Sissinghurst Gardens, ferry terminal/Channel Tunnel for France. Weekly £250 to £450 including electricity, metered oil central heating. Linen £6 per person per week.

See also Colour Display Advertisement **SOUTHERN ENGLAND. Fairhaven Holiday Cottages.** An extensive selection of personally inspected holiday homes. Various shapes, sizes and locations in Southern England and Wales. Available throughout the year. Long and short winter lets. Featuring KENT and the KINGSDOWN LEISURE PARK NEAR DEAL. Contact: **Fairhaven Holiday Cottages, Derby House, 123 Watling Street, Gillingham ME7 2YY (01634 570157).**

WROTHAM. Sheila and Gerry Morel, Butts Hill Farm, Labour-in-Vain Road, Wrotham, Sevenoaks

TN15 7PA (Tel & Fax: 01732 822415). 🐾🐾🐾 *HIGHLY COMMENDED.* Two and three bedroomed timber lodges in peaceful woodland location, yet close to junction of M20 and M26. Each lodge is fully equipped with all modern conveniences for self catering. These include microwave, fridge, cooker and well equipped kitchen with dining area. Large bath/shower room, comfortably furnished lounge with radio, TV and large gas fire. Good quality bed linen and towels are provided. Secure car parking, safe for children and a peaceful location in which to relax or use as a tour base for London, the South East of England and even a trip to the Continent.

LANCASHIRE

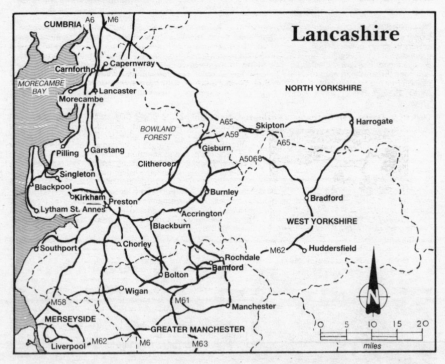

CLITHEROE. Ingledene, Rimington, Near Clitheroe. ♀♀♀ *COMMENDED.* **Sleeps 6.** Ingledene is an extremely comfortable and fully equipped cottage located in the heart of Rimington village, in the lovely Ribble Valley. It has a small garden at the front and a large garden to the rear and the cottage enjoys some beautiful views from all windows. Accommodation for six in two double rooms with bed-settee in lounge. Children welcome — cot, high chair. Pets allowed. There are all-weather tennis courts in the village, and riding facilities. Golf, swimming, snooker locally. Ideal for walking or touring, easy access to Lake District and Yorkshire Dales or Lancashire Coast. Clitheroe four miles. Weekly terms from £100 to £145. Further details on request. **Mrs Brenda Lund, Fernlea, Rimington, Near Clitheroe BB7 4DS (01200 445640).**

CLITHEROE near. Mrs S. Parker, Horns Farm, Church Street, Slaidburn, Near Clitheroe BB7 3ER (01200 446288). ♀♀♀ *APPROVED.* **Working farm.** Two cosy semi-detached cottages situated in small picturesque village and overlooking farmland, make ideal bases from which to explore the Forest of Bowland, an area of outstanding natural beauty. Within easy reach of Yorkshire Dales, Lake District and seaside. Fishing at Stooks reservoir two miles away. On North Lancashire Cycle Way. Sorry no pets. No. 24 sleeps five in two bedrooms and No. 22 has just one twin-bedded room. Garden up steps at rear. Linen and electricity included in the rent of £110 to £145 per week or £20 to £26 per night for out of season Short Breaks. Open all year. Our farmhouse is nearby.

LIVERPOOL. John Moores University. One of the largest new Universities with in excess of 20,000 students. As you would expect from a first class University we have the finest lecture theatres and catering facilities, which in turn means that we are able to offer some of the finest conference and self catering facilities in the country. Prestigious accommodation and catering for all occasions. For further information please contact: **Jonathan M. Chinn, Liverpool John Moores University, JMU Services Ltd, 2 Rodney Street, Liverpool L3 5UX (Tel & Fax: 0151-231 3369).**

PLEASE SEND A STAMPED ADDRESSED ENVELOPE WITH ENQUIRIES

LINCOLNSHIRE

CUMBERWORTH. Old Rectory, Cumberworth, Alford. Sleeps 6. Situated one mile off A52 on a working farm 10 miles from Skegness, four miles coast, 40 miles Lincoln. Within five miles there is easy access to sandy beaches, golf, trout/coarse fishing, Lincolnshire Wolds. This is a large house in its own grounds with a play/parking area. Accommodation comprises three double bedrooms, bathroom, kitchen/diner, lounge, playroom. Electric cooker, fridge, microwave, washer, colour TV, cot, log/electric fire. Fully equipped for six. Linen not provided. Open April — October. Children and pets welcome. Terms from £100 per week including electricity. Apply **Mrs S.M. Ward, Hillcrest, Cumberworth, Alford LN13 9LB (01507 490313).**

LINCOLN. Dorrington Cottages, Dorrington, Near Lincoln. 💡💡💡💡 *COMMENDED.* **Sleep 5.** Semi

detached Victorian cottages, beautifully modernised and fully equipped for comfortable family accommodation in three bedrooms. Tastefully furnished and decorated with lots of personal care and attention. Price includes bed linen and central heating. Electric cooker, colour TV, washer/dryer, private parking, secluded garden, patio furniture and barbecue. Cot and high chair available. Pets welcome. Dorrington is an unspoilt and friendly village with a duck pond in pleasant Lincolnshire countryside. Easy access to Lincoln (15 miles), Sleaford (six miles), Grantham, Newark, Boston and the coast. Prices £145 to £260 per week. Two cottages, open all year. Short breaks available October to April (prices on application). Best time to phone for details Tuesdays to Fridays 10am to 5pm, Sunday 1pm to 4pm and evenings. Contact: **Janet Crafer, 12 Church Lane, Timberland, Lincoln LN4 3SB (01526 378222).**

WOODHALL SPA. "Kirkstead Old Mill Cottage", Woodhall Spa. 💡💡💡💡 *HIGHLY COMMENDED.*

Sleeps 7-10 + baby. Kirkstead Old Mill Cottage is our isolated, three-bedroomed holiday home which is only let to NON-SMOKERS. The sunny house is over a mile off the Tattershall Road on the outskirts of WOODHALL SPA, LINCOLNSHIRE. It is set beside the wide but quiet RIVER WITHAM that is noted for its fishing. A small rowing boat is provided. There is also a large, grassy garden and a three acre nature reserve for picnics. The house is extremely well-equipped with colour TV, dishwasher, automatic washing machine, tumble dryer, fridge/freezer, microwave and piano etc. There is plenty of parking space, and a home help is provided for two hours midweek. Membership of local leisure club with swimming pool is included. Weekly rates from £99 to £400. Apply **Mrs Barbara Hodgkinson, "Hodge's Lodges", 52 Kelso Close, Worth, Crawley, West Sussex RH10 7XH (01293 882008; Fax: 01293 883352).**

FREE and REDUCED RATE Holiday Visits!
See our Reader's Offer Vouchers for details!

PUBLISHER'S NOTE

While every effort is made to ensure accuracy, we regret that FHG Publications cannot accept responsibility for errors, omissions or misrepresentation in our entries or any consequences thereof. Prices in particular should be checked because we go to press early. We will follow up complaints but cannot act as arbiters or agents for either party.

NORFOLK

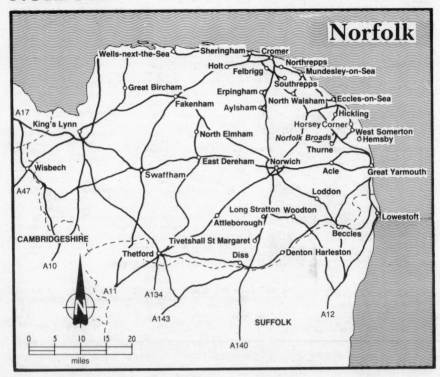

BRISLEY. Church Farm Cottages, Brisley, East Dereham NR20 5LL. ♀♀♀♀ *COMMENDED/HIGHLY COMMENDED.* **Properties sleep 2/5.** Situated just off the village green between East Dereham and Fakenham, these cottages are on a mixed working farm of 230 acres. Kept to a very high standard of cleanliness and comfort, they have full central heating, log fires, colour TV, video, washing machine, etc. Each has a garden and plenty of parking space. Open all year. Short Breaks available. Linen, logs and heating included in price. Terms from £170 to £400. Swimming pool, golf, sports and leisure centre all within easy reach. Ideal for cycling and bird watching. For further details telephone **Gillian Howes (01362 668332).**

CLIPPESBY. Mrs Jean Lindsay, Clippesby Holidays, Clippesby NR29 3BJ (01493 369367). ♀♀ to

♀♀♀♀ APPROVED, √ √ √ √ √ Excellent. Set in the Broadlands National Park where the tranquil waterways are a traditional haunt of fishermen, naturalists and sailors and where the nearby golden sand beaches stretch for miles. Broadland abounds in nature reserves and tourist attractions and Clippesby is perfectly placed for exploring these. When a change from exploring is called for guests can enjoy the amenities of the park itself — lawn tennis and swimming are just two of the things that families can enjoy together. Clippesby Holidays is a family-run country park with 23 courtyard cottages and an award-winning touring park in its spacious wooded grounds. Send for colour brochure!

CROMER. Kings Chalet Park, Overstrand Road, Cromer. Sleeps 4. Comfortable, fully equipped,

self-contained, detached and semi-detached chalets on a quiet and pleasant landscaped site close to woods, cliffs, sands and golf course. Within 10 minutes' cliff top walk to Cromer town centre. There are two bedrooms, one double and one twin, fully equipped kitchen, lounge/diner with colour TV, bathroom and toilet. Duvets, duvet covers, pillowcases provided. Terms: Spring/Autumn £60 to £150; Summer £115 to £190. Electricity extra on meter. Open 1st March to 31st October. Contact: **G.A. Hunt, Field View House, Norwich Road, Roughton, Norwich NR11 8SJ (01263 768324).**

CROMER. 3 Chesterfield Villas, West Street, Cromer. Sleeps 8. Spacious three bedroomed, two

bathroomed Listed cottage within 100 yards of sea, town centre and railway station. All modern facilities. Sleeping up to eight people plus child's cot. Parking at rear of property. Pets welcome. £225 to £300 per week. For full details contact **Mrs Pam Newman, "Eastcote", 16 Heath Road, Sheringham NR26 8JH (01263 823555).**

CROMER. Mr and Mrs J.N. Julian, Roman Camp Brick Chalets, Roman Camp Caravan Park, West

Runton, Cromer NR27 9ND (01263 837256). If you want a peaceful holiday in modern elegant comfort then look no further. Our four-berth chalets have full mains services with hot and cold running water, room heater, fridge, gas cooker, TV, plus all crockery, cutlery and cooking utensils. There is a large open-plan living room, kitchen and dining area; one double bedroom, one bunk room; shower room, washbasin and electric razor point. Linen not provided. Sorry, no pets. We are situated three-quarters of a mile from buses and trains, one and a quarter miles from the sea and within easy motoring distance of Norwich, Yarmouth, Lowestoft, Wells, King's Lynn, Hunstanton, the Queen's estate of Sandringham and many other places of interest. Open from Easter to end of October. Terms from £175 to £210 per week.

NORFOLK – THE BROADS!

Formed by the flooding of medieval peat diggings, the Broads have a unique quality which attracts thousands of visitors each year. Slow moving waterways are bounded by reed and sedge, and despite the pressures of the modern world are home to rare birds, butterflies and plants. Motor boats and sailing boats can be hired in most towns and villages and there are lots of lively riverbank pubs to round off a day afloat.

CROMER. 13 Chesterfield Cottages, Cromer. A charming flint cottage sleeping four/five, situated three

minutes from the town centre, sea front, beach and all amenities. The property is small but well-furnished and equipped. Lounge with colour TV, electric heater; kitchen with electric cooker, fridge, spin dryer etc; bathroom with shower, washbasin and WC; two bedrooms — one double with Z-bed, one with bunk beds. Small rear garden, parking close by. Rentals include electricity and night storage heating. Small pets by arrangement. Within easy reach of places of interest, sailing, ornithology, riding, fishing and rambling. Terms from £80. Apply: **Mr and Mrs Rigg, 124 Waterfall Road, Southgate, London N14 7JN (0181-886 4811).**

EAST RAYNHAM. Mrs Susan Panter, "Clebar", Colkirk Road, East Raynham, Fakenham NR21 7EJ

(01328 855118). Cottages sleep 3+2,2; Mobile home sleeps 2+2. BARCLE COTTAGES: A friendly welcome in our refurbished holiday cottages in private landscaped gardens. Very well equipped, fitted carpets, colour TV and heating throughout. Ground floor bedrooms. Linen provided. Owner supervised. Parking. Sorry no pets. Open all year. Quiet village, central for all North Norfolk, 15 minutes from coast, local for Sandringham and Walsingham. Luxury mobile home with same facilities and a five caravan touring site also available. Short Breaks catered for. Please send for terms and further details.

FAKENHAM. Mrs P. Borlase, Yew Tree Farm, Barney, Fakenham NR21 0AD (01328 878237).

Country views can be enjoyed from this spacious cottage in a peaceful village setting situated next to the owners' working farm. Barney is close to Walsingham (six miles) and the North Norfolk coast with Blakeney and Wells approximately eight to 10 miles away. Accommodation comprises one double-bedded room, two rooms with two single beds in each; cot, high chair and fireguard provided. Comfortable lounge with colour TV and electric fire; kitchen/diner — electric cooker, fridge, fire and automatic washing machine; bathroom. Fully equipped for six persons, linen and tea towels supplied. Fully lawned gardens with furniture and parking for two cars. Pets welcome (£12 extra each per week). Short breaks available. Please write or telephone for brochure.

FAKENHAM. Saddlery Cottage and Hillside Cottage, Colkirk, Fakenham. Sleep 7 and 6

respectively. Both cottages are situated near the farm on the outskirts of Colkirk village, overlooking farmland. Saddlery Cottage (shown in picture) has large and light sittingroom with beams and woodburner, fully fitted kitchen/dining room with fridge and electric cooker, utility room with automatic washing machine. Garage, parking and fenced garden. Hillside Cottage has sittingroom with colour TV, large airy kitchen/dining room with fitted units and washing machine. Fenced garden, parking. Saddlery Cottage is suitable for disabled visitors. Both have central heating/Calor gas heating. Children and pets welcome. Cots available; linen supplied. Apply **Mrs C. Joice, Colkirk Hall, Fakenham NR21 7ND (01328 862261).**

Located on a working farm, a courtyard of seven 2/3 bedroomed SELF CATERING CHALETS. All fully equipped, and all with central heating which is included in the letting fee. Situated 20 miles from the coast and 15 miles from Norwich and the Broads. 365 acres of mature woodland adjoining owners' farm – ideal for walking. Fishing close by.

MOOR FARM HOLIDAYS
FOXLEY, NORFOLK NR20 4QN Tel & Fax: 01362 688523

GREAT WALSINGHAM. Folgate Cottage, Scarborough Road, Great Walsingham, Norfolk. Sleeps 8. This detached cottage is located just opposite the Post Office in this small village, adjoining Little Walsingham, renowned for its shrine and places of historical interest. The North Norfolk coast is within four miles (Wells-next-the-Sea) and nature and bird reserves are also close by at Titchwell, Holme and Cley. Built in 1984, in traditional Norfolk style of flint and red brick, the cottage is fully insulated and double glazed for winter use. Cot available. Storage heaters are installed on the ground floor together with a wood-burning stove in the lounge. Fan heaters are also provided. All rooms are fully carpeted. Kitchen and bathroom are tiled throughout and fitted to a high standard. Please supply own linen except duvet covers. Terms from £167 to £364 per week. SAE to **Mrs M. Matthews, Greenside, Church Lane, Reed, Royston, Herts. SG8 8AS (01763 848461).**

GREAT YARMOUTH. Anchor Holiday Flats, Great Yarmouth. The Anchor holiday flats are pleasantly situated in a select area of Great Yarmouth. Close by are the sea and the Venetian Waterways. Accommodation is in one and two bedroomed flats, all of which are completely self contained and have their own shower and toilet. Kitchen/diner/lounge with sink unit, cooker, refrigerator, automatic kettle and iron. Colour TV and electric fire. All bed linen, crockery and utensils are supplied at no extra cost. Electricity is metered (50p) but all hot water to sink units is free of charge. Conveniently situated for coach station, free public car park, post office and newsagents. Children and pets welcome. Reduced terms early and late season. Contact: **Mrs Pauline Smith, 21 North Denes Road, Great Yarmouth NR30 4LW (01493 844339).**

GREAT YARMOUTH. near. Chalet 18G, Sundowner Holiday Park, Newport Road, Hemsby, Near Great Yarmouth. ♀♀♀ Sleeps 6. Chalet accommodation for hire on an excellent holiday park situated near Great Yarmouth with its many attractions. Chalet comprises two bedrooms; lounge with studio couch; kitchen and bathroom. All rooms nicely furnished. Site facilities include indoor heated swimming pool, night club and bar with cabaret, dancing, bingo and children's club; large site shop and laundry. Children and pets welcome. Terms from £75 to £150 per week. Further details and bookings to: **Mrs Gloria White, 2 Cherry Tree Lane, North Walsham NR28 0HR (01692 403461; Fax: 01692 431500).**

HEMSBY. Bermuda Holiday Park, Hemsby, Near Great Yarmouth. Properties sleep 6/8. Fully equipped two/three bedroom chalets, cottage and bungalow style, at Bermuda Holiday Park. All chalets have the benefit of colour TV. Bermuda Holiday Park is a popular, well-maintained holiday centre situated within easy walking distance of beautiful sandy beaches. On-site facilities include excellent clubhouse with free entertainment for our clients, heated indoor swimming pool, shops, sauna, solarium, games room, play areas. We regret pets are not allowed. Our prices are probably as low as you will find anywhere for a similar standard of accommodation. Electricity by slot meter. Weekly terms from £50 to £220. For full details please contact **Mr P. Jeffery, 40 Marshalls Way, Wheathampstead, Hertfordshire AL4 8HY (01582 460315).**

HOCKWOLD-CUM-WILTON. Mrs B. Deacon, Deacon's Cottages, South Street, Hockwold, Thetford IP26 4JG (01842 828023/878739). ♀♀ APPROVED. Sleep 4. Two cottages in the Breckland Forest area on the Norfolk/Suffolk border, with views of rolling meadows leading to canal and river. Riding, golf and coarse fishing all within easy reach, and various walks and trails in the Breckland Forest. Historic cities of Ely, Cambridge and Norwich within 40 miles, other characteristic East Anglian market towns nearby. Accommodation comprises double bedroom and bedroom with two single beds (camp bed available if required); kitchen/diner; lounge with electric fire and TV; bathroom and WC. Bed linen available at small extra charge. Electricity by meter reading. Ample parking space. Terms from £75 to £150 per week.

HOLT. Roger and Marjorie Doy, Pippin Heath, Holt NR25 6SS (01263 713751). Sleeps 6 plus cot.

This attractive semi-detached farmhouse is situated one mile from the busy market town of Holt. A short drive takes you to the coast and the resorts of Wells, Sheringham and Cromer, the bird sanctuaries of Cley and Blakeney, Sandringham House and Norwich. Downstairs: large lounge/diner with Sky TV; kitchen with cooker, fridge and microwave; hall and shower room. Upstairs: double, twin and bunk-bedded rooms, bed linen and cot available. Electric heating/immersion. Ample parking and spacious garden. Regret no pets. £140 to £175 per week plus electricity. Open April to October.

HOLT. Honeysuckle Cottage, 1 Mill Lane, Briston, Holt. Sleeps 4 plus cot. A comfortable two bedroomed end cottage with a large kitchen on a quiet byroad, nicely furnished, personally supervised, with an enclosed garden. Parking for two cars. Also available, stable conversion at TOFTREES near Fakenham sleeping four plus two with enclosed garden and parking. Situated 12 miles from the coast. Terms from £120 to £250 weekly depending on season and property. Open all year. Contact: **Mrs S. Balderstone, Hawthorn Cottage, Toftrees, Fakenham NR21 7DX (01328 863915).**

HOLT near. 8 Marryat's Loke, Langham, Near Holt. Sleeps 5. A modern red brick house on the edge of a small village. Ideal for bird watching on nearby Cley and Blakeney Marshes, and near beaches such as Cromer, Sheringham and Wells. It is also within easy reach of Norwich and the Norfolk Broads. There are many places of historic interest to visit such as Sandringham and Holkham Hall. The house accommodates five people in three bedrooms. Cot available. Fully equipped except linen. Electricity £1 meter. Heating costs extra in winter. Sorry no pets. Terms from £70 to £230 per week. SAE or telephone for details to: **Mrs L. Thirtle, Rectory Road, Bodham, Holt NR25 6PR (01263 822274).**

HORNING. Mrs C.R. Saxelby, Silver Birches Holidays, Grebe Island, Lower Street, Horning, Norwich NR12 8PF (01692 630858). Fall in love with beautiful Broadland. Situated on a tranquil little island in private waterways off the River Bure, this peaceful retreat offers a spacious bungalow together with five houseboats and all-weather motor day launches. Rowing boats are available free of charge. Children and pets are most welcome. The waterways provide fishing and the keen angler will be able to go further afield and fish "Broadswide". The individual properties are surrounded by lawns with adjacent car parking area. Note: we provide one motor day launch adapted for wheelchair use and our bungalow also has a ramp leading to the property. Call **Cathy Saxelby** for further details.

HUNSTANTON. Mrs L.D. Poore, 3 Wodehouse Road, Old Hunstanton PE36 6JD (01485 534036). ♀♀♀ Near Royal Sandringham/Norfolk Lavender, 500 yards to beach, pubs and restaurants. The ground floor annexe has an airy open plan lounge with storage heater, feature pitch pine ceiling, kitchenette, breakfast bar and hallway, leading to double bedroom with en suite shower and loo. Fully equipped and finished to a high standard. A small garden totally enclosed by an ornamental wrought iron fence. Pets by arrangement. Covered drying area and private parking just outside. No steps, but the path is gravel. Birdwatching at Snettisham and Titchwell approximately six miles in either direction. The post office/village stores are approximately 600 yards. Weekly terms from £110 to £195.

Terms quoted in this publication may be subject to increase if rises in costs necessitate

THOMPSON BRANCASTER FARMS
Brancaster – North West Norfolk

Various properties sleep 2/15. Recently restored flint and brick farm cottages in beautiful countryside near the Norfolk coast. Various sizes available from cottages sleeping 4 people to a large Edwardian House for 14/15 people. All include central heating, open fires (logs provided). Mostly double glazed, modern kitchens and bathrooms with shower attachments and shaving points, colour TV, garden with Bar-B-Q and chairs. Payphone. Grass and all-weather tennis courts on estate, communal washing machines and tumble dryers. Prices are inclusive of electricity, linen and towels. Two miles away are sandy beaches for sailing and windsurfing also bird sanctuary and nature reserve.

Bookings: Telephone Sue on (0585) 269538 (Mobile Phone)
(Mon to Fri 3pm–8pm and Sat/Sun 11am–7pm

English Tourist Board
COMMENDED

HUNSTANTON. Upper and Lower Fieldsend, Homefields Road, Hunstanton PE36 5HL (01485 532593). Up to 𝖸𝖸𝖸𝖸 *COMMENDED*. Fieldsend is a large Edwardian carrstone house with Bed and Breakfast accommodation and two apartments, both sleeping five, one with superb panoramic sea views and the other with patio and garden. Both apartments have their own separate entrance, central heating, lounge with colour TV, kitchen and bathroom. Artistically decorated throughout, with interesting soft furnishings and paint effects yet retaining its original character. Linen, cots, high chairs provided. Fieldsend is within 10 minutes' walking distance of sandy beaches, swimming and golf and four minutes from the town centre. Sandringham, Norfolk Lavender, bird reserves, historic houses, craft centres, village pubs and gourmet restaurants are nearby. Contact **Mrs Sheila Tweedy Smith** for details.

LITTLE WALSINGHAM. Candlemas Cottage, 2 Guild Street, Little Walsingham NR22 6BU. Sleeps 6/8. Detached 18th century Grade II Listed Candlemaker's cottage of intriguing charm and character in unspoilt medieval shrine village, nestling amongst rolling countryside, within easy reach of pine-edged beaches, birdwatching, sailing, riding, Royal Sandringham, etc. Two sitting rooms, open fires (logs provided), colour TVs, books, beams. Dining room, breakfast room (Rayburn). Kitchen (dishwasher, fridge, freezer, electric cooker, washing machine). Three bedrooms; one twin, one double and one kingsize (converts to twins). Shower/toilet/basin/radiator, bath/toilet/basin/radiator. Small magical attic bedroom, sleeps two, up steep narrow stairs (not suitable for aged). Each room a cosy haven of curios, creativity, comfort. Secluded walled garden. Parking. House trained pet extra, children welcome but care taken please. From £190 per week Winter/Summer. Details **Valerie Goodsell, Candlemas Barns (next door) 01328 820748).**

MUNDESLEY near. The Cottage, Knapton. 𝖸𝖸𝖸 *APPROVED*. **Sleeps 9 plus.** Charming country home with beams and inglenook fireplace. Spacious and well appointed with sheltered sunny garden and patio, with views of open countryside. Knapton is a quiet village lying off the B1145 road from North Walsham to Mundesley and the cottage is one and a half miles from the sea and about eight miles from the Broads. Four double bedrooms, all with fitted washbasins and two with en-suite showers. Luxury kitchen/diningroom with dishwasher, etc. Utility room with automatic washing machine. Large sittingroom with colour TV. Terms from £300 to £525 per week. **Mrs A. Michaels, 23 Laura Dale Road, Fortis Green, London N2 9LT (0181-444 7678).**

FHG PUBLICATIONS LIMITED publish a large range of well-known accommodation guides. We will be happy to send you details or you can use the order form at the back of this book.

NORTH NORFOLK. Our comfortable, privately owned, family holiday chalet is situated on a small quiet site with many facilities on the outskirts of North Walsham. The chalet is fully equipped for four people and is well furnished with two bedrooms, colour TV, electric fire, etc., and faces west looking out onto trees and a large grassy area. It is within easy reach of many areas of outstanding natural beauty, stately homes, steam trains, sandy beaches, the pier at Cromer and Wroxham, the heart of the Norfolk Broads. Terms from £100 to £180 per week. For further details, please telephone **Mrs Ann Seal on 01689 837363 after 6pm.**

NORWICH. Mr Codling, Church Farm Guest House, 20 Church Street, Southrepps, Norwich NR11 8NP (01263 833248). British Tourist Board Category 3. Five delightful luxury cottages available in this charming village. Situated near the Church, all have the use of the grounds of Church Farm Guest House. Rose Cottage is suitable for the disabled as there is a ground floor bedroom, and ramps are provided for easy access of wheelchairs. All the cottages are centrally heated and have automatic washing machines. Two of the cottages have three bedrooms and the other three have two bedrooms. Children and pets are welcome, cot, high chair and stair gates provided if required. Linen hire extra on request. Fresh produce and pick-your-own fruit available at certain times of the year. Terms from £70. Winter breaks available.

SHERINGHAM. Flat 2, 16 Augusta Street, Sheringham. ♀ ♀ ♀ Sleeps 2/5/8. Self catering flat to let in the coastal resort of Sheringham. Children welcome. Available all year. For full details contact: **Mrs V.L. Muggeridge, "Laburnum", 8 Warren Close, High Kelling, Holt NR25 6QX (01263 712688 after 3pm).**

SWAFFHAM. Nar Valley Cottages. Sleep 4. Two charming detached cottages in the unspoilt village of

Westacre, each with its own secluded garden. Both are fully furnished with washing machine, colour TV, garden furniture, etc. Linen, heating and logs for the open fires are included. It is an excellent base for exploring West Norfolk with its many beaches, coastal villages, great houses, gardens, craft centres, wildlife parks, etc., and for sailing, golf, fishing or whatever. Well behaved pets are welcome. Weekly from £165 to £225 and Winter bookings from £30 per night. For brochure please telephone **(01760 755254).**

See also Colour Display Advertisement **THURNE. Hedera House and Plantation Bungalows, Thurne. Properties sleep 12.** Hedera House is a comfortably furnished Georgian style house which can sleep up to 12 people. Plantation Bungalows are a select group of individual holiday homes, roomy, comfortably furnished and carpeted. Colour TV in all properties. Beautiful beaches, Broads, villages and countryside all within easy motoring distance of Thurne. Fishing, boating, riding nearby. SAE to **Miss Carol Delf, Thurne Cottage, The Staithe, Thurne NR29 3BU (01692 670242 or 01493 844568).**

TOFT MONKS. Mrs I.B. Birt, Bay Cottage, Maypole Green, Toft Monks, Near Beccles NR34 0EY (01502 677405). Sleeps 4. Detached 19th-century boarded cottage on Maypole Green in a scattered rural parish. Open plan beamed lounge with colour TV, fully equipped kitchen/dining area. Shower room which includes washbasin and WC. Upstairs is bedroom with double bed and a second bedroom with full sized bunk beds. Carpeted throughout; electric heaters; table and bed linen supplied. Secluded garden. Pleasant country walks, five miles from Beccles and the River Waveney, 12 miles from Great Yarmouth, 16 miles from Norwich. £90 to £130 weekly. Further particulars on application.

WELLS-NEXT-THE-SEA. Brig Square Holiday Cottages, Freeman Street, Wells-next-the-Sea. Cottages sleep 2/8; Bungalows/Maisonettes sleep 2/3. Charming group of cottages and bungalows set in attractive square — some listed buildings dating to 17th century. Situated in small, pleasant fishing port on north Norfolk coast between Hunstanton (16 miles) and Cromer (18 miles). Beautiful sandy beach, pine wood walks, fishing, riding and boat trips. Cottages have been completely modernised, some retaining old beams and character, some with central heating. Fully furnished, provided with all amenities to comply with EATB. Maximum sleeping capacity eight. Cot, high chair, colour TV. Communal laundry room available. Car parking within square. Close to shops, quayside and beach. Everything supplied except linen. Sorry, no pets. Open all year. Further details on request. **Mr R. Hewitt, 5 Brig Square, Freeman Street, Wells-next-the-Sea NR23 1BA (01328 710440).**

**If you've found
FARM HOLIDAY GUIDES
of service please tell your friends**

WINTERTON-ON-SEA. Timbers, The Lane, Winterton-on-Sea. Sleeps 5. Comfortable, well-furnished ground floor flat in timber cottage, situated in quiet seaside village, just eight miles north of Great Yarmouth. Broad sandy beach and sand dunes (Nature Reserve) for pleasant walks. Three miles from Norfolk Broads (boating and fishing). Flat is carpeted throughout, and fully equipped for self-catering family holiday. Ideal for children, and pets welcome. One double, one twin-bedded room and one small single bedroom. Sleeps five plus cot. Bed linen provided, and maid service every other day for general cleaning. Attractive beamed sittingroom with colour TV. Secluded garden. Car parking. Available May to September. Terms £140 to £300 per week. For full details write to: **Mr M.J. Isherwood, 79 Oakleigh Avenue, London N20 9JG (0181-445 2192).**

WIVETON. Laneway Cottage, Wiveton, Holt. This lovely flint cottage, which is all on one floor, faces south, with a flint-walled garden with garden furniture. The large sittingroom with open fire and colour TV opens out onto a patio. It has one double and one twin bedroom with fitted carpets and cupboards, and is fully equipped for four people. Kitchen/dining room with fitted units, electric cooker, Aga and fridge. Utility room with washing machine. Cloakroom with shower, toilet and washbasin, bathroom with washbasin and WC. Oil-fired central heating. Telephone. Garage and parking area. Contact: **Mrs C. Joice, Colkirk Hall, Fakenham NR21 7ND (01328 862261).**

NORTHAMPTONSHIRE

BRACKLEY. Richard and Pauline Harrison, Walltree House Farm, Steane, Brackley NH13 5NS (01295 811235; Fax: 01295 811147). ♀♀♀♀ COMMENDED. **Sleep 2/4/6.** Overlooking lawns and mature trees in a courtyard of converted farm buildings and stables adjacent to the farmhouse. In the middle of our arable farm with woods and nature trails to explore, our cosy cottages are fully equipped to a very high standard. The 24 hour heating has individually controlled radiators and electricity and all linen is inclusive. Although we are in the middle of nowhere we are at the centre of everything. Shopping, leisure centres, golf, fishing, stately homes, Oxford, Warwick Castle, Blenheim, etc., are all easily accessible. Good restaurants and pubs nearby. Ample parking. Barbecue. Bed and Breakfast is available. Easy access to M40 Junctions 10 and 11. Weekly terms from £220 to £460. Access and Visa accepted.

NORTH NORTHAMPTONSHIRE. Sleeps 4/6. The Garden House at historic Southwick Hall is three miles north of Oundle. Accommodation — one double, one twin-bedded room, plus bed settee; cot available. Bathroom; cloakroom; kitchen/diner; large sittingroom with open fire and TV. Central heating. Ample parking and access to large grounds. Everything supplied except linen/towels. Sorry no pets. Six other stately homes, Nene Valley Railway, Rutland Water and Country Parks within 15 miles. Available from April. Terms £120 to £140 plus electricity and fuel. Further details from **W.J. Richardson (Manager), Stable Cottage, Southwick Hall, Peterborough PE8 5BL (01832 274064).**

NORTHAMPTONSHIRE – WHAT TO DO AND SEE!

Rolling farmland and woods contrasted against industrial towns such as Corby and Kettering, this is what makes up Northamptonshire. The canal centre at Stoke Bruerne, the coloured stone church at Stanford-on-Avon and the country parks at Barnwell and Irchester all make for interesting visits.

NORTHUMBERLAND

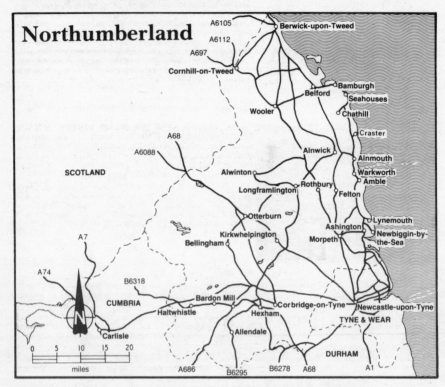

Northumberland

ALNMOUTH. Sheila and Gordon Inkster, Marine House Private Hotel, 1 Marine Road, Alnmouth NE66 2RW (01665 830349). ♀ ♀ ♀ *HIGHLY COMMEN-DED.* **Sleeps 4 adults; 2 children.** This cottage, expertly converted from a coach house and hay loft, stands next to the main building. It faces a nine hole golf links and sea, ensuring uninterrupted panoramic views. Alnmouth is an excellent centre for exploring the magnificent Northumbrian coastline with its castles, wildlife sanctuaries and white sandy beaches. The Cheviot Hills and Roman Wall are within easy reach by car. The cottage has one double, one twin-bedded and one small room with three-foot bunk beds (Z-bed or cot available). Shower room, toilet and vanity basin; Tudor style lounge/diningroom with colour TV; kitchen with electric cooker, fridge, iron. No linen supplied. Metered (50p) electricity. Parking. Pets permitted. Shops 200 yards; regular bus service. Guests may use hotel facilities. Evening Dinner and packed lunches can be ordered. Weekly terms from Low Season from £207 to £288; High Season from £256 to £448.

ALNMOUTH. Mrs A. Stanton, Mount Pleasant Farm, Alnmouth, Alnwick NE66 3BY (01665 830215).

Mount Pleasant is situated on top of a hill on the outskirts of the seaside village of Alnmouth with spectacular views of surrounding countryside. We offer fresh air, sea breezes, green fields, beautiful beaches, country roads and peace and quiet. There are two golf courses and a river meanders around the farm with all its bird life. Convenient for historic castles, Holy Island, the Farnes and the Cheviots. The farmhouse has an annexe which is self contained with open plan kitchen, shower room and sleeps two adults and one child. From £120 to £150 per week.

ALNWICK. Mrs V. Purvis, Titlington Hall Farm, Alnwick NE66 2EB (01665 578253). ♀♀♀♀

COMMENDED. **Sleep 2-10.** Two lovely country cottages available for holiday lets all year round. They are situated in a quiet and beautiful area with many interesting places just a short drive away. Facilities include central heating, TV, fridge, microwave, washing machine, tumble dryer, and linen. Children welcome. Pets by arrangement. Prices from £155 to £295 per week.

BELFORD. Mrs J.B. Sutherland, Ross Farm, Belford NE70 7EN (01668 213336; Fax: 01668 213174). ♀♀♀♀ up to *HIGHLY COMMENDED.* Working farm. Sleeps 2/4/5/6/11. Good cottages at Ross Farm and good cottages and farmhouse at Outchester Farm, both working farms, in superb countryside between Bamburgh and Holy Island, one mile from Budle Bay which is part of the Lindisfarne National Nature Reserve. Access to magnificent stretches of clean, sandy beach. All the properties are comfortably furnished, well heated and fully equipped. Colour TV. Children welcome. Linen and towels supplied. Ample car parking space. Sorry, no pets. From £120 to £625 per week. Please write or phone for a brochure.

BELFORD. 4 Church Street, Belford. Sleeps 5/6. Small Listed town house (stone and slate) with small walled garden in centre of attractive small town of Belford. Comprises twin bedded room with single off and one double bedroom; sittingroom, hallway; diningroom; kitchen, bathroom/WC. Fully equipped including electric cooker, gas central heating, colour TV. Pillows and duvets provided. Berwick and Alnwick 13 miles, Bamburgh and Holy Island under 10 miles. Terms from £180 to £240 per week. Bookings to **Mr L. Tait, 7 Church Street, Belford NE70 7LS (01668 213811). If no answer ring J.M. Clark's office on 01434 320363.**

BENDON MILL. The Old Vicarage, Beltingham, Bendon Mill. ♀♀♀♀ *HIGHLY COMMENDED.* A Grade

II Listed property, idyllically situated in one of Northumberland's most beautiful hamlets surrounded by the magnificent South Tyne countryside and on the edge of the National Park. This cosy, centrally heated house comprises two double rooms, three twin rooms; bathroom, shower room; living room, dining room; kitchen; games room. Ideal for two families or small groups. Concessions for small numbers. Dogs welcome. Facilities include washing machine, tumble dryer, dishwasher, microwave, fridge/freezer, small barbecue. Linen provided. Electricity and fuel included. Please contact **Dr and Mrs R. Nelson, Four Gables, Brampton, Cumbria CA8 2HZ (01697 72635).**

NORTHUMBERLAND – BORDER COUNTRY!
You cannot go any further north and remain in England! There is much outstanding scenery, both inland and on the coast, and a host of interesting places to visit. Border Forest Park has everything you would expect, plus many interesting Roman remains. There are also remains at Housesteads and other places of interest include Lindisfarne, the "conserved" village of Blanchland, Hexham, Heatherslaw Mill and Craster.

BYRNESS. A well equipped former Forester's home, providing an ideal centre for touring Northumberland, Borders, Kielder, Hadrian's Wall. Situated on the Pennine Way surrounded by the Cheviot and Simonside Hills, with the magnificent coastline only a short drive away. Accommodation comprises three bedrooms — one double, one with three single beds, and the third with one single bed and bunk beds. Bathroom; lounge, dining room; kitchen; drying room. Facilities include central heating, washing machine, fridge/freezer, microwave, colour TV. Terms from £120 per week. Available all year. Short Break details available. Further information contact: **Mr and Mrs I. Leslie, 9 Farne Avenue, Gosforth, Newcastle-upon-Tyne NE3 2BJ (0191 285 3538).**

CORBRIDGE. Mr F.J. Matthews, The Hayes, Newcastle Road, Corbridge NE45 5LP (01434

632010). ♀♀ *COMMENDED*. Spacious attractive stone-built guesthouse. Set in seven acres of grounds. Single, double, twin, family bedrooms, all with tea/coffee making facilities, two with showers. Lounge and dining rooms. Open 11 months of the year. Bed and Breakfast £16. Children's reductions. Stair lift for disabled guests. Also self catering properties — three cottages, flat and caravan. Awarded two Farm Holiday Guide Diplomas. Car parking. Brochure/booking, SAE or phone.

HADRIAN'S WALL. Mark Chaplin, Hadrian Lodge, Mindshield Moss, North Road, Haydon Bridge NE47 6NF (01434 688688). Sleeps 1-6. A recent conversion of a former hunting and fishing lodge in the heart of Hadrian's Wall country. Self catering accommodation comprises three well equipped stone-built cottages set around a secluded courtyard garden. Hadrian Lodge makes the ideal base from which to explore Hadrian's Wall and the beautiful North Pennines. Set in lush pastureland above Haydon Bridge, Hadrian Lodge provides a social environment with a large residents' lounge/bar, a games room and free trout fishing on our own lake. Only two miles from both Vindolanda Museum and Housteads Roman Fort. Rates from £100 to £280 per week. Brochure available, please phone.

HALTWHISTLE. Mr J.M. Clark, Featherstone Castle, Haltwhistle NE49 0JG. I can offer at HALT-

WHISTLE, two cottages — Horse Close (illustrated) and Greenriggs. Both sleep five to six. Haltwhistle is five miles, Alston 12 miles and Carlisle and Hexham 20 miles. Scottish Borders, Solway Coast, Lake District, Kielder and Durham City all within one hour. Both are traditional stone and slate shepherd's cottages remotely situated above the South Tyne Valley with garden area, sittingroom with log fire and kitchen with electric cooker and open fire, off peak background heating. Horse Close has three small bedrooms, bathroom/WC upstairs and a separate WC downstairs. Greenriggs has two large bedrooms, downstairs bathroom/WC and front and back porch/lobby. Black and white TV. Pillows and duvets are provided. Terms £175 to £225. Bookings to **Mr J. Rutherford, Featherstone Castle, Haltwhistle (01434 320202). If no answer ring J.M. Clark's office on 01434 320363.**

HEXHAM near. R.A. & A.G. Dodsworth, Station House, Catton, Allendale, Near Hexham NE47 9QF

(01434 683362). ♀♀♀ *APPROVED*. **Sleeps up to 6.** Station House was the terminal station of the Hexham to Allendale Railway, closed in 1950. The Flat is the ground floor front of Station House and is made up of the former Station Master's Office, Staff Room, Booking Office and Waiting Room. Facing south west the rooms are in a line with the second bedroom opening out of the first: Bedroom 1 — two singles, Bedroom 2 — two singles plus full size double bunk; living room with open fire, colour TV; kitchen with electric cooker, microwave, washing machine; bathroom with shower. Central heating by storage heaters included in weekly charge. Electricity for cooking, lighting, etc by meter reading. Weekly terms from £100 to £150. Brochure available.

KIELDER WATER LAKE. Mrs Joyce Gaskin, Lyndale, Bellingham, Near Kielder Water, Hexham

NE48 2AW (01434 220361). ♀♀♀♀ *COMMENDED*. Our charming cottage with lovely views stands just off the main square of Bellingham, a village set in unspoiled rural splendour amidst splendid moorland and scenery. Make a visit to Wallington Hall and Cragside, both National Trust properties; enjoy a cruise on the lake or walk on Hadrian's Wall. There are many attractions locally including good pubs, shops, bowling, golf, fishing, pony trekking, watersports, swimming, sauna. A good walking area — we are on the Pennine Way (famous 175-mile walk). Weekly terms £220 to £370. Providing garage or parking, colour TV, washer/dryer, microwave, linen. A warm welcome awaits you in this extremely well furnished property including a table set with candles, fruit and wine.

ROTHBURY. Mrs H. Farr, Lorbottle West Steads, Thropton, Morpeth NE65 7JT (01665 574672).

♀♀♀ *COMMENDED.* **Working farm. Sleeps 5.** Semi-detached newly modernised cottage on 320 acre mixed farm, lying in the beautiful Whittingham Vale, surrounded by peaceful rolling hills and unspoilt countryside, four and a half miles Rothbury. Double glazed, full gas central heating and fire. Well equipped modern kitchen. Cooking by electricity (included in price), own parking and back garden. Panoramic views from all windows. Colour TV. Very central and ideal for visiting all parts of Northumbria. Gas by meter reading. Children allowed to look around the farm. Alnwick 15, Border region 25, Kielder Water and Hadrian's Wall 30 miles. All bed linen supplied. Single, twin and double beds. No dogs please (sheep nearby). Details on request.

ROTHBURY. "The Lodge", Whitton Grange, Rothbury. ♀♀♀♀ *COMMENDED.* **Sleeps 6 plus.** The

Lodge, originally the stone-built coach house of Whitton Grange, has recently been converted and entirely modernised to provide a delightful family holiday home. Accommodation comprises large sittingroom, a dining area and a fully fitted kitchen including dishwasher and all the equipment you will require; WC and a storage area containing a washing machine; three bedrooms (two twins and one double); bathroom and WC. Centrally heated throughout. All linen, bedding and towels supplied. Colour TV and video. Children welcome, cot and high chair can be arranged. Dogs welcome, kennels provided. Terms from £200 to £400 per week. Brochure available. Contact: **R.E. Thorn Esq., Whitton Grange, Rothbury, Via Morpeth NE65 7RL (01669 620929).**

STOCKSFIELD. The Old Bakery Cottages. Sleep 2/3/4. The three cottages are completely renovated and modernised, in the village of Stocksfield which lies in the heart of Thomas Bewick Country. They have extensive views over a picturesque area of the Tyne Valley close to the historic village of Carbridge with Hexham Abbey and Hadrian's Wall within easy reach. Included in other local attractions are two new golf courses at Slaley and Matfen, and Europe's largest shopping complex is 30 minutes' drive away. Open from January to December. Prices from £150 to £250 per week. Apply **Mr and Mrs Bolton, 56 New Ridley Road, Stocksfield NE43 7EE (01661 843217).**

WOOLER. Kimmerston Country Holidays, Kimmerston Cottage, Wooler (01668 216283). Kimmer-

THE BRITISH HORSE SOCIETY

APPROVED RIDING ESTABLISHMENT

ston Cottages, suitable for riding holidays, are situated on Kimmerston Farm, close to a quiet country road with a breathtaking view of the Cheviot Hills. There is a riding school on the farm for beginners and experts alike; trout and salmon fishing can be easily arranged. The area boasts many hills and links golf courses, and the nearby Cheviots can offer challenging hikes. Ford Castle is a 15 minute walk, and Bamburgh Castle, Holy Island and the Farne Islands are all less than a 25-minute drive. In the evening visitors can walk to the local pub, or drive to any of the fine hotels and restaurants in the area. Babysitters can usually be arranged. Facilities in the cottages include colour TV and washing machine. Pets welcome. Terms from £120 to £280 per week. Contact **Dickie and Jane Jeffreys** at above.

NOTTINGHAMSHIRE

CROPWELL BUTLER. The Old Coach House, The Green, Cropwell Butler. Sleeps 2/4. The Old Coach House is a newly converted cottage offering quality accommodation in a quiet conservation village. Nottingham 10 miles, Leicester 18 miles, Grantham 16 miles and Newark 12 miles; an ideal base from which to visit many places of interest including Belvoir Castle, Newark Castle, Sherwood Forest Country Park and lots more. Terms from £120 to £250 per week. Open all year. Short Breaks available. Bed and Breakfast accommodation also available. Please send for our brochure giving full details, apply **Mrs Walker, The Court, Cropwell Butler NG12 3AD. (0115 9334731).**

MANSFIELD. Mr and Mrs Bennett, Bridleways Guest House, Newlands Road, Forest Town, Mansfield NG19 0HU (01623 635725).

PLOUGHMAN'S COTTAGE — that special place for that special person. Set in three acres, surrounded by bridlepaths — near enough to civilization yet far enough away to forget it. Delightful country cottage with two bedrooms one of which has four-poster; luxury bathroom (gold fittings); fully fitted oak-panelled kitchen; family size lounge with TV and video. Disabled access. Prices from £250 per week or £50 per night. Brochure available.

OXFORDSHIRE

BURFORD. Park House Lodge, Burford. ♀ ♀ ♀ *COMMENDED.* **Sleeps 2.**

Charming Cotswold cottage in lovely grounds of 17th century property, ideal centre for touring an area rich in history and natural beauty. The Lodge is quiet and secluded, only minutes from good shops, restaurants and inns. The warm, comfortable accommodation comprises twin bedroom; bathroom with bath, shower, WC; beamed sittingroom; pine-fitted kitchen/diner with electric cooker and fridge. Night storage heaters in all rooms; fitted carpets, TV and telephone. Bed linen and towels provided free. Private access and parking. Regret, no pets. Terms £140 to £260. **Kennard, Park House, 34 Witney Street, Burford OX8 4SN (Tel & Fax: 01993 823460).**

BURFORD. Manor Cottages, Village Farm, Little Barrington, Burford OX18 4TE (01451 844643; Fax: 01451 844607).

Set in some of the prettiest villages in England, our properties are all furnished to a high standard whilst retaining their essential character. Their rural location in unrivalled scenery will ensure a relaxing stay, whether driving to nearby places of interest or discovering the countryside on foot. Rolling hills dotted with sheep, villages of natural golden stone, historic houses and local heritage combine to give the Cotswolds their unique charm. Add this to the surrounding towns of Oxford, Stratford-upon-Avon, Cheltenham and Bath — you can see why we think you'll like it! We are a small company and can give individual help with the selection of your cottage. Free brochure.

PLEASE ENCLOSE A STAMPED ADDRESSED ENVELOPE WITH ENQUIRIES

COTSWOLD RETREATS

for comfortable self-catering holidays
and short breaks in peaceful locations.
Sleep 2-10, C.H., open fires, gardens,
Pets and children welcome.
call Sue: 01608 684310 or Paula: 01608 737222

COTSWOLDS. Hill View Cottage, Swinbrook, Oxford OX18 4EF (01993 823440). Sleeps 3. At village edge in the beautiful Windrush Valley, this 18th century stone cottage was recently renovated providing comfortable accommodation for three people. Adjoining owner's cottage in peaceful garden setting, it is ideally situated for exploring the Cotswolds. Nearest shops at Burford, three miles. Accommodation comprises (downstairs) well equipped kitchen/dinette leading to single bedroom and bathroom; upstairs the large, bright double bed/sittingroom with lovely views is well furnished. Colour TV, washing machine. Weekly rates include linen but not towels. Children and pets by arrangement. Parking space. Heating by night store heaters; electricity paid by meter reading. SAE, or telephone, for further details.

See also Colour Display Advertisement

COTSWOLDS. Culworth Manor Cottages, Culworth. ♟♟♟♟ *HIGHLY COMMENDED.* Quietly situated overlooking the village green, these charming Grade II Listed Cottages adjoin the owner's historic 17th century Manor House where Charles I stayed in 1644 during the English Civil War. Traditionally furnished, Cavaliers Cottage is warm and cosy, sleeps four and offers every amenity including a four-poster bed. Also next door, and beautifully renovated in 1995, is the Old Dairy which sleeps five. Set amidst rolling countryside with far reaching views. The Cotswolds, Oxford, Woodstock, Warwick and Stratford-upon-Avon are all within easy reach. Open all year. Terms from £100 to £360. Short Breaks available. Illustrated brochure on request. **Mrs Beth Soar, Culworth Manor, Culworth OX17 2BB (01295 760099; Fax: 01295 760098).**

SHROPSHIRE

BISHOP'S CASTLE. Walcot Hall, Lydbury North, Bishop's Castle. Flats sleep 4/9. Spacious flats at Stately Home. Secluded location in own grounds; splendid scenery and ideal area for peaceful holiday for young and old. All flats fully furnished and recently decorated, and sleep four/nine. Larger parties by arrangement. Village shop half-a-mile; local market towns, castles, villages and hill country of the Border Counties provide opportunities for exploration and walking. Boats and bicycles available; riding locally. Coarse fishing available in pools and Lake. Terms from £182 to £287. **Mrs M. Smith, 41 Cheval Place, London SW7 1EW (0171-581 2782).**

CHURCH STRETTON. Mr D.V. Jones, Ley Hill Farm, Cardington SY6 7LA (01694 771366). Sleeps 4. Newly built stone annexe to farmhouse, equipped and furnished to highest standard, set in area of outstanding natural beauty. Apartment has double bedroom and sittingroom (including TV and bed settee) upstairs facing south with panoramic views towards Caer Caradoc Hill and Wenlock Edge; downstairs bathroom and fully equipped fitted kitchen including washing machine. Ceramic tiled floors downstairs, fitted carpets upstairs. Oil central heating system, self controlled. Double glazed. Separate entrance. No pets. No smoking. £90 to £150 per week (inclusive of fuel and linen). Also at farm, small caravan site with toilet block and electric hook-ups.

CRAVEN ARMS near. The Riddings Cottage, Newcastle-on-Clun, Near Craven Arms. Sleeps 6 plus cot. Cottage stands in an acre of rough ground, facing south, with glorious views down a wide valley to Radnor Forest. Within easy reach of historic Montgomery, Ludlow (castles and fine half-timbered houses), Offa's Dyke, Clun Castle and various ancient British hill forts. Fishing, pony trekking in area. All main windows double glazed. Accommodation for six in three double bedrooms; cot; bathroom, toilet; sittingroom; diningroom/kitchen (fully equipped). Everything supplied except linen. 50p coin-operated slot meter for electric heating and domestic use. Wood-burning stove in kitchen/diner. There is one shop at Newcastle-on-Clun four miles away and other shops at Clun and Newtown, eight miles away. Car essential, garage. Pets permitted on request. Available between April and November, but we're not allowed to exceed a total of 139 days, so first come first served. Terms from £95 to £135 per week. SAE, please to **Mrs N.J. Monk, The Vicarage, Verwood Close, Park North, Swindon, Wiltshire SN3 2LE (01793 611473).**

LUDLOW. Mrs S.D. Hall, The Leighs, Richard's Castle, Near Ashford Bowdler, Ludlow SY8 4DL (01584 831200). Sleeps 4. Cottage three miles from the

historic town of Ludlow on the beautiful borders of South Shropshire and North Herefordshire. Centrally placed for visits of historic interest including the castles of Ludlow, Stokesay Croft and Richard's Castle. Situated on a small farm in quiet countryside away from public roads, the comfortable cottage with exposed beams is fully furnished and carpeted throughout. The accommodation sleeps four persons and has a large lounge/diner with woodburning stove and TV. The fully equipped kitchenette has hot and cold water, the shower room/WC has electric shower and shaver point. Cot and high chair available. Ample parking space. Open all year round. £130 to £150 including electricity, fuel and linen.

LUDLOW. R.E. Meredith, The Avenue, Ashford Carbonell, Ludlow SY8 4DA (01584 831616). ♀♀♀ *APPROVED.* **Sleeps 6.** Spacious self-contained flat in large attractive country residence set in its own quiet grounds on edge of village three miles from historic Ludlow. With easy access by wide outside staircase, the flat affords excellent views and is furnished to a high standard of comfort. Two double, one twin bedrooms; bathroom/WC; fully equipped kitchen/diner, electric cooker, fridge, automatic washing machine, microwave; lounge; colour TV; cot/high chair. Electric fires, immersion heater by meter; full night storage central heating by separate meter. Ample parking and private lawn. Linen and garage on request. Open all year. HETB registered, Holiday Homes Approval Scheme Approved. Terms on request.

LUDLOW. Hazel Cottage, Duxmoor, Onibury, Craven Arms. ♀♀♀♀ *HIGHLY COMMENDED.* **Sleeps 4.** Beautifully restored semi-detached, yet private, period cottage, set in its own extensive cottage garden with drive and ample parking space. It has panoramic views of the surrounding countryside and is situated five miles north of historic Ludlow. The cottage comprises a comfortable livingroom with colour TV, radio and telephone, diningroom, fully equipped kitchen, hall, bathroom, two bedrooms (one double and one twin-bedded) with washbasins. Electric central heating throughout. All linen included. No pets. The cottage retains all the original features having been decorated traditionally and furnished with antiques throughout. Tourist information. Winter Breaks. Terms from £130 to £300 per week. **Mrs Rachel Sanders, Duxmoor Farm, Onibury, Craven Arms SY7 9BQ (01584 856342).**

LUDLOW. Miss H. Morris, Coldoak Cottages, Snitton Lane, Knowbury, Ludlow SY8 3LB (01584 890491). ♀♀♀ *COMMENDED.* A traditional stone semi-

detached cottage, set in beautiful, quiet surroundings 130 yards from the road. South facing with panoramic views of Herefordshire and Wales. Large attractive garden with sitting out area. Ample parking space. Cottage sleeps five in one double, one twin bedded and one single room. Two small beamed sitting rooms with TV and radio. Bathroom with W.C. and shower; shower/toilet on ground floor. Very well equipped large kitchen with fridge/freezer, microwave, electric cooker with fan oven, automatic washer, spindryer. Pay phone. Milk and paper delivery. Bed linen, tea cloths, tablecloths and towels provided. Domestic electricity by 50p meter. Pets by arrangement. Terms weekly £185 high season, £170 low season.

NEWCASTLE ON CLUN. Mr and Mrs J.K. Goslin, The Riddings Firs, Crossways, Newcastle-on-Clun, Craven Arms SY7 8OT (01686 670467). Sleeps 2 adults, 3 children. Ideal holiday location on the Welsh Borders, at 1300 feet, in an area designated as being of Outstanding Natural Beauty. For those seeking complete peace and relaxation, this attractive self-catering family accommodation, suitable for four to five people, is in a self-contained traditional farmhouse annexe with own private entrance. Fully equipped and attractively furnished including colour TV, wood burning stove. Open plan arrangement comprises one double, two bunk beds and bed settee; electric cooker, fridge, etc,; shower, toilet, washbasin. Children especially welcome. Pleasantly situated in excellent walking country; several interesting market towns, hospitable inns with dining facilities, Castle within easy reach. Pony trekking and trout fishing can be arranged; area is suitable for mountain bikes. Grazing available for visitors' ponies. No pets. Babysitting available. Self-catering terms from £80 per week. Linen supplied at extra cost if required. Out of season and weekend visitors welcome.

OSWESTRY. David and Hilda Arnott, Coed-Y-Go Holiday Centre, Morda, Oswestry SY10 9AD

(01691 656037). Unique development that tastefully blends olde worlde charm with modern comforts. The centre is open all year round and situated amongst rolling hills on the Welsh border, one and a half miles from the market town of Oswestry. Ideal for touring; north and mid Wales coasts about one and a half hours' drive. Attractive terraced cottages, all with two bedrooms, sleep four/six; farmhouse can be divided into three or used communally by group of up to 20; barn (eight bedrooms) suitable for group of up to 24. All fully equipped except linen. Site facilities include newly built conference hall, games room, shop, crazy golf park, children's play areas, barbecue area and equipment, telephone, etc. Please write or telephone for brochure and full tariff.

SHREWSBURY, Burlton. Sleeps 4/6. Enjoy a relaxed break in our delightful "Jemima's Cottage" set in

lovely surroundings. Conveniently situated for Shrewsbury (eight miles), Ellesmere Lakes (seven miles), Ironbridge, Chester, Hawkstone Park and many other places of interest. "Jemima's" was originally the Dairy Cottage and was lovingly restored four years ago. It is extremely comfortable and convenient, has a pretty garden with patio furniture, and accommodates guests in two bedrooms, two bathrooms, large sitting/dining room, and fitted kitchen. The owners live nearby and will extend a warm welcome and do all they can to make your holiday enjoyable. Children welcome. Sorry, no animals. Terms from £130 to £240 per week; cleaning extra if required (£10). Electricity included in price, also all linen except towels. Brochure available. **Mrs E.J. Martin, The Grove, Burlton, Shrewsbury SY4 5SZ (01939 270310).**

Key to Tourist Board Ratings

The Crown Scheme
(England, Scotland & Wales)

Covering hotels, motels, private hotels, guesthouses, inns, bed & breakfast, farmhouses. Every Crown classified place to stay is inspected annually. *The classification:* Listed then 1-5 Crown indicates the range of facilities and services. Higher quality standards are indicated by the terms APPROVED, COMMENDED, HIGHLY COMMENDED and DELUXE.

The Key Scheme
(also operates in Scotland using a Crown symbol)

Covering self-catering in cottages, bungalows, flats, houseboats, houses, chalets, etc. Every Key classified holiday home is inspected annually. *The classification:* 1-5 Key indicates the range of facilities and equipment. Higher quality standards are indicated by the terms APPROVED, COMMENDED, HIGHLY COMMENDED and DELUXE.

The Q Scheme
(England, Scotland & Wales)

Covering holiday, caravan, chalet and camping parks. Every Q rated park is inspected annually for its quality standards. The more √ in the Q – up to 5 – the higher the standard of what is provided.

SOMERSET

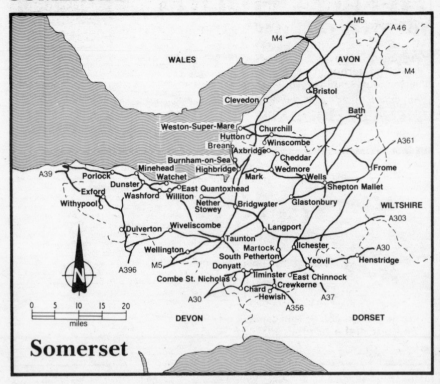

Somerset

BLUE ANCHOR. Keepers Cottage, Chapel Cleeve, Near Minehead. Sleeps 6 adults, 2 children. This large Edwardian cottage is situated in Chapel Cleeve, 10 minutes' walk from beach at Blue Anchor and six miles from Minehead. Marvellous views of Brendon Hills, secluded quarter acre garden. The cottage has recently been renovated but retains many original features. Full central heating, fitted kitchen with oven/hob, fridge/freezer, washer/dryer; dining room with patio doors to garden; sitting room with log effect gas fire; lounge with colour TV and video; bathroom includes electric shower; three spacious bedrooms — double, twin and family, cot available. Payphone. No smokers. Pets by arrangement. £180 to £320 per week including fuel, linen extra. Contact **Mrs R.E.M. Holden, Trotter Cottage, Lower Warborough, Swindon, Wiltshire SN4 0AT (Tel & Fax: 01793 790578).**

SOMERSET – THE CREAM AND CIDER COUNTY!

Wookey Hole, the great cave near Wells, is the first known home of man in Great Britain. Other places of interest in this green and hilly county include The Mendips, Exmoor National Park, Cheddar Gorge, Meare Lake Village and The Somerset Rural Life Museum. The villages and wildlife of the Quantocks, Poldens and Brendons should not be missed.

BURNHAM-ON-SEA near. Mrs W. Baker, Withy Grove Farm, East Huntspill, Near Burnham-on-Sea TA9 3NP (01278 784471). Properties sleep 4/6.

Come and enjoy a relaxing and friendly holiday "Down on the Farm" set in beautiful Somerset countryside. Peaceful rural setting adjoining River Huntspill, famed for its coarse fishing. The farm is ideally situated for visiting the many local attractions including Cheddar Gorge, Glastonbury, Weston-super-Mare and the lovely sandy beaches of Burnham-on-Sea. Self catering Barns and Cottages are tastefully converted sleeping four/six. Fully equipped including colour TV. Facilities also include heated swimming pool, licensed bar and entertainment in high season, games room, skittle alley. Reasonable rates. Please write or telephone for further details.

BURNHAM-ON-SEA. Chapel Cottage, Church Road, Brean, Burnham-on-Sea. Sleeps 5 plus cot.

Large comfortably furnished and well equipped cottage sleeping five adults in three bedrooms in popular coastal holiday village. Pleasant views to Mendip Hills. Convenient for shops and access to flat sandy beach. Electric heating and cooking. Linen provided. Cot available. Safe car parking. Pets by arrangement. Excellent base for exploring tourist attractions of Weston-super-Mare, Bath, Wells, Cheddar, Taunton and cider country by car or coach. This accommodation particularly enjoyed by the over 40's. Personal supervision. Midweek bookings welcome. Terms £200 to £300 weekly including electricity. SAE for brochure. **Mrs M. Hicks, Ataraxia, Church Road, Brean, Burnham-on-Sea TA8 2SF (01278 751626).**

CATCOTT. Mrs Eileen Chilcott, 5 Langland Lane, Catcott, Bridgwater TA7 9HR (01278 722085).

M5 six miles, midway Wells/Quantocks, edge of Levels; waterfowl, bird watching (particularly winter/spring), coast 11 miles, coarse fishing two miles; quiet picturesque village. Shop; hairdresser; play area; two pubs serving good food. Homely, comfortable three bedroomed bungalow sleeps five plus, all beds have king size duvets, electric blankets, matching curtains. Lounge with open fire (logs free), colour TV. Night storage central heating and immersion heaters. All electricity by slot meter. Payphone. Bathroom with shower over bath, washbasin and toilet. Kitchen with dishwasher, washing machine, full cooker, microwave, fridge, etc. All linen, towels, etc supplied. Children welcome, cot available. Pets by arrangement. Large garden, patio set and barbecue. Off road parking. Terms from £100 to £225.

CHARD. Andrew and Kay Clegg, Pulleys Barn, Wambrook, Near Chard TA20 3DF (01460 62583).

This delightful Victorian Barn is situated in an area of outstanding natural beauty. The tiny hamlet of Wambrook is two miles from Chard, 14 miles from Lyme Regis with its beach and picturesque harbour. The accommodation adjoins the main barn and comprises double gallery bedroom, twin bedroom, bathroom, fully fitted kitchen, sittingroom with woodburning stove; french doors to patio; garden furniture for guests to relax and enjoy views of hills and countryside. The pub with its excellent food is within walking distance. Prices from £145 to £245 inclusive of bed linen and electricity. Out of season Short Breaks. Regret no pets.

CHARD. Mrs Karen Ousley, Barnfields, Parrocks Lane, Tatworth, Chard TA20 2PB (01460 220817). Situated just off the A358 two and a half miles south of Chard. Kennels converted into a two bedroom detached bungalow on a working smallholding 20 minutes from M5 and 20 minutes from the Devon/Dorset coast. Close to Cricket St. Thomas Park, Forde Abbey and Yeovilton Air Museum, very good village amenities (butcher's, grocer's, post office, etc); there is also a very good old pub just down the road serving excellent food. Accommodation comprises one double bedroom, one single bedroom (upstairs) and a bed settee in the lounge; cot; dining room; kitchen with cooker, fridge, etc; shower room with toilet and basin. Central heating. Duvets and pillows supplied, bed linen can be hired. Children and pets welcome. Open April to October. Terms from £145 to £250.

CHARD. Mrs Guppy, Hornsbury Hill Farm, Chard TA20 3DB (01460 65516). Situated on the main A358 road, one and a quarter miles from Chard, this detached farmhouse makes an ideal centre for touring Somerset, Devon and Dorset. The accommodation comprises three double bedrooms, lounge with colour TV, diningroom, kitchen with fridge, cooker etc. Bathroom downstairs with hot and cold water. Cot available, babysitting if required. Several lovely coastal resorts approximately 12 miles away; Cricket St. Thomas Wildlife Park three miles; Forde Abbey Gardens four miles; Arts and Crafts Museum quarter of a mile. General Store just down the road. Ample parking. Open Easter to October. Children and pets welcome. Terms from £180 to £210 per week.

CHEDDAR. Mrs K. Thompson, "Hillside", Venns Gate, Cheddar BS27 3LW (01934 742493). 👑👑👑

COMMENDED. **Sleeps 2/4.** Four comfortable, well maintained holiday cottages in converted barn and farmhouse, on southern slopes of the Mendips. Sleep two/four persons in one/two bedrooms, some en-suite (extra sofa beds and cot available). All fully equipped including linen, central heating, colour TVs and garden furniture. Ample car parking. Cheddar with its famous Gorge, caves and many tourist attractions is within walking distance. Ideally situated for touring West Country, with Bath, Wells, Weston-super-Mare, Bristol and coast all within easy travelling distance. Nearby activities include walking, golfing, fishing, swimming, sailing, riding and caving. Prices from £120 per week low season to £260 per week high season.

SOMERSET HAS IT ALL!

Peaceful thatched cottages, stately homes, sandy beaches, breathtaking caves, churches and cathedrals, romantic legends, heather-covered moorland — Somerset has something for everyone! Much of West Somerset lies within Exmoor National Park, and the county's many areas of upland make it ideal for a walking or nature-study holiday.

DULVERTON. Mrs J. Nicholls, Lower Chilcott Farm, Dulverton TA22 9QQ (01398 323439). Sleeps 2/6 adults; 2 children. Edge of Exmoor National Park, near Barle Valley. Superb riding, walking and touring — fishing and other sports — naturalists' paradise. Two cottages in renovated barn conversion in farmyard, sleep two to six, fitted carpets throughout, colour TV, fitted kitchen, laundry facilities. One ground floor en suite double if required. Riding stables next door. Children, pets and mothers-in-law welcome. Linen provided. Terms £100 to £300 per week.

EAST COKER, Near Yeovil. Mrs C. Williams, Prymleigh, East Coker, Near Yeovil BA22 9HW (01935 863313). ♀♀♀ *HIGHLY COMMENDED.* **Sleeps 2.** LITTLE

PRYMLEIGH — not only was this well furnished cottage for two built to a high standard with two bathrooms, but it also enjoys fantastic views over miles of nearby Dorset hills. The cottage lies in owners' pleasant garden with fields adjoining, on edge of beautiful village, 12 miles Somerset Levels, 20 miles Dorset coast. Yeovil two miles, Sherborne eight miles. Village church, pub, shop, Sutton Bingham Reservoir (bird-watching, sailing, angling). Cottage has lounge/diner with French window. Colour TV. Well equipped kitchen, electric cooker/fridge. Downstairs bathroom, second bathroom upstairs beside twin-bedded room. Linen, electricity, central heating included. £120 to £260. Open January to November.

EXMOOR. Jane and Barry Styles, Wintershead Farm, Simonsbath, Exmoor TA24 7LF (01643 831222; Fax: 01643 831628). ♀♀ to ♀♀♀♀ *HIGHLY*

COMMENDED. Four tastefully furnished and well equipped spacious cottages offering all the comforts of home, situated in the midst of beautiful Exmoor with panoramic views. The area is ideal for enjoying the country pursuits of walking, riding, fishing or just relaxing, taking in the spectacular scenery. A safe place for children and pets with a recreation room for those not so sunny days. The cottages sleep from two to six people plus cots. There is also a small bedsit flat for one or two people. All are centrally heated, two also have open fires. Situated 10 miles from Lynmouth Wintershead makes an ideal base for exploring North Devon and Exmoor. Children and pets welcome. Terms from £105 to £440 per week. Short Breaks out of season. Please telephone, Fax or write for colour brochure.

ILMINSTER. Toll House, 12 Bay Hill, Ilminster. Sleeps 6 plus cot. The Toll House (Grade II) was built in

1816 by the Ilminster Turnpike Trust in the local hamstone and is located at the eastern edge of the town. Recently renovated, it is well appointed yet retains many of its old features. Three double bedrooms (one double with wash-basins, two twin-bedded) and a cot and high chair are available. Bathroom with shower and WC, separate WC downstairs. Well equipped kitchen and utility room, separate living and dining rooms. Full central heating and colour TV. Large south-facing garden with open views and ample parking. Pets by arrangement. Available all year. £160 to £310 per week — includes all linen, towels, gas and electricity. Contact: **Mr and Mrs K. Crowhurst, 8 Drakes Way, Portishead, Bristol BS20 9LB (01275 847181).**

SHEPTON MALLET. Mrs J.A. Boyce, Knowle Farm, West Compton, Shepton Mallet BA4 4PD (01749 890482; Fax: 01749 890405). ♀♀♀♀ *APPROVED.* **Working farm. Cottages sleep 2/5/8.** Knowle

Farm Cottages are converted from the old cowstall and stables, set around the old farmyard now laid out as a pleasant garden. Quiet location at the end of a private drive. Excellent views and plenty of wildlife. All cottages furnished to a high standard — bathroom (bath, shower, toilet, wash-basin); fully fitted kitchen (automatic washing machine, fridge/freezer, full size gas cooker). Two cottages have kitchen/diner, separate lounge with colour TV, the other two have kitchen, lounge/diner, colour TV. Cot, high chair by prior arrangement. Bed linen supplied, towels by request. Surrounding area full of interesting places to visit. Good golf courses, fishing, selection of pubs and restaurants. Around the farm plenty of walks, play area for children. Sorry, no pets. Terms: low season £145 to £230; high season £160 to £360. Car essential, ample parking. Payphone for guests. Open all year.

Anchor Cottages

Set in glorious rural Somerset, 'twixt Taunton and Wellington, lies the famous 17th century Anchor Inn, known for miles around for its charm, atmosphere and high standard of food. Recently three self catering cottages were opened, each of which can sleep up to 4 people. Double glazed, with central heating, colour TV and separate bath and toilet, they are tastefully furnished to a very high standard. Each cottage has a private garden. Car parking. Full details from Mike and Angela Ford.

Anchor Cottages, The Anchor Inn, Hillfarrance, Taunton, Somerset TA4 1AW. Telephone: 01823 461334.

TAUNTON. Mr and Mrs P. Bray, Meare Court Farm, Wrantage, Taunton TA3 6DA (01823 480570).

♀ ♀ ♀ *APPROVED.* **Sleeps 2/4.** The Old Dairy, ground floor holiday cottage in peaceful surroundings on family dairy farm. Four miles from county town of Taunton with Somerset Cricket Ground, Castle, large shopping centre, golf, countryside walks, etc. One mile to shop and post office. Accommodation comprises open plan kitchen/diner/sitting room with colour TV, one double bedroom, bathroom, kitchen equipped with electric cooker, fridge, iron, etc. Two folding beds for lounge. Fully heated. Ample parking. Children welcome, cot and high chair available. Dogs by arrangement. Linen and towels available. Price includes electric heating. Brochure. Terms from £170 to £220 per week. Open all year. Short Breaks available.

WEDMORE. Many Stones, Cocklake, Wedmore. Sleeps 6. Charming country cottage with its own secluded garden, situated in the hamlet of Cocklake, one mile from the attractive village of Wedmore, three miles from Cheddar. Ideally situated for touring Mendips and Quantocks. Recently modernised, yet retaining many of its old features and charm. Many Stones is well appointed to accommodate six/seven people in three double bedrooms plus cot. High chair (babysitting may be arranged). Bathroom. Large well-equipped kitchen/diningroom; sittingroom with woodburner stove and colour TV; downstairs cloakroom. Everything supplied except linen. Sorry, no pets. Car essential — ample parking. Weekly terms from £160 to £210 (includes fuel for wood-burner and electricity). Automatic washing machine. Night storage heating. Available Easter to end September. Booking forms, etc from **Mrs S.M. Wills, Rose Farm, Cocklake, Wedmore BS28 4HB (01934 712129).**

WELLS (Panborough). Tigger's Cottage. Sleeps 8 plus cot. Heart of Somerset Levels, looking across to Mendip Hills and Glastonbury Tor. Fine cottage with four double bedrooms. Fitted kitchen with washing machine, 28' lounge/diner, TV, downstairs cloakroom. Full central heating. Upstairs bedrooms, bathroom, separate WC. Fitted carpets. Fishing and riding available locally. Close to Wookey, Cheddar, Burnham. Weston 16 miles. Terms from £240. No linen supplied. Also attractive flat for two in 300-year-old farmhouse. Fitted kitchen, lounge/diner, large bedroom with inglenook fireplace, shower room. Colour TV. Fitted carpets. Area of Outstanding Natural Beauty. Terms from £110. Winter Breaks for both properties available. **Mrs P. Borthwick, Panborough Batch House, Panborough, Near Wells BA5 1PN (01934 712882).**

WINSFORD (near Dulverton). Ball Cottage, Winsford. Sleeps 6 plus cot. 17th century cottage in one of the prettiest villages of the Exmoor National Park. The River Exe runs through the large garden. Redecorated and furnished very comfortably for six people plus baby (two double bedrooms, two singles, sittingroom, kitchen/diner, bathroom). All-electric except for an open fire with free logs. Colour TV. Washer/dryer. Excellent village shop but car essential for exploring Exmoor or reaching the sea at Minehead. Own garage. No linen provided, and no pets, please. Open all year round. £200 to £260 per week. SAE to **Mrs Mary Wilkinson, 44 Guildford Road, London SW8 2BU (0171-622 6757).**

WIVELISCOMBE near. Oddwell and Cridland Cottages, Brompton Ralph, Near Wiveliscombe.

♀♀♀ *COMMENDED.* **Cottages sleep 6.** Charming 300-year-old cottages with beamed ceilings and inglenook fireplaces for cosy coal fires, standing in garden at foot of Brendon Hills. Equipped for six, plus a cot in each. Two bedrooms, one with three single beds, other with double bed; bed/sitting room with put-u-up; modern bathroom, toilet, with extra toilet/washroom upstairs in Oddwell and downstairs in Cridland; dining/living room; kitchen with oil-fired Rayburn (in Oddwell only), both with electric cooker, fridge, immerser, iron, toaster, spin dryer, etc; separate larder in Oddwell. Available all year. Indoor games, books provided. Cot, high chair. Trout fishing, riding, walking, pony trekking. Nine miles to sea and half a mile to shop/post office. Car essential, ample parking; garage in keeping with character of cottage. Pets by arrangement. Weekly terms from £90 to £210. **Adrian and Pippa Blizzard, Talgarth, Bentley, Near Farnham, Surrey GU10 5LN (01420 23839).**

SUFFOLK

ALDEBURGH. Fairhaven, Thorpeness, Near Leiston. Sleeps 9. Reach the beach through garden gate with no road to cross! All-electric bungalow with one double, one twin-bedded, two bunk-bedded and one single rooms, to sleep nine. Bathroom, two WC's; sittingroom/sun room; diningroom; kitchen. Five minutes' walk to Thorpeness Meare (large man-made lake only two feet deep with islands) on which children can learn to row, sail, canoe, punt and fish for coarse fish. Golf course 15 minutes' walk. Aldeburgh one-and-a-quarter miles, with excellent shops, yacht club, tennis, golf, cinema. Concerts at The Maltings, Snape. Nature Reserves at Minsmere and Avocet Island. Nearest station Saxmundham. From £275 to £400 per week. Electricity extra. No linen provided. Open all year. Apply: **Mrs K.V.F. Pawson, Haggas Hall, Weeton, Near Leeds, West Yorkshire LS17 0BH (01423 734200).**

DEBENHAM near. Mrs T. Webb, Wetheringsett Hall, Hall Lane, Wetheringsett, Stowmarket IP14 5PW (01449 766120). ♀♀ An interesting barn conversion centrally situated a mile from the A140 and half a mile down our private drive amidst farmland and our own horses' paddocks. The accommodation provides large living area with colour TV, fitted kitchen, bathroom with shower and a galleried double bedroom. There are bed settees downstairs if needed. Property features many exposed beams and is decorated in true country style. Electricity is by meter. Linen and towels can be provided. There is also a covered swimming pool. Well-mannered pets are welcome. Short Breaks available. Terms from £130 to £215.

DUNWICH. Middlegate Cottages. The cottage illustrated is one of three situated in a quiet, private road 200 yards from the sea. They are ideal for those seeking a peaceful holiday. Dunwich is a small, historic village which was once an important town washed away by the sea and is situated in a protected "area of outstanding natural beauty". The cottages are furnished and equipped to a high standard, centrally heated and available throughout the year. Children and well behaved pets welcome. Over half our guests return for another holiday. Early booking is advisable since the cottages were fully booked for last year. For a brochure please contact **Mrs Elizabeth Cole, Middlegate Barn, Dunwich IP17 3DW (01728 648741).**

HALESWORTH. Beck's End Cottage, Westhall, Halesworth. ♀♀♀ *COMMENDED.* This delightful red

brick house, converted from the one-time village school with landscaped gardens and lawns, set on the hillside of a charming Suffolk village overlooking a valley of quiet countryside, is available for holiday letting all the year round. Westhall is an interesting village with its 12th century Norman Church, typical village pub, and rolling farmlands. Only seven miles from Southwold and Suffolk's Heritage Coastline, this is an excellent base from which to tour Norfolk and Suffolk. Many places of interest both historical and scenic within easy driving distance. Lovely walking terrain. The accommodation comprises large lounge/diner, entrance hall, two large bedrooms, cot for baby, bathroom, toilet. Modern fitted kitchen with electric cooker, fridge, kettle, toaster, cutlery, crockery and cooking utensils. Electric heating. Car essential, parking. Children welcome. Pets permitted. Bargain breaks November to April. From £125 to £250 weekly. SAE, please, or telephone (evenings) to **O.A. Johnson, Becks End Farm, Westhall, Halesworth IP19 8QZ (01502 575239).**

KESSINGLAND. Alandale Holiday Bungalows, Bethel Drive, Kessingland, Lowestoft. Sleep 4/6. Two-bedroomed bungalows on peaceful grassed site, right next to the beach yet only yards from the village centre. The bungalows are comfortably furnished and fully equipped; they are all-electric (fridge, cooker, heaters, colour TV etc), and can sleep up to six using studio couch in the lounge. Linen, cots and some electricity included. Easy parking. Ideal for all the family, pets welcome too. Easy access to A12, Lowestoft, Yarmouth, Broadlands, Pleasurewood Hills, Wildlife Park. Weekly terms from £118 to £239. Open March to January. Proprietor **Mike Lyne (01502 740610).**

KESSINGLAND. Kessingland Cottages, Rider Haggard Lane, Kessingland. Sleeps 6. An exciting

three-bedroom recently built semi-detached cottage situated on the beach, three miles south of sandy beach at Lowestoft. Fully and attractively furnished with colour TV. Delightful sea and lawn views from floor-to-ceiling windows of lounge. Accommodation for up to six people. Well-equipped kitchen with electric cooker, fridge, hot and cold water; immersion heater. Electricity by 50p meter. Luxurious bathroom with coloured suite. No linen or towels provided. Only 30 yards to beach and sea fishing. One mile to wildlife country park with mini-train. Buses quarter of a mile and shopping centre half a mile. Parking, but car not essential. Children and disabled persons welcome. Available 1st March to 7th January. Weekly terms from £50 in early March and late December to £245 in peak season. SAE to **Mr S. Mahmood, 156 Bromley Road, Beckenham, Kent BR3 2PG (0181-650 0539).**

SAXMUNDHAM. Mrs Ann Ratcliffe, Fir Tree Farm, Kelsale IP17 2RH (01728 668356). Midway

Southwold/Aldeburgh, standing in seven acres; self contained wing of farmhouse with pretty views over garden, fields and pond with moorhens. Newly converted accommodation includes one double bedroom with extra single bed; living/dining room with kitchen area; shower and toilet. Electric cooker, fridge, fire, etc. Inclusive terms from £140 per week. Situated one mile from Yoxford with its pottery, art gallery and many inns and restaurants. Beautiful Heritage Coast area; five miles Dunwich beach and Minsmere Bird Sanctuary. Norwich City, American Theme Park, wild life parks all within easy distance. Six berth caravan and Bed and Breakfast also available. SAE, please.

SOUTHWOLD/WALBERSWICK. H.A. Adnams, Estate Agents, 98 High Street, Southwold IP18 6DP (01502 723292; Fax: 01502 724794). Furnished Holiday Cottages, Houses and Flats, available in this charming unspoilt seaside town, within easy reach of the south east and south west Midlands and London. Convenient for sandy beaches, with safe bathing, sailing, fishing, golf and tennis. Near to 300 acres of open Common. Attractive country walks and historic churches are to be found in this area, also the fine City of Norwich, the Festival Town of Aldeburgh and the Bird Sanctuary at Minsmere, all within easy driving distance. SAE, please, for brochure with full details.

STOWMARKET near. Fern and Jason Cottages, Hitcham. ♀♀ *COMMENDED.* **Sleep 2.** Two superbly appointed cottages in peaceful rural setting. Luxury accommodation each with own conservatory. Delightful outlooks over extensive gardens, tennis court and mill ponds. Hitcham is in the very heart of Suffolk and near historic villages and towns such as Lavenham and Long Melford. It is a region of lovely countryside, pretty villages with fine churches. Easy driving distance of the coast, Norwich, Colchester and "Constable" country. Each cottage comprises lounge, kitchen, bedroom, bath/shower room and conservatory. Fitted carpets, central heating, colour TV. Free linen. Parking. Regret no smokers. Open all year. Terms from £120 to £175 including electricity. Details from **Mrs Judith White, Mill House, Water Run, Hitcham, Ipswich IP7 7LN (01449 740315 or 0836 717189 mobile).**

SUSSEX

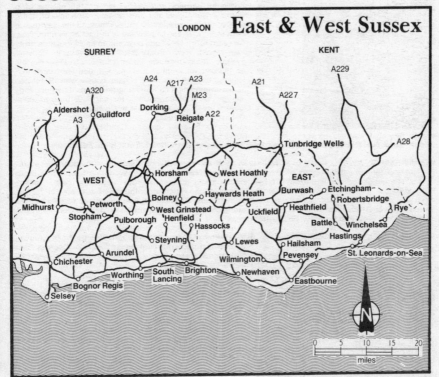

East & West Sussex

EAST SUSSEX

ALFRISTON. Mr and Mrs G. Burgess, Polhills, Arlington, Polegate BN26 6SB (01323 870004).

Idyllically situated on shore of reservoir and edge of Sussex Downs within easy reach of the sea. Fully furnished period cottage (approached by own drive along the water's edge) available for self-catering holidays from April to October (inclusive). Fly fishing for trout can be arranged during season. Accommodation consists of two main bedrooms; tiled bathroom. Lounge with colour TV; large well-fitted kitchen with fridge freezer, electric cooker, microwave, washing machine; dining room with put-u-up settee; sun lounge. Central heating. Everything supplied except linen. Most rooms contain a wealth of oak beams. Children and pets welcome. Car essential. Ample parking. Shops two miles. Golf, hill climbing locally. Sea eight miles. Weekly terms from £165 to £210 (electricity included).

BATTLE. Mrs Brenda Ware, 2 Loose Farm Barns, Hastings Road, Battle TN33 0TG (Tel & Fax: 01424 773829). Sleeps 5.

Great Barn, a converted stone farm building, is quietly situated at the end of a farm lane, one third of a mile from the main road. There are panoramic views and country walks from the building. The seaside is 15 minutes away. This open plan apartment has been decorated and furnished to a high standard, with a well equipped kitchen, bathroom with shower, central heating; access independent of the main building. There is a colour TV, radio, washing machine and a swing from one of the high beams. All linen supplied. Details, maps and photographs on request. From £210 a week.

BRIGHTON. Best of Brighton and Sussex Cottages, Horseshoe Cottage, Whipping Post Lane, Rottingdean BN2 7HZ (01273 308779; Fax: 01273 300266). ♀♀♀ *COMMENDED* **up to** ♀♀♀♀♀ *DE LUXE.*

Sleep 2-18. A wide selection of personally inspected, high quality properties throughout Brighton, Hove, Lewes, Rottingdean and in the country areas of East and West Sussex. Ranging from a small one bedroomed flat in Brighton up to a magnificent 15th century Manor House in the heart of Sussex. One cottage has the best view in Sussex — is right on the edge of Brighton giving you town, sea and countryside right on your doorstep. Children and pets are welcome. There is non smoking accommodation and accommodation suitable for disabled visitors. Terms from £155 to £1580 per week. Three-day Short Breaks available.

EASTBOURNE (EAST DEAN). "Birlingdean", 81 Michel Dene Road, East Dean, Eastbourne. Sleeps 6 plus cot. Detached Chalet-Bungalow with garage. Situated

in quiet and peaceful surroundings with superb views over the South Downs to the sea at Birling Gap. Three double bedrooms (one on ground floor with cloakroom). Gas-fired central heating throughout, refrigerator, colour TV, spin dryer, telephone (incoming calls only), replacement double-glazed windows and doors. Pets accepted. Personally supervised and visitors met on arrival. Available all year for summer holidays, long or short winter lets and mini breaks. Weekly terms from £190 to £400, winter from £150. Contact: **Miss P.G. Elkins, 26 Lymington Court, All Saints Road, Sutton, Surrey SM1 3DE (0181-644 7271 or 01323 422303).**

HASTINGS TOWN CENTRE. Amberley Holiday Flats and Flatlets, Devonshire Road, Hastings. Close to Hastings rail/bus stations. A few minutes' level walk to the beach, shops and entertainments. Flatlets for one or two people each with its own well equipped catering facilities, two on ground floor. Family flat sleeps up to six; self contained with kitchen diner, fridge/freezer, colour TV. All very clean, comfortable accommodation of a high standard. Double glazing, TVs, heaters, etc. Unrestricted street parking. Open all year. Sorry no pets. Weekly prices: Flatlets from £55 to £100; Family Flat from £110 to £220. Out of season Short Breaks. Details from **Win and Bob Steele, Amberlene Guest House, 12 Cambridge Gardens, Hastings TN34 1EH (01424 439447).**

ROTTINGDEAN/BRIGHTON SEAFRONTS. 28A Marine Drive, Rottingdean and Metropole Court, Metropole Hotel, Kings Road, Brighton. ♀♀♀ *HIGHLY*

COMMENDED. Superb self-contained twin-bedded flat adjacent to sea front and central to picturesque village; own ground floor front entrance and parking space. Also private self-contained apartments located above the renowned four star Brighton Metropole with direct access to Hotel facilities including FREE use of luxury heated indoor swimming pool. All accommodation is generously equipped including household linen, colour TVs, stereo music centres, fridge/freezers, automatic washing machines and payphones. Prices from £230 to £610 per week with off peak three-night Short Breaks. Details from **Harold or Valerie Williams, Cliff Edge, 28 Marine Drive, Rottingdean BN2 7HQ (01273 302431; Fax: 01273 307744).**

RYE. Hardy's Cottage, Military Road, Rye. 18th century weatherboard character cottage, with views over River Rother and Romney Marshes. Within easy walking distance of the centre of Rye and bus and railway stations. The cottage has been completely modernised, with fitted carpets and gas central heating. The lounge has a beamed ceiling, colour TV and the large modern kitchen has gas cooker, microwave, fridge and freezer. Upstairs there are two bedrooms, one double, one twin, both with washbasins, and a beamed bathroom with bath and WC. Cot available. Linen available. Pets welcome by arrangement. Garden and garage. Tennis courts nearby. Available all year round and weekend lets from November to Easter. Terms from £115 to £225 per week. SAE to **Mrs J.J. Henderson, 18 Chipstead Park, Sevenoaks, Kent TN13 2SN (01732 457837).**

See also Colour Display Advertisement SOUTHERN ENGLAND. **Fairhaven Holiday Cottages.** An extensive selection of personally inspected holiday homes — various shapes, sizes and locations, coast, countryside and town, in Southern England and Wales. Available throughout the year, and for long and short winter lets. Many situated in SUSSEX. Contact: **Fairhaven Holiday Cottages, Derby House, 123 Watling Street, Gillingham, Kent ME7 2YY (01634 570157).**

WEST SUSSEX

CRAWLEY. "Above Par", Forestfield, Furnace Green, Crawley. ♀♀♀♀ *HIGHLY COMMENDED.*

Modern semi-detached home on a quiet garden estate that overlooks a public golf course and Tilgate Forest, but is only five miles from GATWICK AIRPORT (15 minutes by car). The start of the M23 is less than three miles. Main line railway access to LONDON, GATWICK, and BRIGHTON on the south coast is a mile walk by footpath. The spacious accommodation, which has warm air central heating, comprises lounge with colour TV and video, open plan diningroom and fitted kitchen with all you could need including microwave, fridge/freezer, dishwasher and automatic washer/dryer, plus a separate cloakroom and WC. Upstairs there is a double bedroom with bed settee, twin bedroom and the bathroom. There is plenty of room for children to play on the grass in front of the house plus a small walled garden with furniture and barbecue. Sorry, no pets. NON-SMOKERS ONLY please. Linen hire and cot available. Telephone for incoming and outgoing calls. Weekly rent £150 to £275 plus electricity and gas by meter readings but available for shorter periods. Booking forms from **Mrs Barbara Hodgkinson, "Hodge's Lodges", 52 Kelso Close, Worth, Crawley RH10 7XH (01293 882008; Fax: 01293 883352).**

HENFIELD. The Holiday Flat and Cottage, New Hall, Small Dole, Henfield. ♀♀♀ *COMMENDED.* New Hall, the manor house of Henfield, stands in three and a half acres of mature gardens, surrounded by farmland with abundant footpaths. The holiday cottage is the orginal 1600 farmhouse. It has one en suite bedroom, a large livingroom with a folding bed, dining room and kitchen; a door opens into the walled garden. The holiday flat is the upper part of the dairy wing. Its front door opens from a Georgian courtyard and it has three bedrooms sleeping five, lounge/diner, kitchen and bathroom. Both units are fully equipped and comfortably furnished. Children welcome. Open all year. Terms from £100 to £260 per week. Send SAE for details to **Mrs M.W. Carreck, New Hall, Small Dole, Henfield BN5 9YJ** or phone **(01273 492546).**

HENFIELD. The Granary, Great Betley Farm, Henfield. Sleeps 6. Detached period Granary lovingly restored to a high standard providing comfortable and spacious accommodation of great character with superb views of the Downs. Set in a secluded 200 acre working farm near the River Adur. Coarse fishing permits available. Ample parking. Facilities include fitted kitchen/diner, washer/dryer, colour TV/video, gramophone, selection of videos/records old and new, piano, payphone. 50p electric meter. Duvets provided, linen, cot and high chair available. Terms from £105 low season to £230 high season. Short Breaks by arrangement. Details from **John How, Weppons, Wiston, Steyning BN4 3DN (01903 813270).**

HORSHAM. Mrs G. Drake, Newdenne House, Church Street, Warnham, Horsham RH12 3QP

(01403 251965). Self-contained purpose-built ground floor flat with own entrance but attached to large family house in centre of charming Warnham village, with three-quarter acre garden bordering open farmland. Five minutes Horsham, one hour London, half an hour South Coast. Sleeps four. One double and one twin-bedded rooms, lounge/diningroom, large modern fitted kitchen, bathroom, toilet, conservatory with door to garden, garage. Central heating, electric fires, colour TV, washing machine, fridge, microwave. Comfortable, clean and enough equipment to entertain visitors. Village post office and shops. A warm welcome from the owners in residence. Terms from £150 to £300 per week inclusive of electricity and linen.

WARWICKSHIRE

SHIPSTON-ON-STOUR. Church View Cottage, Great Wolford, Shipston-on-Stour. Working farm, join in. Sleeps 2 adults, 2 children. Church View Cottage

adjoins a delightful old Cotswolds farmhouse, one of the original houses in the little village of Great Wolford, on a 90 acre dairy farm; also three acre lake for coarse fishing. The accommodation, for four people, contains a charming 10'6" × 17' lounge with leaded windows and oak beam, comfortably furnished with colour TV and double bed settee. Fully fitted kitchen has electric cooker and fridge, ample working surfaces. Small bathroom/toilet with hand basin and electric shower. Bedroom is equipped with bunk beds and wash-basin. Continental quilts and linen provided. Children welcome. Car essential — parking. Milk is provided free of charge. Great Wolford is an ideal base for a touring holiday; central to Stratford, Broadway and Stow. Available all year; weekly terms from £80 (low season) to £150 (high season). **Mrs S. Wrench, Hillside Farm, Great Wolford, Shipston-on-Stour CV36 5NQ (01608 674389).**

STRATFORD-UPON-AVON. Meadow View Cottage. ♀♀♀ *APPROVED.* **Sleeps 4.** Immaculate detached bungalow, two and a half miles from Stratford, surrounded by open countryside near to owner's property. Convenient for Cotswolds, Stow, Broadway, Oxford, Worcester, Malverns, Warwick Castle, Blenheim Palace. Spacious lounge/diner, colour TV. Fully fitted kitchen; shower room, all towels provided. Two attractive bedrooms, matching linen and drapes; all bed linen provided. Carpeted, double glazed, heating in all rooms. Patio with garden furniture overlooking open countryside. Ample secure parking. No smoking. No pets. Open all year. £140 to £270 per week inclusive of hot water, towels, bed linen. Details **Mrs Sue Cox, Spring Farm House, Warwick Road, Blackhill, Stratford-upon-Avon CV37 0PZ (01789 731046).**

STRATFORD-UPON-AVON. Mr and Mrs A. Jenkins, King's Lodge, Long Marston, Stratford-upon-Avon CV37 8RL (Tel & Fax: 01789 720705). ♀♀♀

APPROVED. **Properties sleep 2/4/6.** Set in four and a half acres of parkland, King's Lodge was a refuge for Charles II in 1651 after defeat at the Battle of Worcester. The village of Long Marston is quite small, but has a fine old church, shop and Post Office and local hostelry. There are three self-contained units, two apartments adjoining the main house with two and three bedrooms each, and a one-bedroomed cottage in the garden. Six miles from Stratford-upon-Avon, off the B439 or B4632 roads, and at the foot of the Cotswolds, this area abounds in attractions — stately homes, castles, museums, farm parks, Cotswold villages, riverside walks, riding, fishing etc. Weekly rates from £140 to £265. Open from January to December.

WARWICK. Copes Flat, Brook Lane, Warwick. ♀♀♀♀ *COMMENDED.* Warwick town centre, secluded first floor flat dating from the mid 17th century has its own entrance and high level garden, ideal for al fresco meals. The timber framed sitting/dining room is comfortably furnished for eating and relaxing and has a colour TV and telephone. A bathroom, bedroom with twin or double bed and fully fitted kitchen with washing machine and tumble dryer complete this charming accommodation in the interesting historic town of Warwick. Pets by arrangement only. Children welcome. We are ideally situated for visiting Stratford-upon-Avon, Oxford, the Cotswolds and the main towns and attractions in the Heart of England. Terms from £140 to £260. **Mrs Elizabeth Draisey, Forth House, 44 High Street, Warwick CV34 4AX (01926 401512).**

WILTSHIRE

DEVIZES. Colin and Cynthia Fletcher, Lower Foxhangers Farm, Rowde, Devizes SN10 1SS (01380 828254). ♀ Sleep 4. Tranquillity awaits you on our 18th century working farm situated alongside the Kennet and Avon Canal at the base of the staircase of 29 locks. Assist boats through locks. Scenic walks to pubs. Fish and boat to heart's desire. Ideal for cycling. Four mobile homes situated in orchard with patios and garden furniture plus barbecue. Accommodation comprises double bedroom and two singles or twin plus bed settee in lounge. Each unit sleeps four/five. Separate bathroom, kitchen, lounge with TV. From £150 to £200. Open Easter to end October. Bed and Breakfast can be obtained in farmhouse and a small camp site with electricity, toilets and shower is also available. Brochure on request.

DEVIZES. Mr and Mrs C. Butcher, Sleight Farm, Devizes SN10 3HR (01380 722907). Spacious self-catering accommodation in annexe of a farmhouse, completely self-contained. Sleight Farm is a working farm situated two miles from Devizes and half a mile from the main road. Ideal touring base for Bath, Avebury and Stonehenge. The flat comprises lounge/diner, open plan kitchen, two bedrooms, bathroom, hall. Fully carpeted, electric heating, automatic washing machine, telephone, colour TV. Ample parking and private garden. Children and pets welcome. Available all year. Terms from £95 to £145 weekly (linen included, electricity extra). Phone or write for details.

TROWBRIDGE. John and Elizabeth Moody, Gaston Farm, Holt, Trowbridge BA14 6QA (01225 782203). The accommodation is part of a farmhouse, which dates from the 16th century, on the edge of the village of Holt with views across open farmland. Within 10 miles of Bath, Bradford-on-Avon two miles, Lacock eight miles. Private fishing on River Avon available. The apartment consists of a large lounge/dining room with open fire and sofa which converts into a double bed; two generously proportioned bedrooms upstairs, one twin-bedded, one with a double bed, both with washbasins; a separate toilet (downstairs); a large kitchen in the single storey wing, fitted with light oak finish units, electric cooker, microwave, refrigerator and automatic washing machine; shower room which opens off the kitchen. Off road parking. Choice of pubs in village. Terms £110 to £140. Brochure and further details available.

NORTH YORKSHIRE

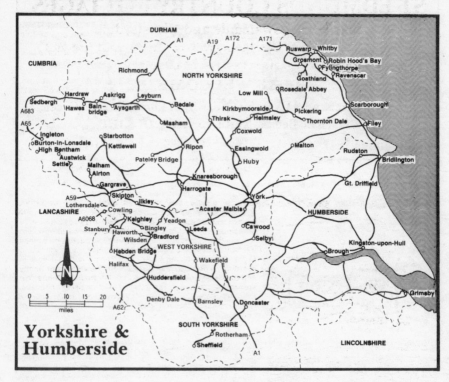

Yorkshire & Humberside

AMPLEFORTH. Pam and Mike Noble, "Hillside", West End, Ampleforth YO6 4DY (01439 788303).

♀♀♀♀ *COMMENDED.* **Sleeps 1/4.** Situated within the half-acre grounds of the main house within the boundary of the National Park, "Hillside Cottage" is an attractive property, stone built and enjoying splendid views. Accommodation consists of oak-beamed living room/kitchen with open stone walls; two bedrooms (one double, one twin) complete with duvets; downstairs bathroom with bath and shower (also houses an automatic washing machine). Nightstore heating and fitted carpets throughout. Linen, heating, etc. fully inclusive. Sorry, no pets. Private off-street parking. There are many local attractions including museums, golf courses, steam railway and the beautiful cities of York, Ripon and Harrogate. Terms from £170 to £270 per week. Personal attention by resident owners.

CARLTON-IN-COVERDALE. Mrs Shirley M. Bowles, Waterforth, Carlton-in-Coverdale, Leyburn DL8 4BD (01969 640626). Sleeps 4. Waterforth is a

modern flat in a Dales house within the Yorkshire Dales National Park in Herriot country enjoying easy access to Wensleydale, Wharfedale and Swaledale which are ideal for walking. This self-contained ground floor flat is south-facing, fully carpeted, centrally heated, with UPVC windows, fully fitted kitchen with fridge/freezer, cooker, microwave, lounge/dining room with open fire, colour TV, VCR; two bedrooms, one with bunk beds; bathroom with electric shower. All linen provided for one week or more. Car parking space. Use of garden. Open all year. Terms from £135 to £275. Regret no pets. Non-smokers preferred. Tourist Board registered.

ST EDMUNDS COUNTRY COTTAGES

Cottages in Swaledale and Wensleydale

Properties sleeping two to seven persons plus cot. These recently renovated cottages are fully equipped and are an ideal base for exploring the Dales and Moors.

PETS WELCOME

For a brochure send SAE to: Sue Cooper, St Edmunds, The Green, Crakehall, Bedale, North Yorkshire DL8 1HP

Telephone 01677 423584   Up to ⸮ ⸮ ⸮ ⸮ COMMENDED

DANBY. Mrs Gillian M. Rhys, Blackmires Farm, Danby, Whitby YO21 2NN (01287 660352).

⸮ ⸮ ⸮ ⸮ *APPROVED.* Self catering cottage for six, storage heaters, three bedrooms, prices — from £125 to £325 weekly — include electricity and linen. It adjoins the farmhouse and has a lawned garden with swing and sand pit. It is on a small working farm where we keep sheep, goats, cattle, hens and ducks. Situated in the North York Moors National Park in beautiful Danby Dale, three miles from the villages of Danby and Castleton and the National Park Information Centre. We are ideally situated for touring and walking holidays. Flamingo Park, Castle Howard, Rievaulx and other abbeys, folk museums and many picturesque villages within 30 minutes' drive.

FILEY. Sleeps 6. A delightful rural location surrounded by beautiful country views to the Yorkshire Wolds

and the coast. Off A165, two miles from Filey, six miles Scarborough. Gristhorpe is a pretty village with shop/Post Office, church and pub. Quiet and convenient for all tourist attractions in Yorkshire. Modern, bright and sunny accommodation comprises downstairs all-electric kitchen — fridge, cooker, washing machine etc.; bathroom/toilet; lounge with colour TV, satellite TV and video; small bedroom with bunk beds. Upstairs a very large family room (two double beds and one single). Cot and high chair. There is a 50p electric meter and £1 gas meter, gas central heating. A large secluded play lawn. Ample car parking space. Bed linen not provided. Terms from £150 to £210 per week. SAE please to **Mrs A. Linley, "Bonnie-Marie", 1 Filey Road, Gristhorpe, Filey YO14 9PH (01723 514951).**

GOATHLAND, near Whitby. Abbot's Farm Cottage, Goathland. ⸮ ⸮ ⸮ *APPROVED.* **Sleeps 6.** Set in

the heart of the North Yorkshire Moors, facing south, overlooking a small river in a secluded part of the farm. Sleeps six in three bedrooms, with part central heating, colour TV, bath and electric shower. Fully equipped kitchen/diningroom, with electric cooker, fridge/freezer, microwave etc. All bed linen, towels and cot provided. Enclosed garden with sandpit and swing. Open all year. Goathland, which is only 10 miles from the sea, is famous for its open moorlands with excellent walks and is now well-known as a location for the TV series "Heartbeat". The North Yorkshire Moors Steam Railway runs through the farm. Terms from £160 to £260. SAE to **J.H. and K.M. Smailes, Abbot's House Farm, Goathland, Whitby YO22 5NH (01947 896270).**

FREE and REDUCED RATE Holiday Visits!
See our Reader's Offer Vouchers for details!

GRASSINGTON. Mrs Judith M. Joy, Jerry and Ben's, Hebden, Skipton BD23 5DL (01756 752369; Fax: 01756 753370). Properties sleep 3/6/8/9. Jerry and Ben's stands in two acres of grounds in one of the most attractive parts of the Yorkshire Dales National Park. Seven properties; Ghyll Cottage (sleeps eight); Mamie's Cottage (sleeps eight); Paradise End (sleeps six); Robin Middle (sleeps six); High Close (sleeps nine); Cruck Rise (sleeps six); Raikes Side (sleeps two/three). All have parking, electric cooker, microwave, toaster, fridge, colour TV, electric heating and immersion heater; lounge, dining area, bathroom and shower; cots if required. Fully equipped, including linen if requested. Washing machine and telephone available. Well behaved pets accepted. Open all year. Fishing and bathing close by. Terms from £70 to £250. SAE, please, for detailed brochure. Suitable for disabled guests.

FOR THE MUTUAL GUIDANCE
OF GUEST AND HOST

Every year literally thousands of holidays, short-breaks and overnight stops are arranged through our guides, the vast majority without any problems at all. In a handful of cases, however, difficulties do arise about bookings, which often could have been prevented from the outset.

It is important to remember that when accommodation has been booked, both parties — guests and hosts — have entered into a form of contract. We hope that the following points will provide helpful guidance.

GUESTS: When enquiring about accommodation, be as precise as possible. Give exact dates, numbers in your party and the ages of any children. State the number and type of rooms wanted and also what catering you require — bed and breakfast, full board, etc. Make sure that the position about evening meals is clear — and about pets, reductions for children or any other special points.

Read our reviews carefully to ensure that the proprietors you are going to contact can supply what you want. Ask for a letter confirming all arrangements, if possible.

If you have to cancel, do so as soon as possible. Proprietors do have the right to retain deposits and under certain circumstances to charge for cancelled holidays if adequate notice is not given and they cannot re-let the accommodation.

HOSTS: Give details about your facilities and about any special conditions. Explain your deposit system clearly and arrangements for cancellations, charges, etc, and whether or not your terms include VAT.

If for any reason you are unable to fulfil an agreed booking without adequate notice, you may be under an obligation to arrange alternative suitable accommodation or to make some form of compensation.

While every effort is made to ensure accuracy, we regret that FHG Publications cannot accept responsibility for errors, omissions or misrepresentation in our entries or any consequences thereof. Prices in particular should be checked because we go to press early. We will follow up complaints but cannot act as arbiters or agents for either party.

HELMSLEY. Mrs Sally Robinson, Valley View Farm, Old Byland, Helmsley, York YO6 5LG (01439 798221). Three holiday cottages sleeping two, four and six persons respectively. Each with colour TV, video, washer, dishwasher, microwave. Peaceful rural surroundings on a working farm with pigs, sheep and cattle. Winter and Spring Breaks available. Short Breaks from £80 and High Season weeks up to £380. Please telephone for brochure.

HELMSLEY near. Bank Cottage, Sproxton, Helmsley. Sleeps 7 plus cot. Beautiful detached stone cottage near Sproxton, one and a half miles from picturesque market town of Helmsley. Accommodation comprises — downstairs: sitting/diningroom with double glazing, beamed ceiling, open fire and colour TV; fully equipped kitchen; twin-bedded room, bathroom with shower, airing cupboard; upstairs: double bedroom, bunk-bedded room and single bedroom. Electric heating. Large lawned garden with barbecue available. Garage and additional parking. Pets by arrangement. Indoor sports centre nearby. Other cottages including converted mill sleeping two/eight available. Prices from £90 to £400 per week. Brochure from **Mrs Armstrong's Holiday Cottages, Golden Square Farm, Oswaldkirk, Near Helmsley, York YO6 5YQ (01439 788269).**

LANGTHWAITE. Mrs E.M. Lundberg, Arkle Town, Arkengarthdale, Richmond DL11 6RB (01748 884398). North Yorkshire Dales Park. Two lovely stone cottages in the heart of Herriot's walking country. Dating from 17th century they have been fully equipped to provide for your every need including linen; modernised without losing their charm. Situated three miles west of Reeth and 15 miles from Richmond, ''The Cottage'' sleeps four; terms £120 to £240; ''The Brae'' sleeps seven, terms £160 to £330. Please write or telephone for further details.

NORTH YORKSHIRE – RICH IN TOURIST ATTRACTIONS!
Dales, moors, castles, abbeys, cathedrals – you name it and you're almost sure to find it in North Yorkshire. Leading attractions include Castle Howard, the moorlands walks at Goathland, the Waterfalls at Falling Foss, Skipton, Richmond, Wensleydale, Bridestones Moor, Ripon Cathedral, Whitby, Settle and, of course, York itself.

LEYBURN (Wensleydale). Thorney Cottages, Spennithorne, Leyburn. ♀♀♀ & ♀♀♀♀ *COMMEN-*

DED. **Sleep 2/8.** Three cottages and one flat in delightful village of Spennithorne. Modernised to a high standard, with one, two or three bedrooms; fully equipped with microwave ovens, colour TV; bed linen and towels provided. Children welcome, pets by arrangement only. Car is not essential, shop in the village. Cottages are available all year, weekend bookings taken; wood-burning stoves and night storage heaters for chilly evenings. FREE electricity. Set in their own grounds, these cottages provide comfortable accommodation for a stay in "Herriot" country, with its castles, waterfalls, museums, fishing, walks and magnificent views. Terms £75 to £300. Details from **Michael and Ann Gaines, No.1 Thorney Cottage, Spennithorne, Leyburn DL8 5PR (01969 622496).**

LOCKTON. Barn Cottage, Lockton, Pickering. Sleeps 6 plus cot. A cosy stone built bungalow offering

quality holiday accommodation with pretty fabrics complementing old pine furniture. Superbly located in a quiet cul-de-sac in the unspoilt village of Lockton, four miles north of Pickering, surrounded by picturesque valleys and heather-clad moors. An ideal base for walking or touring the North Yorkshire Moors with Scarborough, Whitby and York within easy reach. Three bedrooms — one double, one twin, one with full size bunk beds. Gas central heating included, electricity by £1 meter; bed linen for hire; cot; colour TV, radio; electric cooker, fridge, washing machine; enclosed rear garden with parking for two cars. From £170 to £315 weekly. Contact: **Gill Grant, East Farm, Buslingthorpe, Lincoln LN3 5AQ (01673 842283).**

LOW BENTHAM. Mrs L.J. Story, Holmes Farm, Low Bentham, Lancaster LA2 7DE (015242 61198). ♀♀♀ *COMMENDED.* **Sleeps 4.** High quality cottage, centrally heated and fully equipped with cot, high chair, fridge, colour TV, etc. Adjacent to farmhouse in peaceful countryside with patio, playroom, washer and deep freeze facilities, sleeps four. Close to Lakes, coast and Yorkshire Dales. All rates inclusive. Children and pets welcome. Terms from £145 to £220 per week. Open all year round. Please send for details.

MALHAMDALE (Yorkshire Dales). Mrs Pamela J. Hall, Scalegill, Kirkby Malham, Skipton BD21 4BN (Tel & Fax: 01729 830293). ETB ♀♀♀♀ *HIGHLY COMMENDED.* Converted watermill in peaceful and idyllic riverside location. A choice of properties in the old mill or individual cottages in the grounds. Super walking in spectacular National Park scenery and good centre for exploring the Dales in general. Trout fishing on our own lake. Children are most welcome and we are happy to accommodate dogs in the cottages. Very high standard of furnishings and equipment including dishwashers, colour TVs and videos. We were originally in the Domesday Book. Weekly terms £160 to £395 inclusive of linen, towels, electricity and hot water. Short Breaks by arrangement. Colour brochure available.

MALTON. Bulmer Farm House, Ryton, Malton. ♀♀♀♀ *COMMENDED.* Delightfully renovated to a very

high standard, Bulmer Farm is situated in lovely open countryside in the heart of rural Ryedale, yet is within easy reach of the old market towns of Malton and Pickering. This very attractive farmhouse, set in farmland, near a country woodyard, surrounded by fields and trees, is extremely spacious and very nicely furnished and equipped for five people. Double glazed and with electric heating throughout, the first-class accommodation comprises a new kitchen, large dining room, large lounge with patio windows, entrance hall with cloakroom and WC, and utility room. Upstairs are three bedrooms (one with en suite bath, shower, bidet, WC), and all bed linen is provided (inclusive). Two rooms have double beds, one has single. Colour TV. All electric (coin meter). Large south-facing garden for guests' use. Sorry, no pets. No smoking. Bulmer Farm is ideal for country lovers who like to relax in natural surroundings, yet it is central for all of North Yorkshire. Send a stamp, please, for our brochure and terms, or phone **Marion Shaw, Abbotts Farm, Ryton, Malton YO17 0SA (01653 694970).**

MALTON. Mrs S. Armitage, Mount Pleasant Farm, Swinton, Malton YO17 0SP (01653 695890).

♀♀♀ *HIGHLY COMMENDED.* **Sleep 4 and 6 plus cot.** Come and visit beautiful Ryedale. Two spacious cottages situated in small village close to pretty market town of Malton. Converted from magnificent barns in quiet courtyard setting adjoining owners' working farm with splendid open views over Ryedale. Furnished and equipped to high standard. Ideal base for exploring the Moors, Heritage Coast, York, market towns of Malton, Pickering and Helmsley and Castle Howard. Golf, riding, swimming, fishing nearby. Cottages comprise farmhouse-style kitchen, lounge with fire, bathroom. Central heating, colour TV, automatic washing machine, microwave. Own garden. Parking. One three-bedroomed cottage with en suite shower, one single storey two-bedroomed cottage. **Please telephone for terms.**

MASHAM. Mr John D. Airton, Sunnyside, Masham, Ripon HG4 4HH (Tel & Fax: 01765 689327). ♀♀♀♀ *APPROVED.* **Sleeps 7.** Our charmingly converted coach house is ideally located for visits to the Dales; Harrogate and York are within easy driving distance. Masham has two breweries with visitor centres, craft workshops and excellent sporting facilities. Accommodation for seven includes gas-fired central heating and fitted carpets. A family room with three singles and en suite shower and WC. A double and a twin-bedded room with separate luxurious bathroom. Living/dining room with remote control TV. The fitted kitchen includes an automatic washing machine and microwave. Linen and towels provided. Payphone. Safe parking in walled grounds. No pets please. All inclusive charges £140 to £320.

OLD MALTON. Priory View, Lascelles Lane, Old Malton. Sleeps 6. A delightful three-bedroomed

detached bungalow with separate garage and own garden. Fully equipped and maintained to a high standard. Centrally heated with cleanliness guaranteed. Set in a quiet village lane overlooking river, with two public houses, both serving food, Post Office and General Store all within two minutes' walk. Ideally situated near main A64 road, York 18 miles, Coast 22 miles, National Park, Moors and Forest ten miles, Steam Railway eight miles. Bookings accepted all year. For further details and information please contact **Mrs Barbara Dimmey, Croft House, Amotherby, Malton YO17 0TG (01653 693658).**

PATELEY BRIDGE. Cobble House, Mews, Gallery Apartment and Cottage. ♀-♀♀♀♀ **up to**

COMMENDED. Ground and first floor flats, apartments and detached cottage in own private close near centre of small market town 12 miles from Harrogate. Double or family accommodation from £100 to £350 weekly. TV and full linen service. All fully equipped and self contained. Laundry, dryer. Parking. Children welcome, cot and high chair. Pets by arrangement. Ideal walking, riding and fishing country. Central to many interesting, entertaining and historic places. Old town with riverside walks, bowls, tennis and children's recreation area. Apply: **N.E. & T.A., Cobble House, Fog Close, Church Street, Pately Bridge HG3 5LB (01423 711725 or 565735).**

PICKERING. Mrs Livesey, Sands Farm Country Cottages, Wilton, Pickering YO18 7JY (01751 474405). Quietly secluded in 15 acres of fields, gardens and

a wildlife pond. The delightfully renovated four/five/six and eight-bedded cottages are grouped round an attractive courtyard amidst shrubs, roses and honeysuckle. They are individually designed, luxuriously decorated with exposed beams; some four-poster beds, colour TV, gas central heating, real-flame gas fires and farmhouse-style kitchens. Bed linen and towels are provided and beds are made up for your arrival. All the cottages have private parking. Also adjacent to the cottages stands Sands Farm Country Hotel with beautifully designed en suite bedrooms, dining room, tea room, gift shop. Bed and Breakfast with Evening Meal is also available from the main Hotel. NO SMOKING. Wilton is an ideal base for visiting the Moors, coast, stately homes, North York Moors Railway and the ancient attractive city of York. Fishing, riding, swimming less than five miles away. Please send SAE for brochure.

PLEASE SEND A STAMPED ADDRESSED ENVELOPE WITH ENQUIRIES

PICKERING/ALLERSTON. Jean and Lorraine Allanson, Rains Farm, Allerston, Pickering YO18 7PQ (01723 859333). Sleep 2/6. Newly renovated for 1996, barns in a sunny courtyard nestling in very peaceful open countryside in the Vale of Pickering, enjoying unrivalled views to the moors and wolds. Furnished, decorated and equipped to the resident owners' exacting standards, retaining many of the original features including a wealth of old beams, plus some deft touches which have enhanced the charm of these lovely cottages. Within a few minutes' drive are the North Yorkshire Moors, forest, steam railway, coast, York and many attractions. Five cottages; single storey. Children welcome. Pets/smokers by arrangement. Terms from £120 to £350 per week; meters read. Bed and Breakfast available in farmhouse, also short breaks.

ROBIN HOOD'S BAY. Northlands, Sledgates, Fylingthorpe. Northlands is a three bedroomed semi detached house situated on the fringe of Fylingthorpe village, close to local amenities. Set in delightful countryside within the North Yorkshire Moors National Park with magnificent unsurpassed country, sea and moorland views. Gardens to front and rear. Comfortably furnished and attractively decorated with fitted carpets throughout. Fire alarms fitted. Entrance hall, kitchen with double oven cooker, microwave, fridge, automatic washing machine, dryer, etc. Lounge/dining room with colour TV, coal fire (coal allowance in winter); night storage heaters throughout. Three bedrooms sleeping six plus cot; separate toilet and bathroom with immersion heater. One small well behaved dog allowed. Electricity by £1 coin meter. Car parking space off road. Available all year including Christmas and New Year. SAE for terms and brochure from **Mrs E. Beeforth, Marnadale, 8 Sledgates, Fylingthorpe, Whitby YO22 4TZ (01947 880027).**

ROBIN HOOD'S BAY. "Lingers Hill", Thorpe Lane, Robin Hood's Bay, Whitby. Sleeps 4. OPEN ALL YEAR, this character cottage offers clean and comfortable accommodation for two/four guests. It is close to all local amenities and within easy reach of many other places of interest. Ideal walking area with lovely views to sea and countryside, a perfect setting for a truly relaxing holiday. Accommodation: two double bedded rooms (cot provided on request), bathroom and toilet, lounge with beamed ceiling and colour TV, kitchen/diner, microwave, pantry with fridge. Gas fire and central heating (included in rent). Fitted carpets throughout. Electric cooker, spin dryer, iron, duvets (linen hire available). Garden. Parking. Short Breaks available November to March. Weekly terms from £125 to £220. SAE or phone for brochure and terms **Mrs F. Harland, Lingers Hill Farm, Thorpe Lane, Robin Hood's Bay, Whitby YO22 4TQ (01947 880608).**

SLEIGHTS, near Whitby. Mrs June Roberts, White Rose Holiday Cottages (FG), 5 Brook Park, Sleights, Near Whitby YO21 1RT (01947 810763).

A detached stone house set in its own attractive grounds with private parking. Sleeps five adults, two children, plus cot. Two attractive stone cottages with small front gardens, sleep four/five, plus cot. Both fully equipped and attractively furnished, high chairs available. Linen can be hired. Available all year, with reduced rates early and late season. Personally supervised, cleanliness guaranteed. The village of Sleights is one of the prettiest in Yorkshire, winding up the hillside from the River Esk to Blue Bank and the Moors. Approximately three miles from Whitby. Terms from £135 to £380 per week. SAE please for brochure.

STAITHES. Garth End Cottage, Staithes. Sleeps 5/6.

Victorian cottage situated on sea wall in this old fishing village in the North Yorkshire Moors National Park. Excellent walking centre. Small sandy beach with numerous rock pools. Cottage has feature fireplace, beamed ceilings, pine panelled room, well equipped kitchen including microwave. Warm, comfortable, well equipped with central heating, electricity and bed linen included in rent. Two lounges, front one with picture window giving uninterrupted panoramic views of sea, harbour and cliffs. Dining kitchen; bathroom with toilet; three bedrooms, one double, one twin, one single (two with sea views); colour TV. Front terrace overlooking the sea. Sorry, no pets. Terms from £170 — £300. Apply **Mrs Hobbs (01132 665501).**

STOCKTON-ON-FOREST. Orillia Cottages, Stockton-on-Forest, York. Three converted farm workers' cottages in a courtyard setting at the rear of the 300 year old farmhouse in Stockton-on-Forest three miles from York. Golf course nearby, pub 200 yards away serving good food; post office, newsagents and general stores within easy reach. Convenient half hourly bus service to York and the coast. Fully furnished and equipped for four, the cottages comprise lounge with sofa bed, colour TV, etc; kitchen area with microwave, oven, grill and hob; bedroom has one double and one single beds. Gas central heating. Non-smokers preferred. Children and pets welcome. Available Easter to October — Short Breaks may be available. Terms from £150 to £200 weekly includes heating, linen, etc. Please contact **Mrs Jackie Cundall, Orillia House, 89 The Village, Stockton-on-Forest, York (01904 738595).**

SWALEDALE. Brooklyn Cottage, Gunnerside, Swaledale. ♀ ♀ ♀ COMMENDED. **Sleeps 4.** Situated in

the most unspoilt of all the Yorkshire Dales, in the National Park, this delightful cottage is newly furnished throughout with pine. Accommodation consists of one double bedroom and one twin-bedded room (this has an additional colour TV); lounge/dining room with oak beamed ceiling, Victorian fireplace, colour TV; bathroom; new fitted kitchen with cooker, fridge and dishwasher. Heating and fuel included in price. Children over five years welcome. One dog only. Ideal for walking or touring, Gunnerside is 15 miles from Richmond, 10 miles from Hawes. Reasonable rates. **Mrs S. Emmott, Leford, Birchover Road, Stanton in Peak, Matlock, Derbyshire DE4 2LW (01629 636547 or 01335 390345).**

THIRSK. Foxhills Hideaways, Felixkirk, Thirsk YO7 2DS (01845 537575). Cosy log cabins sitting

snugly between North York Moors and the Dale National Park; the coast and City of York are also within easy reach. Village pub around the corner. Pets welcome. Fully inclusive prices (£150 to £325 per week) including free pony riding. Short or long breaks. Open all year. Brochure available.

THIRSK. School House, Sutton-under-Whitestonecliffe, Thirsk. Sleeps 6. This renovated cottage

HOLIDAY COTTAGE

SCHOOL HOUSE,
SUTTON UNDER WHITESTONE CT
Nr. THIRSK, NORTH YORKSHIRE.

offers warm, comfortable and homely accommodation for up to six people plus cot. Fully equipped with new furniture and fittings including colour TV, fridge, electric cooker, washing machine and toaster. Open all year. Suitable for the disabled. Central heating. Car essential, parking. Linen supplied. Situated at the foot of Hambleton Hills, it makes an ideal walking and touring centre with good pubs locally for meals and a shop for milk, etc 100 yards away. Hill climbing on your doorstep with golf, fishing, riding and bathing all within easy distance. Immersion heater and shower. Electricity included in terms from £120 to £295 per week. Other cottages available sleeping from two to eight persons. For further information contact: **Mr and Mrs T. Williamson, Thornborough House Farm, Kilvington, Thirsk YO7 2NP (Tel & Fax: 01845 522103).**

THORNTON DALE (near Pickering). Beechwood, Peaslands Lane, Thornton Dale. Sleeps 4. This

popular touring and walking centre, on the edge of the North Yorkshire Moors National Park, offers riding stable, ample shops, eating places and bus service. Moors Railway, swimming pool, historic houses and Flamingoland nearby. Beechwood is a detached two-bedroomed bungalow with own parking and gardens; sleeps four plus cot. It offers lounge, diningroom, kitchen, bathroom. Uninterrupted view of the Vale of Pickering. Fully equipped with electric cooker, fridge, fires, colour TV and immersion heater. Storage heaters and linen available. Sorry, no pets. Weekly rates £195 to £278. SAE, please to **Mrs J. Clayton, Low Mill Garth, Maltongate, Thornton Dale YO18 7SE (01751 474365).**

Terms quoted in this publication may be subject to increase if rises in costs necessitate

THORNTON-LE-DALE. Easthill House and Gardens, Thornton-le-Dale, Near Pickering. ♟♟♟/

♟♟♟♟ *HIGHLY COMMENDED.* One of Yorkshire's most attractive villages, ideally situated for visiting North York Moors or coast. Large friendly family house recently converted to form luxurious, spacious self contained apartments, also one cottage with choice to suit two to eight plus cot (most bedrooms en suite). Set in two and a half acres of private landscaped gardens and woodland with sweeping views over Vale of Pickering. Nestling in the pine trees we also have three Scandinavian-style chalets sleeping four/ five. Grass tennis court, putting green, adventure play area, table tennis, snooker. Ample parking. No pets. Bed linen, heating, electricity all inclusive. Open all year. Terms from £150 per week. Special terms for short winter breaks. For brochure write or telephone **Martin and Jennie Green, Easthill, Thornton-le-Dale YO18 7QP (01751 474561).**

WENSLEYDALE. Simonstone, Hawes. Cottages sleep 3/5. Two well equipped cottages on working farm, personally supervised for cleanliness and comfort. Small enclosed gardens and ample parking. Panoramic views. Centre of the Dales National Park, chosen location for filming Herriot's "Darrowby Show". Ideal for walking, touring and fishing, and only one hour from the Lakes and West Coast. One cottage has a family bedroom, kitchen, lounge/diner; the other has one family room and one double bedroom, kitchen/diner, lounge, central heating. Both fully modernised with bathrooms/WCs and all electric appliances, colour TV, etc. Optional coal fires in Autumn and Winter. Children welcome. Pets by arrangement. Terms from £80 to £250 per week. SAE, please, for brochure. **Mrs I. Sunter, Nova Farm, Simonstone, Hawes DL8 3LY (01969 667204 and 667186).**

WHITBY. Harbourside Flats, 7 Pier Road, Whitby. Flats sleep 7. Two large holiday flats situated on the harbourside of the picturesque old fishing town of Whitby. The properties, both accommodating seven people (one two bedroomed, the other three bedroomed), are spacious — lounge bay windows have panoramic views over the harbour; fully equipped kitchen; bathroom; immersion heater; electric fires; TV. Electricity by 50p meter. Children welcome, cot and high chair provided. Pets accepted at £5 extra. Guests to bring own linen. Whitby — the home of Captain Cook — offers ideal sandy beaches, leisure amenities, fishing trips, golf and tennis. Excellent location for touring North Yorkshire Moors National Park, unique coastal villages and many other places of local interest. Available Easter to November. Terms from £100 to £280 per week. Further details on request — **Mrs P. Dale, 2 The Crescent, Glaisdale, Whitby YO21 2PQ (01947 897570 or 602059).**

YORK. "Baile Gate House". ♟♟♟♟♟ *DE LUXE.* **Sleeps up to 6 plus 2 plus baby.** This is a new

semi-detached luxury town house. The view from the rear of the house is of the medieval city wall. From the south-facing balcony you can see more of the prestigious Bishop's Wharf development and the River Ouse. All the attractions of this historic, compact city are within easy walking distance, and there is private parking. This well-equipped home has a double bedroom, cloakroom and utility room on the ground floor; livingroom and oak kitchen on the first floor; a master bedroom and en suite shower room on the top floor, plus twin bedroom and bathroom. Home help for two hours midweek. NON-SMOKERS only please. Not suitable for pets. Weekly rates from £180 to £500 plus electricity, gas and phone by meter reading. Apply **Mrs Barbara Hodgkinson, "Hodge's Lodges", 52 Kelso Close, Worth, Crawley, West Sussex RH10 7XH (01293 882008; Fax: 01293 883352).**

YORK. Mrs Rachel Ritchie, The Old Rectory, Thormanby, Easingwold, York YO6 3NN (01845

501417). The Old Rectory's Coach House and Stable have been lovingly converted into two holiday cottages and enjoy a delightful setting in quiet country lane. Just out of the small village of Thormanby (three miles north of Easingwold), it is an excellent base for visiting York (17 miles), the North Yorkshire Moors to the east and Dales to the west. There are many country houses, abbeys and castles in the area. Stable Cottage has one double and one twin room plus cot. The Coach House has one double and two twin rooms plus cot. Both properties are fully equipped. All linen and towels supplied. Colour TV, open fires (fuel provided), night storage heaters when required. Children and well behaved pets welcome. Electricity by meter reading. SAE for brochure. Terms from £130/£140 to £240/£300. Open all year.

YORK. Mrs M.S.A. Woodliffe, Mill Farm, Yapham, Pocklington, York YO4 2PH (01759 302172). Three attractive self-catering choices on the farm. 12 miles from York with fine views of the Yorkshire Wolds. WOODLEA, a detached house, sleeping five/six people with fully equipped kitchen, dining area, large lounge with colour TV, bathroom, downstairs cloakroom and three bedrooms. BUNGALOW adjacent to farmhouse sleeps two/four with kitchen, bathroom, lounge/diningroom with colour TV and double bed settee, twin room with cot. Children and pets welcome. STUDIO adjacent to farmhouse, sleeps two with modern kitchen, lounge/diningroom with colour TV, twin bedroom, bathroom/toilet. Parking for all. Open all year. Shopping and other amenities at Pocklington (two miles). Eating out, stately homes, activities available locally; coast 28 miles. SAE for details.

YORK LAKESIDE LODGES

Moor Lane, York YO2 2QU
Tel: (01904) 702346 Mobile: (0831) 885824
Fax: (01904) 701631
Unique in a city! Luxurious Scandinavian lodges, and cottages in mature parkland overlooking large private fishing lake. Nearby superstore with coach to centre every 10 minutes. Easy access to ring road for touring. Open year round.

🗝🗝🗝🗝 *UP TO DELUXE*

YORKSHIRE & HUMBERSIDE
TOURIST BOARD
WHITE ROSE AWARDS
FOR TOURISM
WINNER

Award – British
Holiday Home
Parks Association

TERRINGTON HOLIDAY COTTAGES

🗝🗝🗝 *Commended.*

Come and enjoy comfort and rest in one of our four superb holiday cottages, sleeping 2-8 people. A peaceful, unspoilt farming village just 14 miles N.E. of York and within 4 miles of Castle Howard, Terrington is in an ideal position for your discovery of a beautiful area. Illustrated brochure. S.A.E. for full particulars to:
Mrs S. Goodrick, Springfield Court, Terrington, York YO6 4PX.
Telephone (01653) 648370

YORK. "Wheel Cottage" and "Anvil Cottage", 30 York Street, Dunnington, York. Sleep 6/2.

Delightful 18th-century "Wheel Cottage" is in the rural village of Dunnington, convenient for shops, buses and amenities. York four miles, coast and North Yorkshire Moors within one hour's drive. Fully equipped for six people (always clean and comfortable); modern all-electric kitchen with cooker, fridge and washer; diningroom. Comfortable lounge with colour TV; modern bathroom with toilet; bedrooms have hot/cold washbasins. Two double and one twin, which can be divided to make two single rooms; also cot available. All rooms damp-proofed, have electric heating and fitted carpets. Lawned gardens, parking. Also "Anvil Cottage" for couples. Terms £65 to £195 per week. SAE, please. **Mr R. Hornshaw, 66 Mill Lane, Wigginton, York YO3 8PZ (01904 761725).**

YORKSHIRE DALES. Selside Farm Cottage, Horton-in-Ribblesdale, Settle.

Selside Farm Cottage is situated in the heart of the Three Peaks — Ingleborough, Whernside, Pen-y-Ghent. Ideal centre for walking, touring, Yorkshire Dales, Lake District, West Coast. It has two bedrooms, one with twin beds, one with double and single; three-piece bathroom suite; immersion heater; large lounge with dining area; coal fire; TV. Well-equipped kitchen, electric cooker, fridge, spin dryer etc. Electricity on meter. Coal, storage heaters included in rent. Has small lawn to front, with access to larger walled-in garden. Ample parking. Sorry, no pets. From £100 to £195 per week. SAE, please, to **Mrs S.E. Lambert, Selside Farm, Selside, Horton-in-Ribblesdale, Settle BD24 0HZ (01729 860367).**

FREE and REDUCED RATE Holiday Visits! See our Reader's Offer Vouchers for details!

YORKSHIRE DALES (Horton-in-Ribblesdale). Mr and Mrs Colin and Joan Horsfall, Studfold House, Horton-in-Ribblesdale, Near Settle BD24 0ER (01729 860200). Georgian house set in one acre of beautiful gardens with panoramic views, near the Three Peaks in the Dales National Park. Ideal centre for visiting the Dales, Lake District and Bronte country. Village pub half-a-mile. The self-contained cottage is attached to the main house, and comprises two double bedrooms, each with a double bed, one with additional full-size bunk beds. Lounge with colour TV; kitchen with fridge etc.; bathroom with shower. Hot water and central heating included in the rent. Bed linen provided. Electricity by 50p meter. Children and pets also welcome. Bikes for hire. Terms from £95 — £195. SAE, please.

WEST YORKSHIRE

HAWORTH. 1 & 2 Royd Wood Cottages, Oxenhope, Keighley. ♀♀♀ *COMMENDED.* **Sleep 2/3 plus cot.** Two 18th century cottages of charm and character situated near the historic village of Haworth, enjoying splendid rural views up the Worth Valley, home of the popular steam railway. An excellent centre for walking and exploring the countryside of "The Railway Children", the Brontes, "Emmerdale Farm" and the Yorkshire Dales. Both cottages have a large sittingroom with a heavily beamed ceiling, comfortable traditional furniture, colour TV and heating. Well equipped kitchens with fitted oak units. Garden and parking area. Well behaved dogs accepted. Linen optional. Available April to November. Terms from £100 to £155 per week. Long SAE please for details and brochure to: **Mrs D.S. Kinghorn, 16 South Close, Guiseley, Leeds LS20 8JD (01943 872767).**

SADDLEWORTH. Mr and Mrs R.S. Burke, "Friar Lodge", Delph, Saddleworth OL3 5HG (01457 872718). ♀♀♀ *COMMENDED.* FHG Diploma Winner. Situated in the picturesque Pennine village of Delph this 18th century semi-detached stone cottage offers comfortable and spacious accommodation for five. Two bedrooms — one double, one family; cot available. Bathroom, including cubicle shower. Lounge with colour TV. Dining/kitchen with electric cooker, refrigerator, microwave, washer. Gas fire heating. Garden and parking. Gas, electricity and bed linen are inclusive. Shops five minutes. Bordered by West Yorkshire and Peak District National Park, Saddleworth is ideal walking country. Also good touring base being only 10 minutes from M62 Junction 22. Easy access to Lancashire coast, Lakes, Yorkshire Dales. Terms from £110 per week.

ISLE OF WIGHT

FRESHWATER. Cliff End, Freshwater. ♀♀ *COMMENDED.* **Sleeps 4.** Delightful purpose built holiday bungalow adjacent to the Solent and overlooking rolling countryside. Easy access to Colwell Bay with views to The Needles and Hurst Castle. Accommodation comprises two bedrooms — one double and one twin; an open plan lounge with colour TV; fully fitted kitchen area with full oven, fridge and microwave; bathroom with bath and shower. All electricity charges are included. Excellent walking and lovely scenery all over the island and attractions and theme parks for children. Many letters of recommendation. From £90 to £210 weekly. Please telephone, or write, for a brochure to: **Mrs Helen Long, 12 Hollis Drive, Brighstone PO30 4AF (01983 740651).**

FRESHWATER. 1 Cliff End, Monks Lane, Freshwater. Sleep 4/6. A small attractive coastal development

of brick built bungalows on high ground with beautiful views over the sea and rolling countryside. It overlooks Colwell beach. There is a clubhouse with a bar, heated swimming pool, a small shop and family entertainment for which membership is available. There are telephones, reception office and a launderette on site. The Bungalow is well furnished and carpeted throughout and comprises two bedrooms; bathroom with electric shower; kitchen/lounge with put-u-up bed, colour TV, electric cooker, fridge, toaster, etc. Electric heating. Bed linen, high chairs and cots can be hired. Sorry, no pets. Please write or telephone for our brochures which give full accommodation details plus Island information to **Mr and Mrs N. Timmins, "Westward Ho!", 1 Marlborough Close, Fleet, Hampshire GU13 9HY (01252 621700).**

CHANNEL ISLANDS

St. Andrews.

SCOTLAND

ABERDEENSHIRE

See also Colour Display Advertisement **DISCOVER SCOTLAND. Sleep 2/18.** Over 100 delightful cottages, houses and chalets, many set in beautiful locations with panoramic views over white sandy beaches, miles of coastline, lochs, islands and mountain peaks. All are comfortable, well equipped and regularly inspected by us. Ideal for golfing and fishing holidays, touring or simply relaxing on sandy beaches. So whether you want the superb coastline of the West, the long sandy shores and quaint fishing villages of the North East or the spectacular scenery and wildlife of the Highlands contact **Discover Scotland, 27 Turretbank Drive, Crieff, Perthshire PH7 4LW (01764 656666; Fax: 01764 656665).**

See also Colour Display Advertisement **HUNTLY. Mrs Rhona M. Cruickshank, Logie Newton, Huntly AB54 6BB (01464 841229; Fax: 01464 841277).** ♥♥♥ *HIGHLY COMMENDED.* Set in the heart of north east Scotland, eight miles due east of Huntly, Logie Newton Holiday Cottages are ideally located for exploring the Grampian Highlands. The cottages have been fully modernised to a high standard yet their original character has been retained. Well equipped including microwave oven, colour TV, midi hi-fi, pay phone, toys and games. A laundry room is attached to the cottages. Garden with play area, barbecue and seating. Electric central heating. Bed linen provided. Ample parking. Brochure available.

AWAY FROM IT ALL

Forglen HOLIDAY COTTAGES

Visitors are free to wander and explore the gardens, forests, farmlands and riverside of one of the ancient Baronies of Scotland.

The Estate lies along the beautiful Deveron River and our traditional stone cottages (modernised and well equipped) nestle in individual seclusion. However, the sea is only 9 miles distant, the nearest market town of Turriff only 2 miles (with good sporting facilities), and Aberdeen, Inverness, the Cairngorms, famous Aviemore, picturesque fishing villages, castles and historic sites all within easy reach on uncrowded roads. Wildlife haven. See our Highland Cattle.

Children and pets are welcome. 1,000 acres to explore. Cottages sleep 6-9.

Terms: £90 to £285 (inc. VAT and firewood)
Grades: ♥♥♥ Approved and Commended.

Please 'phone for further details or write to:

The Secretary, Home Farm Office,
FORGLEN ESTATE,
Turriff AB53 7JP

Telephone Turriff
(01888) 562918 / 562518
(01888) 563565 "gatehouse"

Key to
Tourist Board Ratings

The Crown Scheme
(England, Scotland & Wales)

Covering hotels, motels, private hotels, guesthouses, inns, bed & breakfast, farmhouses. Every Crown classified place to stay is inspected annually. *The classification:* Listed then 1-5 Crown indicates the range of facilities and services. Higher quality standards are indicated by the terms APPROVED, COMMENDED, HIGHLY COMMENDED and DELUXE.

The Key Scheme
(also operates in Scotland using a Crown symbol)

Covering self-catering in cottages, bungalows, flats, houseboats, houses, chalets, etc. Every Key classified holiday home is inspected annually. *The classification:* 1-5 Key indicates the range of facilities and equipment. Higher quality standards are indicated by the terms APPROVED, COMMENDED, HIGHLY COMMENDED and DELUXE.

The Q Scheme
(England, Scotland & Wales)

Covering holiday, caravan, chalet and camping parks. Every Q rated park is inspected annually for its quality standards. The more √ in the Q – up to 5 – the higher the standard of what is provided.

ANGUS

FORFAR. Mr and Mrs Bruce Hunter, Hunters Cabins, Resten-neth, Forfar DD8 2SZ (01307 463101). ❦ ❦ ❦ *HIGHLY COMMENDED.* Our red cedarwood Cabins are situated five miles north of Forfar in a tranquil meadow overlooking the River South Esk with magnificent panoramic views of the Glens of Angus. These luxuriously equipped cabins are the ideal location for golf, fishing, rambling, birdwatching and castle haunting. A choice of either two or three bedrooms, all linen is provided and every room has a heater. Colour TV (videos and microwaves available for a nominal extra charge). Cots available. Pets welcome. Ample play area for children and a barbecue for added enjoyment. We are the perfect venue for your holiday at any time of year.

❦ The National Trust for Scotland

For a special holiday this year, why not try one of The National Trust for Scotland's self-catering flats or cottages which are situated in or around some of the most attractive Castles and Mansion Houses in Scotland.

To receive a copy of the 1996 brochure, please send a cheque/PO for 50p to:

Holiday Cottages (FHG)
The National Trust
for Scotland
5 Charlotte Square
Edinburgh EH2 4DU
Tel. 0131-243 9331

Available from most bookshops, the 1996 edition of THE GOLF GUIDE covers details of every UK golf course – well over 2000 entries – for holiday or business golf. Hundreds of hotel entries offer convenient accommodation, accompanying details of the courses – the 'pro', par score, length etc.

Endorsed by The Professional Golfers' Association (PGA) and including Holiday Golf in Ireland, France, Portugal, Spain and the USA.

£8.99 from bookshops or £9.80 including postage (UK only) from FHG Publications, Abbey Mill Business Centre, Paisley PA1 1TJ.

ARGYLL

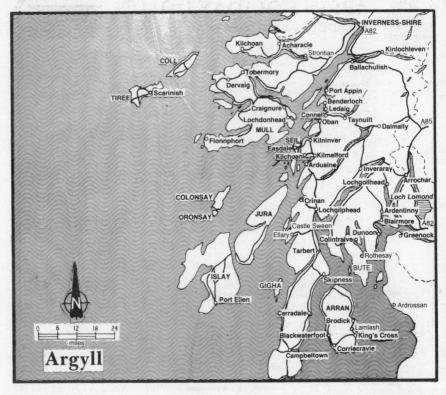

BALLYGRANT. Robolls Cottage, Ballygrant, Isle of Islay. Situated in wooded farming surroundings beside the main road, the Cottage has two bedrooms, sittingroom/livingroom, kitchenette and bathroom. Can sleep six. Bed linen is provided and peat for the open fire. Electricity is by 50p coin meter. Pets are welcome. Property surrounded by its own hedged garden with Hotel and shop only five minutes' walk away. Golf, pony trekking, swimming pool and numerous beaches nearby. A haven for bird watchers and walkers. Terms from £50 to £150 per week. Further details from **Mrs Elizabeth Morris, Main Street, Ballygrant, Isle of Islay PA45 7QR (01496 840670).**

CAIRNDOW near. Upper Croitachonie, Near Cairndow. ♛ ♛ ♛ Enjoy an exciting holiday in this

comfortable traditional cottage in the Scottish Western Highlands. Located in the magnificent Argyll landscape on its own three acre site the cottage sits on a hillside with a panoramic view of Loch Fyne. Two public rooms on ground floor, one with open fire, colour TV and radio. Wood in barn behind cottage. Upstairs one double bedroom and one bedroom with two single beds (stairs quite steep). Linen supplied. Kitchen — cooker, fridge, washing machine. Bathroom — bath and shower. No phone. Night storage central heating all rooms. One hour's drive from Glasgow, 11 miles from Inveraray. Many places to visit. Terms per week £220 to £250. For free brochure with full details phone **Jim McCluskey 0181-892 5704).**

FREE and REDUCED RATE Holiday Visits!
See our Reader's Offer Vouchers for details!

APPIN HOLIDAY HOMES
Beautifully situated overlooking loch
FHG DIPLOMA WINNER

ESTABLISHED 1964

10 chalet-bungalows and three traditional cottages, fully serviced and equipped.
Ideally set midway Oban and Fort William. Launderette, recreation room, play area and babysitting.
FREE fishing (salt and freshwater). Boating and sailing, great hill walks.
Pony trekking and Licensed Inn nearby.
Special Spring, Autumn and Winter terms. Price Guide – £135 to £345 per unit weekly.
DISCOUNTS FOR COUPLES.
Please send SAE for colour brochure giving dates required.

**Mr & Mrs C. Weir, Appin Holiday Homes, Appin, Argyll PA38 4BQ
Telephone: Appin (01631) 730287.**

For more details see colour advertisement.

CAMPBELTOWN. Colonel and Mrs W.T.C. Angus, Kilchrist Castle, Campbeltown PA28 6PH (Tel and Fax: 01586 553210). ✿✿ & ✿✿✿ COMMENDED. Six small, cosy, bright, comfortably furnished, fully-equipped, self-contained cottages sleeping two to six persons in the 13 acre grounds of Kilchrist Castle, near Campbeltown, sandy beaches, golf and the Mull of Kintyre. Colour TV and bed linen included, with beds made-up. Towels for hire but free for overseas visitors. All electric with microwave, convector heaters and coal-effect fires. Meet Gabrielle and her daughter Loretta, our black Shetland ponies. Maybe encounter Billeonie, our fabled kindly Kilchrist brownie at his Wishing Well. Children welcome. Pets allowed. Personally supervised by the resident proprietors. Terms £110 to £270 weekly per cottage.

CARRADALE. Ruth Watson, Carradale Chalets, Carradale Caravan Park, Carradale PA28 6QG (01583 431665). ✿✿✿ COMMENDED. Cosy and comfortable log cabins with panoramic views in quiet area of caravan park with own sandy beach. Ideally situated on Carradale Bay adjacent to the beach and River Carra with exceptional opportunities for boat launching and fishing; canoeing instruction. Trout and salmon fishing; forest walks and 9 hole golf course within one mile and within easy day trip of Gigha, Arran and Islay. Pets welcome. Open April to October. Terms from £150 per week.

**Terms quoted in this publication may be subject to increase
if rises in costs necessitate**

See also Colour Display Advertisement DALMALLY by. Ardchonnel Farms, Lochaweside, By Dalmally PA33 1BW (01866 844242; Fax: 01866 844227). Ardchonnel is a 4000 acre hill farm found 11 miles along the B840 East Lochaweside road with Ardchonnel Cottage situated at the edge of the farm land. Four bedrooms, two bathrooms, large sitting/dining room and spacious fitted kitchen ensures comfortable accommodation for up to eight people. Full central heating and double glazing. Very well equipped including microwave, payphone, washer and dryer, dishwasher, colour TV, etc. All linen, towels and tea towels supplied. Cot and high chair available. One dog welcome. Contact Mrs J. MacKay who will be delighted to send further details.

DALMALLY by. Mrs D. Fellowes, Inistrynich, By Dalmally PA33 1BQ (01838 200256; Fax: 01838

200253). ♛ ♛ ♛ ♛ COMMENDED. Three cottages situated on a private estate surrounded by beautiful scenery: Garden Cottage (four bedrooms), Millside Cottage (two bedrooms) and Inistrynich Cottage (two bedrooms). Situated five miles from Dalmally, 11 miles from Inveraray, 28 miles from Oban. The cottages overlook Loch Awe and each has a garden. They are furnished to a high standard with heaters in all rooms and an open fire in the livingroom. All have electric cookers, fridge, immersion heater, electric kettle, iron, hoover, washing machine and colour TV. Cot and high chair available on request. Dogs allowed by arrangement. Car essential — ample parking space. Ideal centre for touring mainland and Western Isles. Good restaurants, hill walking, forest walks, fishing, boat trips, pony trekking and golf all within easy reach. SAE, please, for brochure and terms.

STRATHCLYDE REGION – WHERE TO START?
Scotland's most densely populated region houses more people than many small countries. At its centre is Glasgow where you will find many attractions including the Art Gallery and the Burrell Collection. Heading further out this Region includes such popular places as Oban, the Mull of Kintyre, the Clyde Valley, the Ayrshire Coast and Argyll Forest Park.

DUNOON. Mr and Mrs I. Webber, Slatefield House, 105 Marine Parade, Kirn, Dunoon PA23 8HH

(01369 704348). Sea front location. Cottage (divided into upper and lower flats) in garden setting with private parking. UPPER FLAT: one double bedroom, one twin (adult sized bunk beds), open plan lounge/diner/kitchen; bathroom/ toilet and second toilet. Central heating. LOWER FLAT: one double bedroom, one twin (adult sized bunk beds), small lounge/diner, separate kitchen; shower room/toilet. Central heating. Both flats well equipped. All linen except towels supplied. Superb location for boating, sailing and golf (concessionary green fees). Terms, inclusive of electricity, Upper Flat: £120 to £180; Lower Flat: £100 to £150.

DUROR OF APPIN. Mrs Elspeth Malcolm, Achadh Nan Sgiath, Cuil Bay, Duror of Appin PA38 4DA (01631 740259). Working farm, join in. Sleeps 4 adults; 2 children. This spacious flat is on the first floor of a large house set in its own grounds at end of side road, one mile from A828 Ballachulish — Oban road. Own private entrance and uninterrupted views of Loch Linnhe. One double and two twin-bedded rooms, all with washbasins; sittingroom; bathroom/toilet; kitchen/breakfast room — fully equipped and all electric. Linen provided at small extra charge. Three hotels near; village shop one mile, sea 500 yards. Pets allowed. Car essential, parking. Open all year. Sailing, boat hiring and pony trekking nearby and opportunities for climbing, walking and bird watching. Several historical connections of interest. The owners farm sheep and beef and have fish smoking business. Weekly terms from £80 to £230 according to season.

`See also Colour Display Advertisement` **EASDALE. "Misty Isles", Easdale, Seil Island. Sleeps 2. NON SMOKERS.** In a row of harbourside cottages with stunning views of the Isles, this cosy studio cottage has replaced one of the original buildings. The famous village of Easdale, 16 miles south of Oban, is on Seil Island, reached by the "Bridge over the Atlantic" and has a Post Office, hotel, gift/craft shops. There are many coach and sea trips available from Oban. It is also a good area for loch and sea fishing. There is private mooring, sorry no divers; because of the steep drop we do not accept children. Pets by arrangement. Open-plan living/sleeping/kitchen area, pine panelled throughout, double glazed, hall and bathroom (bath/shower). There are two single divan beds which can be pushed together to form large double bed. Cooking and lighting by electricity (50p meter). Free night storage heating and coal for multi-fuel stove; fridge, microwave and colour TV. Rates from £110 to £230 per week. Short Breaks negotiable. For details please contact **West Highland Holidays, Albany Street, Oban PA34 4AR (01631 566606; Fax: 01631 566888).**

`See also Colour Display Advertisement` **EASDALE — Isle of Seil. Harbour Cottage.** Modernised quarrier's cottage in the village of Easdale on the edge of the sea. It has a patio and private garden area. There are magnificent views from the kitchen and patio to the Islands of the Inner Hebrides. The cottage was used in the film "Ring of Bright Water" and the TV series "Para Handy Tales". There are two bedrooms (one has double bed, the other has three single beds), a lounge (colour TV), dining room, bathroom (bath/shower) and a toilet; cooking by electricity, night storage heaters and two open fires. There is a steep boxed staircase which may cause problems for elderly visitors and small children. Rates are from £155 to £260 per week. Available all year. For details please write to **Hank and Maureen Clare, Harbour Crafts, Easdale, By Oban PA34 4RQ** or telephone **01852 300424 (1st April to 31st October)** or **0191 4880346 (1st November to 31st March).**

EASDALE, near Oban. Mrs Helen Simcox, Seaview, Easdale, By Oban PA34 4RG (01852 300222). Property sleeps 4. Cross the famous "Bridge over the Atlantic", 16 miles south of Oban, to the picturesque conservation village of Ellenabeich on the edge of the Atlantic Ocean facing the harbour. All modern conveniences. Ample heating. Open all year. Grocery shop, post office, restaurant and pub within walking distance. Hill walking, coastal walking, fishing, golf, boat trips and beach near by. Terms on request.

WHEN MAKING ENQUIRIES PLEASE MENTION
FARM HOLIDAY GUIDES

EASDALE (Oban 16 miles). Self catering holiday home (sleeps five), Cottage (sleeps four) and Chalet

(sleeps two) to let. Cross the "Bridge over the Atlantic" and drive to the picturesque village of Ellenabeich with its views over the Firth of Lorne and Mull. The house faces the pier at Ellenabeich and the attached cottage looks into the grounds where the chalet is situated. The properties are all electric (50p meter) and are fully equipped including linen. There is ample parking 50 metres from the properties. Weekly rates £100 to £250. SAE to **Mrs Nathan, Caolas, Ellenabeich, By Oban (01852 300209).**

FORD by. Ederline Estate, By Ford. The Estate has three stone-built cottages to let, all with mains

SOUTH LODGE

electricity and equipped with fridge, electric cooker and immersion heater. Each cottage is comfortably furnished and has a basic range of kitchen utensils, crockery and cutlery. Each bed is provided with a duvet and a pillow; bed linen and towels are not provided. Suitable for fishing and walking holidays. In a quiet location near Ford village and Loch Awe in one of the most historic and picturesque parts of Argyll; four miles from Kilmartin, 14 miles from Lochgilphead and 32 miles from Oban. Terms from £60 to £210 per week. For further information contact: **Mrs Pat Cairns, Finchcairn Farm, Ford PA31 8RJ (01546 810223).**

INVERARAY. Kilblaan Farmhouse, Inveraray. Sleeps 8. A Victorian farmhouse situated in a beautiful

glen close to Loch Fyne with lovely views down the glen and to the hills behind. Within close distance of Inveraray, but a car is essential. Wonderful hill walks and bird watching, sea and trout fishing locally. The house offers comfortable accommodation. Sleeps eight with two downstairs bedrooms, sittingroom, large country kitchen with fridge/freezer, cloakroom. Upstairs two bedrooms and bathroom. Part oil heating, part night storage. A well kept garden, safe for animals. Car parking. Open March to October. SAE to **Mrs MacLean, Brickmakers Cottage, Lambourn Woodlands, Hungerford, Berkshire RG17 7TS (01488 71474).**

`See also Colour Display Advertisement` **INVERARAY near. Mr and Mrs D. Crawford, Brenchoille Farm, Inveraray PA32 8XN (01499 500662).** ✿✿✿✿ *COMMENDED.* **Working farm. Houses sleep 6.** Braleckan, a mid-19th century stone building comprises three houses, fully modernised and equipped to a high standard of comfort. All electric, cots, high chairs, colour TVs and payphone. Electric storage heaters and carpets throughout and welcoming old-style fires in sittingrooms. Kitchens have electric cooker, washing machine, fridge, microwave oven, kettle, toaster, iron, vacuum cleaner and immersion heater. Bedrooms are fully furnished including linen. Bathrooms have heaters and shaver points. Large parking area. Regretfully no pets. Situated on hill farm yet within easy reach of A83 leading to many attractions including nearby Auchindrain Museum and Crarae Gardens. Open all year. Special winter rates. Charges include linen and VAT. SAE, please, or telephone for details.

`See also Colour Display Advertisement` **KINTYRE. Torrisdale Castle, Kintyre.** ✿ *APPROVED* **to** ✿✿✿✿ *HIGHLY COMMENDED.* Superb accommodation in castle or cottage in absolutely fabulous surroundings on Kintyre's scenic East Coast. Three lovely garden flats in the castle sleeping four to six and five stone-built cottages on the estate sleeping two to 10. Two miles from the picturesque fishing village of Carradale; visit the islands of Arran, Islay, Jura and Gigha. Ideal for walkers, birdwatchers and children. Well behaved pets welcome. Boat available. Golf and fishing offers. Rates from £120 to £330 per week; electricity extra. Colour brochure from **Mary MacAlister Hall, Torrisdale Castle, Carradale, Campbeltown PA28 6QT (Tel & Fax: 01583 431233).**

DUNTRUNE CASTLE
ARGYLL

🏵🏵🏵 HIGHLY COMMENDED

A selection of charming self-catering cottages, each unique in its history and character, and enhanced by the natural Duntrune

beauty of Loch Crinan. All have been attractively modernised and furnished, with care taken in the retention of many traditional and historically interesting features. The cottages offer varying accommodation for two to five persons in comfort. Eating out is no problem with many good restaurants in the area. Salmon fishing, hill walking and safe, sandy beaches

Mother Brown's

can all be enjoyed on the estate. Terms and further details on application. SAE requested:

**Contact: Susan Malcolm
Duntrune Castle, Kilmartin, Argyll PA31 8QQ
Telephone: 01546 510283**

Castle Cottage

LOCH AWE. Innis Chonain, Lochawe, Dalmally (01838 200220). Attractive three bedroom cottage on private 20 acre island (vehicle access by bridge from main A85 road). Superb situation on this beautiful loch with complete privacy, but only half-a-mile to shops. Ideal touring centre, Inveraray 17 miles, Oban 20 miles. Cottage has three bedrooms, sleeps five/six persons. Modern furnishings, colour TV, electric heating, gas cooking, spin and tumble dryers. Linen not provided. Boat with free fishing on loch. Children welcome, pets with permission. Ample parking. Rates from £155 to £335 per week. Full details from: **J.C.D. Somerville, Ashton House, Pattingham Road, Perton, Wolverhampton WV6 7HD (01902 700644 evenings or 01902 351806 day).**

LOCHGILPHEAD. Cottages sleep 4/8. Stone-built seaside cottages, mid-Argyll. Fully equipped to STB requirements. Open fires, electric cooking and heating. Cots and high chair. Colour TV. Duvets with freshly laundered covers. Nearby watersports, fishing, horse riding, unrestricted countryside, castles, gardens, restaurants. Pets by arrangement. For further details and brochure please apply to: **Mrs Margaret MacLachlan, Coulaghailtro Farm, Kilberry, By Tarbert PA29 6YD (01880 770237 or 0185 2500270).**

ELLARY ESTATE

While you are at ELLARY you are free to go wherever you please. There are hill walks, numerous lochs and burns where you can fish, a wealth of ancient ruins for archaeologists, numerous wild animals and flowers for naturalists and plenty of scope for the nautical people.

Chalets and cottages are available on the Estate. All are fully modernised with all-electric kitchens and modern bathrooms. Most accommodate parties of six, but one will take eight and full details are available on request.

The Estate staff are very helpful and can often point out an attractive place for a picnic or an interesting walk. Cars may be driven on the Estate roads and once you know Ellary you will want to return.

All correspondence to:
ELLARY ESTATE OFFICE,
LOCHGILPHEAD, ARGYLL.
(01880) 770209 / 770232
or 01546 850223.

LOCHGOILHEAD. 2 Drimsynie Court, Lochgoilhead. ♥♥ *APPROVED.* **Sleeps 8.** Lochside cottage, situated 300 yards from the loch and the River Goil, and half a mile from the village, with magnificent views. Well equipped for eight in four double bedrooms, one room with bunk beds (plus cot and high chair); sitting/diningroom; kitchen with cooker, fridge/freezer and automatic washing machine; bathroom with toilet; fully equipped except linen. Pets welcome. Shops half a mile. Children welcome, ideal area for family holiday with walking, boating and fishing; facilities nearby for pony trekking, golf, tennis, bowling, curling, swimming and sailing. Within easy reach of Loch Lomond, Glasgow and Western Highlands. Terms from £195 weekly. Brochure on application with SAE to **Mrs A.M. Lee, 51 School Lane, Solihull, West Midlands B91 2QG (0121-705 0201).**

OBAN. Albany Apartments, Oban. Two luxury flats with excellent views overlooking Oban Bay and surrounding Islands. Centrally situated for public transport, shops, restaurants; Oban itself is an ideal centre for touring the West Highlands. Both flats sleep four/five and are decorated and furnished to a very high standard. Two bedrooms (one double and one twin), folding bed/cot available; living/dining room; kitchen with cooker, microwave, washer/dryer, refrigerator; bathroom with bath and shower. Entry phone. Private parking. Electricity, linen, towels included in rent. Open all year. £140 to £335 weekly. Short Breaks November to March. Also eight miles from Oban — Luxury cottage with garden — indentical facilities as in flats. For a brochure please telephone **Miss A. Colthart 01631 710569.**

Terms quoted in this publication may be subject to increase if rises in costs necessitate

ELERAIG HIGHLAND CHALETS

Fully equipped Scandinavian chalets on secluded Eleraig estate near Oban, Argyll

🏵🏵 to 🏵🏵🏵 Commended

Seven fully equipped chalets are set in breathtaking scenery in a private glen 12 miles south of Oban, gateway to the Highlands and Islands. The chalets are widely spaced, and close to Loch Tralaig where there is free brown trout fishing and boating – or bring your own boat. Chalets sleep 4-7. Peace and tranquillity are features of the site, located within an 1,800-acre working sheep farm.

Children and pets are especially welcome. Cots and high chairs are available.

Walkers' and bird-watchers' paradise. Pony-trekking, sailing, golf, diving, gliding, water ski-ing and other sports, pastimes and evening entertainment are available locally. Car parking by each chalet.

Open March-October. From £190/week/chalet including electricity.

Colour brochure from
resident owners:
Gill and Andrew Stevens,
Eleraig Highland Chalets, Kilninver,
by Oban, Argyll PA34 4UX.
Telephone:
Kilmelford (01852) 200225.

Other specialised

FHG PUBLICATIONS

* Recommended SHORT BREAK HOLIDAYS IN BRITAIN   £3.99

* Recommended COUNTRY HOTELS OF BRITAIN   £3.99

* PETS WELCOME!   £4.50

* BED AND BREAKFAST IN BRITAIN   £3.20

Published annually. Please add 50p postage (U.K. only)
when ordering from the publishers:

FHG PUBLICATIONS LTD
Abbey Mill Business Centre, Seedhill,
Paisley, Renfrewshire PA1 1TJ

OBAN. Lag-na-Keil Chalets, Lerags, Oban PA34 4SE (01631 01631 562746). Up to 🌸🌸🌸 *COMMENDED.* **Properties sleep 2/6.** Lag-na-Keil offers peace and quiet in Lerags Glen, just three and a half miles from Oban, a traditional fishing port and popular tourist resort. Perfectly situated for touring the Highlands or taking a ferry trip to the Western Isles, and also for enjoying many outdoor activities including walking, fishing, diving, sailing, horse riding, golf and mountain biking. Accommodation comprises one, two or three bedroomed chalets and cottages, which are fully equipped including linen. Very safe for children and pets are welcome on our family-run site. Good free fishing on Loch Scammadale, deer stalking on our own forestry blocks. Please write, or phone, for further details to **John and Fiona Turnbull.**

OBAN. Major J.W. MacDougall, Gallanach, Oban PA34 4QL (01631 562176). Sleeps 8. Self contained cottage attached to mansion house on an estate near Oban, sitting in own grounds overlooking the Sound of Kerrera and one mile from public road, five miles from Oban. Beautiful situation by the sea with one or two secluded places suitable for bathing and plenty of hill ground for walkers close at hand. Oban is starting point for steamers for trips to the Islands. The cottage has accommodation for eight persons and is fully furnished and equipped apart from linen, with black and white TV. Children welcome, also well behaved pets. Four miles from shops and public transport. Car essential, parking. Open from May to October. SAE, please, for full details.

OBAN by. Henry and Val Woodman, Cologin Chalets, Lerags, By Oban PA34 4SE (01631 564501 anytime). 🌸🌸🌸 **and** 🌸🌸🌸🌸 *COMMENDED.* **Working farm. Bungalows sleep 2/6.** Open all year round — modern luxury timber bungalows on Cologin Farm, three miles south of Oban, set in peaceful private glen amongst the hills in wild and open countryside. Country pub/restaurant on site serving outstanding home-made bar meals at sensible prices. Use our dinghy (and fishing rods) on our trout loch in the hills; ride on a bike; join in the fun on Ceildh Night (Scottish entertainment). Every bungalow is centrally heated, double glazed, has electric heaters, cooker, fridge (most of the electricity included in rentals). Livingroom, bathroom, double/twin bedrooms all fully equipped; colour TV in all bungalows. Shop and launderette on site; babysitting available, also cots and high chairs. Linen included in rental. Site is ideal for children. Pets welcome. SAE, please, for details.

OBAN by. Mrs A. Robertson, Ardoran Marine, Lerags, By Oban PA34 4SE (01631 566123; Fax: 01631 566611). One chalet and two caravans to let on shores of Loch Feochan, five miles south of Oban on the rugged west coast of Scotland. Situated on a private site and overlooking the yachts moored at the marina, each unit is fully serviced with own shower, toilet, Satellite TV. Ardoran, also a farm breeding pedigree Highland Cattle and sheep, is the natural setting for buzzards, pheasants, herons, otters and seals. For those who enjoy the outdoor life Ardoran offers not only excellent sailing opportunities but also walking, bird watching, canoeing and fishing, making it an ideal base for an all-round holiday.

•

AWARDED FARM HOLIDAY GUIDE DIPLOMA

•

Approved

Be independent with a cottage and a boat on

SKIPNESS ESTATE

On this unspoiled, peaceful, West Highland estate with its own historic castle and mediaeval chapel there are traditional estate-workers' cottages available to let all year round. Each cottage is well-equipped, including television, dinghy (except in winter months) and open fires. Laundry facilities available alongside the Seafood Cabin at Skipness Castle. Properties sleep four to ten people. Children and pets welcome. All cottages have magnificent views and beautiful surrounding countryside and coastline. Rocky coasts and sandy bays make for safe swimming, with sea, river and loch fishing, walks, pony-trekking and golf all nearby. Stalking can be arranged in season. Nearby ferries to Arran, Gigha, Islay and Jura. Apply for rates and further details to:

**Sophie James, Skipness Castle, By Tarbert, Argyll PA29 6XU
Telephone: (Skipness) 01880 760207; Fax: 01880 760208**

See also Colour Display Advertisement **TARBERT near. Dunmore Estate, Near Tarbert. Up to** 👑👑👑👑👑 *COMMENDED.* Luxury villa, also a bungalow and four cottages in architect-designed conversion of home farm all on 1200 acre estate with three miles of shore on West Loch Tarbert. Furnished to the highest standard, all have stone fireplaces for log fires. Electricity by £1 meter; linen can be hired at a charge of £10 per person. Birdwatching, sailing, sea fishing, unrestricted walking. Pets welcome. Open all year. Member of ASSC. Brochure available. Terms from £150 to £695. Contact: **Mrs Meg MacKinnon, Dunmore, Near Tarbert PA29 6XS (01880 820654).**

TAYNUILT. Mrs S. Thomson, Clach-ma-Nessaig, Airds Bay, Taynuilt PA35 1JR (01428 654441 or 01866 822663). At the end of a country lane on the shores of Loch Etive, self-contained flat sleeping four/five people in comfort. Children and pets welcome. Cot available. Near Oban; beautiful walks, scenery and ample opportunity to enjoy a really relaxing holiday. Accommodation comprises two twin-bedded rooms with occasional extra bed. Bathroom. Well equipped modern kitchen, washing machine, drying room; large sunny sittingroom with TV. Payphone. Shops and 9 hole golf course two miles. Car essential. £150 to £220 weekly. SAE, please, for more details.

FREE and REDUCED RATE
Holiday Visits!
See our Reader's Offer Vouchers
for details!

AYRSHIRE

GIRVAN. Carlenrig, Poundland, Pinwherry, Girvan. ✿✿✿✿ *HIGHLY COMMENDED.* **Sleeps 6.**

Carlenrig is a luxury holiday cottage in the hamlet of Poundland with views of River Stinchar and surrounding hills. Come and relax in unspoilt countryside. Excellent base for coast or hills. Enjoy many places of interest including Culzean Castle, Burns' country and Glentrool Forest Park. Fishing, golfing, pony trekking, hill walking nearby. Cottage furnished, decorated and carpeted to a high standard. Sleeping six plus baby. Three bedrooms; bathroom, toilet; lounge with colour TV; pine style dining room; oak fitted kitchen with electric cooker, fridge, freezer, washing machine, tumble dryer. Sun porch, attractive secluded shrub and flower garden. Payphone. Car essential, parking. Pets and children welcome. Suitable for disabled guests; one double bedroom and bathroom on the ground floor. Available all year from £85 to £260. Electricity extra. Storage heaters. SAE, please, for details. **Mrs Anne Shankland, 19 Main Street, Colmonell, Girvan KA26 0RY (01465 881265 or 881220).**

KILMARNOCK. Mrs Mary Howie, Hill House Farm, Kilmarnock KA3 6HG (01563 523370). Sleeps 9.

Large very comfortable farmhouse situated in open countryside two miles east of Kilmarnock. Excellent touring base with easy access to all major routes in central and southern Scotland. Ayrshire Coast, sports centres, golf courses all nearby. House furnished to a high standard and fully equipped. Accommodation consists of three bedrooms; large lounge and breakfasting kitchen; bathroom with shower; cot available. Storage heaters, open fire, colour TV, fridge, washing machine, microwave, etc. Linen supplied. Weekly rates from £120 to £295. Smaller cottage is also available and Bed and Breakfast can be obtained in the farmhouse.

MAUCHLINE. Mrs H. Templeton, Syke Farm, Mauchline KA5 5JT (01290 551252). One cottage and

one flat, sleeping four and two respectively, quarter of a mile from A76 situated in the heart of Burns Country, one mile south of Mauchline. Open all year. Both are clean and comfortable, heated throughout; open fire. Linen on request. Children and pets welcome. Very central for touring. Beautiful beaches nearby and castles to visit. Shops one mile. The accommodation is private but not isolated with fishing in the grounds, a golf course adjoining and lovely walks by the river. Prices from £75.

BANFFSHIRE

BALLINDALLOCH. Beechgrove Cottages, Tomnavoulin and Glenlivet. ✿✿✿✿ *COMMENDED.*

Properties sleep 2/6. Traditional Highland Cottages situated in one of the most beautiful areas in Scotland, near the Rivers Livet and Avon. Each has accommodation for up to six people and comprises two double bedrooms; bathroom/shower; fully equipped dining/kitchen and livingroom with colour TV. Heating, lighting and cooking, all electric. Linen supplied. Central for coast, Spey Valley, Aviemore, Dee Valley, Balmoral. Ski-ing available at Lecht Ski Centre 20 minutes away and Glen Shee three-quarters of an hour distant. Children and pets welcome. Car essential. Open all year. Terms from £180 to £260 per week. **Mrs J. White, Beechgrove, Tomnavoulin, Ballindalloch AB3 9JA (01807 590 220).**

DUMFRIESSHIRE

DALBEATTIE. 10 Copeland Street, Dalbeattie. Midway Dumfries, Castle Douglas, By Galloway Coast.

Small detached cottage with one family bedroom (one double bed, one single bed) and living room with bed settee. Electric fire and storage heaters, colour TV. Shower room, toilet and washbasin; kitchen/diner with cooker, fridge, microwave, washing machine. Fully equipped. Small rear garden and car parking. Holiday complex, golf, beautiful scenic walks (guided walks available) nearby. Sandy beach four miles, shops, post office, park, banks within easy walking distance. Electricity included in rental, bed linen not provided. Small dogs allowed. Terms from £80 weekly. Short Breaks available. Telephone **Miss Bailey on 01768351466 or 0860 711411).**

MOFFAT. Mr Terence Hull, Alton House, Moffat DG10 9LB (01683 220903). Sleeps 2 adults and up to 2 children. Attractive first floor flat situated within a historic country house. The flat has been carefully created and retains many period features. It is tastefully and attractively decorated (a Scottish Tourist Board grading has been applied for). Having evolved over several centuries, Alton House is a property of great architectural and historical interest. It is a former home of Chiefs of the Moffat Clan. The property sits in three acres of secluded grounds at the end of a long, private lane. Weekly rentals from £110 to £190. Bed and Breakfast also available.

DUNBARTONSHIRE

Inchmurrin Island
Self Catering Apartments

Situated on Loch Lomond's largest island, ideal for watersports and fishing. Adjacent to fully licensed bar and restaurant. Free moorings.

STB 🏵🏵🏵🏵 COMMENDED

Sleeps 4–6.

Lounge, bathroom with shower, fully equipped kitchen/dining area. £200–£300 per week.

Inchmurrin, Loch Lomond G63 0JY Telephone 01389 850245

STRATHCLYDE REGION – WHERE TO START?
Scotland's most densely populated region houses more people than many small countries. At its centre is Glasgow where you will find many attractions including the Art Gallery and the Burrell Collection. Heading further out this Region includes such popular places as Oban, the Mull of Kintyre, the Clyde Valley, the Ayrshire Coast and Argyll Forest Park.

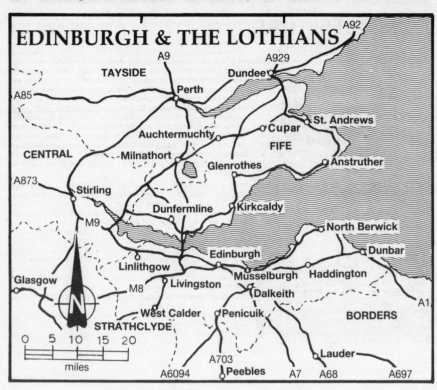

EDINBURGH & THE LOTHIANS

TAYSIDE

A9 A92 A929

Dundee

A85 Perth

CENTRAL Auchtermuchty Cupar St. Andrews

Milnathort FIFE

Glenrothes Anstruther

A873 Stirling

M9 Dunfermline Kirkcaldy

North Berwick

Edinburgh Dunbar

Linlithgow

Glasgow M8 Livingston Musselburgh Haddington

West Calder Dalkeith A1

STRATHCLYDE Penicuik BORDERS

0 5 10 15 20
miles

A6094 A703 Peebles A7 A68 Lauder A697

DUNBAR. Mrs Moira S. Marrian, Bowerhouse Cottages, Bowerhouse, Dunbar EH42 1RE (01368 862293). ☙☙☙ *COMMENDED.* **Sleep 4/8 (total sleeping capacity 16).** Lovely secluded gardens and woodland surround Bowerhouse and the fields are full of farm animals and pets to amuse the children. Guests can choose between the compact Laundry Cottage, the attractive Gardener's Cottage or the spacious east wing of the 19th century mansion house. Ground floor accommodation available. Bus one and a half miles, railway two and a half miles, airport 40 miles. An ideal area for leisure activities including golf, fishing, riding, etc. Pets welcome. Open January to December. Terms from £100 to £290 per week.

EDINBURGH. Glen House Apartments. ☙☙☙ **and** ☙☙☙☙ *COMMENDED.* **Properties sleep 1/7.** Centrally located self catering apartments close to Castle, Royal Mile, Usher Hall, King's and Lyceum Theatres, Meadows Park and a wide variety of bars, restaurants and shops. Apartments are studios, one, two, three or four bedroomed, and all have central heating, colour TV, private telephone; full linen service. Comfortably furnished and with modern fitted kitchens and bathrooms. Housekeeping service available. Ideal for all holiday and business stays. From £168 per week. Access and Visa accepted. Contact: **Hilary Dunlop, 22 Glen Street, Edinburgh EH3 9JE (0131-228 4043; Fax: 0131-229 8873).**

WHEN MAKING ENQUIRIES PLEASE MENTION
THIS *FHG* PUBLICATION

LINLITHGOW (near Edinburgh). Mr and Mrs John and Greetje Howie, Craigs Chalet Park, Williamscraig, Linlithgow EH49 6QF (01506 845025).

👑👑👑 *COMMENDED*. The ten A-frame lodges stand on a wooded hillside, overlooking the River Forth Valley. Each has two bedrooms, one with double bed, the other with two singles; some living rooms have a bunk bed for another occupant. Bed linen supplied. The bathroom is fully fitted; the kitchen has an electric cooker and fridge; colour television. Cot available. Pets by arrangement. Many activities can be enjoyed nearby, Linlithgow golf course and swimming pool are within walking distance. There are two country parks and fishing within four miles. This is an ideal place from which to enjoy day trips to Edinburgh, Glasgow, the Trossachs, the Borders and the sandy beaches of Fife. Open all year. Rates from £137 to £329 weekly.

WEST CALDER by. Mrs Geraldine Hamilton, Crosswoodhill Farm, By West Calder EH55 8LP (01501 785205; Fax: 01501 785308). 👑👑👑

COMMENDED to 👑👑👑👑👑 *HIGHLY COMMENDED*. **Sleep 4/6.** Choose between a self-contained wing of our spacious 200 year old farmhouse with your own garden or Midcrosswood, a beautifully converted detached stone cottage one mile distant on the scenic Pentland Hills. Comfort, charm, warmth, tradition and a friendly welcome await you in either. Why not settle for the best of both worlds on this working 1700 acre livestock hill farm? Rural seclusion, yet a half-hour drive takes you into historic Edinburgh with its museums, palaces, galleries, theatres and fine shops. Glasgow 33 miles, spectacular New Lanark 16 miles. Perfect base for touring the Borders, Trossachs and travelling over the Forth to Fife and Perthshire. Boat trips, pony trekking, golfing, fishing and hill walking within easy reach. Both properties are superbly equipped including colour TV, electric cooker, microwave, washing machine, tumble dryer, dishwasher (cottage only), fridge, freezer, payphone, all bed linen and towels. Full central heating. Dogs by arrangement. Own transport essential. Rates from £140 weekly. Telephone or SAE for brochures.

FIFE

ABERDOUR. Mrs S. Inglis, Dalachy Farm, Aberdour KY3 0RL (01383 860340). 👑👑👑👑 *COMMENDED*. **Sleeps 4.** Spend your holiday on our family run farm set in scenic countryside with panoramic views over the River Forth. Aberdour village one and a half miles away offers two beaches, golf, harbour, castle and railway station. Edinburgh, St. Andrews, Perth and Stirling nearby. The farmhouse flat is on the ground floor and has its own door. Sleeps four plus cot. Babysitting available. Colour TV. Wonderful children's garden. From £160 weekly which includes bed linen. Out of season breaks — minimum two nights, £40 per night.

See also Colour Display Advertisement **AUCHTERMUCHTY. Mrs A. Dunlop, Auchtermuchty Holiday Homes, 6 Gladgate, Auchtermuchty KY14 7AY (01337 828496). Up to** 👑👑👑👑👑 *COMMENDED* **and** *HIGHLY COMMENDED*. Warm and comfortable modernised traditional stone houses in this friendly rural village in North Fife. Ideally placed for exploring east and central Scotland and superbly situated for the many golf courses to suit golfers irrespective of ability. All houses have all linen and towels provided and all gas and electricity included in the price. Good selection of books and jigsaws and some properties have video and membership of nearby leisure centre and tennis club. Short breaks available September to May. Weekly terms from £260 to £525. Free colour brochure available.

See also Colour Display Advertisement **ST. ANDREWS. Mr Tom Scott, Dron Court, South Dron, St. Andrews KY16 9YA (01334 870835).** 👑👑👑 *HIGHLY COMMENDED*. We offer 10 cottages varying in size and outlook but each with its own distinctive character. All have access to the courtyard which has been landscaped around a well and fountain adjacent to the clubhouse. Each cottage has been named after a winner of the British Open Golf Championship which seems appropriate when the complex is situated so close to the Old Course, St. Andrews — the accepted home of golf. The history of the winner who gives his name to your cottage will be found in the wallet (each cottage has one) which also contains information on many local facilities which we think will interest you during your stay. Car parking space. Please write or telephone for our information leaflet giving further details, terms and directions, etc.

See also Colour Display Advertisement **ST. ANDREWS near. Mr Andrew Wedderburn, Mountquhanie Holiday Homes, Cupar, Near St. Andrews KY15 4QJ (01382 330252; Fax: 01382 330480).** 👑👑👑👑 *COMMENDED* to 👑👑👑👑👑 *DE LUXE*. **Sleep 2/12.** A super selection of high quality self catering properties in the St. Andrews area with the huge range of leisure, cultural and historical attractions which this interesting part of the Kingdom of Fife offers. Choose from elegant town houses, country cottages, farmhouses or apartments in a Georgian country house for the ideal holiday for those who want to relax, escape, explore, enjoy their family or take advantage of the golfing opportunities. Children and pets welcome. Please write or telephone for further details and booking.

INVERNESS-SHIRE

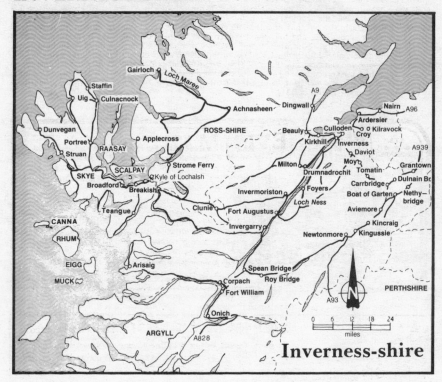

Inverness-shire

ARISAIG. Mr A.A. Gillies, Kilmartin, Kinloid Farm, Arisaig PH39 4NS (01687 450366). 🦢🦢 *APPROVED.* **Cottages sleep 6.** Three new holiday cottages, widely spaced back, commanding magnificent views across Arisaig to the sea and the islands of Skye, Rhum, Eigg. Five minutes by car from the wonderful sands. Ideal area for fishing, hill walking and golf. The cottages are roomy and comfortable and sleep six people. Two bedrooms, furnished lounge with colour TV; bathroom with bath and shower; fully fitted kitchen with electric cooker and fridge. Electricity for heating and lighting. Terms from £180 per week. SAE, please, for brochure.

See also Colour Display Advertisement **AVIEMORE. Mr Colin Webb, Pine Bank Chalets, Dalfaber Road, Aviemore PH22 1PX (01479 810000; Fax: 01479 811469).** 🦢🦢/🦢🦢🦢🦢 *DE LUXE.* ASSC. Cosy log cabins and quality chalets in a lovely setting by the River Spey and the Cairngorm Mountains in the heart of the Scottish Highlands. An ideal touring base for exploring the "Whisky" Trail, lochs and castles and for enjoying attractions like the nearby Steam Railway and walking, cycling, watersports, birdwatching, fishing, golf and ski-ing. Country Inn and Leisure Pool nearby. Mountain bikes, Sky TV. Open all year. Pets welcome. Short Breaks available. Please contact Colin Webb for brochure and details of great holiday value.

CARR-BRIDGE by. Liz and Ian Bishop, Slochd Cottages, By Carr-Bridge PH23 3AY (01479 841666; Fax: 01479 841699). Cottages sleep 6.

A row of three cottages set in their own grounds, off the new A9, four miles north of Carr-Bridge. Ideally placed for touring and convenient for Aviemore and the Cairngorms. Inverness and Loch Ness 20 miles. Cross-country ski and mountain bike hire and wonderful forest and mountain trails from the doorstep. Ski-ing, sailing, windsurfing, canoeing, golfing, fishing, pony trekking, etc within easy reach. Each cottage has sittingroom, central heating and wood burning stove; double bedroom; fully equipped kitchen; shower room with toilet and washbasin; upstairs bedroom with four single beds. Fully equipped including linen. Cot available. Well behaved pets welcome. Open all year. Terms from £115. Fuel extra. Weekend and short stays by arrangement. SAE for further details please.

GLENMORISTON. Sleeps 6. Adjacent to woods. Three bedroomed secluded, semi-detached forester's

cottage, fully equipped and with all amenities. Open fire and electric heating. Sky TV and video. Freezer, automatic washer, etc. River Moriston 250 yards away for fishing and lochs nearby. Superb walking and touring base (ferry for Skye three-quarters of an hour away). Excellent for viewing wildlife. Inverness 35 miles, Fort Augustus 14 miles where there are golf courses. Electricity extra. Well behaved dogs allowed. Please supply own linen and towels. Short off-season breaks available. All dates including Christmas and New Year. SAE for brochure from **Mrs N.J. Wood, 30 Main Avenue, Allestree Park, Derby DE22 2EG (01332 558372).**

GLENMORISTON. Caledonia House, By Torgoyle Bridge. Sleeps 10. Spacious house set in landscaped

gardens, peaceful surroundings with views of hills and forests. Nine miles from Loch Ness. Walking, fishing and golf all nearby. House is comfortable and equipped to a high standard. Five bedrooms (one en suite), two further bath/shower rooms; games room with pool table; large lounge with TV and video; kitchen with dishwasher, fridge, freezer, cooker, microwave; utility room with washing machine, dryer, woodburning stove. Electric central heating. All linen except towels provided. Logs supplied. Dogs welcome. Patio, barbecue. Ideal for two families. Terms from £200 to £525. **Mr and Mrs S. MacLellan, Bracarina House, Invermoriston, Inverness IV3 6YA (01320 351279).**

INVERGARRY. Miss J. Ellice, Taigh-an-Lianach, Aberchalder Farm, Invergarry PH35 4HN (01809 501287). Three self catering properties, all ideal for hill walkers and country lovers. Salmon and trout fishing available. Aberchalder Lodge, traditional Highland shooting lodge, extensively modernised to give high standard of comfort, sleeps 12. Taigh-an-Lianach, modern self-contained bed-sit, secluded and peaceful, sleeps two. Leac Cottage, a secluded cottage which combines old world charm with a high standard of comfort, sleeps three. Regret no pets.

See also Colour Display Advertisement **INVERNESS. Mr Robert M. Pottie, Easter Dalziel Farm Holiday Cottages, Dalcross, Inverness IV1 2JL (Tel & Fax: 01667 462213). Up to** ❦❦❦❦ *HIGHLY COMMENDED.* Relax on our stock/arable farm seven miles east of Inverness. Our three cosy traditional stone built cottages are in a superb central location and make an excellent base from which to explore the Highlands. The area offers a wide range of activities to suit the sports minded, tourist or walker. The surrounding habitat provides a rich haven for wildlife. Look out for dolphins, roe deer and buzzards. Visit locally Cawdor Castle, Fort George, Culloden Battlefield and Loch Ness. Woodland and coastal walks. Cottages are fully equipped including linen and towels. Pets by arrangement. Low Season from £120, High season up to £350 per cottage per week. Recommended in the Good Holiday Cottage Guide. Long stays or short breaks — you are welcome all year. Brochure available.

KIRKHILL, by Inverness. Pine Chalets, Newtonhill, Lentran, Inverness. ❦❦❦ & ❦❦❦❦

COMMENDED. Five chalet site on a magnificent hillside location, each chalet having its own breathtaking view of the Beauly Firth and mountains beyond. Central for Glen Affric, Culloden Moor, Aviemore, Speyside, Isle of Skye, Ullapool and the North West. The chalets consist of lounge with colour TV, fully fitted kitchen with automatic washing machine; bathroom has shower unit in bath; one bedroom with double divan, second bedroom has twin divan beds. Bed linen supplied free and beds made up in readiness for your arrival. Chalets are all electric with immersion heater. Pony trekking, walking, fishing, golf, etc all available in the area. Weekly terms from £120 to £280. Contact: **Archie Chisholm, Fernlea, Kirkhill, By Inverness IV5 7NZ (01463 831619).**

See also Colour Display Advertisement **KIRKHILL (near Inverness). Mr M.R. Fraser, Reelig Glen, Kirkhill, Near Inverness IV5 7PR (01463 831208).** ❦❦❦ *APPROVED* to ❦❦❦❦ *COMMENDED.* **Properties sleep 4/5.** Holiday cottages and chalets in secluded woodland positions only eight miles from Inverness, capital of the Highlands. People staying here have enjoyed the freedom and the solitude; the tall trees and water of the Fairy Glen; the countryside with all the untrammelled joys of nature is at the door, butterflies find what butterflies need. Yet they have been glad of the nearness to shops, the pleasures of Inverness and of Beauly only 10 minutes' drive away. Pony trekking, sandy beaches and organised pastimes not far off. Central for touring West Coast to North, Central Highlands, Glen Affric, Culloden, Aviemore, Speyside and Moray Firth coast. The holiday homes sleep from four to five people and are fully equipped except for linen and towels (unless these are specially asked for), with electric fires, night storage heater, fridge, shaving socket and colour TV. Reduced rates spring and autumn. Brochure available.

KIRKHILL/AIGAS. Mr and Mrs E.S.C. Fraser, Kingillie, Kirkhill, Inverness IV5 7PU (01463 831275).

wwww COMMENDED. Sleep 4/6. Available from April to September, two Highland cottages eight miles apart have accommodation for six and four persons respectively. Comfortable and modernised to a high standard, both have telephone, automatic washer/dryer, colour TV, sittingroom, kitchen, bathroom, toilet, two double bedrooms (larger also has two single bedrooms). Night storage central heating. Secluded but not isolated, this makes an ideal centre for touring North and West. Facilities of Inverness only 25 minutes by car with much of architectural, historic and archaeological interest within easy reach. Golf, fishing, pony trekking all within seven miles with tennis on site. We concentrate on providing a high degree of personal attention. Children welcome. Cot available (extra), plus high chair. Electricity in addition to rental of £154 to £285 weekly, less 5% for two weeks. Linen supplied at £3 per bed per week.

NETHY BRIDGE (Spey Valley). John F. Fleming, Dell of Abernethy, Nethy Bridge PH25 3DL (01463 224358 or 01479 821643). wwww COMMENDED.

Now with easy access from the south, on roads with little traffic, enjoy the peace and tranquillity of Speyside in the shadow of the Cairgorm Mountains. With its fresh air and crystal clear water Nethy Bridge is ideal for walking, bicycling, golf, fishing, tennis and as a centre for touring the countryside and the Moray coast, visiting castles, exhibitions, wildlife parks, etc. Dell of Abernethy Cottages are one mile outside Nethy Bridge on the edge of Abernethy RSPB Nature Reserve. They are warm and comfortable, stone-built, of individual character, set in two and a half acres of lawn and mature woodland. From £170 per week. Colour brochure available.

See also Colour Display Advertisement **NETHYBRIDGE. Up to wwww HIGHLY COMMENDED. Sleeps 2/9.** ASSC. In glorious Strathspey and individually set in this beautiful Highland village, comfortable modern cottages ideal for peaceful holidays. Nethybridge is an excellent touring centre for the Cairngorms and Inverness, for river and forest walks, fishing, golf and birdwatching. Village pub meals. The cottages have central heating, duvets, linen; some with open fires. Children and pets welcome. Prices from £150 to £520 with Short Breaks available. For details and bookings please contact the local owners **Mr and Mrs Bruce Patrick, 1 Chapelton Place, Forres, Morayshire IV36 ONL (Tel & Fax: 01309 672505).**

NEWTONMORE. Ard Chattan, Craigdhu Road, Newtonmore. Family-owned holiday cottage, furnished

and equipped to a high standard, sleeping five/six persons in three bedrooms (double, twin, single plus extra bed). Electric heating throughout plus coal-effect gas fire in lounge and electric blankets. Facilities include washing and drying machines, microwave, payphone, colour TV and VHS video recorder. Linen and towels provided, electricity extra at net rates. Central location (12 miles south of Aviemore) ideal for access to all major Highland activities and attractions. Off-road parking for two vehicles. Open all year. Prices from £175 to £275 per week. Please phone or write for brochure with full details from **Mr and Mrs D. Howson, 9 Homestead Road, Caterham, Surrey CR3 5RN (01883 341259).**

NEWTONMORE. Crubenbeg Farm Steading, Newtonmore PH20 1BE (01540 673566; Fax: 01540 673509). www HIGHLY COMMENDED to wwww HIGHLY COMMENDED. Sleep 2/5 (total capacity 24). Small complex comprising seven cottages in sympathetically converted 18th century steading in the heart of the Highlands. Leisure facilities include sauna, solarium, fitness room and pond stocked with rainbow trout for fishing. An ideal area for outdoor pursuits — golf, riding, sailing, canoeing, ski-ing, etc. Four miles from bus and railway station, airport 50 miles. Kitchens are well equipped but guests may order dinner to be brought to their cottage. Children and pets welcome. One cottage is designed for guests in wheelchairs. Open January to December. Terms from £180 to £330 per week.

SPEAN BRIDGE. Barbagianni Chalet, C/o Barbagianni Guesthouse, Spean Bridge PH34 4EU (01397 712437). ✿ ✿ ✿ ✿ HIGHLY COMMENDED. Sleep

4. One chalet in own grounds finished to high standard with panoramic views of Ben Nevis mountain range. Two bedrooms (one twin and one double); bath and shower; modern kitchen fully equipped; lounge and dining area. Electric heating, washer/dryer, microwave, colour TV. Available all year round. Children and pets welcome. Excellent touring base and lots of interesting walks. Only six miles from Nevis Range ski slope. Weekly terms from £195 to £299.

KIRKCUDBRIGHTSHIRE

CASTLE DOUGLAS. Mr H.G. Ball, Barncrosh, Castle Douglas DG7 1TX (01556 680216; Fax: 01556

680442). Up to ✿ ✿ ✿ ✿ COMMENDED. Properties sleep 2/4/6/8. BARNCROSH FARM, our home, nestles amid the rolling Galloway countryside. Visitors are welcome to wander in the fields and woods. All the accommodation is of a high standard, electrically heated, fully equipped, with all linen supplied and colour TV. The OLD FARMHOUSE sleeps six in three double bedrooms upstairs, one with a double bed, two with twin beds. Ground floor has a spacious kitchen/dining room adjoining a utility room with washing machine. There is also a large lounge with electric heating. A downstairs cloakroom supplements the upstairs bathroom. The FLATS have been converted from the old stone-built stable block and are self-contained with individual access. Accommodation is of a high standard for two/three/four/five people. GALLOWAY has something special to offer all the family. Prices range from £90 to £400 weekly. Please do not hesitate to write or phone for further details. A warm welcome is assured to all our guests.

CASTLE DOUGLAS by. Mrs S. Ward, Auchenshore, Auchencairn, By Castle Douglas DG7 1QZ (01556 640244). ✿ ✿ COMMENDED. Properties sleep

2/5/6. The accommodation, situated by Balcary Bay, consists of three cottages, within 100 yards of the sea, in beautiful countryside. Ideal area for walking, bird watching, fishing, wind surfing and other sporting activities, including golf and riding. Dundrennan Abbey and Thrieve Gardens (National Trust) nearby. "Courtyard Cottage" accommodates five in two double and one single rooms, "Long Cottage" sleeps six in three double bedrooms and "Studio" takes two in one room. Properties are well heated, comfortably furnished and fully equipped. Two cottages suitable for disabled visitors. Shops two miles — car essential. Pets welcome. Play area. Weekly rates £75 to £225. Colour brochure on application.

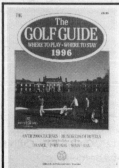

LANARKSHIRE (including the Clyde Valley)

BIGGAR. Carmichael Country Cottages, Carmichael Estate Office, Westmains, Carmichael, Biggar ML12 6PG (01899 308336; Fax: 01899 308481). 🐾🐾, 🐾🐾🐾, 🐾🐾🐾🐾 *COMMENDED* **to** *HIGHLY COMMENDED.* **Working farm, join in. Sleep 2/9.** These 200 year old stone cottages nestle among the woods and fields of our 700 year old family estate, still managed by the descendants of the original Chief of Carmichael. We guarantee comfort, warmth and a friendly welcome in an accessible, unique, rural and historic time capsule. We farm deer, cattle and sheep and sell meats and tartan — Carmichael of course! Children and pets welcome. Open all year. Terms from £160 to £430. FHB Member. ASSC Member. 12 cottages with a total of 25 bedrooms. We have the ideal cottage for you. Private tennis court and fishing loch. Cafe and farm shop. Visitor centre.

MORAYSHIRE

See also Colour Display Advertisement FORRES. Tulloch Holiday Lodges, Rafford, Forres IV36 0RY (Tel & Fax: 01309 673311). 🐾🐾🐾 *HIGHLY COMMENDED.* Our Scandinavian-style lodges are totally at home in their beautiful natural setting. The three-bedroomed lodges are beautifully equipped throughout and provide a wonderful, relaxing holiday atmosphere. The equally delightful two-bedroomed lodges are for smaller parties and young families. Forres is just four miles away, at the start of the Malt Whisky Trail, Findhorn and miles of unspoilt sandy beaches are 15 minutes' drive away. Other pursuits readily available include fishing, riding, birdwatching and walking and there are many interesting places to visit nearby. Prices from £220 to £450 per week for three-bedroomed lodges; £160 to £310 for two-bedroomed lodges. Colour brochure available.

GRANTOWN-ON-SPEY. Mr & Mrs J.R. Taylor, Milton of Cromdale, Grantown-on-Spey PH26 3PH (01479 872415). Sleeps 4. Fully modernised cottage available Easter to October. Excellent centre for touring with golf, tennis and trekking within easy reach. Large garden with views of River Spey and Cromdale Hills. Fully equipped except linen. Refrigerator, electric cooker. Two double bedrooms sleeping four. Bathroom with shower. Colour TV. Children and pets welcome. Car desirable.

See also Colour Display Advertisement ELGIN. Mrs J.M. Shaw, North East Farm Chalets, Sheriffston, Elgin IV30 3LA (01343 842695). 🐾🐾🐾 *COMMENDED.* ASSC Member. Three "A" frame Chalets near Keith and Elgin on separate working farms. "Habitat" furnished, fully equipped for two to six people, colour TV, bed linen, duvets. Beautiful rural locations in Moray — famous for flowers — district of lowlands, highlands, rivers, forests, lovely beaches, historic towns, welcoming people. Excellent local facilities. Moray golf tickets available. From £145 to £275 January to December.

LOSSIEMOUTH. Beachview Luxury Flats, Stotfield Road, Lossiemouth. 🐾🐾🐾🐾 *COMMENDED.*

Sleep 6. Situated on the beautiful Moray Firth, these two spacious flats sleep six people each in three bedrooms. Overlooking golf course, yachting station and west beach. Ideal for golfing holiday and touring Scottish Highlands. Pets welcome. Open April to October. Terms from £280 to £340 per week. For a brochure and details contact **Mrs A. Reedie, 33 Henderland Road, Bearsden, Glasgow G61 1JF (0141-942 4135).**

GRAMPIAN REGION – RICH IN CHOICES.

Whether you are looking for castles to visit, mountains to climb, beaches to lie on or rivers to fish Grampian Region will satisfy all of these and many more demands. Try and visit Crathes Castle, Tomintoul, Elgin, Pitmedden House, Cullen Bay, Culbin Forest and it hardly needs to be said, the granite city of Aberdeen itself.

NAIRNSHIRE

See also Colour Display Advertisement **AULDEARN. Mrs Julia Porter, Newton of Park Farm, Auldearn, Nairn IV12 5HY (Tel & Fax: 01667 453261). Working farm. Sleeps 4 plus cot.** Comfortable attractive cottage set in its own interesting landscaped garden in a quiet location just three miles from Nairn and 15 from Inverness. Nairn is a holiday town with clean sandy beaches, two golf courses, tennis courts and bowling green. Accommodation comprises one double and one twin bedrooms; lounge; dining room; breakfast kitchen; shower room with toilet and basin; sun porch. Facilities include colour TV, radio, automatic washing machine, tumble dryer, microwave, incoming telephone, etc. Children welcome. Sorry, no pets. Terms from £110 to £320; fuel and linen available. Directions: one and a half miles from Auldearn on B9101.

See also Colour Display Advertisement **NAIRN. Mrs Therese Muskus, Laikenbuie Holidays, Grantown Road, Nairn IV12 5QN (01667 454630).** ❦ ❦ ❦ ❦ *HIGHLY COMMENDED.* **Sleep 6.** ASSC. Watch deer and osprey on tranquil croft with beautiful outlook over loch amid birch woods. Free range hens, organic garden, sheep, fishing. Large warm chalet and two residential caravans provide luxury accommodation by the Moray Firth with its dolphins. Excellent holiday centre, four miles from Nairn with low rainfall, plentiful sunshine and sandy beaches. Near Loch Ness, Cairngorm Mountains, Cawdor Castle. All that's missing is you! No smoking inside properties. Pets by arrangement. Chalet £148 to £412; Caravans £96 to £260. Colour brochure available.

PEEBLESSHIRE

WEST LINTON. Mrs C.M. Kilpatrick, Slipperfield House, West Linton EH46 7AA (Tel & Fax: 01968 660401). ❦ ❦ ❦ *COMMENDED.* **Cottages sleep 4/6.** Two cottages a mile from West Linton at the foot of the Pentland Hills, set in 100 acres of lochs and woodlands. AMERICA COTTAGE which sleeps six in three double bedrooms is secluded and has been completely modernised. LOCH COTTAGE which sleeps four in two bedrooms is attached to the owner's house and has magnificent views over a seven acre loch. Both cottages have sittingrooms with dining areas and colour TV; modern bathrooms and excellently equipped kitchens with washing and drying machines, microwave oven and telephone. Controlled pets allowed. Ample parking; car essential. Edinburgh 19 miles. Golf and private fishing. Available all year. SAE, please, for terms.

PERTHSHIRE

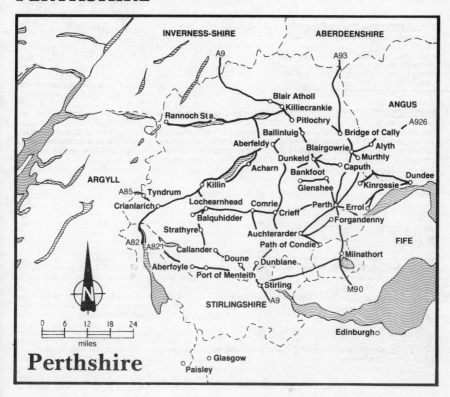

Perthshire

ABERFELDY. Loch Tay Lodges, Acharn. ❀❀❀❀ *HIGHLY COMMENDED.* **Lodges sleep 2/8.** These lodges are in a recently converted stone-built terrace listed as of special historic and architectural interest, situated on the outskirts of the picturesque Highland village of Acharn on the shores of Loch Tay. There is free trout fishing on the loch; salmon and other fishing by arrangement. Special facilities for sailing: many scenic walks. Golf at Taymouth two and a half miles and five other courses within 20 miles. The lodges are fully equipped to the highest modern standard, including colour TV. Four of the units have log fires. Open all year, with terms from £150 to £400. For free brochure, please apply to **Mrs F. Millar, Remony, Acharn, Aberfeldy PH15 2HR (Tel & Fax: 01887 830209).**

ABERFELDY by. Laigh of Cluny Steading, Edradynate, Aberfeldy PH15 2JU (01887 840469/01789 763938). ❀❀❀ *COMMENDED.* **Sleeps 6/8.** Fully furnished self-catering house with outstanding views. Sleeps six/eight people in two bedrooms. Central heating, log burner, washing machine, microwave, payphone. Linen can be supplied on request. Pets accepted by arrangement. Open from January to December for Saturday to Saturday bookings from £240 to £340 weekly, all inclusive. No extra charges for gas, electricity or firewood. Salmon fishing is available on Weem Water, River Tay, at prices ranging from £23 to £28 per day, and £4 per day for trout and grayling. Fishing is let with or without accommodation. Telephone for further details.

BLAIRGOWRIE. Cruachan Flats, Victoria Street, Rattray, Blairgowrie PH10 7AG. ✦✦✦

COMMENDED. Two fully equipped flats, each sleeping four, situated in a quiet, residential area within a few minutes of town centre. Ideal base for touring, relaxing, golfing, fishing, hill walking, theatre visits and ski-ing. Fitted kitchens including washer/dryer and microwave; shower rooms; lounge with TV, video and hi-fi. Electric blankets, radio alarms and hair dryers in bedrooms. Payphone. Cot, babysitting available. Private patio in garden, barbecue and picnic hamper and rug available. Linen, towels, washing powders and hot water (excluding instant shower) inclusive. Terms £165 to £295. Electricity extra. Midweek Breaks and weekends also available. Open all year. For brochure telephone **Miss C. Robertson 01250 874133.**

BRIDGE OF GAUR — Grampian Mountains. Mrs N. Robertson, Camusericht Farm, Bridge of Gaur, By Pitlochry PH17 2QD (01882 633219). Sleeps 5. Situated in the rugged and romantic hills of Scotland where River Gaur runs into Loch Rannoch: Bothy Cottage. Contains livingroom with multi-fuel stove; kitchenette; shower and toilet; two bedrooms with one single and two double beds. Fully furnished except linen. Children welcome. Tariff £95 per week, excluding electricity. Plenty of swimming and fishing. Also Bed and Breakfast in farmhouse. SAE for further details.

COMRIE. Lady Jauncey, Tullichettle, Comrie (01764 670349). The Bothy is an unusual 18th century

cottage, converted from a stable into a modernised, comfortable holiday home. Peaceful location with magnificent views of the Aberuchill Hills which lie across fields beyond the River Ruchill. Fishing available in Rivers Earn and Ruchill and Loch Earn. Many interesting and scenic walks. Golf course in village; bowling 10 minutes' walk. Accommodation for four persons in two twin-bedded rooms; bathroom; sitting/diningroom; kitchen with all electrical equipment, cooker, fridge, dishwasher, kettle, clothes machine/dryer, microwave oven. Everything except linen supplied. Shops one mile, car advisable — parking. Garden area. Dogs only by prior arrangement. Available March to October. Weekly terms from £180 to £280. Further details on request.

CRIEFF by. Stormont, Harrietfield, Logiealmond, By Perth. ✦✦ Traditional stone-built house on the edge of a small hamlet in a peaceful farming area in the Highlands. Crieff 10 miles, Perth nine miles, Edinburgh one hour; excellent centre for touring. Owner's own holiday house, very comfortable and convenient; all electric with one open fire. Downstairs: sittingroom, sitting/diningroom, large fitted kitchen, cloakroom with automatic washing machine, tumble dryer; deep freeze. Upstairs: large double bedroom with basin, twin room and small bunk bedded room, bathroom and airing cupboard. Carpets fitted throughout. Cot available. Duvets supplied — please bring your own linen. TV. Sheltered garden and ample parking space in yard. Caretaker 50 yards away and very helpful. Dogs by arrangement. Terms £70 to £250 per week inclusive. Full details from **Mrs J.D. Drysdale, Brill House, Brill, Buckinghamshire HP18 9RU (01844 238206).**

DUNKELD by. Laighwood Holidays, Butterstone, By Dunkeld PH8 0HB (01350 724241; Fax: 01350 724259). ✦✦✦ COMMENDED to ✦✦✦✦ DE

LUXE. Properties sleep 3/8. A de luxe detached house, comfortably accommodating eight, created from the West Wing of a 19th century Shooting Lodge with panoramic views. Two popular cottages sleeping four, situated on our hill farm, with beautiful views. Two well-equipped flats adjoining Butterglen House near Butterstone Loch. Butterstone lies in magnificent countryside (especially Spring/Autumn), adjacent to Nature Reserve (Ospreys). Central for walking, touring, historic houses, golf and fishing. Private squash court and hill loch (wild brown trout) on the farm. Sorry no pets. Terms: House £320 to £500; Cottages and Flats £90 to £200 per week.

See also Colour Display Advertisement **DUNNING. Duncrub Holidays, Dalreoch, Dunning PH2 0QJ (01764 684368; Fax: 01764 684633).** ✦✦✦ COMMENDED to ✦✦✦✦ HIGHLY COMMENDED. **Sleep 4/6.** A warm welcome awaits visitors to our two family-run holiday homes set in the beautiful Strathearn Valley with Craig Rossie in the background. This is an ideal setting from which to explore Scotland's glorious scenery, history and culture. Please write or telephone for our colour brochure.

LOCHEARNHEAD. Mrs E.O. Hendry, Immeroin Farm, Balquhidder, Lochearnhead FK19 8PF (01877 384254). Sleep 6. Rob Roy country. Two charming cottages in delightful Highland Glen each sleeping six in three double bedrooms (one with bunk beds). Cot and baby chair available. Tastefully and immaculately furnished, warm and comfortable. Fully equipped except linen which can be supplied at extra charge by arrangement. Open log fire and electric fires; fridge, electric cooker, immersion heater, spin dryer and colour TV. Excellent hill walking, canoeing, sailing, fishing, wind surfing available locally. Children and pets welcomed. Weekly terms from £120 to £210. SAE, please, for further particulars. Registered Loch Lomond, Stirling, Trossachs Tourist Board.

LOCHEARNHEAD. Pamela and Lawrence Hopkins, Earnknowe, Lochearnhead FK19 8PY (01567 830238). 🌷🌷🌷 to 🌷🌷🌷🌷 *COMMENDED.*

EARNKNOWE — Four attractive cottages sleeping two/six persons in quiet location with superb views across Loch Earn to Glen Ample and the Ben Vorlich Mountains. Ideal centre for touring the Trossachs and Central Highlands, walking, fishing and water sports. Own jetty on Loch with boat available. Launching facilities for visitors' boats nearby. A 10-minute walk to village with shop, post office, restaurants and Watersports Centre. Pets welcome. Comprehensively furnished and fully equipped, including colour TV and wood-burning stoves. Linen supplied. Weekly terms from £100 to £335. Colour brochure available.

See also Colour Display Advertisement **METHVEN. David and Moyra Smythe, Cloag Farm Cottages, Methven PH1 3RR (01738 840239).** 🌷🌷🌷 *COMMENDED.* Three cottages located on the farm away from the main road in a peaceful setting. They have extensive panoramic southerly views, yet are within walking distance of Methven Village which is seven miles west of Perth. Each cottage is well equipped, centrally heated and sleeps four. This is an excellent base from which to explore east and central Scotland or visit friends and relatives in the area. Prices from £190 inclusive of VAT per week; short breaks available. Open all year.

PERTH. Mrs K. Rowan, Beech Hedge Caravan Park, Cargill, Perth PH2 6DU (01250 883249). Small, quiet caravan park with panoramic views of the Grampian Mountains. Two caravans (maximum five persons) available April to October. Two chalets (maximum five persons) available all year. Chalets suitable for disabled visitors, with wheelchair access and wide doors. Car parking next to unit. All fully equipped except linen. Colour TV, fridge, showers, etc. Small laundry room on site; washing machine in chalets. Ideal touring centre with Dunkeld, Glamis, Braemar, Pitlochry, Scone Palace and Perth easily visited. A warm welcome assured. Terms from £60 to £225 per week.

PITLOCHRY. Michael MacPhail, Prime Perthshire Properties, Burnview House, Strathtay, Dowally Craft Centre, By Pitlochry PH9 0NT (01350 727604).

Prime Perthshire Properties. Three country retreats in showroom condition. All the properties are very well equipped and each has a dishwasher, washing machine, tumble dryer, microwave, TV etc. The three choices are: a three-bedroom, idyllic cottage in scenic Glenlyon, set beside a mountain river and amongst high hills; a four-bedroom house in the village of Strathtay beside a hill stream and just three minutes' walk from a nine-hole golf course; a five/six bedroom house, with balcony, also in Strathtay and close to the golf course. **Dowally Craft Centre, By Pitlochry, Perthshire PH9 0NT (01350 727604).**

See also Colour Display Advertisement **PITLOCHRY by. Mr and Mrs J. MacFarlane, Logierait Pine Lodges, By Pitlochry PH9 0LH (Tel & Fax: 01796 482253).** 🌷🌷🌷 *COMMENDED.* Sleep 2/8. Luxurious Scandinavian pine lodges. So peaceful with wonderful views, these chalets are beautifully situated on the banks of the River Tay. Fitted out to the highest standard for self catering comfort and open all year. Extremely warm with double glazing and electric heating. All have colour TV, refrigerators and full-size cookers, quality beds and fitted carpets. Bath and shower. Ideal centre for touring, golfing, birdwatching or just relaxing. Private fishing on River Tay, also coarse fishing free to residents. Shooting and stalking by arrangement. From £125 to £400 weekly. Colour brochure available.

ROSS-SHIRE

See also Colour Display Advertisement **AULTBEA. Mrs H. Lister, Oran Na Mara, Aultbea IV22 2HU (01445 731394).** 👑 👑 👑 *COMMENDED* to *HIGHLY COMMENDED.* **Sleep 2/8.** On the hill above the crofting/fishing village of Aultbea in the heart of scenic Wester Ross, Oran Na Mara has two luxuriously furnished flats (sleeping two) and a house (ground floor, sleeping eight). Each flat has its own entrance and is fully equipped including colour TV, bath, shower and linen. 50p meter for electricity in the flats including heating. House price includes central heating, etc. Post office, shops and two hotels within walking distance. Caravan also available. Pets welcome in house and caravan. Details of prices on request.

AULTBEA. Lochview Holidays, Aultbea. House 👑 👑 👑 👑 *HIGHLY COMMENDED.* **Sleep 4/5/7.** Overlooking Loch Ewe with panoramic views of Torridon Hills, these well equipped and comfortable properties are an ideal base for walking, climbing, fishing, painting or just to relax and enjoy the magnificent scenery. The two detached bungalows are enclosed in their own grounds with ample parking. The house is also enclosed in its own garden which has a garage as well as parking space. This property has been designed to suit disabled guests. Bed linen, towels and electricity are included in the tariff — £105 to £450 per week. For further details contact: **Mrs K. Mitchell, Riverside, Poolewe IV22 2LA (01445 781484).**

DORNIE. Tigh-na-Mara, Dornie, By Kyle. Tigh-na-Mara is a very comfortable three bedroomed detached cottage in the West Highland village of Dornie. The garden is lapped by Loch Long with Dornie Hill behind with its views of Skye. Cottage sleeps six with bathroom upstairs and shower downstairs. Oil-fired Rayburn, electric cooker, microwave, washing and drying machines, refrigerator, freezer, TV. Dinghy and outboard also available. Excellent village shop, marvellous mountain scenery, good base for walking, touring, fishing. Very well equipped, personal linen only required. £250 to £300 per week coal, oil and electricity included. **J.R.S. Gerard-Pearse, Enbrook House, 170 Offham Road, West Malling, Kent ME19 6RF (01732 842375).**

KYLE OF LOCHALSH. Zoë MacLeod, "Shore Cottages", 23 Camuslongart, Dornie, Kyle of Lochalsh IV40 8EX (01599 555357). STB 👑 👑 👑 *COMMENDED.* These charming self catering cottages are situated on the beautiful, quiet shores of Loch Long with views to Eilean Donan Castle and the mountains of Kintail. Heron Cottage sleeps four and Tigh-Na-Fasgadh sleeps six. Colour TV, shower room, washing machine. Bed linen and towels provided. Washbasins in all bedrooms. Dinghy available on request. Ideal for walking, boating, golfing, fishing. Fresh sea food delivered.

See also Colour Display Advertisement **KYLE OF LOCHALSH. Mackinnon Hathway, "Seawinds", Church Road, Kyle of Lochalsh IV40 8DD (01599 534567; Fax: 01599 534864).** Peace and tranquillity by Scottish lochs. We offer a large range of high class holiday homes accommodating from four to 12 people, all fully furnished with colour TV and washing machines. Situated in ideal positions for touring Wester Ross and Isle of Skye. Pursuits include fishing, golf, pony trekking, sailing, hill walking or simply watching otters play, all close by. Properties available from April to October. Varied prices. Please write for brochure to the above address.

LOCH TORRIDON (Wester Ross). 12 Annat, Torridon. Sleeps 4. Comfortable, well equipped, detached house in enclosed garden on the shores of Loch Torridon, in an area of spectacular scenic beauty. Ideal centre for hillwalking, fishing, sailing, birdwatching, wildlife. Close to National Trust property and Visitor Centre, and 10 miles from Beinn Eighe National Nature Reserve, and Loch Maree. Two bedrooms (one double, one twin) with washbasins; sitting room, kitchen/dining room; bathroom. All electric. Available April to October. Rates from £200. Sorry, no pets. Linen and electricity supplied inclusive. Details from **Mrs M. MacLean, School House, Kinlochewe IV22 2PA (01445 760218).**

POOLEWE. "Seabank", Poolewe, By Achnasheen. Sleeps 7. Beautifully situated cottage with large garden on seafront. Three bedrooms (two double and one with double and single beds), two with washbasins; bathroom; sittingroom with electric fire and colour TV; kitchen equipped with electric cooker, fridge, washing machine, etc. Dimplex wall panel heaters fitted in bedrooms. Ideally situated for hill walking, sandy beaches; Inverewe Gardens 10 minutes' walk; hotels, shop and heated swimming pool in village. Families and pets welcome. Available April to October. Terms from £100 to £150 per week. Electricity by 50p meter. Contact: **Mrs Doreen Robertson, 174 Culduthel Road, Inverness IV2 4BH (01463 238901).**

SUTHERLAND

LAIRG. Fernlea, Main Street, Lairg. Sleeps 6 plus cot. The house has gardens back and front and is situated in the village of Lairg, an ideal centre for touring the north and making daily return trips to Orkney and Outer Hebrides. This area also offers a wealth of opportunity for hill walking, forest walks, fishing, bird watching, boating etc. Golf course 11 miles away and sandy beaches 18 miles to the east and 35 miles to the west. The house is double glazed and fully equipped including linen; available from March to October. Fernlea has three bedrooms; two double beds and two single beds and a cot. Shower room, lounge/dining-room with colour TV; kitchen with electric cooker, microwave, washing machine and fridge, immersion heater and electric fires. Storage heater in lounge. Ample car parking. Terms from £140 to £170 per week. Rowing boat available on Loch Shin, inclusive in rent. Apply to **Mrs R. Corbett, An-Airidh, 24 Achfrish, Shinness, Lairg IV27 4DN (01549 402223).**

See also Colour Display Advertisement **LOCHINVER. Baddidarroch Holiday Chalets, Lochinver.** ❦❦❦ *HIGHLY COMMENDED.* **Sleep 4.** Our superb holiday chalets are set in their own grounds overlooking Lochinver Bay with spectacular sea and mountain views. Built to a high quality, they are comfortably furnished, well equipped and have high standards of cleanliness. Each has two bedrooms, bath/shower room, fitted kitchen with microwave and coffee-maker, suite, dining table and chairs, colour TV, fitted carpets, electric heating and balcony with patio furniture. Separate laundry room has automatic washing machine, tumble dryer, iron and ironing board and clothes airer. Ideal for fishing, birdwatching, walking or for just enjoying the Highland life. Open all year. From £175 to £425 weekly. Short Breaks available. Colour brochure on request from **Mrs J.C. MacLeod, 74 Baddidarroch, Lochinver IV27 4LP (01571 844457).**

WIGTOWNSHIRE

See also Colour Display Advertisement **DRUMMORE. Mrs S. Colman, 4 Coastguard Cottages, Drummore DG9 9QX (01776 840631).** ❦❦❦ *HIGHLY COMMENDED.* Tom Gray the Edinburgh architect has created his third holiday complex for prestige self-catering holidays in the form of a row of fishermen's cottages with a semi-detached house to finish off the row and effectively end the old village as seen from the sea. Each cottage has been named after an island off the west coast of Scotland and has tartan carpets in the lounge and dining areas. French windows at the rear open onto a patio where the southerly aspect affords the best of the sunshine to those using the garden furniture. The village is within walking distance and has several shops and two licensed hotels; there is also a bowling green and play park. Car parking. Please send for our information leaflet giving full details, terms and map.

See also Colour Display Advertisement **NEWTON STEWART. Conifers Leisure Park, Kirroughtree, Newton Stewart DG8 6AN (01671 402107; Fax: 01671 403576).** 29 self-catering luxury furnished chalets, sleep four/six persons, and attractively set amidst pine woods. All electric with colour TV. Two saunas and solarium on site, as well as heated swimming pool, tennis court and barbecues. FREE salmon and sea trout fishing, and FREE golf to our visitors. Tour the beautiful countryside; for the sportsman, river, loch and sea angling, riding and shooting are all within easy reach. There is a privately owned hotel adjacent, and a nine-hole golf course close by. Open all year. Brochure and details on request.

PORTPATRICK. Mrs Orr Ewing, Dunskey, Portpatrick, Stranraer DG9 8TJ (01776 810211; Fax: 01776 810581). ❦❦❦ *COMMENDED.* Traditional country cottages with gardens set in glorious individual locations are for people who enjoy utter peace and tranquillity and love to be surrounded by wildlife with all the amenities of a pretty harbour village only one and a half miles away. Ranger, loch fishing (fly only) tuition available, some shooting; in the village there are two golf courses, tennis, bowls, sea fishing and trips available. Excellent pubs and restaurants. Renowned gardens nearby, wonderful area for walks, wildflowers, birds and to explore topics of history and archaeology. Approach by unmetalled private roads. One cottage 100 yards from sea. Dogs welcome. Open all year. From £150 to £300 weekly. Telephone for brochure.

DUMFRIES AND GALLOWAY REGION – BURNS' COUNTRY.
A fair sprinkling of castles, the Solway Firth coast and, of course, Burns' Country makes this region an interesting tourist destination. Other attractions include the Grey Mare's Tail, Galloway Forest Park, Caerlaverock and Clatteringshaws deer museum.

SCOTTISH ISLES

ISLE OF ARRAN

Majestic .. breathtaking .. splendid .. grand ..

... all words describing Dippin Lodge, originally the Hunting Lodge of the Duke of Montrose, situated on the beautiful Isle of Arran. Dippin will be yours for as long as you like, the total seclusion offered in the 80 acres of tended gardens, meandering woodland walks, cliff top paths, and tranquil burnside strolls, leading to quite breathtaking vistas of the Firth of Clyde.

Contact Ronald & Barbara Stewart
Dippin Lodge, Dippin, Isle of Arran   Telephone: 01770 820213

We invite you to explore the Dippin Estate, and then enjoy the comfort offered throughout this rather splendid property.

See our colour advertisement on the back of this book.

PIRNMILL. Margaret Craig, Hazelwood, Pirnmill KA27 8HP (01770 850222). Working farm, join in. Sleeps 6 plus cot. Hill farm with splendid views towards the Mull of Kintyre. Interesting shoreline with sandy beaches and plenty of wildlife within 10 minutes' drive. Accommodation offered in wing of farmhouse. Large fenced garden at front. Two double bedrooms and two single. Modernised kitchen with automatic washing machine, fridge/freezer and microwave. Lounge with open fire. Night storage heating. Children and pets welcome. Weekly terms from £165 to £275.

PUBLISHER'S NOTE

While every effort is made to ensure accuracy, we regret that FHG Publications cannot accept responsibility for errors, omissions or mis-representation in our entries or any consequences thereof. Prices in particular should be checked because we go to press early. We will follow up complaints but cannot act as arbiters or agents for either party.

ISLE OF ISLAY

BALLYGRANT. Mrs Catriona Bell, Knocklearach Farm, Ballygrant PA45 7QL (Tel & Fax: 01496 840209). *COMMENDED.*

Islay — friendly people, endless sandy beaches, quiet country roads, rich in wildlife, internationally famous for birdlife. Ballygrant village is surrounded by working farms, within a mile radius there are five brown trout lochs and many historical remains including the ancient seat of the Lord of the Isles. Craigard, a traditional stone building, has been converted into three spacious self-contained flats sleeping two to eight people. Linen provided, full elelctric heating, microwave ovens, electricity included in rental, private parking. Pets welcome. Weekly terms from £120 to £250. Under personal supervision.

ISLE OF SKYE

PORTREE by. No 1 and No 2 Sca View, Upper Edinbane, By Portree. 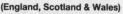 *COMMENDED.* **Sleep 6 each.** Two semi-detached houses to let. Edinbane is situated on the shores of Loch Greshornish, 14 miles from Portree and only nine miles from Dunvegan Castle. Enjoy a relaxing holiday in modern, well equipped bungalows, each containing three bedrooms, lounge, kitchen/dining room, bathroom. Double glazing and electric heating throughout. Fridge, microwave, colour TV and washing machine included in facilities. Fully equipped including linen. Cot and highchair available. Centrally located for touring Skye. Pony trekking, sea and loch fishing by arrangement, and a boat is available. Children and pets welcome. Terms from £100 to £290. Open all year. Further details from **R. MacFarlane, 15 Edinbane, By Portree, Isle of Skye IV51 9PR (Tel & Fax: 01470 582270).**

Key to Tourist Board Ratings

The Crown Scheme
(England, Scotland & Wales)

Covering hotels, motels, private hotels, guesthouses, inns, bed & breakfast, farmhouses. Every Crown classified place to stay is inspected annually. *The classification:* Listed then 1-5 Crown indicates the range of facilities and services. Higher quality standards are indicated by the terms APPROVED, COMMENDED, HIGHLY COMMENDED and DELUXE.

The Key Scheme
(also operates in Scotland using a Crown symbol)

Covering self-catering in cottages, bungalows, flats, houseboats, houses, chalets, etc. Every Key classified holiday home is inspected annually. *The classification:* 1-5 Key indicates the range of facilities and equipment. Higher quality standards are indicated by the terms APPROVED, COMMENDED, HIGHLY COMMENDED and DELUXE.

The Q Scheme
(England, Scotland & Wales)

Covering holiday, caravan, chalet and camping parks. Every Q rated park is inspected annually for its quality standards. The more ✓ in the Q – up to 5 – the higher the standard of what is provided.

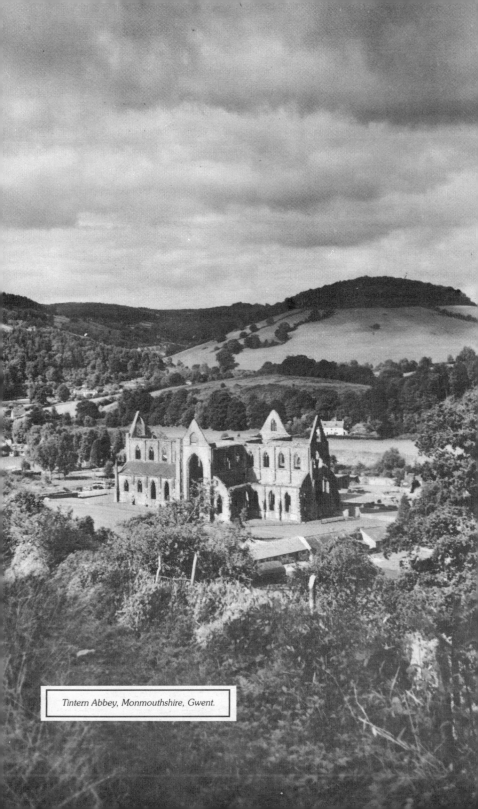

Tintern Abbey, Monmouthshire, Gwent.

WALES

CLWYD

EGLWYSBACH. Glan Aber, Eglwysbach. Sleeps 6. 🍷🍷🍷🍷 Attractive detached holiday house with orchard and parking space. Situated in the Conwy Valley amid beautiful scenery. Peaceful setting only five minutes' walk from the famous Bodnant Gardens. Six miles from beaches, 10 miles from Snowdonia and Betws-y-Coed. Ideal for touring, walking, climbing, fishing, and golf. Accommodation comprises kitchen, morning room, diningroom, lounge with TV, two family and one double bedrooms, bathroom. Night storage heaters and open fires. Children welcome, pets by arrangement. Weekly terms from £170 to £360. Short Breaks available. Personal supervision. **Mrs P. Williams, "Highways", 31 Cayley Promenade, Rhos-on-Sea LL28 4DU (01492 548268).**

OLD COLWYN. Mrs H. Gabbatt, Camelot, 127 Peulwys Lane, Old Colwyn LL29 8YF (01492 516388). Self-contained wing of bungalow in quiet elevated rural setting, sea and country views. Half a mile from beach and village, one and a half miles from Leisure Centre with swimming pool. Bedroom with double bed, bathroom, WC and shower en suite. Living room/kitchen with bed settee. Colour TV, cooker, fridge. Fully equipped except for sheets and pillow cases. All electric cooking, heating and lighting by 50p meter. Parking space. Pets and cot by arrangement. Non smokers preferred. Terms from £70 to £90 weekly. Short Breaks available out of season.

WREXHAM. "Alyn Cottages", Stoneleigh, Willow Court, Bangor-on-Dee, Wrexham LL13 0BT (01978 780679 24 hours or Tel/Fax; 01978 780770). SELF CATERING HOLIDAYS IN REGIONS FOR ALL SEASONS — North Wales/Borderlands, Cheshire and Shropshire. For all year round holidays and short breaks, Alyn Cottages provide a personal friendly service with a selection of quality properties, all fully equipped for comfort and giving value for money. Discount vouchers to visit attractions given with each booking. Properties graded by Tourist Boards of which Alyn Cottages are members, and are all fully described in our FREE brochure.

CLWYD – MOUNTAINS, RESORTS AND CASTLES
A mountainous county with pleasant resorts such as Colwyn Bay and Rhyl on its north coast and a number of castles, including Chirk, Denbigh, Ewloe, Flint, Hawarden and Ruthin. Gresford parish church, Corwen, Ruthin, the church at Llanrhaeadr and the Pontcysyllte aqueduct are also worth visiting.

DYFED

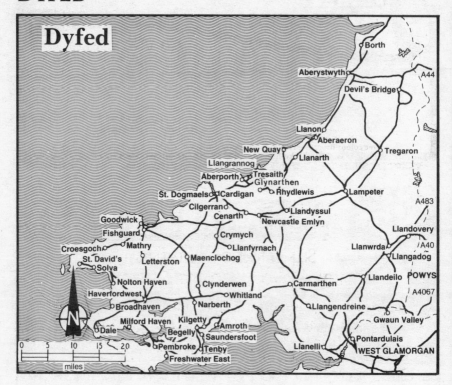

ABERPORTH. Quality Cottages. Around the magnificent Welsh Coast. Away from the madding crowd. Near safe, sandy beaches. A small specialist agency offering privacy, peace and unashamed luxury. The first WTB Self Catering Gold Medal Award Winners. Residential standards — dishwashers, microwaves, washing machines, central heating, log fires. No slot meters. Linen provided. Pets welcome free. All in coastal areas famed for scenery, walks, wild flowers, birds, badgers and foxes. Free colour brochure **S.C. Rees, "Quality Cottages", Cerbid, Solva, Haverfordwest, Pembrokeshire SA62 6YE (01348 837871).** See also our full colour advertisement on the Inside Back Cover.

ABERPORTH. Yr Ysgubor, Pantyffwrn, Aberporth. Sleeps 2 adults. Delightful, small stone cottage in beautiful and unspoilt West Wales. Ideal for retired couples. Good base for touring. Situated on a quiet lane one mile from safe sandy beach and shops. Large garden. Ample parking space in own grounds. Comfortably furnished and equipped. The accommodation comprises one double bedroom, oil-filled radiator. Sitting/diningroom (folding Z-bed), colour TV, electric fire. Kitchen with electric cooker, kettle, fridge, immersion heater. Shower room with washbasin, toilet, shower and wall heater. Pets by arrangement. Low terms, from £60. Electricity extra. Apply: **Miss M. Allen, Pantyffwrn, Aberporth, Cardigan SA43 2DT (01239 810509).**

ABERPORTH. Neuadd-Wen Holiday Bungalows, Aberporth, Cardigan. Sleep 4/5/6. Neuadd-Wen has six holiday bungalows peacefully situated just off the sea front in the picturesque coastal village of Aberporth, and only 250 yards from sandy beach. Modern brick built construction and fully equipped for up to six (except linen). Lounge, kitchenette, two bedrooms, bathroom with WC. Fridge, electric cooker, electric fires and colour TV. Cleanliness assured. Private parking. Shops, restaurant, cafe and hotel only three minutes' walk. Golf, squash, fishing, pony trekking/riding within easy reach. These bungalows are also ideal for early/late holidays, for the beach, coastal walks or for touring surrounding areas of outstanding natural beauty. Terms from £80 to £200. SAE for brochure to **Mr and Mrs A. Phillips, Orchard House, Aberporth SA43 2HG (01239 811167).**

ABERPORTH. Mrs Jann Tucker, Penffynnon, Aberporth, Cardigan SA43 2DA (01239 810387). ♀♀♀/♀♀♀♀ **Properties sleep 2/6.** Well furnished, comfortable bungalows and large apartments close by the sea in the village of Aberporth. All have sea views and ample parking and most are set in their own grounds reached by private road. Dogs welcome. Aberporth is an unspoilt village with two safe sandy beaches and bathing waters rated amongst the cleanest in Europe. The village has several pubs and a variety of shops. Cardigan is seven miles away for a more extensive range of shops and services. Local attractions include Cardigan Bay Dolphins, golf, riding and walking the Preseli Hills. Children and pets welcome. Terms from £100 to £300 per week. Linen can be hired (£4 per bed).

CROFT FARM COTTAGES, Near Cardigan

Featured in FARM HOLIDAY WHICH? 1995, Croft Farm is situated in unspoilt North Pembrokeshire countryside near sandy beaches, coastal path, Preseli National Park and many local attractions. Our slate cottages sleep 2–7. Wine, flowers, tea-tray and water welcome you. Each is fully equipped with central heating, colour TV, microwave and linen. The farmhouse also has en suite bathrooms, bedroom TVs, dishwasher and fridge freezer. Help feed Tabitha the pig, Pearl the goat and other friendly farm animals. Playground, garden, patio and barbecue for guests' use. Pets welcome.

Short Breaks from £60. Weekly cottages £105–£385.

Brochure from Andrew & Sylvie Gow, Croft Farm, Croft, Near Cardigan, Pembrokeshire SA43 3NT   Tel/Fax: 01239 615179

CARDIGAN. Teifi Gatehouse, Cliff Hotel, Gwbert-on-Sea, Cardigan. Self catering dormer bungalow set in grounds of Cliff Hotel (AA/RAC 3 star) with breathtaking views of Teifi Estuary. All facilities of the hotel are available including free golf on nine hole course, snooker, sauna, gym and outdoor heated pool. Bungalow is well appointed with central heating and has three double bedrooms. Smaller maisonette available. Prices from £100 per week. For details telephone **01239 613241.**

CARDIGAN. Bob and Jennie Donaldson, Gorslwyd Farm, Tanygroes, Cardigan SA43 2HZ (Tel & Fax: 01239 810593). WTB 4 Dragons Award. In the

country by the sea, close to sandy beaches and holiday activities. Country style cottages in beautiful, peaceful setting that includes Prince of Wales Award winning gardens, nature trail, barbecue, adventure play area, countryside museum, farm animals, games room and laundry facilities. Comfortable, well equipped and maintained two or three bedroom cottages. Gorslwyd is secluded but not remote, an ideal base from which to explore and enjoy West and Mid Wales. Weekly terms from £100 to £300 per cottage. Designed and equipped to be ACCESSIBLE TO WHEELCHAIR USERS throughout.

CARDIGAN COAST (Tresaith/Llangranog). Mrs C. Davies, Brynarthen, Glynarthen, Llandysul SA44 6PG (01239 851783). Cottages sleep 6; Caravan sleeps 4. Brynarthen is a small working farm delightfully

situated amidst beautiful unspoilt countryside, minutes from sandy beaches, one mile off the A487 Cardigan/Aberaeron coastal road. Within the grounds are two charming traditional stone cottages and one caravan, each surrounded by pleasant lawns and gardens, ideal for those just wishing to relax and take it easy. The superb cottages are personally maintained to a high standard and whilst retaining all their charm and character, are comfortably furnished to meet family needs. One is also ideal for the elderly or partially disabled. Each cottage sleeps six with three bedrooms, bathroom, fully equipped kitchen/diner, lounge with colour TV, video and fitted carpets throughout. The modern 28' caravan sleeps four with a double bedroom, bunk bedroom, shower room with instant hot water, fully equipped kitchen/diner and spacious lounge with colour TV and fitted carpets throughout. Laundry room, play area. Open all year. Brochure on request.

CRICCIETH. Quality Cottages. Around the magnificent Welsh Coast. Away from the madding crowd. Near safe, sandy beaches. A small specialist agency offering privacy, peace and unashamed luxury. The first WTB Self Catering Gold Medal Award Winners. Residential standards — dishwashers, microwaves, washing machines, central heating, log fires. No slot meters. Linen provided. Pets welcome free. All in coastal areas famed for scenery, walks, wild flowers, birds, badgers and foxes. Free colour brochure **S.C. Rees, "Quality Cottages", Cerbid, Solva, Haverfordwest, Pembrokeshire SA62 6YE (01348 837871).** See also our full colour advertisement on the Inside Back Cover.

FISHGUARD. Mr Richard Collier, Abergwaun Hotel, Market Square, Fishguard SA65 9HA (01348 872077; Fax: 01348 875412). Sleeps 8/9 plus cot. Self contained holiday flat on the second floor of the Abergwaun Hotel in the centre of Fishguard. Convenient for shops, pubs and restaurants. The flat is well equipped with lounge/diner (sea views); bathroom; kitchen; two large double bedrooms and two twin bedrooms (one with bunkbeds). Colour TV, video, baby listening for use in hotel lounge bar and restaurant. Self catering with hotel comforts. Gas, electricity and bed linen are all included. Weekly terms from £120 to £300.

GOODWICK. Mrs M.R. Edwards, Trehowel, Goodwick, Pembrokeshire SA64 0JN (01348 891259). Two select, furnished houses, completely equipped for up to five persons, with electric night storage heaters and all modern conveniences including colour TV, cot if required, electric cooker, fridge, automatic washing machine, etc. Linen and towels not provided. One double bedroom with washbasin, other bedroom with three single beds; studio couch in lounge. Situated in the National Park with beautiful coastal scenery, between Fishguard and Strumble Head. Two miles from Goodwick, three miles from Fishguard. Children welcome. Pets welcome if fully house trained. Open March to October. Let without attendance. Wales Tourist Board Approved. Terms from £100 to £240 per week.

QUALITY COTTAGES

AROUND THE MAGNIFICENT WELSH COAST

Away from the Madding Crowd · Near safe sandy beaches

A small specialist agency with over 33 years experience of providing quality self-catering offers privacy, peace and unashamed luxury.
The first Wales Tourist Board Self-Catering Award Winner. Highest residential standards.
Dishwashers, Microwaves, Washing Machines, Central Heating. No slot meters.
LOG FIRES   LINEN PROVIDED   PETS WELCOME FREE!
All in coastal areas famed for scenery, walks, wild-flowers, birds, badgers and foxes.
Away from the madding crowd.
Free colour Brochure: F.G. Rees, "Quality Cottages", Cerbid, Solva, Haverfordwest,
Pembrokeshire SA62 6YE. Telephone: (01348) 837871.

HAVERFORDWEST. Nolton Haven Farm Cottages in Pembrokeshire National Park. Situated beside Nolton Haven's sandy beach which they overlook, these six stone, slate and pine cottages offer discerning guests the ideal situation to enjoy the superb Pembrokeshire coastline. The cottages are fully equipped with colour TV, microwave, fridge/freezer, etc. 30 yards to the beach, 75 yards to the local inn/restaurant. Pony trekking, surfing, fishing, excellent cliff walks, boating and canoeing are all available nearby. Contact: **Jim Canton, Nolton Haven Farm, Nolton Haven, Haverfordwest SA62 2NH (01437 710263).** Colour brochure on request.

LLANDOVERY. Tyncoed Farm, Myddfai Road, Llandovery. Sleeps 7+. This spacious and very comfortable old farmhouse is beautifully set overlooking the Towy Valley, with magnificent views from the house. Tyncoed is in a secluded and private position, yet very conveniently situated just off the A4069 Llandovery/Llangadog road. The farmhouse retains much character and charm with its original stone fireplace and oak beams. As it is on the fringe of the Brecon Beacons National Park, it makes a perfect base for touring this delightful rural area. Log fires and storage heaters. Fully equipped. Cot and high chair available. Terms from £100 to £220 per week. SAE please for further details to **Mrs Lewis Jones, Llwynmeredydd Farm, Myddfai, Llandovery SA20 0JE (01550 720450).**

LLANELLI. Mrs Rawlings, Dan-y-Quarry, Five Roads, Llanelli SA15 5JA (01269 860187). Sleeps 18. Large farmhouse with panoramic views over countryside and Carmarthen Bay. Ideal centre for touring Gower, Brecon Beacons and Pembrokeshire. A wealth of fine beaches easily accessible as is Swansea with its many attractions. 10 miles from Pembrey Country Park and Motor Sports Centre. Accommodation comprises three very large family rooms with washbasins each sleeping up to five and one family room sleeping three; two bathrooms; lounge with colour TV; separate panelled dining room; kitchen with electric cooker, dishwasher, microwave, washer/dryer. Full central heating. Ample parking, safe playing areas for children. Linen supplied. Please telephone or write for details.

PLEASE SEND A STAMPED ADDRESSED ENVELOPE WITH ENQUIRIES

Castell Howell

Pontshaen, Llandysul,

Dyfed

Telephone 01545 590209

12 well-equipped family cottages sleeping 2/8, converted from 200 year old farm buildings. Set in 90 acres, 9 miles inland from New Quay. Facilities include heated indoor swimming pool with toddlers' splash pool, sauna, squash courts and games room. All-weather tennis court, horse riding, clay pigeon shooting on site. Deer and animal park; rabbits and guinea pigs on lawn. Varied homemade menu and good wines available in the Castle bar. Children welcome.

Contact: Andrew or Lisa Nunn for colour brochure.

LLANGOEDMOR. Glandwr, Llangoedmor, Near Cardigan. Working farm, join in. Sleeps 4 adults; 1 child. Glandwr Holiday House is in the parish of Llangoedmor, on the B4570 one mile from the market town of Cardigan. This charming, well equipped, semi-detached holiday home sits in a sunny position in its own grounds with lawn front and back, small drive and ample parking space. Lovely countryside views and walks, sandy beaches two/eight miles, fishing on River Teifi. Two double bedrooms (double bed in each), single bedroom, all very well equipped; bathroom with over-bath electric shower, washbasin, toilet; downstairs toilet; fitted kitchen/dining area, fully equipped with full size electric stove, microwave oven, all utensils, two fridges; comfortable sittingroom with 20-inch colour TV. Fitted carpets. Central heating, electricity included in charge. Available all year from £90 inclusive, with any extra person charged at an additional £12 per week. Mini-breaks from £65. One well trained pet £8 per week. High standard of comfort, service and heating. SAE to **Mrs B. Evans, Rhydyfuwch Dairy Farm, Near Cardigan, Dyfed SA43 2LB (01239 612064).**

LLANGRANNOG. Quality Cottages. Around the magnificent Welsh Coast. Away from the madding crowd. Near safe, sandy beaches. A small specialist agency offering privacy, peace and unashamed luxury. The first WTB Self Catering Gold Medal Award Winners. Residential standards — dishwashers, microwaves, washing machines, central heating, log fires. No slot meters. Linen provided. Pets welcome free. All in coastal areas famed for scenery, walks, wild flowers, birds, badgers and foxes. Free colour brochure **S.C. Rees, "Quality Cottages", Cerbid, Solva, Haverfordwest, Pembrokeshire SA62 6YE (01348 837871).** See also our full colour advertisement on the Inside Back Cover.

LLANGRANNOG. Miss M.B. Jones, Angorfa, Llangrannog, Llandyssul SA44 6SL (01239 654262).

Two houses and one bungalow with modern conveniences, situated near sea front, with safe sandy beaches, available for self catering holidays from Easter to October. This is an area of outstanding natural beauty and a car is essential for touring the lovely countryside. Magnificent walks along the cliffs with panoramic view of Cardigan Bay. Accommodation for up to six people, cots and high chairs are provided in each house. Bathrooms; sittingrooms and dining/kitchens. Electric cooking facilities and heating. Everything supplied except linen. Children welcome and pets accepted by prior arrangement. Shops and public transport a few yards away. Weekly terms available on request. SAE, please.

See also Colour Display Advertisement **MYDROILYN. Blaenllanarth Holiday Cottages, Mydroilyn, Lampeter SA48 7RJ (01570 470374).** Stone farm buildings, recently converted into four cottages, providing a modern standard of comfort in a traditional setting. Sleep two to three (terms £90 to £180), or sleep four to eight (terms £145 to £300). Gas, electricity and linen included in price. All have shower-room and fully-equipped kitchen. Colour TV; shared laundry-room; facilities for children. Special terms for Short Breaks. Open Easter to October. Situated in a secluded rural area abundant with wildlife. Only five miles from sandy beaches and picturesque harbours of Cardigan Bay. Within easy reach of National Trust coastal footpaths, sites of historic and cultural interest, steam railways, castles and breathtaking mountain scenery. Bird watching, fishing and pony trekking nearby. AA Approved. Full details from **Gil and Mike Kearney.**

NEWGALE. Quality Cottages. Around the magnificent Welsh Coast. Away from the madding crowd. Near safe, sandy beaches. A small specialist agency offering privacy, peace and unashamed luxury. The first WTB Self Catering Gold Medal Award Winnners. Residential standards — dishwashers, microwaves, washing machines, central heating, log fires. No slot meters. Linen provided. Pets welcome free. All in coastal areas famed for scenery, walks, wild flowers, birds, badgers and foxes. Free colour brochure **S.C. Rees, "Quality Cottages", Cerbid, Solva, Haverfordwest, Pembrokeshire SA62 6YE (01348 837871).** See also our full colour advertisement on the Inside Back Cover.

NEWPORT. Quality Cottages. Around the magnificent Welsh Coast. Away from the madding crowd. Near safe, sandy beaches. A small specialist agency offering privacy, peace and unashamed luxury. The first WTB Self Catering Gold Medal Award Winners. Residential standards — dishwashers, microwaves, washing machines, central heating, log fires. No slot meters. Linen provided. Pets welcome free. All in coastal areas famed for scenery, walks, wild flowers, birds, badgers and foxes. Free colour brochure **S.C. Rees, "Quality Cottages", Cerbid, Solva, Haverfordwest, Pembrokeshire SA62 6YE (01348 837871).** See also our full colour advertisement on the Inside Back Cover.

NEWPORT. Llwyngwair Manor Holiday Park, Newport. Set in 36 acres of beautiful parkland, the  apartments lie at the foot of magnificent Carn Ingli, in the romantic Preseli district of North Pembrokeshire. We are only a mile from the sea and enjoy three-quarters of a mile of private fishing on the renowned River Nevern. Fully equipped luxury apartments to rent. Fully licensed Manor Hotel with many facilities. Telephone **(01239 820498).**

SOLVA. Quality Cottages. Around the magnificent Welsh Coast. Away from the madding crowd. Near safe, sandy beaches. A small specialist agency offering privacy, peace and unashamed luxury. The first WTB Self Catering Gold Medal Award Winners. Residential standards — dishwashers, microwaves, washing machines, central heating, log fires. No slot meters. Linen provided. Pets welcome free. All in coastal areas famed for scenery, walks, wild flowers, birds, badgers and foxes. Free colour brochure **S.C. Rees, "Quality Cottages", Cerbid, Solva, Haverfordwest, Pembrokeshire SA62 6YE (01348 837871).** See also our full colour advertisement on the Inside Back Cover.

ST. DAVID'S. Quality Cottages. Around the magnificent Welsh Coast. Away from the madding crowd. Near safe sandy beaches. A small specialist agency offering privacy, peace and unashamed luxury. The first WTB Self Catering Gold Medal Award Winners. Residential standards — dishwashers, microwaves, washing machines, central heating, log fires, no slot meters. Linen provided. Pets welcome free. All in coastal areas famed for scenery, walks, wild flowers, birds, badgers and foxes. Free colour brochure **S.C. Rees, "Quality Cottages", Cerbid, Solva, Haverfordwest, Pembrokeshire SA62 6YE (01348 837871).** See also our full colour advertisement on the Inside Back Cover.

ST. DAVID'S. Llysnewydd, Llanrhian, St. David's, Pembrokeshire. Sleeps 6. A delightful farmhouse  situated in Pembrokeshire's renowned National Park, six miles from St. David's, two miles from Croesgoch and a mile from Llanrhian and the picturesque fishing village of Porthgain. Within a mile of numerous safe sandy beaches. The enchanting coastal path runs through the farmland. Sleeps six in one family bedroom, one double bedroom and one attic bedroom; fully equipped and fitted dining kitchen (microwave oven and new automatic washing machine); TV room and pleasant spacious lounge. Fitted carpets throughout and fresh decor. No linen supplied. Washing, ironing and airing facilities. There is a bathroom with a toilet upstairs and also a toilet downstairs. Storage heaters and radiators for your warmth and comfort. Cot available. Ample parking. Secluded sunny lawn with southerly aspect. Open all year including winter mini breaks. £105 to £285 weekly. Electricity by £1 coin meter. Off peak night storage heaters assessed on meter readings. SAE for prompt reply to **Mrs C.E. Skeel Jones, Arosfyr Farm, Dolgellau, Gwynedd LL402YP (01341 422355).**

WHEN MAKING ENQUIRIES PLEASE MENTION
FARM HOLIDAY GUIDES

TENBY. Quality Cottages. Around the magnificent Welsh Coast. Away from the madding crowd. Near safe, sandy beaches. A small specialist agency offering privacy, peace and unashamed luxury. The first WTB Self Catering Gold Medal Award Winners. Residential standards — dishwashers, microwaves, washing machines, central heating, log fires. No slot meters. Linen provided. Pets welcome free. All in coastal areas famed for scenery, walks, wild flowers, birds, badgers and foxes. Free colour brochure **S.C. Rees, "Quality Cottages", Cerbid, Solva, Haverfordwest, Pembrokeshire SA62 6YE (01348 837871).** See also our full colour advertiement on the Inside Back Cover.

WHITLAND. Mrs Angela Colledge, Gwarmacwydd, Llanfallteg, Whitland SA34 0XH (01437 563260). WTB Grade 4. Gwarmacwydd is a country estate of over 450 acres including two miles of riverbank. Come and see a real farm in action; the hustle and bustle of harvest, cows being milked, new born calves and lambs. Children are welcomed. On the estate are five character stone cottages. Each cottage has been lovingly converted from traditional farm buildings, parts of which are over 200 years old. Each cottage is fully furnished and equipped with all modern conveniences. All electricity and linen included. All cottages are heated for year-round use. Colour brochure available.

GWENT

ABERGAVENNY. Llyweddrog Farm, Llanwenarth, Abergavenny. Sleeps 4 adults, 2 children. Stone built farmhouse high on Sugar Loaf Mountain with panoramic views of Usk Valley. Partial central heating. Large fitted kitchen/diner and spacious lounge with open fire. Double, twin and bunk-bedded rooms. Situated between enclosed farmland and mountainside owned by National Trust — great for nature walks. Ideal base for exploring — Vale of Usk, Golden Valley, historic buildings, Roman remains, industrial heritage.Open May to October. Children welcome. Terms from £150 to £280 per week. Contact: **Mrs N.E. Smith, Penygraig Farm, Llanwenarth Citra, Abergavenny NP7 7LA (01873 853398).**

ABERGAVENNY. Troedrhiwmwn, Llanthony, Abergavenny. Sleeps 9. WTB Grade 4. Our traditional 14th century farmhouse on a working farm, furnished to a high standard, is located in the heart of the Black Mountains and commands spectacular views over Llanthony Priory and Valley. It is the perfect retreat for a relaxing and peaceful holiday; ideal for walking, birdwatching, pony trekking or exploring the beautiful surrounding countryside with its many old churches and castles. Guests are welcome to feed the hens, goats, pony, lambs and calves. The farmhouse has three bedrooms, spacious kitchen, fully equipped with microwave, etc. Lounge with large open fireplace and large garden/play area. Bed linen provided. Weekend and midweek breaks. Brochure available. For terms and full details contact: **Mrs Mary Thomas, Cwmbuchill, Llanthony, Abergavenny NP7 7NN (01873 890619).**

GWENT – BORDER COUNTY
Nestling in the south-east corner of Wales, Gwent is an undulating county which includes the ever popular Wye Valley. Other attractions are Chepstow, Abergavenny, Tintern Forest and Tredegar.

GWYNEDD

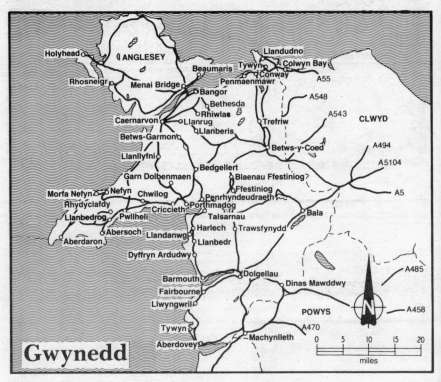

ABERDARON. Mrs M. Parry Roberts, "Ty Fry", Aberdaron, Pwllheli LL53 8BY (01758 760274). Sleeps 5. Working farm. Completely modernised and fully furnished with bed linen supplied, this Welsh cottage has exclusive views over Aberdaron Bay. Few minutes' walk from the local grocery shop. Private drive from main road, and ample parking space. Convenient for many beaches and coves, including the famous Whistling Sands. Mountain walks where the sea views literally surround you, on the extreme tip of the Lleyn Peninsula. Accommodation to let furnished without attendance. Two bedrooms sleeping five, cot available; bathroom; immerser; large lounge with TV; kitchen/diner with electric cooker, fridge. Metered electricity. Pets welcome. Bookings from March to October. For prompt reply SAE, please.

QUALITY COTTAGES

AROUND THE MAGNIFICENT WELSH COAST

Away from the Madding Crowd · Near safe sandy beaches

A small specialist agency with over 33 years experience of providing quality self-catering offers privacy, peace and unashamed luxury.
The first Wales Tourist Board Self-Catering Award Winner. Highest residential standards.
Dishwashers, Microwaves, Washing Machines, Central Heating. No slot meters.
LOG FIRES   LINEN PROVIDED   PETS WELCOME FREE!
All in coastal areas famed for scenery, walks, wild-flowers, birds, badgers and foxes.
Away from the madding crowd.
Free colour Brochure: F.G. Rees, "Quality Cottages", Cerbid, Solva, Haverfordwest, Pembrokeshire SA62 6YE. Telephone: (01348) 837871.

ABERDOVEY. Aberdovey House and Flats. Beach 10 seconds! Sea front, very special maisonettes, flats, also luxury hillside bungalow and house, private balcony, terraces, even a jacuzzi. Guests continually say "CLEANEST AND BEST SELF CATERING THEY HAVE EVER FOUND". Beautifully furnished, equipped, fantastic views. Charming, picturesque village in Snowdonia National Park. Fish, golf. "Luxury Living, Realistic Prices". **Mrs A.D. Bendall, Hafod, Aberdovey LL35 0EB Freephone 0800 212305 for colour brochure. Reservations/administration 01654 767418; Fax: 01654 767078.**

ABERSOCH. Quality Cottages. Around the magnificent Welsh Coast. Away from the madding crowd. Near safe sandy beaches. A small specialist agency offering privacy, peace and unashamed luxury. First Wales Tourist Board Self Catering Gold Award Winner. Residential standards — Dishwashers, Microwaves, Washing Machines, Central Heating, Log Fires, No Slot Meters. Linen provided. Pets welcome free. All in coastal areas famed for scenery, walks, wild flowers, birds, badgers and foxes. Free colour brochure **S.C. Rees, "Quality Cottages", Cerbid, Solva, Haverfordwest, Pembrokeshire SA62 6YE (01348 837871).** See also our colour advertisement on the Inside Back Cover of this guide.

ANGLESEY. Ty Mawr, Llanddaniel, Anglesey. Ty Mawr is for those who appreciate peace and seclusion without being too far off the beaten track. Enjoying uninterrupted views of Snowdonia it is situated on a non-working 50 acre farm and approached by a 400 yard farm lane. Half a mile from a small village and two miles from A5 road; five miles from Menai Bridge and Anglesey's market town Llangefni, six miles from a lovely beach at Newborough. Two twin and one double bedrooms; modern bathroom, toilet and shower; sitting and living room; kitchen with automatic washing machine, fridge/freezer, electric cooker, etc. Ground floor toilet. Telephone. Brochure from **Mrs M.E. Williams, Tyddyn Goblet, Brynsiencyn, Anglesey LL61 6TZ (01248 430296).**

ANGLESEY. Mrs Carol Jones, Tyn Lôn, Llanddona, Beaumaris LL58 8TU (01248 811280). Sleeps

4/6. Tyn Lôn offers luxurious accommodation in an area of outstanding natural beauty close to the historic town of Beaumaris and the breathtakingly beautiful Red Wharf Bay with its unspoilt sandy beaches. The property stands in an acre of garden providing ample car parking and safe grounds for children. Cot and high chair available. Personally supervised, this spacious and tastefully decorated accommodation comprises a well equipped kitchen with automatic washing machine and dryer; lounge/diner; two bedrooms (one double and one twin); bathroom with shower fitment. Bed linen provided. Electricity by 50p meter. Central heating available by arrangement. No pets. Terms from £150 to £250 weekly.

ANGLESEY (Beaumaris). Quality Cottages. Around the magnificent Welsh Coast. Away from the madding crowd. Near safe, sandy beaches. A small specialist agency offering privacy, peace and unashamed luxury. The first WTB Self Catering Gold Medal Award Winners. Residential standards — dishwashers, microwaves, washing machines, central heating, log fires. No slot meters. Linen provided. Pets welcome free. All in coastal areas famed for scenery, walks, wild flowers, birds, badgers and foxes. Free colour brochure **S.C. Rees, "Quality Cottages", Cerbid, Solva, Haverfordwest, Pembrokeshire SA62 6YE (01348 837871).** See also our full colour advertisement on the Inside Back Cover.

ANGLESEY & SNOWDONIA

See Anglesey and Snowdonia from a cottage to suit you. Sleeping 2 to 20, some are luxurious, others are simple and low priced; all are clean and well equipped. Whether by the beach, in the hills or in a village, all are peaceful. Many have washing machines, tumble dryers, microwaves and freezers, and all have colour TV. Contented guests return year after year to our cottages. For our brochure contact:

Menai Holiday Cottages, 1 Greenfield Terrace, Hill Street, Menai Bridge, Anglesey LL59 5AY. Telephone (01248) 717135 Fax: (01248) 717051

BALA. Mr and Mrs Looke, "Rafel", Parc, Bala LL23 7YU (01678 540369). Stone cottage with beams situated in the Snowdonia National Park and well equipped for four people. Double bedroom, lounge with sofa bed, log fire. Central heating. Colour TV. Fitted kitchen with electric cooker; shower, WC, washbasin. Ample parking. Magnificent views. Three miles Bala market town, one and three-quarter miles Bala Lake, the largest natural lake in Wales. Ideal for watersports, fishing, golf, pony trekking, climbing, walking, painting, birdwatching or just relaxing. Well behaved pets welcome. Short term stays available. Weekly terms from £150 to £260. Bed linen, logs, electricity included. Open all year. Beware — can be addictive!

BALA. Mrs M.A. Roberts, Godre'r Aran, Llanuwchllyn, Bala LL23 7UB (01678 540687). WTB Grade 4. Sleeps 4 plus cot. A luxury riverside self-contained apartment on the lower level of modern split-level detached residence on the outskirts of village near Bala Lake. Village shop/post office and village inn serving excellent meals within easy walking distance. Scenic open mountain views, with access to river from garden (free fishing). Ample parking in spacious forecourt. Centrally positioned for Snowdonia and coast, the area is noted for natural beauty and outdoor pursuits — hill walking, bird watching, fishing, sailing, wind surfing, country walks and cycling, miniature railways. The accommodation comprises fully fitted kitchen with microwave and washing machine; open plan lounge/diner with colour TV, electric fire; shower room with toilet, washbasin, shaving point; twin bedroom. Large double bedroom with en-suite toilet facilities on floor above. Cot and Teasmaid. Extra folding single bed available. Centrally heated. One pet permitted. Barbecue and garden furniture. Linen supplied. Terms inclusive of electricity and hot water supply from £150 per week; reduction for Senior Citizens. New Leisure Centre with swimming pool at Bala (five miles). SAE for brochure.

BALA near. Rhyd Fudr, Llanuwchllyn, near Bala. Sleeps 6. Four wheel drive vehicle? This is the cottage for you. This stone farm cottage is set in an isolated position with views of five mountain peaks and Bala Lake. Accommodation comprises three bedrooms, sleeping six plus cot; two sittingrooms; sun room; kitchen; bathroom. Garage. Multi-fuel burning stove and most modern conveniences but no TV. Fully equipped including washing machine and telephone. Linen not supplied. Mountain stream and lovely walks on the doorstep. Sea, 45 minutes by car; Snowdon, one hour. Children welcome. Terms from £150. Apply: **Mrs J.H. Gervis, Nazeing Bury, Nazeing, Essex EN9 2JN (0199-289 2331) or Mrs G.E. Evans, Pant-y-Ceubren, Llanuwchllyn, Bala (016784 252).**

BALA (Snowdonia National Park). Ceunant Isaf, Rhyduchaf, Bala. Beautiful 18th century cottage in

secluded and tranquil setting standing in 12 acres of its own land with large garden and stream. Half mile from village of Rhyduchaf and three miles Bala town and lake. The cottage has a wealth of oak beams and sleeps two to seven plus cot in five bedrooms, two double and three single (three with washbasins); two bathrooms; lounge with colour TV, wood burning stove (free logs); oak fitted kitchen with Neff appliances including dishwasher, fan assisted oven and fridge. Breakfast bar. Economy 7 heating. Linen not provided. Pets welcome. £160 to £245 per week. Contact: **Stephen Webster, Newhaven Farm, Billington, Stafford ST18 9DJ (01785 780253).**

BEDDGELERT. Joan Williams, Colwyn, Beddgelert (01766 890276). Old stone cottage overlooking

river in the centre of a picturesque and unspoilt village at the foot of Snowdon. Surrounded by mountains, forests, lakes, streams. Genuinely old, with warmth, character and imperfections. Fully carpeted, furnished and equipped. All bedrooms en suite with central heating; electric blankets, white linen and towels. Kitchen has washer, dryer, dishwasher, fridge freezer, microwave. Village inns, shops and good food all within 100 yards. Electricity at standard rate. Parking adjacent, no garden. Walkers, muddy boots and wet dogs welcome. Unsuitable for small children or the infirm. Sleeping six £390 per week, sleeping eight £480, open all year. Winter Breaks for six £180, for eight £240. Also to let small cottage sleeping two at £160 March to October.

BEDDGELERT. Bron Eifion, Rhyd Ddu, Beddgelert. Sleeps 6. Attractive semi-detached house on edge of small village in National Park at foot of Snowdon. Splendid mountain, valley and pass walks from village including path up Snowdon. Lakes nearby. Excellent centre for seaside, historic castles and houses, riding, fishing and touring. Three bedrooms; two livingrooms; bathroom; modern kitchen, fridge, airing cupboard, heaters. Well equipped. Mountain view, terrace, rough garden. Inn serving meals nearby. Cot. Sorry, no pets. High season £150 to £240 per week; low season £55 to £140 per week. Short Breaks by arrangement. Open all year. Apply: **Johnson, 12 Chatsworth Way, London SE27 9HR (0181-670 6455).**

BEDDGELERT. Meillionen, Beddgelert. Farmhouse situated in the heart of Snowdonia within one mile of picturesque village. Large house divided into two separate units. One consists of large kitchen/livingroom with colour TV, electric cooker, fridge and Rayburn; stone staircase leads to two double bedrooms and bathroom. Other unit consists of sittingroom, colour TV, open fireplace; kitchen with fridge and electric cooker; downstairs bathroom; three double bedrooms and single bed; cot and high chair available in this larger unit. Bed and table linen not provided. Storage heaters in winter. Electricity on meter. Fishing, pony trekking and sports facilities nearby, also beaches within easy reach. SAE to **Mrs S.H. Owen, Cwm Cloch, Beddgelert, Caernarfon (01766 890241).**

BETWS-Y-COED 6 miles. Two Detached Cottages. Sleep 5/6 plus cot. WTB Grade 4. Situated in a

farming area with panoramic views of Snowdonia and the Conwy Valley, the accommodation is of a high standard and under the owners' personal supervision. Centrally heated, open fire with fuel and electricity supplied free, also bed linen. Colour TV. Modern, well equipped kitchen with automatic washing machine. Ideal location for touring North Wales — within easy reach of sea, lakes, mountains and castles. Ideal for two families holidaying together. Available all year from £140 weekly. Details from **Mrs N. Evans, Pen y Bryn Bach, Maenan, Llanrwst LL26 0UR (01492 640438/640768).**

BETWS-Y-COED. Dol-llech, Capel Curig, Near Betws-y-Coed. Sleeps 7. Detached farmhouse in beautiful Welsh countryside within easy reach of popular climbs and for rambling through magnificent Snowdonia scenery. Its location gives good access for touring Snowdonia and North Wales coast. Lounge, diningroom, kitchen, bathroom and toilet. Four bedrooms — two double, one twin and one single. Microwave, washing machine, tumble dryer, fridge/freezer, cooker; open fire in lounge. Economy 7 heaters. Private parking for three cars. Small sitting-out area with picnic table and barbecue. Electricity on 50p meter. Heaters and bed linen included in rent. Shops and pubs one and a quarter miles. Terms from £115 to £300 per week. Details: **Gwen Williams, Ty'n Twll, Eglwys Bach, Colwyn Bay, Clwyd LL28 5SB (01492 580391).**

BETWS-Y-COED. Jim and Lilian Boughton, Bron Celyn, Llanrwst Road, Betws-y-Coed LL24 0HD (Tel & Fax: 01690 710333). Our cosy 200 year old converted coach house has been tastefully refurbished and offers accommodation for up to four persons. Upstairs: one double room with space for a cot and one bunk-bedded room with full length/width bunk beds. All bed linen is provided but not towels. Downstairs: lounge with colour TV and wood burning stove (ample supply of chopped timber available), kitchen with fridge, electric cooker, microwave, toaster and water heater. Shower room and toilet. Electric storage heaters fitted throughout. Metered electricity (read arrival/departure). Open all year. Ideal centre for walking, climbing, fishing or simply just relaxing! Terms: £120 to £300 per week. Short Breaks available.

BETWS-Y-COED. Mrs E. Thomas, Bryn Farm, Nebo, Llanrwst LL26 0TE (01690 710315). Working farm, join in. Farmhouse flat sleeping two. The perfect place for a peaceful holiday in lovely Conwy Valley close to the North Wales Coast and five miles from Betws-y-Coed in the heart of Snowdonia. The accommodation is private and self-contained and consists of a living room with colour TV; fully equipped kitchen area with fridge and microwave; bathroom, toilet; double bedroom with electric blanket, duvets and bed linen provided free of charge. Also centrally heated during winter. Shop, bakery and Inn two miles. Open all year. Terms from £80 to £150 including heating and electricity. Bed settee also available for additional sleeping accommodation.

Welcome to beautiful Bryn Bras Castle – enchanting castle Apartments, elegant Tower-House, cosy mini-cottage, within unique romantic turreted Regency Castle (Listed Building) in the gentle foothills of Snowdonia. Centrally situated amidst breathtaking scenery, ideal for exploring North Wales' magnificent mountains, beaches, resorts, heritage and history. Near local country inns/restaurants, shops. Each spacious apartment is fully self-contained, gracious, peaceful, clean, with distinctive individual character, comfortable furnishings, generously & conveniently appointed from dishwasher to fresh flowers, etc. Free central heating, hot water, duvets/bed linen. All highest WTB grade (except one). 32 acres of tranquil landscaped gardens, sweeping lawns, woodland walks of natural beauty, panoramic hill walks overlooking the sea, Anglesey and Mount Snowdon. Mild climate. Enjoy the comfort, warmth, privacy & relaxation of this castle of timeless charm in truly serene surroundings. Open all year, including for Short Breaks. **Brochure sent with pleasure. Sleep 2-4 persons.**

Llanrug, Nr. Caernarfon, Gwynedd, N. Wales LL55 4RE Tel. & Fax: Llanberis (01286) 870210

CAERNARFON. Mrs M. Hughes, Glan Llyn, Llanfaglan, Caernarfon LL54 5RD (01286 674700). Sleeps 4. Glan Llyn is a two bedroomed semi-detached cottage, situated in a quiet area, yet only two miles from historic town of Caernarfon and within easy distance of Caernarfon Golf Course and Caernarfon Bay for sea fishing. Ideally situated for touring North Wales, just seven miles from Snowdon and Anglesey and within easy reach of many seaside resorts. Accommodation comprises two double bedrooms; bathroom; lounge with TV; kitchen/diner with fridge, electric stove, electric fires or open fire. Bed linen supplied. Parking space. Cottage available all year round. Mid-week Breaks and Weekend Breaks available during off season. Reduction for winter breaks and weekend bookings during off season period; summer terms and full details on request.

CAERNARVON. Mrs I. Thomas, Llain yr Eglwys, Llandwrog, Caernarvon LL54 5TA (01286 831422). Sleeps 4. Self contained cottage/annexe. Non-smokers. No pets. Situated on the edge of the little hamlet of Llandwrog about one mile from the popular beach at Dinas Dinlle and six miles south west of the historic castle town of Caernarvon; central for touring Snowdonia and Anglesey. Accommodation comprises lounge with colour TV and night storage heater; kitchen/diner; two bedrooms, one double and one twin. The double bedroom has washbasin and en suite shower room with toilet. Small garden and ample parking. Electricity free. Linen not supplied. Available May to October. Reasonable terms.

See also Colour Display Advertisement **CAERNARVON. Beach Holiday Homes, West Point, The Beach, Pontllyfni, Caernarvon LL54 5ET (01286 660400). √ √ √ √ and √ √ √ √ √** Beach Holiday offers bungalow, chalet and caravan accommodation in areas of outstanding natural beauty with sea views. Nearby restaurants, bar snacks and take aways provide good food. Most leisure activities close by including sea/river fishing, golf, rambling, pony trekking. Ideal for touring Snowdonia. Full details of accommodation, prices, etc can be found in the colour section of this guide; brochure also available on request.

GWYNEDD – OUTSTANDING NATURAL BEAUTY!

With Snowdonia National Park and the Lleyn Peninsula, Gwynedd well deserves its designation as an 'Area of Outstanding Natural Beauty'. The tourist is spoiled for choice in this county but should endeavour to visit the hill-fort at Tre'r Ceiri, the Llugwy Valley, Cwm Pennant, Dinas Dinlle hill-fort, the gold mine at Clogau and the railways and quarries at Blaenau Ffestiniog.

CONWY VALLEY. Hafodty Log Cabin No. 2, Tal-y-Cafn, Conwy Valley. This is a comfortable

Norwegian log cabin, one of three on a two-acre site, a peaceful setting with superb views of Snowdonia, southern aspect. It is situated 600 feet up and approached via lovely wooded lanes in beautiful countryside, two miles from Llanrwst-Conwy road. There is fishing, walking; Llandudno and Colwyn Bay beaches; Conwy Castle and harbour — all within easy reach. The cabin has two bedrooms with double beds; one bedroom with bunk beds. Extra bunk beds and cot available. Cabin is carpeted throughout. Bathroom, toilet; sittingroom with TV; kitchen with electric cooker, fridge, spin dryer, and fully equipped with everything except linen. Children and well behaved pet welcome. Bodnant Gardens, two miles. Village of Eglwysbach with store and cafe within three miles. Ideally situated for a relaxing holiday. Spring and Autumn Breaks. SAE to **Mrs J. Smart, 10 Elizabeth Crescent, Queens Park, Chester, Cheshire CH4 7AZ (01244 680145).**

CRICCIETH. Mrs E.W. Roberts, Cae Canol Farm, Criccieth LL52 0NB (01766 522351). Sleeps 2 adults; 3 children. Pleasantly situated with lovely mountain views, this country cottage has two bedrooms sleeping four/five plus cot. Bathroom, toilet; spacious kitchen/diner, fully equipped with fridge, etc. Sittingroom with TV. Everything supplied except linen. Garden in front of cottage with plenty of parking space. Golf, tennis, boating, walks, shooting, fishing and horse riding all within easy reach of cottage. FREE fishing on private river — salmon and trout. Terms on request with SAE, please. Open all months.

CRICCIETH. Mrs K.A. Handcock, 9 Marine Terrace, Criccieth LL52 0EF (01766 522060). Sleep 4. Criccieth, a small picturesque town at the northern end of Cardigan Bay, is ideally located for a quiet, leisurely holiday, also an excellent base for touring North Wales, within easy reach of Caernarvon, Snowdon and Harlech. Two flats, available all year round, accommodating four persons each, situated on the sea front with views across the bay to Harlech. Shops and all local amenities within a few minutes' walk. Flat 1 (first floor) — one double bedroom, one room with two single beds; lounge with colour TV; kitchen; bathroom, separate WC. Flat 2 (second and third floors) — one double bedroom, one twin bedded room; lounge with colour TV; kitchen/diner; bathroom. Fully equipped except linen; cot provided on request. Electricity by slot meter. Terms and further details from Mrs Handcock.

CRICCIETH. Mrs A.M. Jones, Betws-Bach and Rhos Ddu, Ynys, Criccieth LL52 0PB (Tel and Fax:

01758 720047 or 01766 810295). A truly romantic, memorable and special place to stay and relax in comfort. Old world farmhouse and period country cottage. Situated just off the B4411 road, in tranquil surroundings. Equipped to Wales Tourist Board Grade 5 — with washing/drying machines, dishwashers, microwaves, freezers, colour TV; old oak beams, inglenook with log fires, full central heating. Snooker table, pitch and putt, romantic four poster bed, sauna and jacuzzi. Open all year — Winter Weekends welcomed. Ideal for couples. Sleeps two/six plus cot. Own fishing and shooting rights, wonderful walks, peace and quiet with Snowdonia and unspoilt beaches on our doorstep. For friendly personal service phone, fax or write to **Mrs Anwen Jones.**

DOLGELLAU. Cefn Clawdd, Cross Foxes, Dolgellau. WTB 3 DRAGONS. Farm cottage in open valley

situated off A470/A487 from Dolgellau. Very accessible, 200 yards from main road, with hard road to farm. At foot of Cader Idris with panoramic views — Tal-y-Lyn Lake and Pass can be seen a little way along our mountain path. Tiny stream with trout fishing. Low beamed, low ceilinged old world cottage, solidly furnished, accommodates six in three double bedrooms, cot. Bathroom, toilet; sittingroom; dining kitchen with electric cooker, microwave, fridge, vacuum, twin tub washing machine, clothes dryer. Shops five miles, sea eight miles. Car essential — parking. Pets by arrangement. Terms from £70 to £260 per week depending on season. Also converted wing attached to cottage, a separate unit sleeping four persons. Available all year. SAE, please, to **Mrs E. Wyn Price, Glyn Farm, Dolgellau LL40 1YA (01341 422286).**

DOLGELLAU. Mrs C.E. Skeel Jones, Arosfyr Farm, Pen-y-Cefn Road, Dolgellau LL40 2YP (01341 422355). Sleeps 4/2 adults; 1/3 children. "Y Penty" is a farm building converted into a two-bedroomed luxury holiday cottage, half a mile from the quaint market town of Dolgellau, with panoramic views of Cader Idris mountain. Accommodates five persons in two bedrooms, cot available; bathroom, toilet; open-plan colour TV lounge and dining area. Kitchen with Hygena fitments, cooker, fridge-freezer, immerser; storage heaters, automatic washing machine; fitted carpets throughout. Fully equipped except linen. Parking. Small lawn and flower border to the front and grassy area with rotary clothes line at the back. Good centre for visiting castles, slate caverns, gold mines and miniature railways. Dolgellau Golf Course 400 yards, also walking, pony trekking and climbing. Sea eight miles. Weekly terms from £100 to £235, electricity extra. Also luxury first floor flat for two and new luxury farm bungalow for four. Parking. Convenient on foot to shops etc. Well maintained and fully equipped. Bed and Breakfast at the farmhouse from £13.50. Details on request. SAE or telephone for prompt reply.

DOLGELLAU. Mrs R. Le Tissier, Felin Ship, Arran Road, Dolgellau LL40 1LA (01341 423487).
Sleeps 4. Attractively modernised old coach house flat in lovely grounds with spacious car park. Only five minutes' walk into Dolgellau. Very comfortably furnished lounge with colour TV; well equipped kitchen/breakfast room. Two bedrooms (one double, one twin). Bathroom. Personal supervision. Sorry, no pets and no smoking. Amenities include a secluded riverside setting with picnic area and garden furniture. Dolgellau, with its impressive Cader Idris mountain range, is central for many holiday pursuits, with spectacular scenery and sandy beaches. Good eating places in the area. Weekly terms from £150 includes electricity and bed linen. All enquiries to **Mrs R. Le Tissier (01341 423487).**

HARLECH. Quality Cottages. Around the Welsh Coast. Away from the madding crowd. Near safe, sandy beaches. A small specialist agency offering privacy, peace and unashamed luxury. The first WTB Self Catering Gold Medal Award Winners. Residential standards — dishwashers, microwaves, washing machines, central heating, log fires. No slot meters. Linen provided. Pets welcome free. All in coastal areas famed for scenery, walks, wild flowers, birds, badgers and foxes. Free colour brochure **S.C. Rees, "Quality Cottages", Cerbid, Solva, Haverfordwest, Pembrokeshire SA62 6YE (01348 837871).** See also our full colour advertisement on the Inside Back Cover.

LLANDONNA. Quality Cottages. Around the magnificent Welsh Coast. Away from the madding crowd. Near safe, sandy beaches. A small specialist agency offering privacy, peace and unashamed luxury. The first WTB Self Catering Gold Medal Award Winners. Residential standards — dishwashers, microwaves, washing machines, central heating, log fires. No slot meters. Linen provided. Pets welcome free. All in coastal areas famed for scenery, walks, wild flowers, birds, badgers and foxes. Free colour brochure **S.C. Rees, "Quality Cottages", Cerbid, Solva, Haverfordwest, Pembrokeshire SA62 6YE (01348 837871).** See also our full colour advertisement on the Inside Back Cover.

LLANDUDNO. Mrs A.I. Roberts, Oaklands Holiday Flats and Flatlets, 19 Caroline Road, Llandudno LL30 2TY (01492 583820 or 875450). WTB Grade 3.

Situated in a quiet, tree-lined, residential area in central Llandudno — an ideal base for touring beautiful Snowdonia. You are within minutes of all that Llandudno has to offer; main shopping centre, both beaches and promenades, pier, the Oval with cricket, bowling, tennis, theatres, cinemas, gardens, yachting, children's boating and swimming pools. Convenient for Railway Station and coach park. Self-contained flatlets for one, two, three and four persons; two/four room flats for two/six persons (some on ground floor with toilet and shower). Cooking and heating by gas, some electric. Well-furnished with fitted carpets throughout. Private key. No restrictions. Children welcome, cots available and small house-trained pet welcome. Linen, cutlery and crockery provided. Colour TV available for all flats and flatlets. Under personal supervision. Guests' payphone. Reduced terms for early/late season and winter breaks. New fire prevention system. Annually inspected by Wales Tourist Board. Open all year round from £90 to £290 weekly. SAE for brochure stating number of persons and dates required.

LLANDUDNO. Mrs D.E. Maber-Jones, Westbourne Hotel, 8 Arvon Avenue, Llandudno LL30 2DY (01492 877450). WTB 4 Dragons Award. Sleeps 2/4. First class semi-detached holiday house with gardens and private parking. Near to shops, West Shore beach and 15 minutes' walk to main North Shore and shopping centre. Very comfortable house with high standards of cleanliness and fully equipped. No extra charge for linen and power. Weekly terms from £165 to £220. Adults only. Sorry no pets. Please telephone for full details.

LLANRWST. Garthmyn Pella. Sleeps 4 adults, 1 child. Farmhouse overlooking the Conwy Valley,

situated five miles from Betws-y-Coed and close to North Wales coast. Ideally located for walking. Farmhouse comprises one single and two double bedrooms; lounge; dining-room; fully equipped kitchen; bathroom with shower. Colour TV. Heating by electricity which is extra. Linen not supplied. Weekly terms from £170. **Mrs Gaynor Wyn Evans, Belmont, Llanddoged, Llanrwst LL26 0UE (01492 640318).**

LLANRWST near. Mrs Eirian Williams, Llainfadyn, Groesffordd, Llanddoged, Llanrwst LL26 0UA (01492 640599). Sleeps 4/5. "Gwelfro" is a two bedroom cottage one-and-a-quarter miles from the market town of Llanrwst. There are lovely views from the cottage which is excellently situated for exploring the beauties of North Wales. It is approximately 15 miles from the sea and also from the Snowdon Railway. Locally there are first class inns and restaurants, pleasant walks, golf, pony trekking etc. The cottage keeps its high standard of cleanliness and is comfortably furnished, with colour TV; bathroom with bath and shower. Storage heaters. Car space. Open January to December. Rates £100 to £180. Electricity extra by 50p meter. Sorry, no pets. Further details on request with SAE.

LLWYNGWRIL. "Gwastadgoed Ganol", Llwyngwril. Gwastadgoed Ganol is situated on the Tywyn/Dolgellau coast road and commands a magnificent view of Cardigan Bay. Centrally placed for tourists wishing to visit the many interesting places nearby. Walking, fishing, pony trekking, swimming pools, old churches, beautiful mountains and lakes within easy reach. Available all year round (storage heaters in winter). Two double bedrooms (with washbasins) and one room with three single beds; one cot; bathroom with shower; one inside and one outside toilet; sittingroom with TV; kitchen-cum-diningroom; fully equipped electric kitchen; utility room with washing machine and tumble dryer. Everything supplied except linen. Shops one mile; sea half a mile. Car essential — parking. No pets. SAE, please. Terms on request. **Mrs M.E. Davies, "Waun" Farm, Llanegryn, Tywyn LL36 9SY (01654 710408).**

MORFA NEFYN. Quality Cottages. Around the magnificent Welsh Coast. Away from the madding crowd. Near safe, sandy beaches. A small specialist agency offering privacy, peace and unashamed luxury. The first WTB Self Catering Gold Medal Award Winners. Residential standards — dishwashers, microwaves, washing machines, central heating, log fires. No slot meters. Linen provided. Pets welcome free. All in coastal areas famed for scenery, walks, wild flowers, birds, badgers and foxes. Free colour brochure **S.C. Rees, "Quality Cottages", Cerbid, Solva, Haverfordwest, Pembrokeshire SA62 6YE (01348 837871).** See also our full colour advertisement on the Inside Back Cover.

CHOOSE FROM 200 SEASIDE & MOUNTAIN COTTAGES etc.

in superb locations in and around the beautiful Snowdonia National Park. Available all year round. Sleep 1 to 14 persons from as little as £95 per cottage per week in the Low Season.

Central Reservations: SNOWDONIA TOURIST SERVICES (Ref. FHG), PORTHMADOG, GWYNEDD, LL49 9PG. Telephone 01766 513829 or 513837 or 512660.

Please send me your FREE brochure

Name .... Address ....

.... Postcode ....

PORTHMADOG. Quality Cottages. Around the magnificent Welsh Coast. Away from the madding crowd. Near safe, sandy beaches. A small specialist agency offering privacy, peace and unashamed luxury. The first WTB Self Catering Gold Medal Award Winners. Residential standards — dishwashers, microwaves, washing machines, central heating, log fires. No slot meters. Linen provided. Pets welcome free. All in coastal areas famed for scenery, walks, wild flowers, birds, badgers and foxes. Free colour brochure **S.C. Rees, "Quality Cottages", Cerbid, Solva, Haverfordwest, Pembrokeshire SA62 6YE (01348 837871).** See also our full colour advertisement on the Inside Back Cover.

PWLLHELI near. Mrs J.M. Roberts, Tai Cryddion, Llangwnnadl, Pwllheli LL53 8NW (01758 770261). A comfortable, modernised furnished farmhouse situated in the Lleyn Peninsula, on the main road between Nefyn and Aberdaron, within easy reach of all the small sandy beaches. The farmhouse sleeps six persons. Two double and one single bedroom with bunk beds; cot, mattress and high chair provided. Washroom upstairs with basin, hot and cold water and flush toilet. Outside shower room for farmhouse use. Sittingroom with colour TV. Fully equipped kitchen/diner with all-electric equipment including microwave (electricity 50p meter). Sandy and rocky beaches of Llangwnnadl about one-and-a-half miles from farm. Aberdaron five miles; Abersoch 10 miles; Nefyn nine miles. Fishing, hill climbing, bathing, golf, eight miles. Children are welcome. One dog allowed. Available from May to October. Bed linen provided. Electric heating. Terms from £90 per week. Also six berth static caravan with shower, only one on farm, from £75 per week. Touring caravans welcome.

TAL-Y-BONT, near Conwy. "Saronfa", Tal-y-Bont, Near Conwy. Sleeps 4. Pets taken. This stone built cottage on the edge of the National Park is comfortably furnished and modernised yet retaining old world charm. Inglenook fireplace, log or electric fire, storage heaters. Two bedrooms (one double, one twin), kitchen, lounge, bathroom with shower. Secluded rear garden with views of mountains. Parking for two cars. Situated in the beautiful Conwy Valley it provides an ideal base for walking or touring the National Park. Short distance from coastal resorts, the historic town of Conwy, Roman Spa, Woollen Mill and the famous Bodnant Gardens. Shop, inn and country restaurant within walking distance. Weekly terms from £98 to £198. Winter Breaks £15 per night including logs. **Mrs M.C. Waddingham, "Cefn", Tyn-y-Groes, Conwy LL32 8TA (01492 650233).**

TYWYN. Coastal House, 35 Corbett Close, Tywyn. Lovely three bedroomed coastal house with garage, very close to the sea with easy access to sandy beach. Accommodation in one double, one bunk-bedded and one single rooms, blankets provided. Equipped as if it were your own home — new furnishings, washing machine, cooker, microwave, crockery, colour TV and stereo. Large bathroom with additional built-in shower room. Sole use of garden front and rear, patio set provided. 10 minutes' walk from Tywyn centre, within walking distance of Tal-y-Llyn Steam Railway, two minutes from pub with excellent meals and eight doors from shop selling home baked bread, pies, pasties, etc. Very good walks in this beautiful area close to the Snowdonia Park. Pets are most welcome free of charge. Terms from £130 to £199 weekly. Further details from **Mr and Mrs Ian Weston, 18 Elizabeth Road, Basingstoke, Hampshire RG22 6AX (01256 52364).**

POWYS

BRECON. Theresa Jones, Trehenry Farm, Felinfach, Brecon LD3 0UN (01874 754312). ♛♛♛♛

DE LUXE. **Working farm, join in. Sleeps 8.** Trehenry is a 17th century farmhouse on a 200 acre working farm offering tranquillity and surrounded by breathtaking views. Modernised to a high standard yet retaining all its character with oak beams and inglenook fireplaces. Accommodation comprises fitted kitchen with microwave, electric cooker, dishwasher; utility room with washing machine; two double bedrooms en suite, one twin room with private bathroom; dining room; lounge; second lounge with bed-settee. Wood burning stove; video and TV. Oil central heating. Terms from £250 to £400 per week inclusive of linen, electricity and central heating. Open all year. Brochure available. Also Bed and Breakfast accommodation.

LLEWELLYN LEISURE PARK
Cilmery, Builth Wells, Powys LD2 3NU
Tel. 01831 101052 or 01982 552838

✓ ✓ ✓ RAC Appointed, AA, Caravan Club, Caravan & Camping Club Listings

Ideally situated for touring or peaceful relaxation in "secret" heart of Wales. Severn Bridge, Cardiff, Worcester and West/South Coast beaches all within one and a half hours' drive. Panoramic views towards Brecon Beacons from two-bedroomed modern luxury accommodation including colour TV, from £117 to £279 weekly; sleeps six persons. Executive 31' × 12', including video, microwave, stereo, duvets from £178 to £348 weekly. Short Breaks available all season. Touring and camping from £6 to £9 per night; 240V electricity, water and drainage, hook-ups, hard standings. Adjacent Inn/Restaurant. Nearby facilities for fishing, golf, riding, bowls, tennis, swimming; theatre, sports centre. Wales Showground. Bed and Breakfast also offered at £16 per person per night. Conference facility for 30 persons. Under one hour to Brecon Beacons, Hay-on-Wye, Hereford and Elan Reservoirs. Convenient for railway station (200 yards) and bus service.

BUILTH WELLS. Bryn-Llwyd, Llanafan Fawr, Builth Wells. This old fashioned farmhouse is situated in the countryside on the B4358 Newbridge-on-Wye to Beulah road. Six miles north west of Builth Wells and one and a half miles from village of Llanafan (pub and post office). Golf, fishing, horse riding, caves, etc nearby. The farmhouse has one double bedroom and a bedroom with two double beds (please note stairs are a little steep). Bed linen included. Bathroom downstairs. Small kitchen with microwave and spin dryer, livingroom has colour TV, dining room has open fire. Heating by electric fire and storage heaters. 50p coin meter. Telephone for incoming calls. Children and pets welcome. Plenty of parking space and an orchard for children to play in. Terms from £125 to £200 per week. Open all year round. Telephone **Mrs Haines 01591 620324).**

KNIGHTON. Mrs J.M. Morgan, Selley Hall, Llanfair Waterdine, Knighton LD7 1TR (01547 528429). **WTB Grade 3. Sleeps 6 plus cot.** A warm welcome awaits guests to this well furnished and comfortable self-catering accommodation on a working farm overlooking Offa's Dyke. The surrounding countryside is very peaceful with beautiful views; quiet lanes and roads make it an ideal centre for walking and touring. The accommodation comprises two double and one twin-bedded rooms; bathroom, toilet; large lounge with colour TV; diningroom/kitchen, fully fitted, all electric. Ample parking and garden for guests' use. Linen may be hired. Midweek and Short Break bookings taken out of season. Trout fishing in private pool. Many local historic places to visit. Sorry, no pets. Children welcome. Terms from £90 to £200 per week.

LAKE VYRNWY (3 miles). Mrs J. Smith, Felin Wynfa, Llanfihangel, Llanfyllin SY22 5JB (01691 870228). WTB Four Dragons. Cosy, beamed, self contained wing of former 17th century millhouse currently a 10 acre smallholding with sheep and poultry. Picturesque location beside a stream. Ideal walking, bird watching area with an RSPB nature reserve a short distance away. Powis Castle, narrow gauge railway, Bala Lake and Pistyll Rhaeadr Waterfall are within a radius of 18 miles. Accommodation comprises well equipped kitchen/diner with microwave; sitting room; two bedrooms, one double leading through to children's room with bunk beds plus cot; shower room. Bed linen provided. Children welcome. Sorry no pets. Non-smokers preferred. Terms from £90 to £170 per week. Short Breaks available. Please write or telephone for brochure.

LAKE VYRNWY. Mrs M. Jones, Fronheulog, Lake Vyrnwy, Oswestry, Shropshire SY10 0NN (01691 870662). Sleeps 4. Fronheulog Cottage is situated two miles from picturesque Lake Vyrnwy with its scenic nature trails, walks and RSPB hides. Fishing nearby. Central for touring mid-Wales. Set in delightful, peaceful countryside. The cottage is fully furnished except for linen, has three bedrooms sleeping four adults only, dining room, sitting room, kitchen with sink unit, electric stove and fridge. Bathroom with WC and hot and cold water. Electric and open fires. Aerial for TV. Well behaved dogs allowed. Rates £80 to £120 weekly. SAE, please, for replies.

LLANFAIR CAEREINION. Mrs Ann Reed, Madog's Wells, Llanfair Caereinion, Welshpool SY21 0DE (01938 810446). WTB 4 Dragons. Sleeps 5 plus cot. Tastefully furnished bungalow designed for wheelchair access (criteria 2) located on small hill farm in beautiful secluded valley. Also two six/eight berth caravans (self contained, WC, shower, fridge, cooker). Free gas/electricity and linen. Picnic benches, games room and children's play area on site. Farmhouse Bed and Breakfast also available from £14 per person; Evening Meal (optional) £7. Astronomy Breaks — view the night sky through a superb 16 inch Dobsonian telescope. Ideal base for touring mid-Wales. Weekly rates: Bungalow £125 to £220, open all year; Caravans £125 to £160, open April to November. No hidden extras, daily rates available out of main holiday season.

See also Colour Display Advertisement **LLANGURIG. Llangurig School House, Llangurig, Llanidloes. WTB Grade 3. Sleeps 4 adults, 2 children plus cot.** A self contained centrally heated school house in a peaceful mid-Wales village, sleeping six plus a baby's cot. Colour TV. Enjoy excellent walking and superb scenery (the habitat of the rare Red Kite), visit Aberystwyth and the Vale of Rheidol Steam Railway and take up pony trekking or fishing. There is a well equipped leisure centre at Rhayader some eight miles to the south. Price includes all electricity and central heating. For further details and bookings contact: **Gwen Edwards, Estates and Property Division, Powys County Council, County Hall, Llandrindod Wells LD1 5LG (01597 826055; Fax: 01597 826250).**

LLANRHAEADR-YM-MOCHNANT. Aber-Rhaeadr Cottages, Llanrhaeadr-ym-Mochnant. Two river-

side cottages in the heart of the Welsh Uplands (renowned for mountainous views, lakes, forests and waterfalls) having traditional Welsh cottage charm with pointed riverstone walls, beamed inglenook fireplace, open beamed ceiling, winding staircase, low doors and sun trap patio overlooking the riverside lawn and hills to the south. Superbly furnished, carpeted and equipped including cot, TV, radio, fridge, washing machine, spin dryer, airing cupboards, etc. (also sand pit under the damson tree in the riverside garden). Local attractions include Pistyll Rhaeadr Waterfall, Lake Vyrnwy, little trains of Wales, pony trekking, Powys Castle, local markets and character pubs. Associate Member of the Welsh Tourist Board and complying with their standards. Just write for illustrated brochure and terms to **Mrs Susan Lucas, No 2 Aber-Rhaeadr Cottages, Llanrhaeadr-ym-Mochnant SY10 0AG (01691 780083).**

MACHYNLLETH. Penygraean, Llanymawddwy, Machynlleth. Sleeps 6 plus cot. Situated in the upper

part of the Dovey Valley, five miles from the Montgomeryshire Border, this cottage is to let from March to November. Surrounded by farms and mountains, it is a haven for walkers and climbers. Sleeps six in three double bedrooms; cot; lounge with black and white TV, dining room; bathroom, toilet; kitchen with electric cooker, fridge, kettle, immerser, all utensils and hot and cold water. Storage heaters extra. Fully equipped except linen. Pets allowed if under control. Car essential, parking. Fishing by permit. Excellent for touring North and South Wales. Dolgellau 15 miles, Bala Lake 10 miles. Terms from £90 to £120 per week. SAE please to **Mrs Catherine Roberts, Cerddin, Llanymawddwy, Near Machynlleth SY20 9AJ (01650 531234).**

NEWTOWN. Mr and Mrs J.R. Pryce, Aberbechan Farm, Newtown SY16 3BJ (01686 630675).

Working farm, join in. Sleeps 10. This part of quaint Tudor farmhouse with its lovely oak beams is situated in picturesque countryside on a mixed farm with trout fishing and shooting in season. Newtown three miles, Welshpool, Powis Castle and Llanfair Light Railway 14 miles; 45 miles to coast. The sleeping accommodation is for 10 people in four double and two single bedrooms, also cot. Two bathrooms, two toilets. Sitting/diningroom with colour TV. Fully fitted kitchen with fridge, electric cooker, washing machine and dishwasher. Log fires and off-peak heaters. Electricity on meter. Large lawn with swing. Everything supplied for visitors' comfort. Linen available for overseas guests at extra cost. Car essential to obtain the best from your holiday. Farm produce available in season. Village shop one and a half miles away. Open all year. SAE, please.

TALYBONT-ON-USK. 1 Caerfanell Place, Talybont-on-Usk, Brecon. Talybont-on-Usk is a small village

nestling below the Beacons in the National Park. Cottage is built of traditional Welsh slate and stone, situated in the centre of village with garden leading to River Caerfanell. Three bedrooms sleep six plus child's small bed; bathroom and toilet upstairs and shower room and toilet downstairs; comfortable lounge with colour TV and cosy wood/coal stove for winter or chilly nights. A washing machine, dryer, fridge, freezer and microwave are complemented by a full range of smaller kitchen essentials. Roadside parking. Excellent village pubs serve a wide selection of beers. Short Breaks available out of season. Bicycle hire facility in village and canal trips available nearby as are many other sporting activities. Terms from £95 to £265 per week. Winter fuel provided; linen hire. Apply: **Mrs F.I. Smith, Holt's Farm House, Coopers Lane, Fordcombe, Near Tunbridge Wells, Kent TN3 0RN (01892 740338).**

POWYS – MOUNTAINOUS AND LANDLOCKED

With many border castles and the Brecon Beacons, which cover the south of the county, Powys can be very spectacular. You will also find the best stretches of Offa's Dyke, Hay-On-Wye, the steam railway at Llanfair Caereinion, Radnor Forest, the fortified house of Tretower, the farming centre at Builth Wells and the abandoned medieval town of Cefnllys.

IRELAND

CORK

BANTRY. Mrs Sheila O'Shea, Ard-na-Greine, Adrigole, Bantry (00 353 2760018). Ard-na-Greine is a

furnished holiday house on private ground including a field suitable for children's playground. Situated in the Beara Peninsula overlooking Bantry Bay and within 200 yards of the shore of the peaceful sea inlet at Adrigole Harbour. Adrigole is adjacent to the Healy Pass on the Ring of Beara and is an ideal centre for touring, and is within easy reach of Gougane Barra, Glengarriff, the Lakes of Killarney, Ring of Kerry and the fishing town of Castletownbere. Adrigole is adjacent to Hungry Hill, the highest peak in the Caha Mountains with their fishing lakes, waterfall and numerous walks. Accommodation consists of five bedrooms, bathroom with electric shower, sittingroom with colour TV, diningroom, modern kitchen/breakfast room with electric cooker, fridge, automatic washing machine. Open fire, electric fires and off peak storage heater. Meter read on guests' arrival and departure. Linen not supplied. Terms from £150 to £250. International Reply Coupon please.

CASTLETOWNBERE. Mrs Margaret O'Dwyer, Toormore Bungalow, Toormore, Castletownbere, Bantry (027 70598; from UK 00 353 2770598). Luxury

double glazed bungalow in West Cork overlooking the fishing port of Castletownbere, Bere Island and Bantry Bay. Situated among peaceful surroundings with superb views of sea and mountains. One mile from town and sea. Ideal base for touring around the scenic Ring of Beara, Ring of Kerry, Killarney, Blarney, Glengarriff, etc. Golf, fishing, boating, sailing, swimming, cycling, horse riding, mountain climbing, water sports and shooting available locally. Four double rooms, sittingroom with open fire, livingroom with colour TV, bed settee, bathroom with shower, oak kitchen with all modern conveniences. Cot, high chair and babysitting available. Oil and solid fuel central heating. Weekly from £150 to £250. Telephone or write (International Reply Coupon please) for brochure.

PUBLISHER'S NOTE

While every effort is made to ensure accuracy, we regret that FHG Publications cannot accept responsibility for errors, omissions or misrepresentation in our entries or any consequences thereof. Prices in particular should be checked because we go to press early. We will follow up complaints but cannot act as arbiters or agents for either party.

KERRY

SOUTHERN IRELAND
Abbeydorney, Tralee, Co. Kerry

Situated at the Abbey Tavern in Abbeydorney, these self catering flats are ideally placed for touring County Kerry. Both Tralee and Banna Beach are five miles away and Ballyheigue, Killarney, Dingle and the Ring of Kerry are also within easy reach. Near Tralee, Killarney and Ballybunion Golf Courses. Clean and reasonably priced, the flats have shower, toilet; living room/kitchenette with electric cooker, fridge, heater, etc. Electricity by 50p meter. Linen and towels supplied. Cot on request. A car is essential and there is ample parking. Overnight stops welcome. Evening Meal available for self catering guests. Bed and Breakfast and Partial Board also available. Bar Meals served all day. A 4-bedroom self-catering house is also available.

Further details from Mrs Mary O'Connor (00-353-6635145).

TIPPERARY

BORRISLEIGH. Michael & Noreen O'Donnell, Cathy Hackets Cottage, Borrisleigh (0504 51616; from UK 00 353 504 51616).  Traditional Irish farm cottages situated in Tipperary — "the heartland of Ireland" and within easy reach of all the major tourist attractions. The small cottage is a quaint double bedroomed cottage en suite sleeping two persons. It has open fire, stone chimney, roof beams. The farm cottage sleeps six persons in four bedrooms, it has open fires in sitting room and double bedroom. Lots to do locally or just relax on the farm with ponies, sheep, wild flowers, pleasant walks, Bronze Age fort. Comfort and relaxation for guests is our prime concern — "The Hidden Ireland". Weekly terms from £85 (Low Season) to £165 (High Season); weekend lets available. There is also Hotel accommodation available, brochure on request. Selection of self-catering property throughout Ireland.

FREE and REDUCED RATE
Holiday Visits!
See our Reader's Offer Vouchers
for details!

**If you've found
FARM HOLIDAY GUIDES
of service please tell your friends**

Campus Holidays

How about a University holiday this year, or perhaps you'd fancy a College?

If you are interested, you'll be joining thousands of non-students who have discovered the delights of the Campus as a value-for-money holiday destination.

For 1996 around 100,000 places are available during the summer and even during term-time many campuses can offer holiday facilities. The various establishments have organised themselves into two marketing groups, both of which will be more than happy to provide you with brochures and information on request.

THE BRITISH UNIVERSITIES ACCOMMODATION CONSORTIUM (BUAC)

First in the field, the members of BUAC can now offer accommodation at over 60 venues nationwide for individual and family holidays, for conferences and study vacations. From Aberdeen to Exeter, from Aberystwyth to Norwich, you will find comfortable and modern accommodation at affordable prices. *Further details from: Carole Formon, BUAC Ltd., University Park, Nottingham NG7 2RD (0115 950 4571).*

THE HIGHER EDUCATION ACCOMMODATION CONSORTIUM (HEAC)

Representing a wider range of institutions as the name suggests, HEAC now has over 70 members with around 30,000 beds available throughout Britain, in seaside, rural and city centre locations.

For further information you should contact: HEAC Ltd., 36 Collegiate Crescent, Sheffield S10 2BP (0114 268 3759).

Here are just a few different possibilities for Campus Holidays for 1996.

CARLISLE. Mrs D. Carruthers, University of Northumbria, Old Brewery Residencies, Bridge Lane, Caldewgate, Carlisle CA2 5SW (01228 597352). These recently built self-contained flats are ideal for holiday accommodation with a choice of four, five or six bedrooms. Bed linen and tea towels provided but not personal towels. Suitable for disabled visitors. Children welcome, but sorry, no pets. Terms from £196 to £284 per week.

LIVERPOOL. John Moores University. One of largest new Universities. Prestigious accommodation and catering for all occasions. For further information contact: **Jonathan M. Chinn, Liverpool John Moores University, JMU Services Ltd, 2 Rodney Street, Liverpool L3 5UX (Tel & Fax: 0151-231 3369).**

WORCESTER. Self catering flats on a quiet, rural college campus two miles from Worcester's centre, within easy reach of Junction 7 of the M5. The fully equipped flats sleep six people in separate rooms and are available from mid July to mid September. Not suitable for infants/toddlers. No pets. £235 per week. Details from **Colin Fry, Head of Residential Services, Worcester College of Higher Education, Henwick Grove, Worcester WR2 6AJ (01905 855000).** Please quote FHG.

The Old Mill, West Harnham, Salisbury, Wilts.

CARAVAN AND CAMPING HOLIDAYS
ENGLAND

CORNWALL

CARAVANS

ST. IVES BAY HOLIDAY PARK

01736 752274 24 hrs

ON THE BEACH

With private access to your own stunning sandy beach, many units have sea views. We offer you a huge range of Caravans, Chalets and Camping, a large indoor pool (free), 2 Pubs on site (free entertainment) and all facilities you would expect. Ideal for children. Pets welcome.

Ring now for Free 16 page colour brochure or write to Mr. M. White:

ST. IVES BAY HOLIDAY PARK,
Upton Towans, Hayle, TR27 5BH

CORNWALL

NAME

ADDRESS

FH

CORNISH CUISINE!
The traditional Cornish Pasty was originally the tin-miners' portable lunch — shaped like a torpedo to fit in his pocket! The filling is usually mutton mixed with potatoes and swedes, and is enclosed in pastry pinched high along its entire length. Another Cornish speciality is Stargazey Pie, where pilchards are arranged in a dish like the spokes of a wheel, the pastry cover being cut to allow the eyes to gaze out. And to finish off — a clotted cream tea with scones and strawberry jam!

CUMBRIA   CARAVANS

GRANGE-OVER-SANDS. Greaves Farm Caravan Park, Field Broughton, Grange-over-Sands. ✓ ✓ ✓ Luxury holiday caravans for hire on small level quiet site in farm orchard. All units fully serviced and have refrigerator, colour TV. Four/six berths. Personal supervision. Situated in Cartmel Valley, ideal base for exploring the Lake District. Weekly terms from £160 to £200. Also small site for limited number of touring caravans and tents. Booking essential. Contact: **Mrs E. Rigg, Prospect House, Barber Green, Grange-over-Sands LA11 6HU (015395 36329).**

SILLOTH. Mr and Mrs Bowman, Tanglewood Caravan Park, Causeway Head, Silloth-on-Solway CA5 4PE (016973 31253). Tanglewood is a family-run park on the fringes of the Lake District National Park. It is tree-sheltered and situated one mile inland from the port of Silloth on the Solway Firth, with a beautiful view of the Galloway Hills. Large modern holiday homes are available from March to October, with car parking beside each home. Fully equipped, except for bed linen, with end bedroom, electric lighting, hot and cold water, toilet, shower, gas fire, fridge and colour TV, all of which are included in the tariff. Touring pitches also available with electric hook-ups and water/drainage facilities, etc. Play area. Licensed lounge with adjoining children's play room. Pets welcome free but must be kept under control at all times. Full colour brochure available.

LAKE DISTRICT   CARAVANS

See also Colour Display Advertisement **LAKE DISTRICT. Lakeland Leisure Park, Moor Lane, Flook-burgh, Grange-over-Sands (015395 58556).** ✓ ✓ ✓ ✓ Gateway to the Lake District, on the Furness and Cartmel Peninsula. Luxury holiday homes for two to eight people. Facilities on site include heated indoor and outdoor swimming pools, bowling, putting, tennis, horse riding; restaurant, bars, takeaway, live family evening entertainment, Bradley Bear Kids Club and Teen Club. Touring and tent pitches available. Please telephone for our FREE colour brochure.

See also Colour Display Advertisement **WINDERMERE. Fallbarrow Park, Windermere, The Lake District LA23 3DL (015394 44427).** ✓ ✓ ✓ ✓ ✓ Set amidst this wooded parkland that borders the eastern shore of Lake Windermere you may find your ideal holiday. Luxury caravans offering everything you would expect in your holiday home — spacious lounge with colour TV, modern shower with flush toilet, bright and easy kitchen — and comfortable bedrooms. Within the grounds there is a friendly reception and information centre, licensed bar with good food, family lounge, children's playground, mini market with off licence — and of course boat launching facilities. Full colour brochure available. AA Four Pennants.

DEVON   CARAVANS

ASHBURTON. Mrs Rhona Parker, Higher Mead Farm, Ashburton TQ13 7LJ (01364 652598; Fax: 01364 654004). A friendly, family-run farm site set in 400 acres and surrounded by beautiful countryside. 12 miles from the sea and close to Dartmoor National Park. Ideal for touring Devon/Cornwall. Perfect for children and pets with all farm animals, play area and plenty of space to roam, also large area for dogs. Holiday cottages and caravans, fully equipped except for linen. Level touring site with some hard standings. Free showers in fully tiled block, laundry room, games room. Small family bar, shop and telephone. Prices start from £90 to £380 High Season. Good discounts for couples. From Exeter, take A38 to Plymouth; when you see sign "25 miles Plymouth" take second left at Alston Cross signposted to Woodland and Denbury.

PEACE & TRANQUILLITY NEAR EXETER, DEVON

The SALTER family welcomes you to

HALDON LODGE FARM

Kennford, nr. Exeter EX6 7YG

20 minutes from Dawlish and Torbay beaches

Central for South Devon coast and Exeter in delightful setting, four luxury six-berth caravans in a private and friendly park. Relax and enjoy the scenery or stroll along the many forest lanes. Two private coarse fishing lakes and an attraction of farm animals, ponies and horse riding for both novice and experienced riders exploring the Teign Valley Forest. Weekly wood fire barbecue (July and August); many friendly country inns nearby. Excellent facilities including picnic tables and farm shop. Set in glorious rural Devon, the site offers freedom and safety for all the family. Very reasonable prices. Pets accepted – exercising area. OPEN ALL YEAR.

Large 6-berth Caravans, 2 bedrooms, lounge with TV, bathroom/toilet (H/C water); Rates from £70 to £160 High Season. Personal attention and a warm welcome assured by David and Betty Salter.
For brochure telephone Exeter (01392) 832312.

SEATON. Axe Vale Caravan Park, Seaton EX12 2DF (01297 21342). √ √ √ √ A quiet, family run park with 68 modern and luxury caravans for hire. The park overlooks the delightful River Axe Valley and is just a 10 minute walk from the town with its wonderfully long, award-winning beach. Children will love our extensive play area with its sand pit, paddling pool, swings and slide. Laundry facilities are provided and there is a wide selection of goods on sale in the park shop which is open every day. All of our caravans have shower, toilet, fridge and TV with satellite channels, and with no clubhouse, our relaxing atmosphere is ensured. Terms from £65 per week; reductions for three or fewer persons early/late season.

SIDMOUTH. Dunscombe Manor, Sidmouth EX10 0PM (Tel & Fax: 013955 13654). Brand new barn conversion offering self catering apartments sleeping two to four persons. Adjacent to National Trust countryside, Weston Mouth Beach, coastal path, donkey sanctuary and Dunscombe Manor Caravan Park. Ideal for exploring the East Devon Heritage Coastline. The delightful seaside resort of Sidmouth is two and a half miles westward and to the east lies Lyme Regis and the quaint fishing villages of Branscombe and Beer. Main bedroom with en suite facilities (one apartment with electric stair lift), lounge/kitchen with cooker, microwave, hob, refrigerator and breakfast bar. Terms from £100 to £425 inclusive of linen, duvets, colour TV and heating. Regret no pets.

FREE and REDUCED RATE Holiday Visits!
See our Reader's Offer Vouchers for details!

WOOLACOMBE. Twitchen House and Mortehoe Caravan Park. LUXURY CARAVANS AT WOOLA-

COMBE. Have a carefree and comfortable holiday in one of our Executive, luxury or modern caravans on this attractive, well-equipped Rose Award Park graded √ √ √ √. Park facilities include heated pool, licensed club with two bars, snooker, activities room, games and family areas, free entertainment, shop, launderette, putting green, etc. We offer a wide selection of caravans all on concrete bases, with mains water and drainage, flush toilets, hot and cold water to sinks/showers, refrigerators, heating, TV, etc. Fully inclusive terms from £95 per week, with special low rates/Senior Citizens discounts out of season. On-site supervision. Regret, no pets. For colour brochure and tariff, SAE or phone: **Woolacombe Caravan Hirers, Dept SCFH, Garden Cottage, 27 East Street, Braunton, North Devon EX33 2EA (01271 816580).**

WOOLACOMBE SANDS. Caravans to let. Farm site above Rockham Beach (only 500 yards). Delightful

situation in the heart of National Trust land, magnificent sea views. Famous three miles of Woolacombe Sands only one mile away. Marvellous walking, surfing. Magnificent coast for lovers of unspoilt beauty. Wide choice of new kingsize caravans (33ft) with toilet, shower, hot water, fridge, TV, etc. Very well equipped, parking beside caravan. On site shop, laundry, showers, etc. Rates from £99 to £299. SAE please. **Morte Point Caravans, 23 Brooks Road, Wylde Green, Sutton Coldfield B72 1HP (Tel & Fax: 0121-354 1551).**

Key to
Tourist Board Ratings

The Crown Scheme
(England, Scotland & Wales)

Covering hotels, motels, private hotels, guesthouses, inns, bed & breakfast, farmhouses. Every Crown classified place to stay is inspected annually. *The classification:* Listed then 1-5 Crown indicates the range of facilities and services. Higher quality standards are indicated by the terms APPROVED, COMMENDED, HIGHLY COMMENDED and DELUXE.

The Key Scheme
(also operates in Scotland using a Crown symbol)

Covering self-catering in cottages, bungalows, flats, houseboats, houses, chalets, etc. Every Key classified holiday home is inspected annually. *The classification:* 1-5 Key indicates the range of facilities and equipment. Higher quality standards are indicated by the terms APPROVED, COMMENDED, HIGHLY COMMENDED and DELUXE.

The Q Scheme
(England, Scotland & Wales)

Covering holiday, caravan, chalet and camping parks. Every Q rated park is inspected annually for its quality standards. The more √ in the Q – up to 5 – the higher the standard of what is provided.

DORSET

CARAVANS

MANOR FARM HOLIDAY CENTRE
Charmouth, Bridport, Dorset

Situated in a rural valley. Charmouth beach a level ten minutes' walk away.

Luxury 6-berth Caravans for Hire with toilet/shower, refrigerator, full cooker, colour TV, gas fire.

30-acre Tourist Park for touring caravans, dormobiles and tents.

Centre facilities include * Toilets; * Hot showers; * Fish and chip takeaway; * Licensed bar with family room; * Amusement room; * Launderette; * Shop and off-licence; * Swimming pool; * Electric hook-up points; * Calor gas and Camping Gaz; * Ice pack service; * Chemical disposal unit.

Send SAE for colour brochure to Mr R. E. Loosmore or Tel: 01297 560226
See also Colour Display Advertisement in this Guide.

NORFOLK

CARAVANS

KILN CLIFFS CARAVAN PARK

Peaceful family-run site situated around an historic brick kiln. Six-berth caravans for hire, standing on ten acres of grassy cliff-top. Magnificent view out over the sea; private path leads gently down to extensive stretches of unspoilt sandy beach. All caravans fully equipped (except linen) and price includes all gas and electricity. Caravans always available for sale or for hire. Within easy reach are the Broads, Norwich, the Shire Horse Centre, local markets, nature reserves, bird sanctuaries; nearby golf, riding and fishing. Facilities on site include general store, take-away snacks, launderette. Pets welcome.

Substantial discounts for off-peak bookings – phone for details. Call for brochure. Mr G. Malone, Kiln Cliffs Caravan Park, Cromer Road, Mundesley, Norfolk NR11 8DF. Tel: 01263 720449.

SOMERSET

CARAVANS

BREAN SANDS. Dolphin Caravan Park, Brean Sands, Burnham-on-Sea. Caravans sleep 4/6/7. ETB √ √ √ √ *VERY GOOD.* Caravans TO LET and FOR SALE on  this friendly, family run park. Private access to sandy beach; no roads to cross; children's play area, launderette and public phone on the park. Free membership of licensed club on adjacent park. Brean Leisure Park 300 yards; shops 500 yards; Burnham-on-Sea four miles; Weston-super-Mare nine miles. Convenient centre to visit Cheddar, Wookey Hole, Bath, etc. Pets welcome. Car parking by your caravan. From £86 to £299 per week. Member of British Holiday and Home Parks Association. Free brochure from **Dolphin Caravan Park, Coast Road, Brean, Burnham-on-Sea TA8 2QY (01278 751258).**

NORTH YORKSHIRE

CARAVANS

HARROGATE. Mr H.W. Bowe, Pinemoor Caravan Park, Pennypot, Harrogate HG3 1RZ (01423 503980). ✓ ✓ ✓ Three miles west of Harrogate off A59. Modern six/eight berth caravans (with showers, toilets and TCs) for hire on quiet country park. Shop 100 yards. Ideal centre for touring Yorkshire Dales with lovely views towards Pateley Bridge and Brimham Rocks. Places of interest include Fountains Abbey, Studley Park, Newby Hall and Harewood House and Birdgardens. Children's play area, sand pit and swing. Open April to October. SAE or telephone for terms.

ROBIN HOOD'S BAY. Sleeps 6. Luxury three bedroomed caravan in a pleasant garden setting with superb views, picnic and barbecue area on our mixed working farm. One and a half miles from Robin Hood's Bay (less by pleasant footpaths), half a mile from the North Yorkshire Moors. Easy reach of Whitby, Scarborough and "Heartbeat" country. The accommodation comprises one double-bedded room, one twin and one bunk-bedded rooms. Dining area, kitchen with sink unit, fridge and gas cooker. Spacious lounge area with colour TV and full size gas fire. Bathroom with washbasin, toilet and shower. Short Breaks available. Contact: **Mr and Mrs L.E. Hodgson, Low Farm, Robin Hood's Bay, Whitby YO22 4QF (01947 880366).**

ISLE OF MAN

CAMPING

LAXEY. Laxey Camping Site, Quarry Road, Laxey, Isle of Man. This site is in Minorca, Laxey. Quarry Road is opposite the former Minorca Methodist Church. Warden on site. This holiday site is open from April to September and has a kitchen, toilets and showers available for campers. For further details contact: **LAXEY VILLAGE COMMISSIONERS, Commissioners Office, New Road, Laxey (01624 861241).**

CARAVAN AND CAMPING HOLIDAYS
SCOTLAND

ABERDEENSHIRE
CARAVANS

ABOYNE LOCH. Aboyne Loch Caravan Park, Aboyne (013398 86244). Set in a unique eight acre position on a wooded promontory of land surrounded on three side by Aboyne Loch, with fishing boat hire and water ski-ing. The site offers 50 touring pitches all with hardstanding, 40 with electricity, 40 level pitches, 43 static caravans (three of which are for hire) and six chalets. Eight hot showers, 18 WCs, two CWPs. Playground. The village of Aboyne is only half a mile away with a variety of activities — swimming, theatre, squash courts, restaurant and good shopping centre. Pets welcome. Terms: Car and caravan, motor caravan £8; Car and tent £6, plus 50p per adult above two, child 50p; electricity on meter (50p), awning £1. No single-sex groups, no motorcycles. We overlook nothing but the Loch!

ARGYLL

CARAVANS

APPIN HOLIDAY CARAVANS
Truly magnificent setting right on the Lochside
FHG DIPLOMA WINNER

ESTABLISHED 1964

8 very private caravans, 10' and 12' wide units all with free gas and electrics and colour TV. Some with video and microwave ovens. All recent models, each fully serviced. Launderette, recreation room, play area and babysitting. FREE fishing (salt and freshwater). Boating and sailing, great hill walks. Pony trekking and Licensed Inn nearby. Special Spring, Autumn and Winter terms.
Price Guide – £135 to £235 per unit weekly.
Please send SAE for colour brochure giving dates required.

Mr & Mrs C. Weir, Appin Holiday Caravans, Appin, Argyll PA38 4BQ   Telephone: Appin (01631) 730287

For more details see colour advertisement.

HELP IMPROVE BRITISH TOURIST STANDARDS

You are choosing holiday accommodation from our very popular FHG Publications. Whether it be a hotel, guest house, farmhouse or self-catering accommodation, we think you will find it hospitable, comfortable and clean, and your host and hostess friendly and helpful. Why not write and tell us about it?

As a recognition of the generally well-run and excellent holiday accommodation reviewed in our publications, we at FHG Publications Ltd. present a diploma to proprietors who receive the highest recommendation from their guests who are also readers of our Guides. If you care to write to us praising the holiday you have booked through FHG Publications Ltd. – whether this be board, self-catering accommodation, a sporting or a caravan holiday, what you say will be evaluated and the proprietors who reach our final list will be contacted.

The winning proprietor will receive an attractive framed diploma to display on his premises as recognition of a high standard of comfort, amenity and hospitality. FHG Publications Ltd. offer this diploma as a contribution towards the improvement of standards in tourist accommodation in Britain. Help your excellent host or hostess to win it!

FHG DIPLOMA

We nominate ....

....

Because ....

Name ....

Address ....

.... Telephone No. ....

CAITHNESS

CARAVANS

DUNBEATH. Mrs Joyce Polanska, Knockinnon, Dunbeath KW6 6EH (01593 731347). Working farm, join in. Two caravans on quiet croft site on A9, half mile north of Dunbeath village. Willerby Berwick six-berth with bedroom, bathroom with toilet and shower facilities and water heater; gas cooker, heater. Electric lighting, fridge, kettle, toaster, power points. Atlas Aztec has similar facilities. Both sleep six and are fully equipped (except bed linen). Children and pets welcome. Parking space. Picturesque coastal area. Pony trekking nearby. Charges from £80 to £90 per week.

DUMFRIESSHIRE

CARAVANS

MOFFAT. Mrs Jean MacKenzie, Hidden Corner, Beattock Road, Moffat DG10 9SE (01683 220243). Enjoy a self-catering holiday in peaceful surroundings in one of these two very comfortable static homes. Each has one double bedroom with shaver point, one twin room; a second double bed makes down in the spacious lounge/dining area, also extra single bed. Toilet, washbasin and shower room (hot and cold). Fully equipped kitchen, laundry facilities, TV, electric blanket, heating. Sorry, no pets. Ideal base for exploring the Borders and South West Scotland. Edinburgh, Glasgow, East and West coasts within one hour's drive. In and around Moffat there is boating, putting, tennis, green bowling, fishing, 18-hole golf, hill walking, pony trekking. Write or telephone for terms.

INVERNESS-SHIRE

CARAVANS

ARISAIG. Mr A.A. Gillies, Kinloid Farm, Arisaig PH39 4NS (01687 450366). √ √ √ *APPROVED.* **Working farm. Caravans sleep 6/8.** Eight caravans (six-berth) available for hire from Easter to October. Attractively situated occupying an elevated position at Kinloid Farm, a five-minute car run from wonderful sands. The caravans are new models and have hot and cold water, showers, fridges, electric lighting, flush toilets and are completely self-contained. Each van commands magnificent views across Arisaig to the sea and islands of Skye, Rhum and Eigg. Sea cruises from Arisaig village. Children welcome. Well behaved pets allowed. Weekly terms from £140. Huge reductions early/late season. SAE, please.

DULNAIN BRIDGE. Mrs J. Allan, Easter Curr Farm, Dulnain Bridge PH26 3PA (01479 851214). Six berth caravan situated beside farmhouse near to Rivers Spey and Dulnain. It is 12 miles from Aviemore, eight miles from Carrbridge and three miles from Grantown-on-Spey. Accommodation consists of double bed, bunk beds and bed settee. Linen is provided. Pets allowed. Electricity by coin slot meter. Fridge, microwave and TV supplied. Terms £135 per week with £35 deposit two weeks in advance. Further enquiries **(01479 851214).**

ROSS-SHIRE   CARAVANS

POOLEWE. Mrs A.E. Ella, "Sonas", Cove, Poolewe IV22 2LT (01445 781203). ❀ ❀ ❀ ❀ *COMMENDED.* **Sleep 6/8.** Four strategically placed six berth caravans and croft house sleeping eight are situated in a crofting hamlet on the shore of Loch Ewe. All have uninterrupted panoramic views of sea and distant mountains. Bird watching, loch/sea fishing, walking, safe beaches, or just sit relaxing. For the fortunate, seals and otters in the adjacent bay. The two acre landscaped site's perimeter is fenced, making it safe for children and pets. Helpful and friendly atmosphere. All accommodation fully equipped except linen. Open February to December. Weekly terms from £105 inclusive (caravan) and from £160 (house). SAE or phone for details.

FOR THE MUTUAL GUIDANCE OF GUEST AND HOST

Every year literally thousands of holidays, short-breaks and overnight stops are arranged through our guides, the vast majority without any problems at all. In a handful of cases, however, difficulties do arise about bookings, which often could have been prevented from the outset.

It is important to remember that when accommodation has been booked, both parties — guests and hosts — have entered into a form of contract. We hope that the following points will provide helpful guidance.

GUESTS: When enquiring about accommodation, be as precise as possible. Give exact dates, numbers in your party and the ages of any children. State the number and type of rooms wanted and also what catering you require — bed and breakfast, full board, etc. Make sure that the position about evening meals is clear — and about pets, reductions for children or any other special points.

Read our reviews carefully to ensure that the proprietors you are going to contact can supply what you want. Ask for a letter confirming all arrangements, if possible.

If you have to cancel, do so as soon as possible. Proprietors do have the right to retain deposits and under certain circumstances to charge for cancelled holidays if adequate notice is not given and they cannot re-let the accommodation.

HOSTS: Give details about your facilities and about any special conditions. Explain your deposit system clearly and arrangements for cancellations, charges, etc, and whether or not your terms include VAT.

If for any reason you are unable to fulfil an agreed booking without adequate notice, you may be under an obligation to arrange alternative suitable accommodation or to make some form of compensation.

While every effort is made to ensure accuracy, we regret that FHG Publications cannot accept responsibility for errors, omissions or misrepresentation in our entries or any consequences thereof. Prices in particular should be checked because we go to press early. We will follow up complaints but cannot act as arbiters or agents for either party.

CARAVAN AND CAMPING HOLIDAYS
WALES

DYFED   CARAVANS

See also Colour Display Advertisement **CARMARTHEN near. Pendine Sands Holiday Park, Near Carmarthen.** √ √ √ A Welsh holiday park set alongside miles of golden sandy beaches offering luxury holiday homes for two to eight people. Tourers welcome — electric hook-up available. Site facilities include heated indoor swimming pool, children's indoor/outdoor soft play areas, amusement arcade, family putting green, live family evening entertainment, bar, snack food, barbecues and supermarket. Horse riding, bike hire and tennis nearby. For your FREE colour brochure please telephone **0345 443 443** low call rate — 24 hours a day, seven days a week, or see your local travel agent.

HAVERFORDWEST. Scamford Caravan Park, Keeston, Haverfordwest, Pembrokeshire SA62 6HN

(01437 710304). √ √ √ √ √ 25 Dragon-Award luxury holiday caravans on peaceful park in attractive countryside, near Pembrokeshire Coastal Path and many lovely beaches. Every caravan has all mains services, fridge, gas fire, shower and colour TV. Also five touring pitches with electric hook-ups, free hot showers. Excellent children's playground — swings, sand pit, climbing frame and trampoline. Dog welcome. Some caravans "dog-free", for the sake of children with allergies. Telephone, launderette with ironing facilities. Terms from £90. Plenty to do in the area — castles, farm parks, craft shops, boat trips, island bird sanctuaries, surfing, golfing, riding, etc, or spend a day at Oakwood Leisure Park. Colour brochure from resident owners **Jean and Maurice Gould.**

GWYNEDD   CARAVANS

BALA. Mrs S.E. Edwards, Bryn Melyn Farm, Rhyduchaf, Bala LL23 7PG (01678 520376). Sleeps 6. One six-berth caravan is available on Bryn Melyn, a 56 acre mixed farm in the village of Rhyduchaf, two miles from Bala, situated in the beautiful Bala countryside. The caravan has a bathroom, inside flush toilet, hot and cold water, electric light, gas cooker, gas heater, fridge, colour TV. Fully equipped with microwave, blankets, etc. Children are welcome. Sorry no pets allowed. Open from April to September. Seaside 25 miles away. Weekly rates from £80. Reduced rates for Senior Citizens May, June and September. Electricity on slot meter (10p). Bed and Breakfast accommodation (1 Crown Commended) also available on the farm. SAE please for further details.

DOLGELLAU. E. Wynne-Williams, Coed Croes, Dolgellau LL40 1TD (01341 422658). Modern and comfortable caravan, six/eight berth, situated on the foothills of Cader Idris Mountain, 40 yards from farmhouse. Hot and cold shower and basin, toilet; two separate bedrooms; bedding provided but bring own linen. Gas or electric heating, gas cooking, electric fridge and lighting (no meters), TV. Dolgellau town two miles, beach seven miles. All recreational activities and restaurants, etc, within easy reach. Sorry, no pets. Very reasonable terms.

ONE FOR YOUR FRIEND 1996

FHG Publications have a large range of attractive holiday accommodation guides for all kinds of holiday opportunities throughout Britain. They also make useful gifts at any time of year. Our guides are available in most bookshops and larger newsagents but we will be happy to post you a copy direct if you have any difficulty. We will also post abroad but have to charge separately for post or freight. The inclusive cost of posting and packing the guides to you or your friends in the UK is as follows:

Farm Holiday Guide
ENGLAND, WALES and IRELAND
Board, Self-catering, Caravans/Camping,
Activity Holidays. **£4.80**

Farm Holiday Guide SCOTLAND
All kinds of holiday accommodation. **£3.60**

SELF-CATERING & FURNISHED
HOLIDAYS IN BRITAIN
Over 1000 addresses throughout for
Self-catering and caravans in Britain. **£4.60**

BRITAIN'S BEST HOLIDAYS
A quick-reference general guide
for all kinds of holidays. **£3.60**

The FHG Guide to CARAVAN &
CAMPING HOLIDAYS
Caravans for hire, sites and
holiday parks and centres. **£3.60**

BED AND BREAKFAST STOPS
Over 1000 friendly and comfortable
overnight stops. Non-smoking, The
Disabled and Special Diets
Supplements. **£4.80**

CHILDREN WELCOME! FAMILY
HOLIDAY & ATTRACTIONS GUIDE
Family holidays with details of
amenities for children and babies. **£4.60**

SCOTTISH WELCOME
Introduced by Katie Woods.
A new guide to holiday accommodation
and attractions in Scotland. **£4.50**

Recommended SHORT BREAK
HOLIDAYS IN BRITAIN
'Approved' accommodation for
quality bargain breaks. Introduced by
John Carter. **£4.50**

Recommended COUNTRY HOTELS
OF BRITAIN
Including Country Houses, for
the discriminating. **£4.50**

Recommended WAYSIDE AND
COUNTRY INNS OF BRITAIN
Pubs, Inns and small hotels. **£4.50**

PGA GOLF GUIDE
Where to play. Where to stay
Over 2000 golf courses in Britain with
convenient accommodation. Endorsed
by the PGA. Holiday Golf in France,
Portugal, Spain and USA. **£9.80**

PETS WELCOME!
The unique guide for holidays for
pet owners and their pets. **£5.20**

BED AND BREAKFAST IN BRITAIN
Over 1000 choices for touring and
holidays throughout Britain.
Airports and Ferries Supplement. **£3.60**

THE FRENCH FARM AND VILLAGE
HOLIDAY GUIDE
The official guide to self-catering
holidays in the 'Gîtes de France'. **£9.80**

Tick your choice and send your order and payment to FHG PUBLICATIONS, ABBEY MILL BUSINESS CENTRE, SEEDHILL, PAISLEY PA1 1TJ (TEL: 0141-887 0428. FAX: 0141-889 7204). **Deduct** 10% for 2/3 titles or copies; 20% for 4 or more.

Send to: NAME ....

ADDRESS ....

....

.... POST CODE ....

I enclose Cheque/Postal Order for £ ....

SIGNATURE .... DATE ....

Please complete the following to help us improve the service we provide. How did you find out about our guides:

☐ Press   ☐ Magazines   ☐ TV   ☐ Radio   ☐ Family/Friend   ☐ Other.